Mocked with Death

Mocked with Death

Tragic Overliving from Sophocles to Milton

Emily R. Wilson

The Johns Hopkins University Press
Baltimore and London

© 2004 The Johns Hopkins University Press
Printed in the United States of America on acid-free paper
9 8 7 6 5 4 3 2 1

The Johns Hopkins University Press
2715 North Charles Street
Baltimore, Maryland 21218-4363
www.press.jhu.edu

Library of Congress Cataloging-in-Publication Data
Wilson, Emily R., 1971–
    Mocked with death : tragic overliving from Sophocles to Milton /
    Emily R. Wilson.
        p. cm.
    Includes bibliographical references and index.
    ISBN 0-8018-7964-7 (hardcover : alk. paper)
    1. Classical drama (Tragedy) — History and criticism. 2. Milton,
John, 1608–1674 — Characters — Heroes. 3. Literature, Comparative —
Classical and English. 4. Literature, Comparative — English and
Classical. 5. Shakespeare, William, 1564–1616 — Tragedies. 6. English
literature — Classical influences. 7. Tragic, The, in literature.
8. Survival in literature. 9. Heroes in literature. 10. Death in literature.
11. Tragedy. I. Title.
    PA3027.W55 2004
    882'.0109–dc22   2004008931

A catalog record for this book is available from the British Library.

To my Grandmother, E. E. Duncan-Jones

Contents

Preface

I first became interested in the subject of overliving after nursing my supposedly dying grandmother in the summer of 1997. While I was staying with her, she became unable to walk, or get out of bed, or even, most importantly for her, to read. At times she was comatose and absent, at other times she was in a kind of dream, asking, "Are we in Russia, darling?" Sometimes, when she was in pain or feeling too conscious of what was lost, she would say as I fed her sleeping pills, "I wish you could give me a Death Pill, darling." I had no death pill, and in any case I would have been too cowardly to administer it. Instead, we waited. While we were waiting, I held up her head to feed her painkillers and water. The doctor had prescribed antibiotics for her chest infection, and I gave her those for a day, until I realized the paradox of trying to cure someone who wanted to die and who looked almost dead. The doctor and the district nurse told me not to be afraid when the death rattle came. The family gathered round the bedside, but she was unaware of the world. On Sunday morning she revived briefly to talk to the doctor about Hopkins's poem *Spring and Fall;* it seemed an appropriate note on which to die. That evening she seemed to have no life left in her except a faint heartbeat; her eyes showed no response to the doctor's light. But the next day, extraordinarily, she was much better. She came back to life. I felt guilty about giving her those antibiotics: I did her wrong to take her out of the grave. I thought she would have to live on as an empty shell, which would insult what she once was. She lived for almost six years; she died in April 2003, aged ninety-four. She often spoke of death, but she also regained many of the powers that had seemed lost forever. She read, wrote, talked, and enjoyed the company of her friends and family. The present study is an attempt to understand both the horror of the sense of overliving, and the possibility that overliving may be converted into survival.

Acknowledgments

This book began as a doctoral dissertation in the classics and comparative literature departments at Yale University. First thanks go to my two supervisors: Victor Bers, who wanted me to be clear, and David Quint, who wanted me to be sexy.

I am grateful for a Whiting dissertation fellowship, which helped me complete the thesis, and an award from the Yale Center for British Art, which facilitated my work on the Milton chapters. I was also delighted to receive the Charles Bernheimer prize for the dissertation from the American Comparative Literature Association. The ACLA judges, Sarah Suleiman of Harvard and Michael Palencia-Roth of the University of Illinois, and Margaret Higgonet, the chair of the ACLA, provided comments that were encouraging and helpful in the final revision stages of the project.

I have been greatly helped by comments and suggestions from those who have listened to talks based on parts of the book, at Yale, Harvard, Bard College, and Tel Aviv University. I would like to thank all those who have read and commented on all or part of the manuscript at various stages, especially Gordon Braden, Susanna Morton Braund, Cyrus Hamlin, John Kirby, Bridget Murnaghan, and Annabel Patterson. Bridget Murnaghan read the whole manuscript at the final stage of revision and made some very useful and detailed suggestions; I thank her and all my colleagues at the University of Pennsylvania, who have provided a supportive environment in which to finish the book.

My greatest intellectual debt is to Marco Roth, my best critic.

Mocked with Death

Introduction

This book argues that there is a central thread in the tragic tradition that is concerned not with dying too early but with living too long, or "overliving." Lives do not always end at the expected time. Sometimes people go on living even after the moment when they or others feel they should have died. Prolonged old age is one way in which life may seem to go on too long. But even young people may feel that they ought already to have died, when they live on after extraordinary loss. Sophocles, Euripides, Seneca, Shakespeare, and Milton were all concerned with the problem of overliving. Each of these writers presents a character who experiences an apparently intolerable sense of suffering and loss, and feels that he has lived too long but, nevertheless, decides to resist suicide. The sense that the central character "should" have died generates an uneasy feeling in the audience or reader that the text itself "should" have ended. These texts therefore challenge Aristotelian notions of tragic structure, in that they go on after the expected moment of ending. Each writer in the tradition tries to contain or suppress the problem, often by suggesting that from some larger cosmic, historical, or divine perspective, the character's life has not, after all, gone on too long. But these strategies are often not entirely successful. Tragedies of overliving disturb the audience or reader by reminding us that life may feel too long and endings may seem to have come too late.

I take the term "overliving" from Milton, whose Adam asks, after the Fall,

> Why do I overlive,
> Why am I mocked with death, and lengthened out
> To deathless pain?
> (*Paradise Lost* 10.773–75)

It is important that Milton's Adam uses the word "overlive" in a question. Overliving is an essentially questionable, paradoxical form of survival. Although the Latinate word "survival" has precisely the same root meaning as "overliving," the connotations of the two terms are distinct and even opposed. Briefly, "survival" paints the concept of continued existence with positive connotations, "overliving" with tragic ones. The object of the verb "to survive" is usually some event that might have been expected to destroy the survivor. One survives earthquakes and shootings; one overlives oneself. "Survival" implies that continued existence is an unexpected triumph; "overliving" implies that it is a paradox.

I use the absolute form of the verb "to overlive" interchangeably with the reflexive form, in the *Oxford English Dictionary*'s sense (c):

> a. *trans.* To live longer than, or after the death of (a person); to live after or beyond (an event, etc.); to survive, outlive; also *fig.* of things.
> b. *intr.* To survive, continue in life.
> c. *refl.* To live beyond one's proper date or time of action, live too long.[1]

OED cites Milton's Adam (*Paradise Lost* 10.773) for definition b — "to survive, continue in life" — and implies that Adam is asking merely, "Why do I continue to survive?" But the word in Adam's mouth is also tainted with the negative associations of definition c. The prefix "over" suggests excess (*OED*, s.v. 23) and, therefore, implies a normative notion of how long one ought to live. In the context of Adam's speech as a whole, it is clear that he feels he has lived too long because he has lost what made his life worth living.

The notion of excessive life begs the question, "Too long for what?" One possible answer is, "Too long for a human being." There is a philosophical and literary tradition suggesting that human bodies and human minds may be constitutionally unfit for lives longer than three score years and ten.[2] An obvious mythic model for senescent overliving is Tithonus, the mortal man beloved by Aurora, goddess of the dawn, who was given eternal life but not eternal youth.[3]

Other examples of senescent overliving include Nestor in the *Iliad*[4] and Swift's Struldbruggs in *Gulliver's Travels*.[5] Senescence, or physical frailty, may be used as metonymy for tragic overliving.[6]

But there is no necessary connection between tragic overliving and old age or physical incapacity.[7] Sometimes — as in the case of Seneca's Hercules — the retention of physical strength can increase the horror of living on after more important powers have been lost.[8] The tragic tradition links overliving to the loss of a particular quality through a single traumatic event.[9] Relatively few tragic characters who live too long are old in years. Tragic overliving is the result not of a gradual natural decline, but of a single sharply defined event or action after which it seems that life ought to be over — and yet it goes on.

The tragic tradition associates the sense of living too long with disgust at life in general. In *The Birth of Tragedy*, Nietzsche identified this attitude as the voice of Dionysus and, hence, as the first and central truth of tragedy. He quotes an ancient anecdote that Silenus was captured and bound by Midas and forced to tell the truth.[10]

> There is an ancient story that King Midas hunted in the forest a long time for the wise Silenus, the companion of Dionysus, without capturing him. When Silenus at last fell into his hands, the king asked what was the best and most desirable of all things for man. Fixed and immovable, the demigod said not a word; till at last, urged by the king, he gave a shrill laugh and broke out into these words: "Oh, wretched and ephemeral race, children of chance and misery, why do ye compel me to tell you what it were most expedient for you not to hear? What is best of all is beyond your reach forever: not to be born, not to be, to be nothing. But the second best for you — is quickly to die."[11]

For Nietzsche, tragedy is the taming by Apollo, the ordering force of art and civilization, of the primitive, Dionysiac ritual of dismemberment. Tragedy is a form that includes and structures the desires that threaten to overturn all human life, including especially the desire not to be alive.

The maxim that "Never to be born is best" is, as Nietzsche rightly suggests, central to tragic thought. The sentiment has not always been associated with tragedy as a dramatic genre,[12] and Nietzsche's literary history is implausible.[13] But his insight into the essence of tragedy is compelling. Tragic literature reminds us that life always includes pain and loss: we are "wretched and ephemeral, children of chance and misery," and must therefore regret not only the fact that we die, but also the fact that we live at all. Tragedies of overliving suggest an association between the apparently exceptional lives of those who commit or suffer terrible horrors and yet go on living, and the condition of humanity in general. They are an essential thread in the tragic tradition, concerned particularly with the suspicion that death can never come soon enough.

Wittgenstein suggested that we understand the term "game" not by recognizing a single feature shared by all games, but by seeing that games as a group possess "family resemblances."[14] Literary genres are usually like "games" on Wittgenstein's model: we recognize that a work is a novel, a satire, or an elegy through certain cues or associations, not all of which are present in every member of the genre. But among genres, as among the members of any category, some are more typical than others.[15] As a large generic category, "tragedy" includes multiple subgenres.[16] Some are relatively marginal, while others, such as tragedies of overliving, are central in the tradition throughout its history.[17]

My study is confined almost exclusively to works normally considered "tragic." Through rereading even these familiar and uncontroversially tragic texts, I hope to adjust and expand our understanding of the tragic and of the tragic tradition. But although my main focus is on drama, I use the word "tragic" not only for a particular dramatic genre ("tragedy") but also for any literary work within the tragic mode.[18] I would argue that epic in particular (but also history, novels, and even painting or sculpture) may be, in this looser sense, tragic. In chapter 8, I suggest that *Paradise Lost* is an epic that struggles to contain a tragic sense of overliving.

Through the study of tragic overliving, I hope to make some larger claims about tragedy as a whole, which I sketch in this introduction. First, tragedy need not be concerned primarily with death; it may, rather, be about the failure to die, and about the sense that life is worse than death. Related to this is the fact that tragic plots need not be end-driven, need not feel inevitable, and need not produce any sense of psychological purification in the reader or spectator. Tragedy may, rather, be associated with obscurity and bewilderment and the inability to make sense of a story as an orderly whole — a pattern often represented in concrete terms in these texts, through the central character's blindness or his desire to hide. Second, tragedy is usually concerned with time gone wrong; tragedies of overliving invoke complex and contradictory attitudes to time, contrasting impersonal with subjective experiences of temporality. Tragedies of overliving are associated with repetition: time goes on but without the possibility of change. Third, and perhaps most important, tragedy suggests that the apparently exceptional experiences of extraordinary individuals, like Oedipus or Heracles or King

Lear, may be representative of all human life. In tragedies of overliving, there is a slippage between the life of the central character, which goes on beyond normal limits, and the "normal" life-spans of the rest of us, which also go on too long.

Living too long may be as upsetting as dying too soon, or more so, and it is equally "tragic." Tragedies need not end badly, and death is not the ultimate tragic experience.[19] Many Greek tragedies do not end in death, and even early modern and modern tragedies do not always present death as the defining event in life. Some critics, noticing that literal death is often not a prominent feature of tragic plots, have suggested that tragedy is about spiritual or metaphorical death.[20] But tragedy may also be concerned with the postponement of death, or with continuing life. It may concentrate not on the ends of life but on the bewildering middle periods, when it is unclear what the future holds or when the end will come. Tragedy can create expectations of death as an ending only to deny them.

Tragic overliving often blurs the distinction between life and death. Excessive life is presented as a kind of living death. Euripides' Heracles, on emerging from madness, believes he is in Hades, not yet understanding that the world of the living has become, for him, a kind of underworld. Lear says, "You do me wrong to take me out o' the grave."[21] Those who overlive are already experiencing a version of death, while they are still alive.[22] In these texts, death is not an ending that gives final closure to the whole life, but a process that goes on within life, without hope of an end.

One might expect that these characters would want to kill themselves. In his diatribe against the fear of death, Lucretius promises that death will end our "deathly life" on earth.[23] Many of the characters discussed in this study are persuaded not to commit suicide only with great difficulty. But tragedies of overliving suggest that suicide is the female response to the problem, to be contrasted with the male experience of living on.[24] Tragic overliving is usually, though not exclusively, a masculine phenomenon.[25] Female characters in these texts die quickly, often offstage, often by suicide. Jocasta kills herself, but Oedipus remains alive. Megara wants to kill herself and is killed, but Heracles lives on. Lady Macbeth kills herself, but Macbeth can expect "To-morrow, and to-morrow, and to-morrow" (*Macbeth* 5.5.19). Adam asks, "Why do I overlive?" while Eve proposes the simple solution of suicide.[26]

For characters who have lived too long, suicide is often seen not as a solution, but as an irrelevance. There can be no end to their guilt, shame, and sense of pollution; no river could ever make them clean. The pre-Socratic philosopher

Thales, who claimed there was no difference between life and death, was asked, "Why do you not die?" He replied, "Because there is no difference."[27] Oedipus tells the Chorus that he put out his eyes rather than kill himself because suicide would only make his situation worse: he could never bear to look at his father or mother in the underworld.[28] Suicide may be rejected from fear that the afterlife will be no better, or even worse.

The possibility that suicide is morally wrong is raised in Euripides' *Heracles*, and becomes increasingly important in Seneca and then in Christian writers. Seneca suggests that in some circumstances one may have a duty to live, to care for one's family.[29] Shakespeare and Milton both allude to Christian condemnations of suicide;[30] the duty to live is juxtaposed with the desire to die.[31] But there is also a suspicion in Shakespeare and Milton, in *King Lear* in particular, that suicide might be not merely wrong, but impossible. Christian writers examine with new intensity the fear that death may not be the end of life and that death itself may not always be available. Gloucester tries to kill himself but fails.[32] He discovers that even throwing himself down from what he thinks is a cliff cannot set him free from the pains of the world. These characters cannot control the ending of their lives. Suicide is never presented as a wholly satisfactory solution to the problem of overliving because once a character has lived too long, any death must come too late.

One might think that if a man can live too long, it ought to be possible also for him to have lived for the right length of time. To avoid senescent overliving, one should live as long as the body and mind are capable of functioning at the height of their powers, and no longer.[33] Logically, to avoid traumatic overliving one should simply live until immediately before the horrible event and then die. Macbeth exclaims, "Had I but died an hour before this chance / I had lived a blessed time!" (*Macbeth* 2.3.89–90). Similarly, Odysseus cries out that he envies those who had the good fortune to die at Troy: three and four times blessed were those who died before suffering the shipwrecks and despairs of the journey home (*Odyssey* 5.306–12). Odysseus's exclamation shows his awareness that, in surviving the battlefield, he has lost the possibility of honor. He envies those who were able to die nobly, in battle. The proper moment for a heroic death has gone by, and Odysseus must face less honorable forms of death, by drowning, at the hands of some unknown monster, or — if he survives the journey — from old age. Odysseus can only look back in longing at the time at which a noble death might have been possible.

But tragedies of overliving imply that it is impossible to have lived the right length of time, except by avoiding life altogether. When Oedipus wishes he had died at a previous time, as a baby exposed on Mount Cithaeron, he cries, "Cithaeron, why did you receive me? Why did you not take me and kill me immediately, so that I might never have shown myself and my parentage to humanity?"[34] Oedipus, unlike Odysseus, longs not to have died nobly, but to have died as quickly as possible after being born. The tragic sense of overliving is not caused by fear of ignoble death, but by the desire not to be alive. Oedipus is prompted by the realization of what he has done not only to wish that he had died before doing those terrible things, but also to wish that he had never been born. Moreover, these texts often generalize the experience of the tragic protagonist so that overliving becomes not merely the terrible fate of the tragic few who become cut off from the norms of proper human life-spans, but an inextricable part of the human condition. Overliving becomes equated with living: to live at all is to live too long.[35]

Time is always of central importance in tragedy; tragic time is always out of joint.[36] Tragedies of overliving express the fear that time may always be the enemy of humanity. Time is resisted or goes wrong, lives end too soon or too late, the temporal order of human generations is confused by incest or familial murder, and time brings only staleness or repetition or death.[37] Tragic time may, as in tragedies of overliving, seem too long; or it may, as in *Romeo and Juliet*, go too fast. In *Hamlet* the political "times" of Denmark are not as they should be, and Hamlet himself also has a distorted relationship to time; he cannot accept that time passes and that one generation succeeds to another, that "all that lives must die/Passing through nature to eternity."[38] Hamlet wants to stop time, to defer indefinitely the proper moment to act. Macbeth, on the other hand, finds time too slow and tries to leap over it: for him, the right moment has always already slipped by.[39]

Tragic overliving is associated with a tension between different temporal schemes. The central character's "sense of an ending" may compete with alternative possible endings.[40] *Paradise Lost* presents Adam's dilemma as the result of a mismatch between his own experience of time and God's time. Adam believes that his life is not worth living once he has lost his innocence and his happiness. But the poem suggests that, from a divine perspective, Adam's question shows that he misunderstands the plan for human history. The Fall is not the end; Adam must look to the future, when the second Adam and the Apocalypse will come.[41] In Sophocles, Euripides, and Seneca, as in Christian writers like Milton, the sense that life has gone on too long is countered by quite different ways of understanding time. But there remains a strong and often predominant emphasis on the human feeling of resistance and regret.

Three Greek words for time provide a clear way to think about the alternative views of time invoked in these texts:[42] *kairos*, the right moment, or qualitative time (to feel that one has lived too long is to suspect that one's *kairos* has already passed);[43] *chronos*, linear or historical time;[44] and *aion*, time seen as a whole, a lifetime or an age.[45] Tragedies of overliving set the suspicion that the proper moment or *kairos* has gone by, against one or both of the other ways of understanding time. Perhaps in the long course of historical time (*chronos*) there may be new and unexpected events that can redeem the past. Transformation, escape, or successful revenge may overturn the notion that there is nothing left to live for. According to the archangel Michael, Adam thinks he has lived too long only because he fails to understand God's plan for humanity. Alternatively, the sense that the proper moment has passed may be answered by a view of time as a whole (*aion*). Tragedies of overliving often suggest that, from some perspective, it is unimportant how long or short one's life is. Perhaps, as Seneca argues, any life is long enough to be good, and at any moment one ought to be ready to die.[46] It is also possible that the sense of multiple contradictory endings can be expressed simultaneously by a single writer or in a single tragic work. But it is easier to represent the suspicion that the proper moment to end has already passed than to show "eternity, whose end no eye can reach."[47] Action, the essential feature of all narrative, is possible only within time. The appeal to another kind of time cannot entirely repress the feeling that life seems too long.

Repetition, duplication, and listing are used to convey the feeling that things go on the same, without change or growth or death, or connections between one thing and another. Often there is simple verbal repetition: for instance, Oedipus cries, ὦ γάμοι γάμοι (O marriages, marriages, *Oedipus Tyrannus* 1403); Macbeth talks of "To-morrow, and to-morrow, and to-morrow" (*Macbeth* 5.5.19); Lear howls, "Lear, Lear, Lear" (*King Lear* 1.4.262) and "No, no, no" (5.3.304); Samson exclaims, "O dark, dark, dark" (*Samson Agonistes* 79). The use of repetition enacts the anguishing sense that there is mere addition without alteration; Samson longs for the repeated word "life" to include or change into the word "light," but it does not.[48] A variant on simple verbal repetition is the use of plural for singular, as in "Marriages, marriages"; Oedipus suggests that his whole life has consisted of the same thing, "marriages," not only by repeating the word twice but also by making it plural. Listing suggests the lack of pattern or development in a life: Oedipus calls on his marriage, Mount Cithaeron, Polybus and Merope, and the place where the three paths meet; Seneca's Hercules lists all the rivers that will fail to wash him clean: Tanais, the Nile, the Tigris, the Rhine, and the Tagus (*Hercules Furens* 1321–29); Lear asks, "Why should a dog, a horse, a rat have life/And thou no breath at all?" (*King Lear* 305–6). Objects are rhetorically juxtaposed but not related to one another beyond their common place in a single category. The repetitions are often not merely verbal — many of these texts use repetitive argument, dialogue, or narrative to convey the feeling that nothing does or can change until death. In *Paradise Lost*, for example, Adam returns to the words "Yet" and "But," repeating the pattern of argument and counterargument. In the last books of Milton's poem, the same story structure recurs repeatedly, undermining the hope that any new events can happen in human history.

Overliving is always associated with repetition because there is always a contrast between overliving and outliving. Those who feel that they have lived too long see life as mere repetition of the same pattern, over and over again, with no possibility of any new action or new event. Time goes on but without the feature that ought to define time, namely change. In several texts in the tradition, those who are trapped in the endless cycle of repetition are contrasted with those who succeed in breaking free of it and finding some possibility of change. The *Oedipus Coloneus*, *Samson Agonistes*, and *Paradise Lost* raise particularly sharply the question of whether the sense of overliving can ever be resolved. All three texts suggest that the central character who says he has lived too long will achieve some kind of final triumph and transformation. In the *Oedipus Coloneus*, for example, Oedipus himself manages to achieve a new social position and a new value — while the children of Oedipus, and the whole mass of humanity, are condemned to endless repetition of "killings, strife, hatred." *Samson Agonistes*, similarly, raises the possibility that Samson may be able to avoid repeating his own past and may therefore break free from the sense of overliving. But in none of these texts, I suggest, does the ultimate success entirely resolve or eliminate the despair and confusion that has gone before. The emphasis of the narrative often shifts away from what had been its main concern — the inner emotions of the central character. We are distanced from the final triumphs of Oedipus or Samson and led to concentrate on the pain and confusion of those left behind, who are condemned continually to repeat the same pattern of suffering.

These texts dramatize a conflict between the impersonal and personal responses to time. On one level, the divine or historical views of time may seem to correct the characters' fears that they have lived too long. From the perspective of the farsighted archangel Michael, Adam is merely mistaken to believe he has lived too long, being unaware of the whole truth about God's plan. But the long perspective is necessarily impersonal. If our sympathy is engaged with the human characters, our distress cannot be entirely assuaged by a shift to an unemotional mode of understanding. Those who are within time will, these texts suggest, find it too long, even if, from some perspective beyond human life-spans, the problem disappears. The characters' perception of time resists narrative attempts at containment.

Tragic overliving frustrates the reader or audience's hope for an ending that feels permanent. Critics may have been tempted by the idea that tragedy must end with some kind of ultimate closure, if not death itself, because an ordered, final ending might seem the most promising way to effect tragic catharsis in the audience or reader. Perhaps the most popular of Aristotle's pronouncements about tragedy has been his obscure description of tragedy as "achieving through pity and fear the purification (catharsis) of such emotions" (*Poetics* 1449b27–28). Subsequent critics of tragedy have seized eagerly on this dark saying, usually taking it to mean that watching or reading tragedy leaves us feeling better, both morally and emotionally.[49] Aristotle's invocation of the term "catharsis" is probably part of his defense of tragedy, and poetry in general, from Plato's attacks.[50] In the *Republic* (606d), Socrates claims that the tragic poets "foster and water" those emotions which should rather be dammed up and that they must therefore be expelled from the city. Against Plato, Aristotle implies that tragedy encourages civic values and emotional stability. Most tragic theorists have followed Aristotle over Plato and have assumed that tragedy confers some kind of psychological benefit on those who read or watch it. But tragedy is not necessarily cheering, comforting, or redemptive.[51] Plato was right to worry that tragedy might stir up feelings that could threaten the equilibrium of the state or the soul. I argue that tragedies of overliving encourage feelings of despair and longing for death that are never completely eliminated. In many of these texts, other characters try to "cure" the central character's despair, to treat it merely as a diseased passion — as do Samson's three visitors in *Samson Agonistes*. But for the audience or reader, after the text has raised the possibility that life has gone on too long, any ending is liable to feel too late.

Distinctions between classical, early modern, and modern tragedy have often exaggerated the unity, orderliness, and nobility of classical tragedy. The contrast between modern and premodern tragedy is a critical commonplace, and many have argued that tragedy is impossible in the undignified and anarchic modern world.[52] I hope my work shows the limitations of some ways of distinguishing classical and early modern tragedy and suggests that classical tragedy is closer to early modern and modern tragic narratives than has often been thought. Even Sophoclean tragedy resists Aristotelian norms, and even Sophoclean heroes disintegrate.

My focus on tragic overliving highlights one way in which tragic art forms can model themselves on the broken structures of experience.[53] Tragic narratives need not end in a way that feels conclusive. Tragic plots need not seem inexorable or inevitable;[54] indeterminacy has always been a central thread in the tragic tradition.[55] Tragedy tends toward ambivalence, rupture, and irresoluble conflict.[56] Once he has lived too long, the tragic protagonist becomes opaque; the audience no longer knows what to expect from him, his role is no longer clearly defined, and nothing is inevitable. The tragic mode is often concerned with the middle times of life, not its ends. Tragedies of overliving remind us of the illegibility of life when we are in it, and the difficulty or impossibility of making sense of our stories as a coherent narrative.

The representation of overliving suggests that the text itself may have gone on too long. Tragic closure, like the end of tragic lives, may not come when we expect.[57] Aristotle argues that tragedy must deal with a single, complete action.[58] For Aristotle, an ending is that after which there is nothing else (*Poetics* 1450b27–34). But tragedies of overliving create expectations of Aristotelian unity only to defeat them. They present an apparently complete action, but then keep going after what should have been the end. Tragic overliving undermines our confidence that we can understand tragic narrative patterns.

The spectators' inability to make sense of what they see is mirrored by a refusal or inability on the characters' part to see their lives as a whole. The difficulties of spectatorship, consciousness, and insight are often represented in terms of literal blindness. Oedipus puts out his own eyes;[59] Gloucester, Lear's double, has his eyes gouged out;[60] Samson has lost his eyes as well as his strength. Blindness is a terrible loss in itself; Samson develops the ironies and suffering inherent in living a half life, without light.[61] But it is also used to represent the fact that these characters must go on living after they can no longer see or be seen, either literally or metaphorically. Even in those texts where the central character is not actually blind, there is often a concern with darkness and the desire to be hidden. Euripides' Heracles hides under his cloak; Adam prays, "Cover me, ye pines" (*Paradise Lost* 9.1088). Seneca's Hercules finds darkness at noon, when he sees the bodies of his dead children (*Hercules Furens* 939–40). Macbeth says his hands "pluck out mine eyes" (*Macbeth* 2.2.56). All these texts are concerned with characters who have performed actions that are difficult or impossible to look at or contemplate, either for themselves or for the audience or reader. Physical blindness may be associated with other kinds of insight; Oedipus blinds himself after he has "seen" the truth about his parents. But characters who can no longer see also become difficult to look at, both for the other characters and for the spectators of the play. Blindness creates a barrier between the character and the spectator: we are led both to sympathize and to realize that we do not understand.

We share the bewilderment of characters who say that they have lived too long; neither they nor we can make sense of their lives as a whole. Tragedies of overliving show characters who claim that the ending of their story should already have come. Oedipus cannot be the famous riddle-solver after he fails to solve the riddle of himself, and the glorious humanitarian labors of Euripides' Heracles are compromised by their association with his slaughter of his family.[62] These characters express a self-consciousness that undermines the unity of the self and of dramatic character. They become opaque both to themselves and to the reader or audience. On one level, the discontinuity between past and present actions produces a sense of confusion and despair in the character, which must be shared by the audience or reader. But the representation of characters who evade orderly narrative structures and definition may increase the illusion of realism. Characters who question their own stories break the dramatic frame; we are led to find them puzzling in the way that people in real life are puzzling. The characters seem to become free from the constraints of their own narrative form.

My critical approach emphasizes the emotions both of characters and of readers or spectators. I focus on a particular structure of tragic feeling, the sense of having missed the right moment or *kairos*, and suggest that our own emotional responses are shaped by the emotions of the characters. My study will, I hope, build bridges between ethical and formalist ways of reading literature. "Overliving" is a new conceptual tool for thinking about the gap between the characters' view of their story and the narrative structure of the text.[63] Too often — and perhaps particularly among critics of drama — a false distinction is made between "naive" readers or spectators, who want to question the motivations of fictional character as if there could be evidence about them independent of the text, and "formalists," who emphasize the fact that all our responses to a literary work are conditioned by its rhetorical form. In fact, the two sides are entirely compatible; to ignore either is to deny half of one's literary experience. All imaginative literature produces a kind of double consciousness: it pulls us into its fictional world, making us engage with the thoughts and passions of fictional characters; but even as we suffer with those that we see suffer, we also know there's no harm done. I enter into the fiction when I consider Oedipus as someone who has perhaps lived too long. But I also step outside the fiction when I consider the formal aspects of the text, including questions of unity and narrative structure. My study thus addresses the larger theoretical issue of how formal and ethical criticism can meet one another. Both perspectives are necessary, and neither need be reduced to the other.

The *Aeneid* is, before *Paradise Lost*, the epic most concerned with the sense of overliving. A brief explanation of this claim may help to justify the idea that epic can include tragic elements, and also to illustrate the strategies used in both epic and dramatic works to contain or repress the fear that life may be too long. In book 1, Aeneas echoes Odysseus's exclamation in the storm off Calypso's island (*Odyssey* 5.306–12): three and four times blessed were those who died at Troy:

> O terque quaterque beati,
> quis ante ora patrum Troiae sub moenibus altis
> contigit oppetere! o Danaum fortissime gentis
> Tydide! mene Iliacis occumbere campis
> non potuisse tuaque animam hanc effundere dextra,
> saevus ubi Aeacidae telo iacet Hector, ubi ingens
> Sarpedon, ubi tot Simois correpta sub undis
> scuta virum galeasque et fortia corpora volvit!

> O three and four times blessed,
> those who had the chance to die before the faces of their fathers,
> beneath the high walls of Troy! O greatest of the race of Greeks,
> Tydides! That I was unable to lie down on the fields of Ilium
> and pour out this life by your right hand,
> where Hector lies by the weapon of Aeacides, where great
> Sarpedon lies, where the Simois rolls so many
> shields and helms and brave bodies of men, whirled beneath its waves!
> (*Aeneid* 1.94–101)

Odysseus envies those who fell at Troy because they died with honor and on dry land. Aeneas, eliminating the desire for honor and for a dry death, envies the Trojan dead because they never had to make the journey away from their home and their fathers. They were fortunate not because they died well — the death of

Polites in book 2, in front of his father Priam, will show the reader how horrible and gruesome it can be to die before the faces of one's family—but simply because they died sooner, without having to leave home. There is no parallel in Homer for Virgil's mention of the river Simois, which is, in context, a striking detail. Aeneas, lost in a terrible storm at sea, envies not those who died a dry death, but those who are rolled under the waves of the river. The men's bodies, in the final line of the speech (101), are syntactically parallel to their inanimate weapons (*scuta virum galeasque et fortia corpora*); the language makes no distinction between the different objects swept under the waves. The ideal to which Aeneas aspires is the total passivity of death. Unluckily for him, he must go on living and take up the burdens of history.[64]

The long-lived Sibyl, *longaeva Sibylla*, who appears in book 6 — the center of the *Aeneid* — is a female counterpart to Tithonus.[65] Apollo has given her two gifts that allow her to move further into the future than other mortals: the gift of prophecy and the gift of long life without youth.[66] Both are burdens she cannot reject. The god's possession of the prophetess (*Aeneid* 6.45–97) is a reenactment of the time when he raped her and suggests the Sibyl's inability to resist either excessive knowledge or excessive life. The Sibyl in the *Aeneid* is a concentrated image of the longing for death that haunts the whole poem.[67] The apparent purpose of the epic — to describe and celebrate the events that led to the founding of Rome — competes with a deep sense of loss, and a suspicion that it might be most desirable to give up the quest and die. Aeneas himself expresses few wishes other than the hope that he may die as soon as possible. In book 6, when he sees the souls (*animae*) as they huddle eagerly to drink the waters of Lethe and be born again, Aeneas asks,

> o pater, anne aliquas ad caelum hinc ire putandum est
> sublimis animas iterumque ad tarda reverti
> corpora? quae lucis miseris tam dira cupido?

> O father, is it to be thought that any souls go from here
> high up to the sky, and are turned again to sluggish
> bodies? What is this so terrible desire the wretched have for light?
> (*Aeneid* 6.719–21)

The question, prompted by nothing the narrator or Anchises has said immediately before, is surprising. Anchises, indeed, has just promised to make Aeneas rejoice (*laetere*) in the discovery of Italy (*Aeneid* 6.718). Aeneas's question suggests that it is not worth it to make the journey from the underworld up to the light — a journey that parallels his own voyage away from the dead world of Troy to the unknown city of the future.

Anchises gives two answers, two possible reasons why it is better to be born than not. First, he gives an account of reincarnation, which implies that time may be cyclical: human life-spans may not, it seems, be the right way of measuring time. The cosmic time scheme denies any validity to the human experience of "too long" or "too short." Second, he suggests that linear history will bring redemption, in the city of Rome and in the person of Augustus. There are here two possible temporal models for how to answer the suspicion that life is always too long, which run simultaneously through the tragic tradition. *Paradise Lost* also stages a series of debates about the question, and, like the *Aeneid*, Milton's poem holds in balance alternative temporal models for how to respond to the problem: perhaps the proper moment has not passed after all; or perhaps time itself can be redeemed. But in *Paradise Lost*, as in the *Aeneid*, there remains an awareness of human loss, human suffering, and longing for an end.

A further possibility is that tragic overliving may be evaded only by a move to a different kind of tragic narrative: revenge.[68] Aeneas, like Macbeth, turns his desire to die into a willingness to kill;[69] the end of the poem leaves it uncertain whether the death of Turnus is the beginning or the end of a cycle of violent killing. Revenge is often presented as a possible solution to overliving. One tragic subgenre can begin to mutate into another. In *Paradise Lost*, Adam refrains from suicide partly because he remembers that his seed will one day bruise the serpent's head: humanity will finally take revenge on our enemy, Satan.[70] The *Oedipus Coloneus* and *Samson Agonistes* both move from overliving to revenge.[71] Tragic overliving is, in a sense, the opposite of revenge tragedy, in which a primary action of aggression repeats itself from generation to generation: many different people perpetuate the same pattern.[72] In tragedies of overliving, a single character is fragmented when he fails to maintain a consistent pattern of action throughout his life.[73] But these texts do not suggest that revenge is an entirely satisfactory solution to the problem of overliving; rather, it may increase the feeling that all action is only repetition. The shift from overliving to revenge, from an individual sense of belatedness to violent action, may also feel like an evasion of the emotional issue — as it does, I suggest, in *Samson Agonistes*.[74]

Tragedies of overliving are associated with a particular set of problems about order, timing, character, and emotion and with a particular set of rhetorical tropes and images (repetition, blindness, pollution, slavery, torture, and living death). I show how five very different tragic writers — Sophocles, Euripides, Seneca, Shakespeare, and Milton — respond to one another, and how each empha-sizes a different aspect of the common theme. Each chapter stands on its own, although the argument for a tradition of tragic overliving is cumulative.

My aim in juxtaposing these five writers is to chart the literary history of a tragic subgenre but also to analyze a theme that crosses historical and national bound-aries. Shakespeare did not need to have read Sophocles to wonder whether life is worth living. Cross-cultural comparison allows me to examine many different mutations of this central tragic question. The tragic tradition is formed partly by the interaction of each writer with his predecessors. But this is not only an account of literary influence or intertextuality. Shakespeare had probably not read any Greek tragedy, but in some ways King Lear is closer to Sophocles' Oedipus than to any of the Senecan characters Shakespeare did know.[75]

This book is primarily a work of literary criticism rather than literary theory, although, as I have suggested, my readings of particular texts have important theoretical implications about tragedy as a genre, about the representation of time, about closure, about the ways the emotional responses of a spectator or reader may be shaped by those of the characters, and about the use of individual and exceptional figures as models for all human life. I aim to combine literary criticism with both literary theory and literary history, although my emphasis is conceptual, not historicist. My readings are not guided primarily by the position of the text within its particular place and time, although the different inflections of overliving in different writers may be partly the result of different cultural and political circumstances. For instance, Seneca's versions of tragic overliving are shaped by imperialism and by the sense of cultural and political belatedness.[76] In the second half of the book, I suggest that postclassical writers show a greater preoccupation with the possibility of immortality and a greater sense of the body and the material world as a burden. The different permutations of tragic overliv-ing are also informed by the generic and cultural conditions in which the texts were produced. For instance, throughout the tradition, tragic overliving is asso-ciated with repetition and with the distancing of a character from his former roles. But only on the Shakespearean stage, where plays are created for multiple performances — not for a single appearance at a dramatic festival like Greek trag-edies — do the theatrical repetitions of the "poor player" become an image for tragic overliving.[77]

In the first chapter I use the final scene of *Oedipus Tyrannus* as a paradigmatic example of tragic overliving. Oedipus has done terrible things and — unlike earlier in the play — he knows it. He is a polluted figure who can, it would seem, never be accepted back into society; he can never undo what he had done. Neither he nor the audience can reconcile the Oedipus he once was — the king of Thebes and the man who solved the Sphinx's riddle — with the social outcast who killed his own father and married his own mother. Yet he refuses to commit suicide. Instead, he puts out his eyes and goes on living, and he remains on stage. His blindness becomes an image not only for Oedipus's desire not to know what he has done, but also for the audience's inability to make sense of his life as a whole. The continued presence of Oedipus frustrates the spectators' desire for definite endings.

The second chapter is a reading of Sophocles' *Oedipus Coloneus*, as a play that both tries to solve the problem of tragic overliving, and generalizes the experience of Oedipus, so that all human life is seen as too long. Oedipus's terrible past is transformed into a source of power: it enables him both to bless and to curse. Pollution becomes a kind of strength; the hero achieves revenge against his enemies, and escapes from human vulnerability, repetition, and despair. But the power belongs only to Oedipus. The daughters of Oedipus are left to mourn his passing and live an unlivable life, while his sons are left to repeat an endless cycle of killings, bitterness, and loss. The great central ode of the play associates tragic overliving not, paradoxically, with the exceptional figure of Oedipus, but with all human life and all tragic narratives.

In chapter 3 I discuss Euripides' *Heracles* as a play that can be seen as a development of both Sophocles' Oedipus plays. As in the *Oedipus Tyrannus* but even more obviously, the representation of tragic overliving is associated with a denial of audience expectations about closure, unity, and dramatic character. The hero first triumphs, then goes mad, and then decides to go on living. The play implies a different solution to the problem of overliving from that of the *Oedipus Coloneus*. Like Oedipus, Heracles is offered sanctuary in Athens by Theseus. But he does not thereby become transformed or empowered, nor does he escape from the sufferings of common humanity. In this play, the hero himself recognizes that the exceptional experience of overliving is in fact the norm: everyone may be both strong and weak, all may be unclean, and there is no guarantee that life will follow a consistent pattern. Overliving is the mark of human, as opposed to divine life; human beings are enslaved to circumstance and dependent on time and on one another.

In the fourth chapter I show that Seneca uses tragic overliving to represent or enact anxieties about literary and cultural belatedness.[78] Seneca's rhetoric, both in the *Epistles* and in the *Hercules Furens*, suggests a disparity between dying young (which is never a bad thing) and living too long (which is sometimes a duty, but never desirable). Seneca associates tragic overliving with all the conventional tropes of the classical underworld, transferred to the upper earth. Tragic overliving is associated not with horrible discoveries, as in the Greek tragedians, but with the feeling that there can be no more surprises; everything is already known, and yet it goes on. In Seneca, as in Sophocles and Euripides, overliving is associated with pollution and social isolation. But even more than in Euripides, tragic overliving is also associated with slavery and with the sacrifice or suppression of individual desire. Seneca associates overliving with a particular rhetorical mode, which substitutes multiple closural moments for Aristotelian unity. The endless repetitions of a too-long life represent Seneca's own position in tragic literary tradition, and the oppressive sense of living under the Roman Empire.

Between my fourth and fifth chapters I move from antiquity to early modern England. The leap is a large one, but, as I hope to show, important continuities link Shakespeare and Milton to their classical predecessors. In Shakespeare, as in Sophocles, the sense of overliving produces a disintegration of dramatic character and frustrates audience expectations about dramatic and narrative structure. As in the classical tragedies, so in Shakespeare, tragic overliving is associated with blindness and the desire to hide, with repetition, and with living death. Shakespeare, like the classical tragedians, suggests that the exceptional characters who live too long may become representatives of us all. The impact of Christianity is, if anything, to increase the fear of overliving. Both *King Lear* and *Macbeth* use parodic, perverted versions of the Resurrection to suggest the horrors of an unending life in the body.

But there is also an increasing feeling, in postclassical texts, that the sense of overliving may be a mistake — and perhaps a sinful one, which causes further harm. In the classical texts, characters who feel they have lived too long are responding to terrible external circumstances, and their feeling that they should already have died is understood and often shared by the other characters; in the *Oedipus Tyrannus*, for example, the Chorus wonders why Oedipus has not committed suicide. In postclassical tragedies, the sense of overliving becomes increasingly subjective. These texts interrogate the belief that someone could live too long and suggest that the mental and emotional framework associated with the sense of overliving may itself be the root of the trouble. Lear decides that the time has come to divide his kingdom before he is dead; the action that makes his life a living death is the deliberate decision to give up his power — not, as is the case with Oedipus and Heracles, an action performed in ignorance or madness. The possibility that tragic overliving is a sinful and mistaken mental attitude becomes even more apparent in *Macbeth*, where the sense of "the future in an instant" leads to murder. In the poetry of Milton, there is an even greater suspicion that the sense of overliving may be wrong, both empirically and morally. But in both Shakespeare and Milton, as in the classical tragedies, the feeling persists and seems to be not only the characteristic of a few exceptional individuals, but essential to all human life.

In chapter 5 I show how *King Lear* sets Christian injunctions against suicide against the Senecan, Stoic assumption that death is always available. Gloucester tries to kill himself but discovers that he still remains alive, unable to rid himself of the burden of his body. In this play, overliving is associated with material excess and with the pressure of the physical world. The conditions of life in seventeenth-century England suggested torture and binding as the essential images for overliving — a variation on the metaphors of slavery and the torments of the underworld that recurred in the classical texts. Lear gives away his "living," his property, and wants to retain his "living," his life. There is an increasing suggestion that living too long is like physical torture, as Lear is stretched on the "rack" of the world. As in Seneca, overliving is both a personal and a political problem: the "gored state" seems to share the torturous suffering of its citizens. *King Lear*, like earlier tragedies in the tradition, suggests that overliving is both exceptional and universal. The material and temporal excesses of Lear's life are echoed by the superfluity of anyone who is born into the world — even those who do not live as long in years as Lear himself.

In the sixth chapter, on *Macbeth*, I discuss the possibility that the sense of overliving may be the result not of a terrible discovery, but of a mistaken and perhaps sinful view of time — which itself prompts terrible actions and creates an increasing feeling that life has gone on too long. Macbeth is unable to bear the knowledge that he is living in the middle of his life, unable to control its ends. His desire to kill time leads him to kill other people. But in trying to "leap" to the end, he becomes conscious that there are no true ends of life. Even the dead come back to life; the appearance of Banquo's Ghost, like Gloucester's inability to kill himself, reminds us that life may go on and on, even past the apparent moment of death. Macbeth begins to see not only his own life but all life as mere repetition, without ending and hence also without meaning. *Macbeth* associates the sense of overliving with the theater: plays are performed over and over again, by actors whose roles may change from day to day. At the end of the play,

Malcolm tries to make way both for a new kind of theater and for a new set of attitudes toward time and history. But — as is also the case in the work of Milton — the subjective and problematic sense of overliving is presented with intense emotional vividness, which is not matched by Malcolm's attempt to inaugurate a new regime.

My last two chapters are about Milton, for whom overliving is both a literary and a theological problem. Adam's sense that he has lived too long is, from God's perspective, a sinful mistake; but its emotional intensity is not easily forgotten, either by the human characters or by the reader. I argue that *Samson Agonistes* and *Paradise Lost* are Christian tragic works, concerned with the sense of overliving that may afflict all postlapsarian human beings, even those who have a glimpse of God's plan for humanity. Christian tragedy draws attention to the human suffering and despair that may exist even in an ultimately good universe.

In chapter 7, I discuss the book of Job as a model for the representation of overliving, which Milton combines with the classical tradition. The common tropes of tragic overliving recur vividly in Samson's opening speeches, as he cries out at his blindness, expresses his shame and guilt at what he has done, repeats the words "living" and "light," searches in vain for an end to life and its burdens, and imagines his life as a living death. The solutions to overliving in this drama include both the outward triumph and revenge Samson achieves by killing his enemies (which is comparable with the success of Oedipus's final curse) and also his internal "rousing motions," which may or may not be the voice of God. But *Samson Agonistes* implies that the internal cure for overliving may be unrepresentable; instead, the subject shifts to impersonal, historical, and theological modes of interpretation. The tragic theory of the preface to *Samson Agonistes* associates tragic catharsis with the cure of Samson's despair; but Samson's emotions are stirred up, not moderated, in the course of the play. Milton's drama suggests no way to avoid excessive emotions, including the sense that God's timing is wrong — except by eliminating emotions altogether.

In the final chapter, I trace the classical and Shakespearean tragic origins of Adam's question in *Paradise Lost*, "Why do I overlive?" (10.773). Milton brings together Sophocles, Euripides, Seneca, and Shakespeare, and mingles them with biblical and theological traditions. The final books of this epic contain Adam's tragedy of overliving and suggest that all human life after the Fall will feel too long. The poem provides the most extensive exploration in the tradition of the trope of life as living death. "Death," as Adam gradually discovers, means all kinds of different things, since it is the name for everything wrong with postlapsarian human life. But death does not mean the end of life. The final books of *Paradise Lost* revert again and again to the frustrated human longing for an ending and the desire never to have been born. More than any previous text, *Paradise Lost* emphasizes that there was, at one point, a chance for humanity not to have been born or made; the sense of overliving is a central and troubling theme in the poem because it implies that God may have been wrong to create the human race. More, too, than any previous text, *Paradise Lost* suggests that the sense of overliving is not exceptional but universal: Adam's sense of living death and desperate desire for an ending will be shared by all his children, who are the implied readers of the poem. Adam is more like us, more ordinary, than any previous tragic hero; he is exceptional only because he is the first to act and feel as we do. Our sense of identification with Adam and Eve may, therefore, be greater than with previous tragic characters. All fallen human beings will, like Adam, find life too long. But all may also, like Adam and Eve, and like Oedipus, find a kind of freedom in the experience of living death. At the end of *Paradise Lost*, the ancestors of the human race leave the garden, having done all that we knew they would do; and we do not know where they will go. The representation of tragic overliving can offer the reader the impression that fictional characters, like people in real life, may become unpredictable and unknown. *Paradise Lost* is the culmination of my study, since it condenses and defines the discourse of tragic overliving, even as it tries to supersede it.

The texts I discuss here form a tightly knit group — each writer alludes back to and interacts with his predecessor.[79] But this is not, of course, intended as an exhaustive study of all texts that deal with tragic overliving. One could begin the story not with Sophocles but with Homer.[80] The Homeric poems evoke the pathos of senescent overliving: Nestor, for instance, laments the fact that he lives on after his strength in battle is gone, and Laertes in the *Odyssey* lives to see his own loss of political, military, and domestic power.[81] There is a closer precursor to tragic, traumatic overliving in the *Iliad*, which is, as has often been recognized, a tragic poem.[82] When Achilles lives on after the death of Patroclus, it is as if he is himself already dead.[83] Priam's terrible journey to Achilles is like a journey to the underworld, guided by Hermes, a journey to meet someone whose death has already happened. In choosing to stay at Troy, Achilles has already chosen death; the moment of extinction will fulfill what has already taken place in book 24 of the *Iliad*.[84]

It would be quite possible to extend the study to texts after Milton. For modern dramas of overliving, one might look to Beckett, whose characters live on in the middle, between a forgotten beginning and an ending that never quite arrives. Chekhov provides an even closer analogy. In act 4 of *Uncle Vanya*, life on the estate has been shown to be meaningless; there is no reason to go on working, but nothing else to do, and Vanya begs the doctor, Astrov, to give him poison: "Oh, my God! I'm forty-seven. If I live to be sixty, I've got another thirteen years. What a time! How am I to get through those thirteen years?"[85] Vanya steals a bottle of morphia from Astrov, but Sonia persuades him to give it back. She reminds him not of hope but of the necessity to continue, even without meaning:

> *Sonia:* Give it back, Uncle Vanya! I dare say I'm just as unhappy as you are, but I don't despair all the same. I bear it, and I shall continue to bear it till my life comes to its natural end. You must bear it too. [A pause] Give it back! [Kisses his hand] My dear, kind uncle — give it up, dear! [Weeps] You're so good, I know you'll feel sorry for us and give it back. You'll have to bear it, Uncle! You must bear it![86]

Vanya returns the bottle. He submits to Sonia, not to Astrov, because she knows what his decision will mean. She has already experienced the loss of hope or meaning from her life, in the rejection of her love of Astrov. But life must go on.

Beyond the dramatic tradition, there are many analogues to tragic overliving in the novel. One branch of the novel of overliving is concerned with the horrors of living on after a terrible romantic disappointment or loss. *Wuthering Heights* is a novel of romantic overliving in this sense. Heathcliff lives on after the loss of Catherine, despite declaring that she is his life: "Oh God! It is unutterable! I *cannot* live without my life! I *cannot* live without my soul!"[87] Heathcliff has lost not a particular role or capacity but the person whom he regards as his other half. In *Ethan Frome* the main character also has to live on after losing all possibility of erotic fulfillment and tied to a wife who is always dying and never dead.

In Tolstoy there are echoes of tragic overliving in the double ending of *Anna Karenina*, where Anna's suicide is paralleled by Levin's difficult decision to go on living. Anna's decision to kill herself is anticipated by her willingness to use birth control.[88] Dolly is momentarily tempted by the surprising possibility that fertility can be controlled; but almost at once she realizes that it is revolting to try to impose rational control on decisions of life and death. Anna's rational calculation that it would be best for her children not to be conceived is paralleled by Levin's attempt to impose rational, calculated methods on the land, despite the advice of peasants and other landowners.[89] Levin himself begins to long for death, despite his happy marriage, because he cannot accept the irrational life affirmation of faith; instead, he reads Schopenhauer and finds no nourishment in him.

> And Levin, a happy father and husband, in perfect health, was several times so near suicide that he hid a rope so that he might not be tempted to hang himself, and was afraid to go out with his gun for fear of shooting himself.
>
> But Levin did not shoot himself, and did not hang himself; he went on living.[90]

Levin goes on living, although he can see no reason why; he realizes only gradually that his reason is wrong, not his decision to live. In *Anna Karenina*, as in tragedies of overliving, the decision to live is associated with a new understanding of the relationship of the divine and human worlds. The double ending of the novel implies two possible responses to the temptation of suicide — Anna's, to yield, and Levin's, to resist and to go on living.

The literary tradition from the Greeks to Milton, and beyond, is broken by enormous cultural and ideological differences. But we should remember what has remained constant as well as what has changed.[91] Tragedy is important because it speaks to some of our deepest concerns and experiences. Tragic individuals who seem exceptional — like those who commit and suffer atrocities and yet go on living — can represent us all. There are, of course, important distinctions between tragic texts and real tragic events; indeed, it is morally and politically dangerous to equate literary tragedy too closely with the "tragedies" of everyday life.[92] But the representation of suffering in mimetic art may draw our attention to suffering in real life, and our awareness of real suffering can inform our understanding of suffering in literature. People have always wondered whether life is worth living, and tragic narratives have always included a suspicion that life goes on too long, and that never to be born is best.

CHAPTER ONE

"O darkness"

Sophocles' *Oedipus Tyrannus*

Sophocles' Oedipus plays dominate the modern Western canon.[1] Any text as well known as the *Oedipus Tyrannus* is bound to be read and reread in the light of ever changing critical and cultural concerns.[2] But more than canonicity blocks the road to Thebes. The end of the play represents the difficulty of its own reception because it shows the aftermath of the story of Oedipus. It shows us a figure who lives on after it seems as if his life ought to be over, and whose roles seem to have proliferated so that his character no longer makes sense. "Know yourself" (Γνῶθι σεαυτόν), said the Delphic oracle. The *Oedipus Tyrannus* makes one ask, "Which self?"

Until the final episode of the play, the spectators know more than Oedipus does about his life. We all know the story of Oedipus, or we think we do. Oedipus, as everyone who has heard or read the *Odyssey* well knows, killed his father and married his mother.[3] Moreover, the audience of the *Oedipus Tyrannus* is habituated by the play itself to feel in a position of privileged knowledge about the life of Oedipus.[4] The audience of the Greek theater looked down on the stage, and the spectators of the *Oedipus Tyrannus* are led to feel justified in looking down on Oedipus in a metaphorical sense as well. The spectators know Homer;

Oedipus does not. Sophocles relentlessly exploits the gulf between what the audience knows about Oedipus and what Oedipus himself knows.

But everything changes in the last scene of the play, after Oedipus has discovered the truth about his past. In the earlier scenes of the play, there are two incompatible stories and roles associated with Oedipus, one of which is known to him and one that is hidden. There is the story he himself believes, that he is the son of Polybus and Merope, the famous man who solved the riddle of the Sphinx by his own native wit, who liberated the people and married the queen of Thebes, and who now rules like a father to the people. There is also the buried story that the spectators know: that he is the son of Laius whom he killed and Jocasta whom he married. But in the final episode of the play, we are presented with an Oedipus who has not only two different stories, one apparent but false, another hidden but true, but multiple and apparently incompatible roles simultaneously: he is both the killer of Laius and his avenger, and both attributes are out in the open. Now, Oedipus knows as much as the spectators do about who his parents were and what he has done to and with them. The spectators, like the Chorus, look at the blinded Oedipus not only with horror and pity, but also with an awareness that they no longer understand his life or his character any better than he does. His discovery of the truth about himself produces not simple self-recognition, but multiplication of the meanings of "Oedipus." Our desire to judge the life of Oedipus is frustrated by his refusal to die.

When Oedipus realizes the truth about his past, he cries out to the light:

ἰοὺ ἰού· τὰ πάντ' ἂν ἐξήκοι σαφῆ.
ὦ φῶς, τελευταῖόν σε προσβλέψαιμι νῦν,
ὅστις πέφασμαι φύς τ' ἀφ' ὧν οὐ χρῆν, ξὺν οἷς τ'
οὐ χρῆν ὁμιλῶν, οὕς τέ μ' οὐκ ἔδει κτανών.

Ah, ah! Now everything is come clear.
O light, may I now look on you for the last time,
who am revealed as the offspring of those from whom I should not have been born,
companion of those I should not have been with, killer of those I should not have
    killed. (1182–85)

The audience might well assume that Oedipus sees the light for the last time because he is about to kill himself.[5] But when the Messenger comes in, the first news he tells the Chorus is of the death of Jocasta. He begins with the shortest and simplest part of his story: "The shortest of stories to tell and to learn: reverent Jocasta is dead" (ὁ μὲν τάχιστος τῶν λόγων εἰπεῖν τε καὶ / μαθεῖν, τέθνηκε θεῖον Ἰοκάστης κάρα, 1234–35). Jocasta's story is over because she is dead. The contrast between Oedipus and Jocasta suggests that instantaneous death, even of the most violent and pathetic kind, is less upsetting, less incomprehensible, and less tragic than overliving.

Tragic overliving is contrasted also with tragedies of revenge or of inherited guilt. The Messenger suggests that the story of Oedipus is like the *Oresteia*: his sufferings are the result of a curse that passes from one generation to another.[6] The first thing the Messenger says concerns the house of the Labdacids:

> ὦ γῆς μέγιστα τῆσδ' ἀεὶ τιμώμενοι,
> οἷ' ἔργ' ἀκούσεσθ', οἷα δ' εἰσόψεσθ', ὅσον δ'
> ἀρεῖσθε πένθος, εἴπερ εὐγενῶς ἔτι
> τῶν Λαβδακείων ἐντρέπεσθε δωμάτων.
> οἶμαι γὰρ οὔτ' ἂν Ἴστρον οὔτε Φᾶσιν ἂν
> νίψαι καθαρμῷ τήνδε τὴν στέγην, ὅσα
> κεύθει, τὰ δ' αὐτίκ' ἐς τὸ φῶς φανεῖ κακὰ
> ἑκόντα κοὐκ ἄκοντα. τῶν δὲ πημονῶν
> μάλιστα λυποῦσ' αἳ φανῶσ' αὐθαίρετοι.

> Most honored men of this land,
> what actions you shall hear of, what you shall see! And how much
> you will suffer, if you still feel kindly
> toward the house of the Labdacids!
> For I think that neither Ister nor Phasis
> would be able to wash this house with purification; so many things
> it hides, and some evils it will immediately reveal to the light,
> deliberate, not involuntary evils. But the sufferings
> which hurt the most are those which appear through our own choice.
> (1223–31)

The messenger implies that the horrific events in the palace, the suicide of Jocasta and the self-blinding of Oedipus, are the result and the continuation of an ancient ancestral curse. The suffering of the Labdacids will never end; the taint will never be washed away. The allusion to the house of the Labdacids reminds the audience that Oedipus inherits his suffering from his forebears. There is an undying family curse whose taint is passed from generation to generation and can never be cleansed.

But the final scene of the play moves far away from the ancestral curse pattern.

What fails to die in the final scene of the *Oedipus Tyrannus* is not an abstract pollution, the curse on the house of the Labdacids, but Oedipus himself. His sufferings are not only the involuntary inheritance of his past but the results of his own decision: as the Messenger says with emphatic redundancy, they are "deliberate, not involuntary," or "willing and not unwilling" (ἑκόντα κοὐκ ἄκοντα). The narrative pattern in which horror fails to end from one generation to another, and the children inherit the sins and the sufferings of the fathers and mothers, is replaced by a newly individualistic pattern. Oedipus himself fails to die, and his suffering fails to end not only in his household, but also in his own life. Certainly, the children of Oedipus will inherit terrible pain and conflict. But even when he says goodbye to his daughters at the end of the play, the focus remains on Oedipus himself. He refuses to die or to leave the stage, even when he seems to embody multiple incompatible roles. The possibility of an ancestral curse tragedy is replaced by a tragedy of overliving.[7]

The Messenger emphasizes how many things the house hides (ὅσα / κεύθει, 1228–29) but promises that it will immediately reveal some of them to the light (τὰ δ' αὐτίκ' ἐς τὸ φῶς φανεῖ, 1229). The emphasis on what remains hidden could be taken metaphorically: the house of the Labdacids holds yet further horrors in store for Oedipus and for his children. But it can also be taken literally: Oedipus himself is temporarily hidden from the light and from the eyes of the Chorus and the spectators of the play, but in fewer than a hundred lines he will be revealed to the light of the stage as a horror and a thing of darkness. He emerges as both king and outcast, son and husband, the riddle-solver and the solution. But he does not kill himself.

Oedipus expresses the wish that he had died long ago, as a baby. He curses the man who freed his bound ankles and rescued him when he was exposed on the mountain (1349–52), since had he died then, he would not be such a burden to his loved ones and to himself (τότε γὰρ ἂν θανὼν / οὐκ ἦ φίλοισιν οὐδ' ἐμοὶ τοσόνδ' ἄχος, 1354–55). He cries out to the mountain itself:

ἰὼ Κιθαιρών, τί μ' ἐδέχου; τί μ' οὐ λαβὼν
ἔκτεινας εὐθύς, ὡς ἔδειξα μήποτε
ἐμαυτὸν ἀνθρώποισιν ἔνθεν ἦ γεγώς;

O Cithaeron, why did you receive me? Why did you not, taking me,
kill me at once, so that I had never shown
myself to men, the source of my birth?
(1391–93)

Oedipus blames those who kept him alive past infancy. It is interesting that he refrains from addressing his parents; he does not express the wish not to have been conceived, and the mountain, Cithaeron, substitutes for the mother's womb that received him, nourished him, and put him forth into the world. But Oedipus's wish to have died long ago does not translate into a wish to die now. His desire not to have lived is associated with his desire not to have been seen, and it is already too late for the world never to have looked at him.

Instead of killing himself, he puts out his eyes. Oedipus emerges onto the stage at 1297 with his face obviously mutilated.[8] The self-blinding was a feature of the Oedipus myth even before Sophocles, as we know from, for example, Aeschylus's *Seven against Thebes*.[9] But Sophocles puts a new emphasis on the self-blinding as Oedipus's response to his discovery, and creates a new ambivalence about the motives for it. The spectators are led to feel confused by the figure of Oedipus and unable fully to understand his actions. The text offers us several different motives for the self-blinding. Explicit and implicit explanations for the action come at 1271–74, 1329–35, 1336–46, and 1369–90. Oedipus suggests at least five reasons why he blinded himself. In the Messenger's account, as we have seen, he cries out that he longs for his eyes to be unable to see himself or what he has done (1270–72). Later, he tells the Chorus that he blinded himself because "What could be a pleasure for him to see now?" (1334–35). When the Chorus asks why he put out his eyes rather than commit suicide, his answer is that he does not know how he could have looked at his family in the underworld, or at the city, or the temples (1371–74). There are three different suggestions here: (1) he wants to repress knowledge of his horrific actions; (2) nothing in the visual world could any longer could give him pleasure; and (3) he wants to cut himself off from all social contact, not to see either his dead parents, or his living children, or his city. All these motives present the self-blinding as a gesture of denial and avoidance of the truth about the past. Oedipus puts out his eyes because he refuses to look at himself as revealed by the past or in his new social position.

But there are two further motives implied by Oedipus, which are incompatible with the previous ones and also incompatible with one another: (4) because a god made him do it; and (5) to assert his own autonomy. The Chorus asks him, "You have done terrible things! How could you bear to do such things, to mutilate your own eyes? What god incited you?" (ὦ δεινὰ δράσας, πῶς ἔτλης τοιαῦτα σὰς / ὄψεις μαρᾶναι; τίς σ᾽ ἐπῆρε δαιμόνων; 1327–28). Oedipus answers the two questions with two responses:

Ἀπόλλων τάδ᾽ ἦν, Ἀπόλλων, φίλοι,
ὁ κακὰ κακὰ τελῶν ἐμὰ τάδ᾽ ἐμὰ πάθεα.
ἔπαισε δ᾽ αὐτόχειρ νιν οὔ-
τις, ἀλλ᾽ ἐγὼ τλάμων.

Apollo, these things were Apollo, my friends,
who brought about these terrible terrible sufferings of mine, of mine.
But the one who struck with his own hand was
nobody but my own wretched self.

(1329–32)

Oedipus is conceding the Chorus's assumption that he was led to do something so ghastly as blind himself only through divine intervention or compulsion. But he also emphasizes that he performed the self-blinding with his own hands. He draws a contrast between two different levels of agency and, hence, two different types of cause: Apollo was the force behind the self-blinding, Oedipus was the one who struck the blow. Oedipus simultaneously acknowledges his subjection to divine power and asserts his own agency. He emphasizes both Apollo's power and his own subjectivity: he repeats the name "Apollo" (Ἀπόλλων τάδ᾽ ἦν, Ἀπ-όλλων), but he also repeats the first person pronouns, "of mine, of mine" (ἐμὰ τάδ᾽ ἐμὰ) and the emphatic "my own wretched self" (ἐγὼ τλάμων). Moreover, there may be a distinction between his discovery of horrible past events suffered passively, "these sufferings of mine" (ἐμὰ τάδ᾽ ἐμὰ πάθεα), and the present active blow that put out his eyes: "he struck with his own hand" (ἔπαισε δ᾽ αὐτόχειρ).[10] So a further motive for striking his eyes may be to assert his own agency, against the passive suffering of his past life. Self-blinding is both an expression of insight, and a defiant refusal of it.[11]

Oedipus tries to divorce himself from his past by blocking off his vision of it. But the very act of self-blinding is also a reenactment of the things Oedipus does not want to see. Oedipus uses the verb ἔπαισε to describe his self-blinding (1331), and the Messenger uses the same verb to describe Oedipus striking his own eyes — ἔπαισεν (1270). The verb has been used only twice in the play before: first, when Oedipus describes how he killed Laius and struck him: παίω (807); and second, when he bursts through or penetrates the palace gates in search of Jocasta: εἰσέπαισεν (1252). The act of self-blinding is not only an attempt to reject the taint of parricide and incest, but also a reenactment both of striking the father and of penetrating the mother. Moreover, the word Oedipus uses to describe himself as he strikes his own eyes is αὐτόχειρ (1331), which has been used twice in the play before, both times by Oedipus to describe the killer of Laius (231, 266). Oedipus avenges the killing of his father by striking himself just as his father was struck; but he also reenacts that killing by killing his father again in his own body. Oedipus's self-blinding is overdetermined because it represents both a desire to repress the past, and also a reenactment of that past. He blinds himself both because he refuses to recognize what he has done and because he does recognize it.

The *Oedipus Tyrannus* provides Aristotle with the supreme examples of what are, for him, the most important features of tragic plot structure, reversal, περιπέτεια and ἀναγνώρισις, recognition:

> Ἔστι δὲ περιπέτεια μὲν ἡ εἰς τὸ ἐναντίον τῶν πραττομένων μεταβολὴ καθάπερ εἴρηται, καὶ τοῦτο δὲ ὥσπερ λέγομεν κατὰ τὸ εἰκὸς ἢ ἀναγκαῖον, οἷον ἐν τῷ Οἰδίποδι ἐλθὼν ὡς εὐφρανῶν τὸν Οἰδίπουν καὶ ἀπαλλάξων τοῦ πρὸς τὴν μητέρα φόβου, δηλώσας ὃς ἦν, τοὐναντίον ἐποίησεν . . . ἀναγνώρισις δέ, ὥσπερ καὶ τοὔνομα σημαίνει, ἐξ ἀγνοίας εἰς γνῶσιν μεταβολή, ἢ εἰς φιλίαν ἢ εἰς ἔχθραν, τῶν πρὸς εὐτυχίαν ἢ δυστυχίαν ὡρισμένων· καλλίστη δέ ἀναγνώρισις ὅταν ἅμα περιπετείᾳ γένηται, οἷον ἔχει ἡ ἐν τῷ Οἰδίποδι.

"Reversal" is the change of events to the opposite, as has been said. It should happen according to probability or necessity, as in the *Oedipus*, the man coming as if to cheer up Oedipus and relieve him of his fear about his mother, in fact does the opposite because he reveals who he is . . . And "recognition" is, as the name implies, the change from ignorance to knowledge, either in the direction of friendship or enmity, of things defined in relation to good fortune or bad. Recognition is best when it occurs together with reversal, as does the recognition in the *Oedipus*. (*Poetics* 1452a22–26, 1452a29–33)

Aristotle admires Sophocles' conjunction of περιπέτεια with ἀναγνώρισις in a single dramatic moment. The Corinthian messenger came to bring Oedipus the good news of his supposed father's death (*Oedipus Tyrannus* 924–72), but in so doing, he revealed that Polybus and Merope were not Oedipus's parents — in Aristotle's words, δηλώσας ὃς ἦν — revealing who he, Oedipus, was.

Aristotle is quite right that the reversal is combined, in complex ways, with recognition. But although the *Oedipus Tyrannus* is one of Aristotle's favorite examples of ideal dramatic form, the play does not fit at all well into Aristotelian patterns of dramatic structure. The "reversal" in the play is not a straightforward alteration of "events to the opposite," as if Oedipus, who was once fortunate, became unfortunate — the man who was a king becomes a monster and a social outcast. Oedipus does not change into the killer of his father and husband of his mother; rather, it is revealed that he has already been these things, at the same time as being the king of Thebes. It has been well argued that Oedipus is "a man in the shape of a riddle — and this time a riddle to which there is no solution."[12] He is both king and scapegoat, not first the one and then the other. He is both above and below humanity, combining multiple incompatible and inhuman roles. He regards himself as so far beyond the norms of human life that he is not even, he believes, polluted; he tells the Chorus members that they need not be afraid to touch him (1413–15). His continued presence on stage makes the audience aware that his reversal of fortune is not final or the end of the story, and that his recognitions produce not knowledge, but awareness of incomprehension.

Oedipus's self-recognition invites comparison with recognition scenes elsewhere in Greek tragedy, when brothers and sisters or parents and children meet again. In Greek tragedy, as in life, unexpected recognitions are accompanied by exclamations: the syntactical form associated with recognition is apostrophe. When a person recognizes a lost friend or kinsman, the normal thing is to address him or her ("O long-lost relative!"), and often also to address the gods or the light, both of which bear witness to the truth and bring it to the open ("O you who see this!").[13]

But Oedipus's recognition of "who he was" (ὃς ἦν) is far less straightforward in Sophocles' play than Aristotle's account would suggest. Oedipus is certainly led to some kind of recognition by the herdsman: he recognizes the facts that he killed his father and married his mother.[14] But in other recognition scenes in Greek tragedy, the recognition of facts leads without difficulty to the recognition of persons. By contrast, Oedipus's recognition of the facts makes it all but impossible for him to recognize himself. He realizes he has done things that are incompatible not only with being king of Thebes and not only with thinking of himself as the clever solver of riddles, but also with being part of human society. In the final episode of the *Oedipus Tyrannus*, Oedipus becomes unable to recognize a single man in the events of his past life.

Oedipus recognizes all kinds of things and people at the end of the play that are associated with himself or his past life, but in none of them, nor their combination, does he recognize a unified character. It becomes difficult for the spectators to make sense of Oedipus as a king or as an outcast, as a human being, or even as a single entity. When he hears from Jocasta that the killing of Laius happened where the three roads meet, just where he himself killed an old man before arriving in Thebes, the obvious conclusion for Oedipus to draw is that the old man he killed was Laius. His last hope that he may not be Laius's killer himself lies in the witness's supposed claim that the royal party was attacked by a whole group of brigands. One man, Oedipus reassures himself, cannot be equal to many: οὐ γὰρ γένοιτ' ἂν εἷς γε τοῖς πολλοῖς ἴσος (845).[15] It is a striking feature of the plot that this crucial detail is never resolved; there is never an explanation for the inconsistent stories about the number of men who killed Laius.[16] Oedipus realizes that he is the killer of Laius, and in so doing, he also realizes implicitly that he is equivalent to many different characters: the name "Oedipus" refers not to a single man but a conglomerate. The life of the king once the truth is known is figured, both by Oedipus and by others, not merely as shocking but also as plural.

This is partly the result of incest, which necessarily multiplies the number of relationships between family members. Through incest, Oedipus becomes both husband and son to Jocasta, both brother and father to Antigone and Ismene, both brother-in-law and son-in-law to Creon, and both son and murderous replacement to Laius.

But the problem is not just incest but the fact that Oedipus lives on even after he discovers the truth about his relationship to Jocasta. The multiplication of Oedipus's roles is associated specifically with the fact that he does not kill himself, as Jocasta does. When the Messenger tells the Chorus about Jocasta's last words before she hanged herself, Oedipus bursts into his narrative, distracting attention from her and her motives for suicide:

ὅπως γὰρ ὀργῇ χρωμένη παρῆλθ' ἔσω
θυρῶνος, ἵετ' εὐθὺ πρὸς τὰ νυμφικὰ
λέχη, κόμην σπῶσ' ἀμφιδεξίοις ἀκμαῖς·
πύλας δ', ὅπως εἰσῆλθ', ἐπιρράξασ' ἔσω,
καλεῖ τὸν ἤδη Λάιον πάλαι νεκρόν,
μνήμην παλαιῶν σπερμάτων ἔχουσ', ὑφ' ὧν
θάνοι μὲν αὐτός, τὴν δὲ τίκτουσαν λίποι
τοῖς οἷσιν αὐτοῦ δύστεκνον παιδουργίαν.
γοᾶτο δ' εὐνάς, ἔνθα δύστηνος διπλῆ
ἐξ ἀνδρὸς ἄνδρα καὶ τέκν' ἐκ τέκνων τέκοι.
χὤπως μὲν ἐκ τῶνδ' οὐκέτ' οἶδ' ἀπόλλυται·
βοῶν γὰρ εἰσέπαισεν Οἰδίπους, ὑφ' οὗ
οὐκ ἦν τὸ κείνης ἐκθεάσασθαι κακόν,
ἀλλ' εἰς ἐκεῖνον περιπολοῦντ' ἐλεύσσομεν.

When she went through the door in her passion,
she rushed straight to the marriage
bed, tearing her hair with both hands.
When she entered she slammed shut the door panels,
and she called on Laius, now long dead,
remembering their old seeds, through which
he died and left her to bear, by his very own children,
a terrible childbearing accursed in its offspring.
And she lamented her marriage beds, where she wretchedly twice over
bore a husband by a husband and children by children;
and how she died after that I do not know.
For screaming Oedipus burst in, and because of him
it was not possible to look at her suffering,
but we looked at him as he rushed all over the place.
(1241–54)

Jocasta kills herself because she cannot live with the horror that she has slept with both Laius and Oedipus, bearing a new husband by her husband, and then still more children by her own child. The incestuous proliferations of Jocasta's sexuality are veiled forever by her death. Even the final moment of her death is obscured, because Jocasta's last words are interrupted by the scream of Oedipus: βοῶν γὰρ εἰσέπαισεν Οἰδίπους (1252). The line could mean, and is usually taken to mean, "Oedipus burst in screaming." But it is ambiguous: it could also mean, "He burst in, screaming '*Oedipus!*' "[17] Oedipus's arrival is the culmination of the things that were tormenting Jocasta. He is the husband she bore by her husband, he is the child by whom she had children.

Jocasta, according to the Messenger's account of her indirect discourse, explains her motives for suicide in a series of nouns, which are either abstract, like μνήμη (memory) or παιδουργία (childbearing), or plural, like εὐνάς (beds) and τέκνα (children) (1245–50). Jocasta, and/or the Messenger, may be trying to distance themselves from the horrors by these means.[18] But these rhetorical devices also work to suggest that the word "Oedipus" is the name not only for the man but also for all the abstractions and plurals that preceded that name. "Oedipus" becomes associated, and by implication identified, with the old seeds and the memory of them (1246), the terrible childbirth and the beds (1249–50). No single definite description is equivalent to the name "Oedipus."

Recognition, according to Aristotle, can be either of events or of people (*Po-*

etics 1452a34–36). Oedipus recognizes events — that he killed his father and married his mother — and also the true identity of persons: Laius as his father, Jocasta as his mother, himself as the killer of his father and husband of his mother. But when he conveys his recognition of events, he does so in a way that breaks up the narrative and confuses his own revealed character, by describing the facts not by finite verbs but by nouns. In his long speech evoking his discoveries (1369–1415) Oedipus relies on questions, apostrophe, and imperatives, rather than statements. Oedipus tells the story of his past life, but he does not do so by finite verbs ("I killed my father, I slept with my mother"). Instead, he uses indirect questions ("I do not know with what eyes I could look at my father or my mother," 1371–74), rhetorical questions ("Would it be desirable to look at my children now?" 1375–76), and finally, climactically and repeatedly, apostrophe (1391–1408), before, in a series of imperatives (1409–15) urging the people of Thebes to expel him from the city or kill him.[19]

Apostrophe is associated particularly with recognition scenes.[20] Oedipus's moment of multiple apostrophes in 1391–1408 is the central expression of his recognition. But he recognizes, and therefore addresses, not a single man, Oedipus, but the multiplicity of different things that are now associated with him: "O Cithaeron!" (ἰὼ Κιθαιρών, 1391); "O Polybus and Corinth and my old father's home!" (1394–96); "O three-path crossroad, and hidden groves of oak, and passage between the three roads!" (1398–99). Finally and most famously, he cries,

> ὦ γάμοι γάμοι,
> ἐφύσαθ᾿ ἡμᾶς, καὶ φυτεύσαντες πάλιν
> ἀνεῖτε ταὐτὸν σπέρμα, κἀπεδείξατε
> πατέρας ἀδελφούς, παῖδας αἷμ᾿ ἐμφύλιον,
> νύμφας γυναῖκας μητέρας τε, χὠπόσα
> αἴσχιστ᾿ ἐν ἀνθρώποισιν ἔργα γίγνεται.

> O marriages, marriages,
> you produced us, and after begetting, again
> you brought back the same seed, and revealed
> fathers, brothers, children, kindred blood,
> brides, wives and mothers, and all
> the most revolting deeds among humanity.
> (1403–8)

The marriages produced Oedipus, and thereby revealed him to the world (ἀπε-
δείξατε, 1405). His first revelation, the first recognition of his true character,
began at birth. But what was revealed was not a single baby, or even a single
human being, but rather "fathers, brothers, children, kindred blood." The list
includes different things adding up to a plurality (father, brother, child), and the
nouns are also themselves plural. Oedipus's roles are thus multiplied twice over.[21]
He recognizes not a single man but a whole list of entities.

Through his discovery, the roles associated with Oedipus have proliferated: he
"is" Polybus and Corinth and Cithaeron and fathers, brothers, children. Things
were much simpler when he was Oedipus the king. Even the Messenger resorts
to lists of nouns when describing Oedipus's life after his discovery:

> ὁ πρὶν παλαιὸς δ' ὄλβος ἦν πάροιθε μὲν
> ὄλβος δικαίως, νῦν δὲ τῇδε θἠμέρᾳ
> στεναγμός, ἄτη, θάνατος, αἰσχύνη, κακῶν
> ὅσ' ἐστὶ πάντων ὀνόματ', οὐδέν ἐστ' ἀπόν.

> The old happiness in the past
> was true happiness, but now on this day,
> lamentation, ruin, death, shame, of all sufferings
> none of the names is missing.
> (1282–85)

Once, the house of Oedipus could be described by the single noun, "happiness"
(ὄλβος). Now it has multiplied into "lamentation, ruin, death, shame" (στεναγμός, ἄτη, θάνατος, αἰσχύνη, 1284). The multiplication of misery goes beyond
the pluralization of family relationships produced by incest, to a pluralization of
all abstract unhappiness associated with this household. Happy families are all
alike, and happiness is the only name one needs for happiness; but each unhappy
family is unhappy in multiple ways, which produce a proliferation of names for
suffering.

Instead of recognizing himself, Oedipus recognizes others—things, places,
and people associated with himself. The discovery of the truth is preceded and
foreshadowed by Oedipus's recognition of the herdsman who belonged to Laius.
Oedipus draws attention to the process by which he recognizes him: he notices
that he looks like the Corinthian in age, and he recognizes (ἔγνωκα, 1115) the
slaves leading him in. The Chorus picks up the verb ἔγνωκα (I recognize him,
1117). In recognizing the herdsman Oedipus is recognizing someone who is

connected to his own life. Oedipus is, in a more intimate sense than the herds-man, "of Laius" (the word Λαΐου recurs at 1117, 1122, 1139); and the herdsman is the man who will reveal his own life to him. But Oedipus and the herdsman are not in fact identical. Oedipus can recognize himself only by various forms of synecdoche and metonymy: he recognizes all kinds of things associated with himself but not himself as a unity.

The play has confused the question of whether the punishment for the killer of Laius will be exile or death.[22] In the event, the two possibilities are conflated. Oedipus will go into exile, but he presents his future life also as a kind of living death. He asks that he may go to Cithaeron,

οὑμὸς Κιθαιρὼν οὗτος, ὃν μήτηρ τέ μοι
πατήρ τ᾽ ἐθέσθην ζῶντε κύριον τάφον,
ἵν᾽ ἐξ ἐκείνων, οἵ μ᾽ ἀπωλλύτην, θάνω.

That Cithaeron of mine, which my mother
and father, when they were both alive, chose as my own proper tomb,
so that I may die from those two, who destroyed me.
(1452–4)

He will go on living on the mountain as a fulfillment of the death that his parents chose for him. His future life will be an enactment of the death that should already have happened in the past.

There is one faint hint that there may be a reason in the future why Oedipus has remained alive — an anticipation of the *Oedipus Coloneus*. Oedipus says,

καίτοι τοσοῦτόν γ᾽ οἶδα, μήτε μ᾽ ἂν νόσον
μήτ᾽ ἄλλο πέρσαι μηδέν· οὐ γὰρ ἄν ποτε
θνῄσκων ἐσώθην, μὴ ᾽πί τῳ δεινῷ κακῷ.

Nevertheless, I know this much, that neither disease
nor anything else will destroy me; for I would never
have been saved when dying, unless for some strange evil.
(1455–57)

Simple death will not be the end of Oedipus's story. The gods have some strange purpose for him. Oedipus's roles will proliferate still further: one day he will be transformed into a hero.[23] At this stage, he himself has no specific knowledge of what he will be. He assumes that his future must hold something bad, "some strange evil." But he is mistaken even in that; his future holds more unexpected transformations than he can imagine.

The complexity of Oedipus's present and future life is emphasized by the relative simplicity of the future he envisions for his daughters. Oedipus is unable to tell his own story in narrative form. He cannot look at himself or his own life clearly. But he is able to describe in concrete detail his daughters' future lives. The play is framed by two episodes in which Oedipus acts as a father. In the first scene, he promised to be a good father to his metaphorical children, the people of Thebes. His emotional address to his literal children, his daughters, is the climax of the final episode (1478–1514). The daughters will inherit the curse of the house of the Labdacids. Oedipus himself looks forward to a much less clearly defined future.

In reminding his daughters of their kinship to him, Oedipus simultaneously recalls his own birth. "Children, neither seeing nor discovering, I appeared for you as a father from the very place from which I myself was sown" (ὃς ὑμίν, ὦ τέκν', οὔθ' ὁρῶν οὔθ' ἱστορῶν / πατὴρ ἐφάνθην ἔνθεν αὐτὸς ἠρόθην, 1484–85). On one level, this is a reminder of the terrible fact that his daughters are his sisters. But Oedipus also enacts another birth, into a new life beyond the ones that are over, by naming himself as the blind father. He makes an appearance, ἐφάνθην, a word more appropriate to a baby being born than to a man becoming a father.[24] The position of his daughters, as Oedipus describes it, is a version of what his own might be. But Oedipus is able to transfer the role of the suffering outcast from human society onto his daughters, and leave his own future still undefined. He appeared, or was born, as a father; he can anticipate further births, even when his daughters can hope for nothing but repetition and pain. The daughters are still confined in a world of ancestral guilt.

Oedipus pities his daughters, rather than himself.

καὶ σφὼ δακρύω· προσβλέπειν γὰρ οὐ σθένω·
νοούμενος τὰ πικρὰ τοῦ λοιποῦ βίου,
οἷον βιῶναι σφὼ πρὸς ἀνθρώπων χρεών.
ποίας γὰρ ἀστῶν ἥξετ' εἰς ὁμιλίας,
ποίας δ' ἑορτάς, ἔνθεν οὐ κεκλαυμέναι
πρὸς οἶκον ἵξεσθ' ἀντὶ τῆς θεωρίας;

I weep for you — for I do not have the power to look at you
— thinking of the bitterness of the remainder of life,

the life you must live at the hands of mankind.
For which gatherings of citizens will you come to,
which feasts, from which you will not, weeping,
go home instead of [attending] the spectacle?
(1486–91)

He weeps "thinking of the bitterness of the rest of life" (νοούμενος τὰ πικρὰ τοῦ λοιποῦ βίου). But one might expect it would be not only Antigone and Ismene, but also Oedipus himself, who will have to face "the rest of life" in bitterness. The way Oedipus describes the horrors of his daughters' future existence draws attention to parallels between their lives and his own. They will be social outcasts confined to the house, for whom the public world is barred — just as Oedipus himself, only a few lines later (1515–23), is pushed by Creon into the palace, instead of being allowed to stay in the public, visible arena. He emphasizes that he cannot see his daughters, and that they too will be cut off from sight or spectacle (θεωρία, 1491): they will be excluded from public life, a life identified with the ability to see and be seen. Oedipus represents one version of his own future in the future of his daughters; it is his future in a form he can articulate. He transfers appeals for his own future onto his daughters: he prays, at the end of the speech, that they may have a better life than their father (1512–14). On one level, Oedipus is already treating himself as dead, and his life over, as Ajax does when he wishes his son more luck than he had in life (*Ajax* 550–51). But Oedipus, unlike Ajax, is desperately unwilling to let go of either his children or his life. He wants to prescribe and predict the future for his descendants, while he himself remains alive and his own future life remains unknown and unpredictable.[25]

Even before the discovery, Oedipus described himself as the child of τύχη and claimed that he was the child of the moons, waxing and waning like them.[26] His past and present identities evade definition, and Oedipus still resists Creon's desire that he leave the stage.

> Οι. ἄπαγέ νύν μ' ἐντεῦθεν ἤδη.
>
> Κρ.   στεῖχέ νυν, τέκνων δ' ἀφοῦ.
>
> Οι. μηδαμῶς ταύτας γ' ἕλῃ μου.
>
> Κρ.   πάντα μὴ βούλου κρατεῖν.
>
> καὶ γὰρ ἁκράτησας οὔ σοι τῷ βίῳ ξυνέσπετο.
>
> Χο. ὦ πάτρας Θήβης ἔνοικοι, λεύσσετ', Οἰδίπους ὅδε,
>
> ὃς τὰ κλείν' αἰνίγματ' ᾔδει καὶ κράτιστος ἦν ἀνήρ,
>
> οὗ τίς οὐ ζήλῳ πολιτῶν ταῖς τύχαις ἐπέβλεπεν,

εἰς ὅσον κλύδωνα δεινῆς συμφορᾶς ἐλήλυθεν.
ὥστε θνητὸν ὄντ' ἐκείνην τὴν τελευταίαν ἔδει
ἡμέραν ἐπισκοποῦντα μηδέν' ὀλβίζειν, πρὶν ἂν
τέρμα τοῦ βίου περάσῃ μηδὲν ἀλγεινὸν παθών.[27]

Oedipus: Take me away from here now, at once!
Creon: Go now, let go of the children.
Oedipus: No! don't take my daughters away from me!
Creon: Don't try to take control of everything.
What you controlled did not follow you through life.
Chorus: Inhabitants of ancestral Thebes, look, this is Oedipus,
who solved the famous riddle and was the most powerful man,
at whom all the citizens looked in envy in his good fortune;
to such a great wave of terrible misfortune is he come.
So being mortal one should look to that final
day and count no man happy until
he has passed the finishing point of life without suffering.
(1521–30)

Creon reminds Oedipus that he can no longer "control everything." Creon himself tries to take control of Oedipus, but he succeeds only with great difficulty in hustling him into the house. Oedipus may no longer be in control, but he is also not easy for others either to control or to understand. Oedipus's continued existence is an embarrassment for the Thebans, and particularly for Creon, as his brother-in-law. It is a reminder that the city was ruled by a king who is now an abomination. But it is also a problem for the spectators of the play as they try to make sense of what they have seen.

Sophocles' play makes it difficult for the Chorus or the audience to feel secure in concluding from Oedipus's suffering even the banality that life is no stranger to uncertainty, or that fortune conquers all. The choral ode at 1186–1223, after Oedipus's discovery of the truth, is about the impermanence of all human existence. The ode tries to take Oedipus's life as exemplary of all human life. "O generations of mortals" (ἰὼ γενεαὶ βροτῶν, 1186): all generations of men equal nothing. If Oedipus, who seemed to be a great king and the man who saved Thebes from the Sphinx, has fallen, then all men are equal to nothing. The moral was a traditional one to draw from the story of Oedipus.[28] But the continued existence of Oedipus in the final scene of the play suggests that the Chorus's attempt to draw even this gloomy conclusion from the fall of Oedipus may be precipitate. The Oedipus who resists leaving the stage may be an enigma, but he is not dead, and he is hardly equal to nothing.

The Chorus warns that we should not judge any life until it is over.[29] Such advice was probably proverbial.[30] But Sophocles sets apparently obvious folk wisdom in a context where it becomes puzzling and less obviously true. Similarly, Herodotus's Croesus learns to call no man happy until he is dead (1.30.2–34.1, 86.1–90.1). But he learns this lesson, necessarily, before he himself is dead. He learns not to judge life precipitately, but even this lesson is a precipitate judgment.[31] The sentiment at the end of the *Oedipus Tyrannus* suggests a similar paradox. Oedipus, at the end of the play, is not dead and has not crossed over life's finishing line. The final episode shows how many reversals his life may yet hold. It is still too early to call him happy, but it is also too early to call him unhappy. He has lived on past what seemed to be life's finishing line, but he turns out to be still alive. Since it is unclear when the end of Oedipus's life may be, judgment, either on the life or on the play, must be deferred indefinitely. The Chorus's confused attempt to produce a moral from the story only draws attention to how impossible it is to do so conclusively. One cannot judge a life until it is over. But if lives which seem to be over keep going, and plays do the same, it is unclear how we can ever be sure that the time for judgment has truly arrived. Oedipus is not dead, and it is still not at all clear what we see when we obey the Chorus's injunction (1524) to "look at Oedipus."

CHAPTER TWO

"Never to have lived is best"

Oedipus Coloneus

The Chorus in Sophocles' *Oedipus Coloneus* declares,

μὴ φῦναι τὸν ἅπαντα νι-
κᾷ λόγον· τὸ δ', ἐπεὶ φανῇ,
βῆναι κεῖθεν ὅθεν περ ἥ-
κει πολὺ δεύτερον ὡς τάχιστα.

Not to be born conquers every
logos. But when one is born,
to go back where one came from
as fast as possible is by far the second.
(1224–27)[1]

Never to be born is best; to die almost immediately is a distinctly inferior second best. The lines imply that to be born at all is already to have lived too long. All living is therefore overliving. This gloomy sentiment is not original; Sophocles' Chorus is appropriating a phrase that may have been proverbial, and that had already been used by the lyric poets Theognis and Bacchylides.[2] But in its new dramatic context the old dictum acquires a new urgency because the declaration that all human living is overliving is juxtaposed with the specific case of Oedipus. Oedipus lives on not only after the proper time for all human beings to die (namely, before birth), but also after he is no longer the individual he seemed to be, the king of Thebes and famous solver of riddles.

The *Oedipus Tyrannus* confronts the audience with the problem of overliving but offers no possible solution. The *Oedipus Coloneus*, composed many years later and performed only after Sophocles' death,[3] suggests that it may be possible to transform an overdetermined and terrible identity into a source of strength — but only for some lucky few, such as Oedipus himself, who discovers a new role as protector of Athens.[4] According to many critics, the *Oedipus Coloneus* charts the gradual purification and redemption of Oedipus.[5] Others have emphasized Oedipus's continuing anger and bitterness, especially toward his son Polyneices.[6] The play provokes both these apparently incompatible readings. From the perspective either of Oedipus himself or of the gods, the *Oedipus Coloneus* shows the rehabilitation of a broken, blind old man: the most wretched and polluted of men is no longer a social outcast, because he finds a welcome in Athens and assumes almost divine powers as the object of a new hero cult.[7] But the divine perspective is not the only one available. Oedipus withdraws from human life, but the play emphasizes the continuing and indeed increasing suffering of those who remain behind. The children of Oedipus are left with all the most unpleasant aspects of his life, including the sense that all life is living death. Oedipus's past is transformed into a source of power for the hero himself, but his children remain the victims of past actions, who must endlessly reenact their own past lives. Living too long, in Sophocles' last play, becomes associated with all merely human life, and with tragedy.

Oedipus's first utterance in the *Tyrannus* is "O children" (ᾯ τέκνα, 1); in the *Coloneus*, it is "Child" (τέκνον, 1). As the words "children" and "child" suggest, both plays are concerned with the consequences of Oedipus's past life. But at the beginning of the *Oedipus Tyrannus*, Oedipus was not a suppliant but the king to whom his people came in supplication. He was a public figure who called his citizens his children. In the *Oedipus Coloneus*, he has been reduced from the great heights of power and influence he exerted at the beginning of the *Oedipus Tyrannus*, and his sphere has been reduced from the public to the private. The *Oedipus Tyrannus* is about Oedipus the public figure, Oedipus the king: it explores his social relationships in the public and political sphere. *Oedipus Coloneus* is about the private Oedipus, the family man: it explores his relationships with his literal children, and the impact on them of his past history.

All Oedipus has left at the beginning of the play is his broken body, his tainted name, and his daughter. In the course of the play, both body and name become intensely valuable: Thebes and Athens compete to possess the polluted Oedipus, who will protect the city where he dies.[8] On one level, Oedipus's power is the result of the transgressive actions he has performed in the past; the city is strengthened by incorporating into itself the power of the outcast.[9] But Oedipus's power to curse and bless, even after life, is also linked with the ability not to repeat the past, and to reject or distance himself from those who reflect his own past actions — including, most obviously, his own children. The worst aspects of his past seem to be transferred to Thebes, while Oedipus himself finds a new world in Athens.

Oedipus repeatedly encounters figures who recall his own past self. The first of these is the Chorus. The play opens with the arrival of Oedipus and Antigone at Colonus. They discover from the Stranger where they are, and meet the Chorus, the native inhabitants of the place. Now, it is not Oedipus himself, as in the *Tyrannus*, but the old men of Colonus who gradually discover the truth about his past. He is reluctant to let them know who he is; he urges, "Don't, don't ask me who I am!" (210–11). Like Teiresias and Jocasta in the *Oedipus Tyrannus*, Oedipus thinks it would be better to abandon the attempt to learn the truth about parricide and incest; but like Oedipus himself in the earlier play, the Chorus persists. Oedipus leads the old men through the story of his ancestry, dropping clues before the name "Oedipus" emerges, presented not as a new revelation but as something they may already know. Oedipus never tells them who he is, but he allows them to find it out:

Oι. Λαΐου ἴστε τιν' —
Xo.   ὤ· ἰοὺ ἰού.
Oι. τό τε Λαβδακιδᾶν γένος;
Xo.   ὦ Ζεῦ.
Oι. ἄθλιον Οἰδιπόδαν;
Xo.   σὺ γὰρ ὅδ' εἶ;
Oι. δέος ἴσχετε μηδὲν ὅσ' αὐδῶ.
Xo. ἰὼ ὤ ὤ.
Oι.   δύσμορος.
Xo.   ὤ ὤ.

Οι. θύγατερ, τί ποτ' αὐτίκα κύρσει;
Χο. ἔξω πόρσω βαίνετε χώρας.

Oedipus: Do you know of a certain son of Laius . . . ?
Chorus: O! Oh no! Oh no!
Oedipus: . . . of the race of the Labdacids . . . ?
Chorus: O Zeus!
Oedipus: Wretched Oedipus?
Chorus: Are you he?
Oedipus: Do not be frightened by what I say!
Chorus: O! Oh no! Oh no!
Oedipus: How unlucky I am.
Chorus: O! O!
Oedipus: Daughter, what will happen now?
Chorus: Go far away out of the country!
(220–26)

The Chorus had promised to protect Oedipus and allow him to stay where he is (176–77). But as soon as they know his name, they insist that he must be expelled from the city. Oedipus longed for exile or death on Mount Cithaeron when he first discovered the truth; similarly, the Chorus insists that this polluted man cannot remain in the sacred grove, or even in the country of Attica.

The Chorus assumes that it already knows all it needs to know about Oedipus. The comic poet Antiphanes claims people always respond this way to the name "Oedipus." Everyone knows the whole story. Tragedy is easy, compared with comedy, argues Antiphanes' speaker; one only needs to remind the audience of stories they already know:

Οἰδίπουν γὰρ † φῶ
τὰ δ' ἄλλα πάντ' ἴσασιν· ὁ πατὴρ Λάιος,
μήτηρ Ἰοκάστη, θυγατέρες, παῖδες τίνες,
τί πείσεθ' οὗτος, τί πεποίηκεν.

For you say "Oedipus,"
and they know all the rest: his father Laius,
his mother Jocasta, who his daughters were, and his sons,
what he will suffer, what he has done.[10]

The name "Oedipus" alone implies everything else about the story.[11] In the *Coloneus* it seems that any of the names ("Laius," "Jocasta," "Labdacids") implies all the others and triggers a response to the whole story. Oedipus has only to drop the name of "Laius" — "Do you know of a son of Laius?" (Λαΐου ἴστε τιν'; 220), and already the Chorus shrieks in recognition, ἰοὺ ἰού (220). Oedipus repeats three times who he is (the son of Laius, the descendant of the Labdacids, wretched Oedipus); each alone would have been enough to reveal the horrible truth.

The Chorus assumes that Oedipus is defined by his past history and that he is hateful to the gods. The old men are horrified to discover who he is, and their first reaction is to try to expel him from the land. Their fear is greater than their pity. They insist on their own right to take revenge against Oedipus for deceiving them: "fated retribution comes to no one, for the things he suffered first" (οὐδενὶ μοιριδία τίσις ἔρχεται / ὧν προπάθῃ τὸ τίνειν, 229–30).

Antigone tries to make them move from vengeance to mercy (237–53). Her speech is important because Antigone offers a perspective quite different from that of either the Chorus members or Oedipus himself: she, unlike them, defends the idea of forgiveness.[12] She hopes the old men will pity her father's plight and her own, rather than tremble at his terrible story and his terrible name. She reminds them that Oedipus's actions were involuntary (240) and that no man can escape the gods (252–54). The Chorus is afraid that the gods will punish those who protect a polluted man; Antigone reminds the old men that Oedipus's terrible actions were themselves caused by the gods. But the Chorus remains too fearful of the gods to offer any help to the suppliants.

Oedipus speaks in his own defense and shows the Chorus why it is wrong to assume it knows the full story of Oedipus. His speech divides neatly into two parts, each seventeen lines long. In the first (258–74) he discusses the relationship of name to nature. In the second part of the speech (275–91), signaled by "because of these things" (ἀνθ' ὧν, 275), he draws his conclusion about the relationship between the visible and the invisible. The speech associates the visible with the present, the invisible with the past: the gods can see both things invisible and things long past, and will hold men to a past and invisible standard in the present and visible world (276–81). Oedipus shows that there is a parallel between his past (the actions of the *Oedipus Tyrannus*) and his present. A forgotten history has again been uncovered; he has again arrived blindly in a new place, and is again threatened with exile from that place. But he appeals for a new ending for his story, so that the second time round he may be not expelled from the city, but reintegrated into society. The two parts of the speech explore from two different perspectives the unstable relationship between past and present actions. The past seems to repeat itself; but past character is not necessarily a reliable guide to what a person will do in the present or the future.

The first part of the speech sets out two distinctions between name and nature — between what is said about people and what they really are. First, Oedipus reminds the Athenian Chorus members of the historical, and therefore moral, implications of their own city's name. Athens has a reputation for helping suppliants, and yet Athens is not, in the present instance, helping him.[13]

τί δῆτα δόξης, ἢ τί κληδόνος καλῆς
μάτην ῥεούσης ὠφέλημα γίγνεται,
εἰ τάς γ᾿ Ἀθήνας φασὶ θεοσεβεστάτας
εἶναι, μόνας δὲ τὸν κακούμενον ξένον
σῴζειν οἵας τε καὶ μόνας ἀρκεῖν ἔχειν;
κἄμοιγε ποῦ ταῦτ᾿ ἐστίν, οἵτινες βάθρων
ἐκ τῶνδέ μ᾿ ἐξάραντες εἶτ᾿ ἐλαύνετε,
ὄνομα μόνον δείσαντες;

So what benefit comes of fame or good reputation,
if it is poured out in vain,
if they say Athens is the most god-fearing city,
and that only Athens has the power
to save the wronged stranger?
Where is all that for me, if you curse me
and drive me out from this place,
fearing only my name?
(258–65)

His questions about Athens show that the name and reputation of a place or person do not necessarily offer any clue to how they will act. There may be nothing in a name, if "Athens" does not mean "the only city that protects suppliants." Then Oedipus moves to his own case. He suggests that there is a similar disjunction between his own name or what people say about him and his true nature. Past history and reputation would have been a misleading indicator of what Athens is like now; so why should his own history and name not be equally unreliable as signs of his present character? Why then should the Chorus reject him, "fearing only his name" (ὄνομα μόνον δείσαντες)?

Oedipus is hinting at a conventional view of language. The fact that he is called "Oedipus" bears no relation to who he is.[14] One might infer that his name has no connection with how he acts, or has acted. But things become more complicated as Oedipus goes on to explain why his name is not to be feared. It is not only his name but also his body, which one might think would be polluted, and also his apparent deeds, he argues, which bear no relation to his true nature:

> οὐ γὰρ δὴ τό γε
> σῶμ᾽ οὐδὲ τἄργα τἄμ᾽· ἐπεὶ τά γ᾽ ἔργα με
> πεπονθότ᾽ ἴσθι μᾶλλον ἢ δεδρακότα,
> εἴ σοι τὰ μητρὸς καὶ πατρὸς χρείη λέγειν,
> ὧν οὕνεκ᾽ ἐκφοβῇ με·

> For indeed neither
> my body nor my deeds are mine, since as for my deeds,
> know that I suffered them rather than performed them,
> if it should be necessary to tell you the events of my mother and father,
> because of which you fear me.
> (265–69)

The things he did unknowingly with his parents are classified not as action but as suffering. Neither his name nor what he has "done" gives any indication of how he should be treated in the present. Clearly, there is no reason to hold someone morally responsible for what he did in ignorance, any more than people can be held morally responsible for their own names. But Oedipus seems entirely to neglect the possibility of pollution. Neither a man's name nor his body — nor even what he does if those actions were "suffered rather than performed" — gives one any reliable access at all to his nature; nor should any of these have any consequences for how he is treated by others.

But Oedipus's appeal to the members of the Chorus as citizens of Athens relied on the idea that past actions and reputation ought indeed to affect present behavior. His initial question, "What good is reputation if it bears no relation to how people act?" implied that Athens ought to live up to its reputation. The city's name and past deeds are associated with one another, and Athens ought to act to prove that they are deserved. He suggests that the actions of Athens must be determined by the city's reputation, name, and past history. But he insists on his own right to distinguish himself from his own past passive experiences, and from his name. Oedipus's past actions do not in themselves determine how he should be treated or how he should act in the future.

At the beginning of the play, Oedipus's blind arrival in Colonus seemed merely to repeat the blind arrivals of his past, at the crossroads and in Thebes; but he manages in the course of the scene to give a new meaning to his own name. The Chorus members respond to his rhetoric; they already begin to reinterpret the name "Oedipus." They present the name as the bait that will inevitably draw Theseus to come and meet him (ὄνομα is repeated in 301 and 306). The name is powerful because it recalls the terrible actions of the famous Oedipus. But it will cause not only revulsion and horror, like the Chorus's first reaction to learning Oedipus's identity, but also attraction.

Oedipus distinguishes three different periods of the past: the first part of his life in which he killed his father and married his mother; the time immediately after he discovered the truth, in which he was furious with himself and consumed by shame; and the later time when he had distanced himself from his parricide and incest and was no longer consumed by self-hatred, when his sons drove him out of the city. Oedipus insists that only this last period has any relevance for the present; neither his past parricide and incest, nor his past self-blinding and self-hatred, have anything to do with his life now.

οὐ δῆτ', ἐπεί τοι τὴν μὲν αὐτίχ' ἡμέραν,
ὁπηνίκ' ἕζει θυμός, ἥδιστον δέ μοι
τὸ κατθανεῖν ἦν καὶ τὸ λευσθῆναι πέτροις,
οὐδεὶς ἔρωτ' ἐς τόνδ' ἐφαίνετ' ὠφελῶν·
χρόνῳ δ', ὅτ' ἤδη πᾶς ὁ μόχθος ἦν πέπων,
κἀμάνθανον τὸν θυμὸν ἐκδραμόντα μοι
μείζω κολαστὴν τῶν πρὶν ἡμαρτημένων,
τὸ τηνίκ' ἤδη τοῦτο μὲν πόλις βίᾳ
ἤλαυνέ μ' ἐκ γῆς χρόνιον, οἱ δ' ἐπωφελεῖν,
οἱ τοῦ πατρός, τῷ πατρὶ δυνάμενοι, τὸ δρᾶν
οὐκ ἠθέλησαν, ἀλλ' ἔπους σμικροῦ χάριν
φυγάς σφιν ἔξω πτωχὸς ἠλώμην ἀεί·

No indeed, since even on that very day
when my anger was blazing, and it was my dearest wish
to die and be stoned to death with rocks,
nobody appeared to aid this desire;
but in time, when the whole pain had then become softened,
and I realized that my excessive anger was greater
than my former mistakes as a punisher,

then indeed, at that time, the city by force
exiled me for a long time, and they,
the ones who could have helped their father, their own father,
were unwilling to do so, but for lack of one little word from them
I was driven out in exile, wandering forever as a beggar.

(433–44)

His past parricide and marriage to his mother once seemed to him to have a bearing on his present existence, but now he regards these actions as irrelevant to his character or social role. In time (χρόνῳ) Oedipus realized that his proud anger (θυμός) against his own former behavior was excessive. The parricide and incest were, after all, "mistakes" (ἡμαρτημένων, 438). There is an obvious difference between what he did in ignorance, driven by divine compulsion, and the failure of his sons to help him, which was, Oedipus suggests, entirely deliberate and conscious.

In T. S. Eliot's imitation of the play, *The Elder Statesman*, the Oedipus figure, Lord Claverton, finds that the only way to free himself from his own sense of guilt is to acknowledge the figures who appear to him from the past. He tells the Polyneices figure, his son Michael, "Those who flee from their past will always lose the race."[15] He must confess his fault even in those forgotten past actions which do not look, to society, like crimes. Eliot's play is about the liberating power of confession: freedom depends on not running away, on calling an action or a person by the right name, and owning up to one's own responsibility.[16] Sophocles' Oedipus, by contrast, changes the meaning of his past precisely by refusing to acknowledge its worst features as his own.

The other characters in the play try to draw Oedipus back to the horrors of his past life, but he repeatedly and vehemently resists.[17] He will neither repeat what he has done, nor be defined by others as a sinner or a polluted man.[18] The Chorus makes him recount again his past history. Creon and Polyneices try to drag him back to Thebes. But Oedipus insists that he must be free to change and that those who associate him only with his past are doing him a terrible wrong. When the Chorus members ask him about his parricide and incest (at 510–48), he accuses them of striking him by saying the word "father": he cries, "Alas! You have struck me a second time, sickness upon sickness!" (παπαῖ, δευτέραν / ἔπαισας, ἐπὶ νόσῳ νόσον, 543–44).[19] One could see his sensitivity even to the name "father" as a sign of how deeply he is still affected by the memory of his discoveries.[20] But equally striking is his insistence that he must not and will not be held accountable for those actions. He accuses Creon of inflicting his crimes on him by merely talking about them.

ἀλλ᾿ οὐ γὰρ οὔτ᾿ ἐν τοῖσδ᾿ ἀκούσομαι κακὸς
γάμοισιν οὔθ᾿ οὓς αἰὲν ἐμφορεῖς σύ μοι
φόνους πατρῴους ἐξονειδίζων πικρῶς.

But I shall not be convicted as a bad man, neither in these
marriages, nor those paternal killings which you always bring me,
reproaching me bitterly.
(988–90)

The killing of his father is brought by Creon — "you bring them to me" (ἐμφορεῖς σύ μοι) — not performed by Oedipus himself.[21] He contrasts his own past passivity and ignorance with Creon's conscious freedom to speak even things that ought not to be spoken (1000–1003).[22] He claims that because his parricide and incest were destined by the gods (964–73) and ignorantly suffered rather than performed by him (963–64, 976), Creon has no right to make him suffer for those events. Creon has behaved appallingly, according to Oedipus, in even mentioning Jocasta (978–80): Creon's mouth is unholy (ἀνόσιον στόμα, 981), whereas Oedipus suggests — here at least — that he is untainted by the events of his past.[23]

His long speech of self-defense to Creon (960–1013) hinges on the premise that it is unfair to hold someone accountable for anything other than a conscious choice — for what he has incurred by mistake (ἡμάρτανον, 968). How could Oedipus be blamed for the oracle to Laius, or for his birth, when he was yet unborn (969–73)? And how could he be blamed for killing his father, when he did not recognize him (974–77)? He insists that the parricide was something that might have happened to anyone; it was self-defense, a mistake he had to make in order to survive. He asks Creon,

εἴ τίς σε τὸν δίκαιον αὐτίκ᾿ ἐνθάδε
κτείνοι παραστάς, πότερα πυνθάνοι᾿ ἂν εἰ
πατήρ σ᾿ ὁ καίνων, ἢ τίνοι᾿ ἂν εὐθέως;
δοκῶ μέν, εἴπερ ζῆν φιλεῖς, τὸν αἴτιον
τίνοι᾿ ἄν, οὐδὲ τοὔνδικον περιβλέποις.

You are a moral man, but if someone were right there
standing by to kill you, would you ask if
the one killing you was your father, or would you pay him back straight away?
I think, if you love to live, you would pay back
the one responsible, and you would not look around for justice.
(992–96)

Oedipus associates parricide with the desire to go on living: if you "love to live" (ζῆν φιλεῖς), you will kill any man who threatens your life, without worrying about whether he might be your father. The love of life trumps all other kinds of kinship or familial love (φιλία). Laius was the aggressor, ὁ καίνων (literally, "the killer"). Oedipus had to kill his father, to pay him back for the threat he posed to his life; and besides, he was led by the gods (997–98). Oedipus claims that even Laius himself would not disagree, were he alive to discuss it (998–99). Sons may, when necessary, kill their fathers; and Oedipus's treatment of Polyneices suggests that fathers may also, when necessary, cause the deaths of their sons.

The encounter between Oedipus and Polyneices (1254–1446) is the central scene of the play.[24] Polyneices appears in Colonus to ask for his father's help against his brother Eteocles, who has ousted him from the throne and banished him from Thebes. Antigone begs her father to listen to his supplication (1181–1203). She challenges the idea that it is ever justifiable to harm one's family members, even in retribution or self-defense. She tells her father,

> ἔφυσας αὐτόν· ὥστε μηδὲ δρῶντά σε
> τὰ τῶν κακίστων δυσσεβέστατ᾽, ὦ πάτερ,
> θέμις σέ γ᾽ εἶναι κεῖνον ἀντιδρᾶν κακῶς.

> You begat him, so that even if he did to you
> the most unholy of terrible evils, o father,
> it would not be right for you to do that man harm in return.
> (1189–91)

Antigone here, as earlier in the play (237–53), argues for mercy rather than revenge. She implies that the relationship between father and son is more important than the *lex talionis*. The past action of begetting Polyneices has established a relationship that no subsequent action can undo. Kinsmen should not take revenge on one another, even in the most extreme circumstances. Antigone tries to make Oedipus see that there are some obligations, such as the ties of family, that one incurs without any conscious decision.

The obvious difference between Oedipus's killing of Laius and Oedipus's sons' failure to help him is that Polyneices and Eteocles were well aware of who their father was. But Antigone suggests that there may be less difference than Oedipus imagines between his own actions and those of his sons. Other people, she reminds him, have bad offspring, and a sharp temper (θυμὸς ὀξύς) but are willing to be charmed out of their inclinations by their friends (1192–94). The allusion to the others who have "bad fruits" or "bad begettings" (γοναὶ κακαὶ) may be simply an appeal to a general truth. But addressed to Oedipus, it may also be a reminder that Laius, too, had some trouble with his son. Oedipus is not in the best position to argue that it is inexcusable for sons to treat their fathers badly.

Moreover, Antigone reminds Oedipus that he has suffered in the past from his quick temper. She suggests that in taking revenge on Polyneices, Oedipus will be repeating his own mistakes of the past, such as the self-blinding (1195–1200). She urges him to look not at the present circumstances (τὰ νῦν) but at what happened in the past, at the "paternal and maternal miseries you suffered" (πατρῷα καὶ μητρῷα πήμαθ' ἄπαθες, 1196). This phrase may suggest that Oedipus should have learned by now not to act so hastily; he might not have killed Laius, had he not yielded to his anger (θυμός, 1198). He should remember also that he, like Polyneices, has made mistakes. More obviously, it is a reminder that Oedipus made his involuntary sufferings worse, by yielding to his passions and putting out his eyes. Remembering his parents, he will, she claims, recognize that aggression (θυμός) can have bad results, since (γάρ) he has the evidence of his blinded eyes (1195–1200). θυμός was the word that Oedipus himself used (434) to describe the self-hatred that led him to long for death, and which eventually grew more calm. Antigone sees the self-blinding as a previous occasion when he was led by passion to wish to censor his own past. He cannot afford to behave so rashly again. Antigone suggests that he should accept his connection to his past and acknowledge his kinship with all his children, whatever they have done. But Antigone fails to persuade Oedipus that he has any obligation to the ties of the past, or to kinship. He consents to listen to Polyneices but only to give Antigone a burdensome pleasure (βαρεῖαν ἡδονὴν, 1204), not because he has any reason of his own to do so.

Polyneices develops Antigone's suggestion that he and Oedipus may have things in common. He points out the parallels between his own situation, and that of his father:

πρός νύν σε κρηνῶν, πρὸς θεῶν ὁμογνίων
αἰτῶ πιθέσθαι καὶ παρεικαθεῖν, ἐπεὶ
πτωχοὶ μὲν ἡμεῖς καὶ ξένοι, ξένος δὲ σύ·
ἄλλους δὲ θωπεύοντες οἰκοῦμεν σύ τε
κἀγώ, τὸν αὐτὸν δαίμον' ἐξειληχότες.

Now I beg you, by the fountains and the gods of the race we share,
I beg you to be persuaded and to yield, since
we too are beggars and strangers, and you also are a stranger.

We live dependent on others, both you and

I also, sharing the same *daimon*.

(1333–37)

Not only is Polyneices Oedipus's son: he also shares the faith in the same gods, comes from the same place, and shares his suffering as a beggar, a wanderer, and a stranger. Like Oedipus himself, he has been expelled from the throne and country of Thebes. His arrival at Colonus as a suppliant recalls Oedipus's role at the beginning of the play, and Polyneices stresses the parallel (1335–37).[25] Moreover, just as Oedipus claims that his parricide and incest were caused by the gods rather than his own choice (964–65), so Polyneices claims that the interfamilial strife is the result of what he calls Oedipus's own Fury or curse (1299).[26] Polyneices, like Oedipus, has been led astray by divine compulsion; how then can he be blamed? Polyneices uses the same word to describe his own "mistakes" that Oedipus used to describe his parricide and incest: ἡμαρτημένα.[27] Just as Creon had the power to help Oedipus or harm him on the grounds of his past involuntary actions, so Oedipus has the power to help his son or to harm him and hold him responsible for the strife of the past.

But Oedipus rejects Polyneices' claim that he resembles his father. One could argue that Polyneices has made an error of tact in emphasizing Oedipus's weakness and dependency, as well as his own: perhaps the Oedipus of the *Coloneus* has no desire to be seen as pitiable.[28] But Oedipus is quite capable of mentioning his own weakness, as long as he can use it as a form of strength. Polyneices' tactlessness lies, rather, in his attempt to undermine Oedipus's sense of his own uniqueness. Oedipus refuses to admit that he is like anyone else. He accuses Polyneices of having killed his father (1361), with no suggestion that this action might recall anything he has done himself.

Oedipus insists that family relations must be the result of conscious choice, not of unforeseen accidents of birth; his sons are those he chooses to be his sons, those who care for him, not those whom he happens to have begotten. His daughters are his daughters because they have behaved like friends to him; his sons are not his sons because they have betrayed him and ruined his life (1365–69).[29] Oedipus buys back his reintegration into the city at the cost of rejecting his own family — his own sons.[30] He refuses to accept any ties based merely on nature. Although he begat his sons, he incurs no particular obligations toward them because of this. On the other hand, he also insists that his sons have done wrong in failing to recognize their natural obligations to him as their father, the one who begat them. He implies that to betray one's begetter, ὁ φύσας, is to go against nature, φύσις.[31]

His curse compels Polyneices and Eteocles to shed each other's blood, to teach them to honor their natural parents, τοὺς φυτεύσαντας (1377).

It has often been claimed that Oedipus's curse of his sons stands "outside the boundaries of ordinary moral judgement."[32] But Oedipus's condemnation of his sons is a mirror image of his defense of himself: he applies in the one case a moral principle that he withholds in the other. He insists that he is untainted by what he has done in ignorance or under divine compulsion. But he insists that his own sons must suffer indefinitely for what they have done in casting him out, even though those actions were — at least according to Polyneices — "mistakes" that were the result of a divine curse, Oedipus's own curse (the Fury of 1299, or the *daimon* of 1337). Oedipus liberates himself from the demands of his past, by denying any parallel between himself and his sons.

Oedipus invokes his own previous curses to help him curse Polyneices again. Polyneices will never be able to evade either his own past, or his father's old anger (1372–79). He tells him, "Be off with you, spat upon and fatherless as far as I am concerned" (σὺ δ' ἔρρ' ἀπόπτυστός τε κἀπάτωρ ἐμοῦ, 1383). Polyneices will never escape the implications of his own name, which means "man of much strife"; in his curse, Oedipus condemns Polyneices to strife and more strife. As soon as Oedipus has finished his long curse on his son and told him to begone forever, the Chorus addresses Polyneices by name: Πολύνεικες (1397).

Certainly, there is a difference between killing one's father without recognizing him and rejecting one's blind old father, knowing quite well who he is. But it is a difference that is undermined by the play's insistence on the parallels between the events of past, present, and future. Even in cursing his son, Oedipus shows himself like him. Polyneices, like Oedipus himself, insists on indulging his passionate anger against his family members — in his case, his brother. Like Oedipus, Polyneices rejects Antigone's appeal to restrain his anger (θυμοῦσθαι, 1420). He rushes off, to kill and be killed by his brother. One could see Oedipus's actions in relation to his children as conscious repetitions of his unconscious relations with his parents: he destroys his male offspring, and he becomes deeply intimate with his daughters.

Oedipus gives inconsistent signals about whether he regards himself as still tainted by his past.[33] As we have seen, in conversation with Creon he seems to insist that he can be free from his family background: it is Creon's mouth, not Oedipus's body, that is polluted or unholy (ἀνόσιον, 981). He condemns Polyneices and Eteocles to remain under a curse of which he himself is free: it is they, not he, who must continue to repeat and perpetuate the pattern of suffering and the killing of kindred that is associated with the house of the Labdacids. But later, in his conversation with Theseus, Oedipus seems to acknowledge that he might be still polluted by his relations with his parents. He asks for Theseus's hand, but at once withdraws the request:

πῶς σ' ἂν ἄθλιος γεγὼς
θιγεῖν θελήσαιμ' ἀνδρὸς ᾧ τίς οὐκ ἔνι
κηλὶς κακῶν ξύνοικος; οὐκ ἔγωγέ σε,
οὐδ' οὖν ἔασω· τοῖς γὰρ ἐμπείροις βροτῶν
μόνοις οἷόν τε συνταλαιπωρεῖν τάδε.

> How could I, being a wretched man,
> be willing to touch you, a man for whom there is no
> stain of evils dwelling with you? I will not touch you,
> nor will I let you [touch me]; for only those mortals who are experienced,
> only they can jointly suffer these things.
> (1132–36)

Although Oedipus is made angry by others who view him as polluted, in the right company he is himself willing to admit that his body is still in some way unclean. Oedipus resents Creon's accusation of pollution, but to Theseus, who treats him as clean, Oedipus admits that he is tainted.[34]

The difference is not only that Theseus is kinder to Oedipus than Creon is. It is also that Theseus is a stranger. Both his sons and his daughters, and his brother-in-law Creon, must share in the sufferings of Oedipus, whereas Theseus, ruler of Athens, will not and cannot share in the miseries of Thebes.[35] To acknowledge his pollution to Creon would have involved some acknowledgment that he is associated with the continuing suffering of the people of Thebes. In Thebes, Oedipus's parricide and marriage to his mother have become associated with the plague and with the battles between his sons for the throne. But at Colonus, Oedipus is not a scapegoat king, but an outsider whose pollution is not shared by the city. Athens can appropriate Oedipus's otherness as a form of strength. In Athens, Oedipus can be transformed from an outcast to a hero. His status as a man who cannot be touched, a man outside the human community, will bring him closer to the gods.

For Oedipus, there is a way out of the pattern of repetition of the past. Revenge may bring about an endless cycle of violence; but Oedipus himself is able to transform his actions, both the things he did in ignorance and the things he did deliberately. His extreme position, both above and below humanity, becomes a source of power. The gods call him away from the human sphere and ask only why he stays so long: "O you, you, Oedipus, why are we waiting to go? For a long time your affairs have been delayed" (ὦ οὗτος οὗτος, Οἰδίπους, τί μέλλομεν / χωρεῖν; πάλαι δὴ τἀπὸ σοῦ βραδύνεται, 1627–28). From the divine perspective, all human life is only delay. The gods enable Oedipus to escape at last from a life that has gone on too long. He goes out on a note of triumph, having succeeded in taking revenge on those who have done him wrong and blessing those who have served him well; and he is welcomed into the sphere of the gods, where there is no more sense of delay.

But the play is not only about Oedipus. It hints at his triumphant welcome into a divine realm, but it also shows the continued suffering of those who are left behind, who will experience killings, mourning, loss, and the longing for death. Oedipus's children are left to live on in a world that will be overshadowed by their father's past. He tells the girls, "On this day you no longer have a father," or "On this day your father is no more" (οὐκ ἔστ' ἔθ' ὑμῖν τῇδ' ἐν ἡμέρᾳ πατήρ, 1612). He has already rejected Polyneices as a son (1383); now he withdraws even from his daughters. Oedipus says he loved his daughters more than any other man will do (1617–19): the one word that redeems all their suffering is "love" (τὸ φιλεῖν): they suffered for their father, but at least he loved them. But no sooner has Oedipus introduced the redemptive promise of love than he uses it to intensify his daughters' past, present, and future grief. They will never find such love from any man other than their father, and he is gone. The daughters must live out their whole lives without him (1619). They are left with a life that is, they declare, unlivable. Ismene says,

> κατά με φόνιος
> Ἀίδας ἕλοι πατρὶ
> ξυνθανεῖν γεραιῷ
> τάλαιναν, ὡς ἔμοιγ' ὁ μέλ-
> λων βίος οὐ βιωτός.

> May bloody
> Hades take me down
> to die together with my old father,
> wretched me, since for me
> the life to come is not worth living.
> (1689–93)

Oedipus's experience in the grove is unlike any ordinary human death; there is no tomb, and Oedipus's broken, suffering body seems finally to disappear: "He fell without a tomb, away from everyone" (ἄταφος ἔπιτνε δίχα τε παντός, 1732). Antigone and Ismene are frustrated in their desire to mourn their father. It has been suggested that the absence either of corpse or of lamentation reinforces the sense of finality at the end of the play, and perhaps it does.[36] But it also reinforces the suspicion that Oedipus's end is less like death than the lives of those who remain behind. The daughters' unlivable lives and the cycle of killing that awaits their brothers substitute for the death of their father. At the end of the play Antigone asks Theseus to let them go to Thebes, to try to prevent their brothers from killing one another (1768–72); but the audience could not help knowing that no such attempt will succeed.

Oedipus himself claims at the beginning of the play, "For sufferings have taught me to be patient, and long time, my companion, and a third thing, nobility" (στέργειν γὰρ αἱ πάθαι με χὠ χρόνος ξυνὼν / μακρὸς διδάσκει καὶ τὸ γενναῖον τρίτον, 7–8).[37] He tells Theseus that for the gods alone time is nonexistent; all-conquering time confounds everything else (607–9). He himself approaches the condition of godhead by his refusal to take any notice of time in his relationships with others. He lays immutable curses on his sons, and to Theseus and Athens, he gives blessings that will, he claims, be invulnerable to the painful effects of age (γήρως ἄλυπα, 1519). Oedipus tries to impose stability on the relationships he leaves behind, in urging Theseus to care for his children (1631–35). But even Oedipus implicitly acknowledges that beyond the magic world of Theseus's Athens, and beyond the grove, nothing in human life is constant. Time makes most human relationships alter: brothers become enemies, cities move from amity to war. Oedipus's timeless loves and hatreds are set against the mutability of normal human life.

The Athenian spectators may be tempted to congratulate themselves on living in a city where tragedy does not happen.[38] The future looks grim for the children of Oedipus, but they are, after all, only Thebans, while Theseus, the representative of Athens, is offered protection by Oedipus. But Athenian self-congratulation would be premature. The reason Theseus will need the protection of Oedipus is that there is a danger that Athens will once again come into contact with Thebes:

χοὔτως ἀδῆον τήνδ᾽ ἐνοικήσεις πόλιν
σπαρτῶν ἀπ᾽ ἀνδρῶν· αἱ δὲ μυρίαι πόλεις
κἂν εὖ τις οἰκῇ, ῥᾳδίως καθύβρισαν.

θεοὶ γὰρ εὖ μέν, ὀψὲ δ' εἰσορῶσ', ὅταν
τὰ θεῖ' ἀφείς τις ἐς τὸ μαίνεσθαι τραπῇ·
ὅ μὴ σύ, τέκνον Αἰγέως, βούλου παθεῖν.

And thus you will live in this city unravaged
by sown men; but countless cities,
even ones that live well, easily become insolent.
The gods see it clearly though late, whenever
anyone abandons religion and turns to madness.
Son of Aegeus, do not be willing to let that to happen to you!
(1533–38)

Oedipus promises protection to Athens against Thebes (the sown men) in the time to come. But one can read Oedipus's last words as a warning to Athens, rather than a consoling validation. He emphasizes that there is a possibility that the city may degenerate. The protection he promises is entirely conditional: if the city does not act like his daughters and nurture him always, then the *daimon* will produce curses on Athens to rival the curses given to Thebes. The play was composed before 406 (when Sophocles died), perhaps in 409, and first performed in 401.[39] In 404 Athens fell to Sparta, marking the end of the Peloponnesian War. The original audience could well have seen in Sophocles' last play not a final blessing from a lost old man but a premonition of disaster for the city from beyond the grave.[40]

The ending of the play is a triumph for Oedipus himself. He successfully takes revenge on Polyneices and liberates himself from the ill effects of his own past. The god sets him free from the cycle of time. But Oedipus leaves tragedy behind only when he ceases to be human, becoming instead the object of cult worship. In doing so, he also ceases to be the subject of discourse. No one but Theseus and his descendants are allowed to know what happens when Oedipus withdraws into the sacred grove, and they are sworn to silence.[41] The rest of us, like the children of Oedipus, remain in the human world of tragedy, in which we are forced to repeat over and over the same list: killings, uprisings, battles, strife, hatred (φόνοι, στάσεις, ἔρις, μάχαι / καὶ φθόνος, 1234–35), the hangover of a past that refuses to end.

The great choral ode at 1211–48 comes structurally in the center of the play, between Oedipus's confrontations with Creon and with Polyneices, and is also its conceptual center. The ode suggests that most of us struggle in vain to outlive our own past selves. Outliving involves the capacity not to repeat one's past, but to make it new — as Oedipus succeeds in doing. But most people are not summoned away by the gods into magical groves; for most of us, ordinary death is the only end of suffering. We live beyond our proper time without being able to be reborn. The effect of time is, therefore, merely to prolong pain. Most people only repeat suffering until death. Overliving becomes the inevitable condition of all human life.

ὅστις τοῦ πλέονος μέρους
χρῄζει τοῦ μετρίου παρεὶς
ζώειν, σκαιοσύναν φυλάσ-
σων ἐν ἐμοὶ κατάδηλος ἔσται.
ἐπεὶ πολλὰ μὲν αἱ μακραὶ
ἁμέραι κατέθεντο δὴ
λύπας ἐγγυτέρω, τὰ τέρ-
ποντα δ᾽ οὐκ ἂν ἴδοις ὅπου,
ὅταν τις ἐς πλέον πέσῃ
τοῦ δέοντος· ὁ δ᾽ ἐπίκουρος ἰσοτέλεστος,
Ἄϊδος ὅτε μοῖρ᾽ ἀνυμέναιος
ἄλυρος ἄχορος ἀναπέφηνε,
θάνατος ἐς τελευτάν.

μὴ φῦναι τὸν ἅπαντα νι-
κᾷ λόγον· τὸ δ᾽, ἐπεὶ φανῇ,
βῆναι κεῖθεν ὅθεν περ ἥ-
κει πολὺ δεύτερον ὡς τάχιστα.
ὡς εὖτ᾽ ἂν τὸ νέον παρῇ
κούφας ἀφροσύνας φέρον,
τίς πλαγὰ πολύμοχθος ἔ-
ξω; τίς οὐ καμάτων ἔνι;
φόνοι, στάσεις, ἔρις, μάχαι
καὶ φθόνος· τό τε κατάμεμπτον ἐπιλέλογχε
πύματον ἀκρατὲς ἀπροσόμιλον
γῆρας ἄφιλον, ἵνα πρόπαντα
κακὰ κακῶν ξυνοικεῖ.

ἐν ᾧ τλάμων ὅδ᾽ — οὐκ ἐγὼ μόνος —
πάντοθεν βόρειος ὥς τις ἀκτὰ
κυματοπλὴξ χειμερία κλονεῖται,
ὡς καὶ τόνδε κατ᾽ ἄκρας

δειναὶ κυματοαγεῖς
ἆται κλονέουσιν ἀεὶ ξυνοῦσαι,
αἱ μὲν ἀπ' ἀελίου δυσμᾶν,
αἱ δ' ἀνατέλλοντος,
αἱ δ' ἀνὰ μέσσαν ἀκτῖν',
αἱ δ' ἐννυχιᾶν ἀπὸ Ῥιπᾶν.

Whoever desires a greater portion,   *strophe*
passing by moderation
in living, in my opinion he is transparently
a guardian of crookedness.
For long days add many things nearer to sorrow,
but as for pleasures you could not see where they might be,
when a person falls into excess
of what is necessary. But the comrade, the equal-ender,
when fate of Hades, with no marriage song,
no lyre, no choral dance, has been revealed,
is death at the end.

Not to be born conquers every   *antistrophe*
logos. Or, when a man appears,
to go back where he came from,
as fast as possible, is second by far.
When the new creature appears
bearing insubstantial follies,
what blow of suffering is he free from?
What troubles are absent from him?
Killings, fightings, strife, battles,
and hatred. And then he is allotted
despised, final, impotent, lonely,
friendless old age, so that every single
evil of evils lives with him.

In this the unhappy man here — not I alone —   *epode*
is battered from all sides, like a north-facing cliff,
surrounded by storms and buffeted by waves.
So also the terrible wave-bearing
curses whirl over him,

always living with him, breaking over the top,
some from the settings of the sun,
some from its rising, some from the middle beam,
some from the northern forces of night.
(1211–48)

All of us overlive, according to this ode. We live too long from the moment of birth, even if we make no terrible, Oedipal discoveries. If we are fools, we may desire more life, but in fact all deaths come too late. To be born at all is, the ode suggests, already to have lived too long, because the proper time for a man to live is never.

Yeats's *A Man Young and Old* ends with a wonderful imitation of Sophocles' ode:

Endure what life God gives and ask no longer span;
Cease to remember the delights of youth, travel-wearied aged man;
Delight becomes death-longing if all longing else be vain.

Even from that delight memory treasures so,
Death, despair, division of families, all entanglements of mankind grow,
As that old wandering beggar and these God-hated children know.

In the long echoing street the laughing dancers throng,
The bride is carried to the bridegroom's chamber through torchlight and
    tumultuous song;
I celebrate the silent kiss that ends short life or long.

Never to have lived is best, ancient writers say;
Never to have drawn the breath of life, never to have looked into the eye of day;
The second best's a gay goodnight and quickly turn away.[42]

A brief account of the gulf between Yeats and his original may help to show what is distinctive about the Sophoclean representation of overliving. Yeats's poem is about our unending slavery to sex or, more generally, to desire: longing goes on too long. Sophocles' ode makes a tripartite distinction between never being born, dying early, and overliving. In Yeats, the choice between three possible quantities of life becomes a choice between erotic objects; the delights of youth are replaced by the delights of death, who gives his silent kiss: "I celebrate the silent kiss that ends short life or long." There are no kisses in the Sophoclean ode. Delight "becomes" death-longing in Yeats not only because it is appropriate or "becoming" to long for death, but also because death, not sex, becomes what a man longs for if he lives long enough — or, at least, so he hopes. Yeats's poem is about the transformation of erotic desire into the desire for death.

The men in Sophocles' ode, by contrast, have no desires at all. Instead, they are constantly assailed by all the external storms and seas and sufferings that flesh is heir to. The Sophoclean ode entirely deprives humanity of desire, and even of agency: throughout the ode, things are the subjects of verbs, not people. Days pile up misery (πολλὰ μὲν αἱ μακραὶ / ἀμέραι κατέθεντο δὴ / λύπας ἐγγυτέρω, 1215–17); death is our companion in battle (ἐπίκουρος, 1220); every kind of suffering lives with us (πρόπαντα / κακὰ κακῶν ξυνοικεῖ, 1237–38); and the dark fates that are always beside us attack the shores of our lives (δειναὶ κυματοαγεῖς / ἆται κλονέουσιν ἀεὶ ξυνοῦσαι, 1243–44). Human misery "deepens like a coastal shelf."[43]

In Sophocles' ode, the best thing is μὴ φῦναι (not to be born, or not to be begotten). The wording reminds us that those who live are born into a family — in contrast with Yeats's "Never to have lived."[44] Yeats's line suggests that there is some kind of unity to the whole life and to the whole person; the perfect tense implies a retrospective realization that it would have been better never to have lived. It would, after all, have been better not to have experienced the desires, pleasures, and love affairs of life. In Sophocles, by contrast, the trouble begins as soon as one is begotten, conceived, or born. It would have been better for Oedipus himself, and for his children, not to come into being, because simply by existing they became implicated in terrible and inescapable relationships with their parents and ancestors. The suffering of this dysfunctional family becomes, by implication, the model for all our lives. We are all born into a world we did not choose, bound to a family we cannot change, and subject to more and more pain, which will end only with death. For Yeats, all living is longing; for Sophocles, all living is too long. To be born at all is to become subject to the endless sufferings of human life. The language of the Sophoclean ode implies that all human beings, not just Oedipus, are the passive victims of suffering.

Sophocles' strophe begins with a challenge: an aggressive repudiation of anyone fool enough to want to extend life (1211–14). Those who do not realize how undesirable it is to live too long are clearly perverse idiots. To desire longer life, we learn as the strophe goes on, is simply to desire more pain, since more life cannot increase happiness. Our only true friend and companion (ἐπίκουρος, 1220) is therefore death, the one who ends us all equally or who balances life by ending it (ἰσοτέλεστος, 1220). The fate or μοῖρα of Hades, which is presumably equivalent to Death personified, is characterized by a series of alliterating alpha-privative adjectives, which emphasize silence and the lack of any communicative signs: it is without a wedding song, without a lyre, without a choral dance (ἀνυμέναιος, ἄλυρος, ἄχορος, 1222). The choice posed by the strophe is between more life and more pain, or the blessed release of nothingness and death.

One might think that the alliterating adjectives qualifying death in the strophe imply that there is some possibility of pleasure in life: before death, there are such things as marriage and music. But the possibility is repressed when the list is answered in the antistrophe by a second set of alpha-privative adjectives: "impotent, friendless, lonely old age" (ἀκρατὲς ἀπροσόμιλον / γῆρας ἄφιλον). Life is associated not with sex, music, and the joys of youth, as in Yeats, but with the privations of old age. This old age is not, like that of Oedipus, supported by daughters and friends, nor, like that of Sophocles, productive and successful. Rather, the ode suggests that all old age is mere negation, loneliness, and loss. We will live on without any of the companions who make life bearable, and instead all kinds of suffering lives with us: κακὰ κακῶν ξυνοικεῖ (1238).

The climactic ending of death comes too soon in this ode, at the end of the strophe: "death at the end" (θάνατος ἐς τελευτάν). The ode continues, after the word "end" (τελευτάν). The antistrophe shows what lies beyond the moment when death should have happened. It begins by comparing the relative merits of three different possible quantities of human life. The first, never to be born at all, μὴ φῦναι, is by far the best. The second best is to go back where one came from as soon as possible, to die as soon as one can after being born (βῆναι κεῖθεν ὅθεν περ ἥκει, 1225–27). The comparison implies a third term, the worst thing of all. The antistrophe goes on to suggest that the worst is to be born, and then continue to live for a long time, longer than one should. The worst, then, is overliving.

The following lines of the antistrophe (1229–38) enumerate all the evils inherent in living too long. In the strophe, it seemed at least possible to live for a moderate amount of time. The fool is the man who desires to exceed that amount of life, to go beyond moderation, τοῦ μετρίου, and to fall "into excess of what is necessary" (ἐς πλέον. . ./τοῦ δέοντος, 1219–20). But it turns out in the antistrophe that "living too long" is actually synonymous with "living." The right time for life to end is before it begins. All other deaths, and therefore all deaths, come too late. The child comes into this world trailing not clouds of glory but the folly of having been so ill-advised as to be born at all. He is immediately assailed by suffering, and it will only get worse.

The strophe and antistrophe together draw a contrast not only between death and life, and between not living and overliving, but also between silence and the alternatives to silence. The antistrophe begins, μὴ φῦναι τὸν ἄπαντα νι- / κᾷ λόγον· Literally, "not to be born conquers every λόγος." The meaning of λόγος here is, I would suggest, importantly ambiguous. Commentators tend to take the word to mean "account" or "reckoning." The clause means, on the standard reading, "Not to be born conquers every (other) reckoning on what the best thing is; so, not to be born is best."[45] The justification for reading the clause in this way is that Sophocles' Chorus is echoing the lyric poets Theognis and Bacchylides, both of whom use the phrase μὴ φῦναι and claim that it is the best thing.[46] The lyric poets use the phrase as if it were already proverbial: in Bacchylides it is explicitly presented as a quotation. But there is no reason to assume a priori that Sophocles would simply reproduce the use of the proverb in his lyric predecessors, without twisting it to suit his own interests. Sophocles adds the word λόγος to the phrase and, in doing so, introduces a whole new set of associations. Elsewhere in Sophocles, λόγος is rarely used to mean account or calculation or value: at least four times out of five, λόγος means speech, word, story, language, the act of speaking, or the thing said.[47] It is therefore at least possible that Sophocles' audience would have heard connotations of language in the word here too, at least as a secondary meaning. "Not to be born" conquers every story, every language, every word; it makes language impossible — and, especially, it precludes tragic language. On this way of reading the antistrophe, the tripartite comparison becomes less evaluative than descriptive. There are not only three possible quantities of life but also three correspondent kinds of discourse.

"Not to be born" is the best: the best kind of speech is silence, and melodies unheard are sweetest. Never to be born, therefore, conquers every word and every story, because it makes language impossible. Nonexistence, like death, lacks the lyre, song, and a chorus, and therefore can be represented only by silence. Second is the briefest possible speech, which ends almost as soon as it begins. In the *Oedipus Tyrannus*, Jocasta kills herself when she finds out the truth, and the Messenger reports that his news of her is the shortest kind of story (λόγος): "she is dead" (1234–35).[48]

The third possibility is the only one that allows for narrative expansion and, specifically, for tragic narrative. Only if one makes the primary error of being born, and then the secondary error of failing to die immediately, can one's story include slaughter, strife, battle, and friendless old age. "Killings, uprisings, strife, battles and hatred" (φόνοι, στάσεις, ἔρις, μάχαι / καὶ φθόνος, 1234–35): the list reads like an enumeration of the subjects of the *Oedipus Coloneus*, and of tragedy in general. It is comparable with the list of sufferings that are present in *Oedipus Tyrannus* once the truth is known: "lamentation, ruin, death, shame, of all sufferings none of the names is missing" (στεναγμός, ἄτη, θάνατος, αἰσχύνη, κακῶν / ὅσ' ἐστὶ πάντων ὀνόματ', οὐδέν ἐστ' ἀπόν, 1284–85). Tragedy is the opposite of death, which lacks the lyre and song and a chorus. Overliving becomes, in this ode, the necessary precondition for tragedy. Tragedy represents the true horrors of life, including the worst horror—the fact that we live and, therefore, live too long.

As at the end of the *Oedipus Tyrannus*, the Chorus takes Oedipus's life as an image for all our lives. His apparently exceptional story has become representative of all human existence. At the beginning of the *Oedipus Coloneus*, the Chorus was horrified to discover who Oedipus was. Now, it sees his fragmented, violent, and too-long life not as the terrifying exception but as the norm. Oedipus himself escapes from the human world, but the proliferation of suffering will continue both in the lives of his children and in all human lives. In the *Oedipus Tyrannus*, Oedipus himself lives too long. In the *Coloneus*, Oedipus's children inherit their father's suffering, and the conflict and fragmentation associated with living too long become characteristic of all human life. Oedipus's past life has become a model for the human condition.

CHAPTER THREE

"Enslaved to fate"

Euripides' *Heracles*

The *Oedipus Coloneus* constructs two distinct narrative responses to the problem of tragic overliving: Oedipus himself triumphantly curses those who have wronged him and withdraws from human life, while his children, and the rest of humanity, are left to live too long. In Euripides' *Heracles*, the central character himself experiences both triumph and pathetic vulnerability. The play is a combined version of Sophocles' two Oedipus plays.[1] Oedipus kills his father and marries his mother in ignorance, and then goes on living, finding sanctuary for his final end in Athens. Heracles kills his wife and children in a fit of madness, and then goes on living; like Oedipus, he is welcomed to Athens by Theseus. As in the *Oedipus Tyrannus*, tragic overliving causes a fragmentation of dramatic character: Heracles, like Oedipus, struggles to come to terms with his inconsistent actions and multiple roles. Two new aspects of tragic overliving become important in the *Heracles*. First, whereas Oedipus becomes increasingly isolated, the *Heracles* associates overliving with society: in this play, to endure life is to allow oneself to be dependent on others or even enslaved to them. Second, the play uses overliving to undermine the audience's expectations about tragic structure more radically than Sophocles had done.

Many tragic narratives contain only two distinct episodes. Aristotle remarks that the plot structures of tragedy should be "complex" (πεπλεγμένοι), and explains that he means it should include *peripeteia* or *anagnorisis*, or both, and follow an arc from good fortune to bad, or from bad fortune to good.[2] Priam in the *Iliad* provides the most important model for the Greek tragedians of a life that contains both good fortune and bad.[3] This kind of narrative prompts Solon's injunction to Croesus: "Call no man happy until he is dead."[4]

However, the *Heracles* does not conform to this narrative pattern because it has too many distinct episodes. While Heracles is in the underworld completing his final labor, his family is threatened by the tyrant Lycus. His wife Megara recalls that once, she and her children had hope of fortune and happiness; now their luck has changed (480), and all hope is gone (480–84). Megara's fortunes are apparently reversed when Heracles returns, having successfully completed the labors. There is a further reverse, when Iris, sent by Hera, compels Madness (Lyssa), against her will, to drive Heracles out of his mind and make him kill his family. In the final episode of the play, after a long argument with Theseus, Heracles decides to go on living; there will be still more reverses as his life goes on. The representation of overliving in the final episode of the play challenges audience expectations that tragic life stories will—like Priam's—contain only two episodes. The jarring structure of the play forces the spectators to confront a problem parallel to that faced by Heracles himself: whether we can accept wildly diverse forms of experience.[5]

Euripides probably reversed the traditional order of events, in setting the killing of the family after Heracles' labors, not before.[6] The reordering creates a Heracles who finds himself in a domestic world where his physical strength causes terrible destruction. The play contains two episodes in which life seems to have gone on too long. It offers two alternative dramatic presentations of living death, broken up by a central episode in which Heracles is driven mad and kills his family.[7] In the first episode, Heracles' wife, Megara, and his father, Amphitryon, discuss whether it is time to give up on life.[8] Amphitryon, Megara, and the children are suppliants at the altar of Zeus. The first question the tyrant asks, when he emerges to confront the family of suppliants, is, "How long do you seek to prolong your life?" (143). He implies that the suppliants can have no possible motive for resisting death, except a foolish hope that Heracles may return from the underworld.

Megara is ready from the start to submit to Lycus and accept that death is inevitable (90, 92, 94). She uses the striking image of time that "bites": "Time in the middle, being painful, bites me" (94). For Megara, time (χρόνος) is like one of the monstrous animals defeated by her husband; it can be destroyed only by a heroic willingness to submit to death. Amphitryon, on the other hand, argues that it is the mark of the best and bravest kind of man (ἀνὴρ ἄριστος, 105) to rely on hope: "This man is the bravest and best, who always trusts in hopes; to despair is the mark of a coward" (οὗτος δ᾽ ἀνὴρ ἄριστος ὅστις ἐλπίσιν / πέποιθεν αἰεί· τὸ δ᾽ ἀπορεῖν ἀνδρὸς κακοῦ, 105–6). Whereas Megara, like Sophocles' Ajax, associates dishonor with the desire to cling to life, Amphitryon declares that it is brave and honorable to rely on hope, and stay alive as long as possible.[9]

The disagreement between Megara and Amphitryon about when to accept that life is over is associated with another disagreement, about the nature of courage. Is it brave to die honorably? Or does one incur the charge of cowardice by giving up hope of life too early? Lycus accuses Heracles of cowardice since he only killed animals and fought with the coward's weapon, the bow (151–64).[10] His labors were the mark not of courage but of cowardice.[11] Both Megara and Amphitryon defend Heracles, but they use two very different ideas of courage. Amphitryon argues that Heracles was brave because he did the sensible thing (σοφόν, 202): he fought defensively and survived. Megara, on the other hand, thinks that to display courage worthy of her husband, she must accept death and make sure she dies in the most dignified way possible. Since death is, as she thinks, inevitable, she must not die in a manner unworthy of Heracles' wife.[12]

We are prepared by the distinct viewpoints of Lycus, Megara, and Amphitryon to see Heracles himself from at least three incompatible points of view.[13] He is, for Megara, a supremely brave man in a traditional sense: he is someone willing to suffer pain and death rather than dishonor. For Lycus, he is a coward or weakling. For Amphitryon, finally, he is a model for a different kind of heroism, one that includes self-protection not as cowardice (δειλία) but as part of a commitment to life in a community and to the protection of the weak. Amphitryon and the Chorus both present the labors of Heracles as acts of civilization and public benefaction: Heracles is admirable not simply for courage or strength, but for the use of these capacities to preserve and improve human life.[14]

After Lycus threatens to set fire to the altar and burn the whole family (238–46), Megara persuades Amphitryon that it is time to abandon hope of salvation. Death can no longer be postponed. Megara takes the children into the house and brings them back dressed in burial clothes (442–47). The living children already dressed for the grave provide a stark visual image of living death. Death seems so certain to Megara that she describes it as already taking place, in her final appeal to her supposedly dead husband: "O my darling, if any voice of mortals is heard in Hades, I say this to you, Heracles: your father is dying, and your children, and I am being destroyed, I who once was called happy among mortals, because of you" (490–93). It is as if Megara is ready to write her own epitaph: she thinks the time has come to pass judgment on her whole life, and she emphasizes its ironic reversal from good fortune to bad.

But those who seemed dead turn out to have more time to live. Suddenly Heracles appears (514), not as a shadow or a ghost or a dream—the most Megara could expect (494–96, 517–18)—but as a living man and a savior. After vowing to take horrible revenge on Lycus (562–73), Heracles implies that, unless he uses his strength now to protect the weak, his former labors will seem to have been useless. He echoes the controversy between Lycus and Amphitryon about his own character and treats the rescue of his family as a test of his past achievements. His present actions will prove whether he is the kind of man whose strength protects the weak from oppression.

> χαιρόντων πόνοι·
> μάτην γὰρ αὐτοὺς τῶνδε μᾶλλον ἤνυσα.
> καὶ δεῖ μ' ὑπὲρ τῶνδ', εἴπερ οἵδ' ὑπὲρ πατρός,
> θνήισκειν ἀμύνοντ'· ἢ τί φήσομεν καλὸν
> ὕδραι μὲν ἐλθεῖν ἐς μάχην λέοντί τε
> Εὐρυσθέως πομπαῖσι, τῶν δ' ἐμῶν τέκνων
> οὐκ ἐκπονήσω θάνατον; οὐκ ἄρ' Ἡρακλῆς
> ὁ καλλίνικος ὡς πάροιθε λέξομαι.

> Good-bye, labors.
> For it was useless that I performed them, rather than these things.
> And if they should die for their father, I should die for these children,
> defending them; indeed, why shall we say it is noble
> to take up arms against a hydra and a lion,
> on the instructions of Eurystheus, but for my own children
> shall I not labor away death? I shall not then be called, "Heracles
> the nobly victorious," as before.
> (575–82)

Heracles declares that he regards his labors as pointless, if they were mere shows of strength. Clearly, the primary sense is that the labors were worth performing only if they include the final labor of protecting his family, his father, wife, and children. The present and the past are continuous; what Heracles does now will prove the worth of what he has done before. But there is also a submerged suggestion that perhaps the labors should be rejected altogether. "Good-bye, labors" could be heard momentarily not as a conditional but as an absolute declaration of intent. οὐκ ἄρ' Ἡρακλῆς / ὁ καλλίνικος ὡς πάροιθε λέξομαι (I shall not then be called "Heracles the nobly victorious," as before) is syntactically not the apodosis of a conditional but an independent declarative statement. The ambiguity momentarily suggests that there may be a contrast between Heracles' heroic role as killer of monsters and his domestic role as protector of his children.

But it may not be possible for Heracles to distinguish clearly between apparently incompatible actions and apparently incompatible roles. His language associates his present attempt to protect his children with his past labors. The weapons used are the same and are described with the same epithet—"nobly victorious," "fine-victoried" (καλλίνικος, 570, 582).[15] When he asks, "Shall I not labor away the death of my children?" (τῶν δ' ἐμῶν τέκνων / οὐκ ἐκπονήσω θάνατον;), Heracles transfers the language of the labors onto the domestic sphere: he can protect children only by labor, ἐκπονήσω.[16] The phrasing of the question has puzzled editors. Out of context, the phrase would presumably mean, "Will I not complete the labor of killing my children?"[17] In context, either the verb must be understood in some unusual way—as "labor to avert" perhaps, though such a usage is unparalleled—or else by "death" (θάνατον), Heracles means not literal death but the threat of death.[18] Neither reading of the phrase is easy, and the difficulty begets the buried awareness of dramatic irony. The audience would have been conscious on some level of the more obvious meaning of the phrase, although Heracles must be trying to promise that he will save his children's lives. He thinks he is saying that he will labor to prevent the death of his children; in fact, he will labor to kill them.[19] Heracles not only labors against death, his labors also produce death, both for his children and himself. Ostensibly opposite kinds of behavior—such as protection of the weak and the slaughter of children—turn out to be performed by the same man, and to be expressed in the same words.

Heracles' first action as a family man is similar to his previous actions: he kills. Hera tells "Madness" (Λύσσα) to descend upon him; she reluctantly does so, and he slaughters his own wife and children under the delusion that they are the family of his oppressor, Eurystheus. In trying to protect his family, he destroys it; the weapons he took up to protect his wife and children are used to kill them. Of course, the madness is sent by Hera and Iris and might, therefore, be thought to have nothing to do with Heracles' character or with his former life. Certainly he is not morally responsible for the murders, any more than Oedipus is morally responsible for what he did unwittingly with his parents. But Heracles knows that he is polluted by his actions. In the *Oedipus Tyrannus*, the spectators struggle to assimilate the parricide with the king, and the husband of Jocasta with the husband of his mother, in the still-living figure of Oedipus. Similarly, the *Heracles* challenges the audience to relate the Heracles who civilized the world through his labors with the Heracles who kills his own wife and children. The audience has been prepared, by Heracles' own words ("Good-bye, labors"), to associate whatever he does for his family with his former labors. The problem is the more difficult because the labors are presented in this play as a good thing; and yet the performance of the labors seems to be continuous with the destruction of the family.

The Messenger describes the whole household's shock at Heracles' madness (922–1015). The people ask, "Is the master joking with us, or has he gone mad?" (952). It is hard to believe that the rational and kindly Heracles could mistake his own family for that of his enemy, Eurystheus. Heracles, who has killed monsters for the good of humanity, himself becomes like a wild animal, whirling a savage Gorgon's face on the children (990) before slaughtering them — although he himself believes that he is continuing the work of the labors. Moreover, neither the triumphant Heracles of the first episode nor the violent madman of the messenger speech seems to have any connection with the pathetic figure of the last episode, who huddles in shame under his cloak and has to be supported by Theseus as he finally hobbles off the stage. Heracles has rescued Theseus from the underworld; now Theseus himself has to rescue Heracles from the desire for death.

Theseus, in the final episode of the play, tries to persuade Heracles that he need not be disturbed by the unfortunate slaughter of his family but should identify himself only with the glorious "Heracles" who performed the labors; the child-murders were a terrible aberration, which need not be integrated into Heracles' self-image. Heracles can, Theseus thinks, simply ignore those episodes of his life which do not seem to fit his heroic character. But Heracles is the killer of his family as well as the benefactor of mankind. The inclusion of these disparate episodes of his life generates a problem both for Heracles and for the spectators as they struggle to make sense of who Heracles is.[20]

The wildly different versions of Heracles are all presented as aspects of a single figure. One can try to spot a unity or common thread between the different manifestations of the character — a game Heracles himself tries to play. He wants to impose an order on his life. He claims that, contrary to appearances, his actions have all been of a single kind; he traces the common thread of labor and enslavement in everything he has done. His life has consisted only of labor, performed under compulsion from Eurystheus and Hera. But the experience of disparity in the events of the play itself is too strong to be overcome by Heracles' own attempts to impose unity on the narrative of his life. Heracles lives on both as savior of mankind, and as a terrifying killer of wife and children, and as the broken, weeping, ordinary dependent of Theseus.

After his madness, Heracles falls asleep. He wakes to sanity surrounded by the mutilated corpses of his wife and children. In his first speech on waking (1088–1108), he hails the light and expresses his bewilderment: he does not understand where he is or why he is surrounded by dead bodies. One possibility can, he thinks, be ruled out: "I have not, I suppose, gone back down again to Hades?" (1102). This does not look like the underworld; he cannot see its geographical markers, which he well knows — the rock of Sisyphus, Pluto, and the scepter of Persephone (1103–5).

But he will soon realize that in fact the whole upper world has now become for him like the land of the dead. He sees his future life as an anticipation on earth of the horrors of the underworld: "I shall imitate Ixion in chains bound to the wheel" (τὸν ἁρματήλατον / Ἰξίον' ἐν δεσμοῖσιν ἐκμιμήσομαι, 1297–98). Heracles is like Ixion not only because he has shed the blood of his family and suffers for it but also because he cannot move freely. He is bound upon a wheel of fire, so that he moves only under compulsion and with enormous pain.[21] He is physically alive and in the world above, but he is metaphorically dead.

The question, then, is whether he ought to literalize the metaphor and kill himself. With the help of his father, Amphitryon, Heracles gradually understands that the corpses surrounding him are those of his own loved ones and that it was he who killed them.[22] His first response to learning the truth is to ask, "Why should I not kill myself?" "Alas! Why then do I spare my life, when I have become the murderer of my darling children?" (οἴμοι· τί δῆτα φείδομαι ψυχῆς ἐμῆς / τῶν φιλτάτων μοι γενόμενος παίδων φονεύς; 1146–47). Now that he is confronted by the horror of what he has done, he wants to escape back into the land of the dead. He hopes that death will preserve his heroic character — like Megara at the beginning of the play. He sees suicide as the only way to thrust aside the shame or bad reputation (δύσκλεια, 1152) inherent in being alive after having done something so terrible. He is aware that he is polluted by the murders and sees no possibility of reintegration into human society. Moreover, his question implies that suicide is the only way to take revenge for the deaths of his loved ones on the man who murdered his children — himself.[23]

He is prevented from killing himself immediately only by the arrival of Theseus. Theseus will come "in the way of his deathly plans" (ἐμποδών μοι θανασίμων βουλευμάτων, 1153) not merely by showing up but also by his persistent attempts to talk him out of his suicidal impulses. Heracles at first tries to retreat from Theseus under the darkness of his cloak (1159–62). He wishes to hide himself from the gods and men in his state of pollution; he covers himself as an apotropaic gesture. Theseus insists that Heracles uncover his head (1202, 1214–28) and assures him that he will be a true friend in his trouble and pay him back for rescuing him from Hades (1223–25).[24]

The long conversation between Theseus and Heracles (1214–1426) dominates the final scene of the play.[25] Theseus takes over from Amphitryon as Heracles' supporter and interlocutor.[26] As friends, Theseus and Heracles are interchangeable, in a way that a father and son cannot be. Theseus has been saved and brought up from the underworld by Heracles as part of his final labor.[27] Theseus was once dependent on Heracles; now Heracles will depend on Theseus. Heracles has brought Theseus back from the land of the dead; in turn Theseus will try to draw Heracles away from his desire for death and feeling that his life has gone on too long.

Theseus denies that Heracles has any reason to feel dishonored or polluted. Drawing on sophistic philosophy, he rejects traditional ideas about pollution: he denies that any man can pollute the divine elements (1232), and later he will even be willing to touch Heracles' bloody hand.[28] Theseus emphasizes in his first speech to Heracles that he is not the kind of man to desert his friends in time of need (1223–25). The relationship formed when Heracles saved Theseus from Hades has not been forgotten, even now that Heracles' fortunes are different (1236–38).

For Theseus, fortunes may change, but heroes do not — or at least they should not. Theseus tries to hold Heracles up to the mark of his own former heroic character.

Θη. δράσεις δὲ δὴ τί; ποῖ φέρηι θυμούμενος;
Ηρ. θανών, ὅθενπερ ἦλθον, εἶμι γῆς ὕπο.
Θη. εἴρηκας ἐπιτυχόντος ἀνθρώπου λόγους.
Ηρ. σὺ δ᾽ ἐκτὸς ὤν γε συμφορᾶς με νουθετεῖς.
Θη. ὁ πολλὰ δὴ τλὰς Ἡρακλῆς λέγει τάδε;

Ηρ. οὔκουν τοσαῦτά γ'· ἐν μέτρωι μοχθητέον.

Θη. εὐεργέτης βροτοῖσι καὶ μέγας φίλος;

Ηρ. οἱ δ' οὐδὲν ὠφελοῦσί μ', ἀλλ' Ἥρα κρατεῖ.

Theseus: What will you do? Where are you carried, overcome by your passion?

Heracles: Dying, I am going back to the earth from which I came.

Theseus: You have spoken the words of an ordinary man.

Heracles: You give me advice, but you are outside my misfortune.

Theseus: Is it the much-enduring Heracles who says this?

Heracles: Not as much as this. One should suffer [or labor] in moderation.

Theseus: Are you the benefactor of mankind, the great friend?

Heracles: They do me no good, but Hera triumphs.[29]

(1246–53)

Heracles had intended to kill himself in order to preserve his heroic dignity and to avoid the threat of dishonor (δύσκλεια, 1152). But Theseus suggests that the way for Heracles to retain his honor is not to die but to live. He echoes Amphitryon's declaration that it is the mark of the brave man to trust in hope (105–6). To talk about suicide is what an "ordinary man" would do. He tries to persuade Heracles to live by reminding him of who he once was; he suggests that it is unworthy of "Heracles," the savior of mankind and the great protector and friend, to give in to suffering and die. Theseus suggests that Heracles has a responsibility both to himself and to his public to behave heroically; he says, "Greece would not put up with you dying foolishly" (οὐκ ἂν <σ'> ἀνάσχοιθ' Ἑλλὰς ἀμαθίαι θανεῖν, 1254).

Heracles does not seem to dispute Theseus's view that "Heracles" ought not to be bowed down by grief. But he does not agree that he himself, in the present circumstances, should not submit to grief. Such a thing would be impossible. Rather, he is willing to abandon his identity as "Heracles," the hero who performed the labors. He declares that there should be limits to suffering and labor (1251), using a verb — μοχθητέον — whose cognates are associated elsewhere with the labors.[30] By insisting on his desire to die, Heracles is refusing to undergo any further labors. He will no longer act as the man who could do whatever Hera or Eurystheus set him to do. Now it is not his actions that are exceptional, but his sufferings. He declares, "I am full of troubles, and there is no room to add more" (γέμω κακῶν δὴ κοὐκέτ' ἔσθ' ὅπηι τεθῆι, 1245). The language he uses makes him sound passive — no longer either brave or strong but simply a vessel of suffering that can hold no more. He has lost his capacity even for exalted tragic diction.[31] Theseus suggests that the only way Heracles can be "Heracles" and fulfill the promise of his past heroism is to go on living and resist yielding to suffering. But Heracles proposes a new association for his name. He is the man conquered by Hera: "Hera conquers" (Ἥρα κρατεῖ, 1253).[32]

As in the Oedipus plays, there is a temporal paradox generated by tragic overliving. One might expect Heracles would wish to have died before he killed his children; instead, he declares that his life never was worth living. He presents himself as consistently wretched (1255–1310). He begins by claiming emphatically that his life is unlivable, and always has been.

> ἀναπτύξω δέ σοι
> ἀβίωτον ἡμῖν νῦν τε καὶ πάροιθεν ὄν.
> πρῶτον μὲν ἐκ τοῦδ᾽ ἐγενόμην, ὅστις κτανὼν
> μητρὸς γεραιὸν πατέρα προστρόπαιος ὢν
> ἔγημε τὴν τεκοῦσαν Ἀλκμήνην ἐμέ.

> I will unfold to you that
> my life is not worth living now, nor was it in the past.
> First, I was born from a man who killed
> the old father of my mother, and with the guilt of killing on his head,
> he married my mother, Alcmene.
> (1256–60)

After an inauspicious beginning, Heracles' life has become worse and worse.[33] From birth, he has been doomed to be unhappy: when the foundation of a family is not set right, it is inevitable that the children suffer (ἀνάγκη δυστυχεῖν ἐκγόνους, 1262).[34] Theseus shows Heracles a divided self-image, juxtaposing his present pathetic yielding to suffering with his previous heroism. Heracles responds by giving an alternative narrative of his own life. He finds continuity between his past, present, and future selves only on the grounds that he has always been unhappy, and it would always have been better never to live at all. Theseus's vision of him as "Heracles of noble victories" has always been mistaken.

After enumerating the labors he performed for Eurystheus, he presents his current situation as the culmination of a life of slavery to misfortune: "I have come to this point of necessity" (ἥκω δ᾽ ἀνάγκης ἐς τόδ᾽, 1281). The phrasing suggests that necessity is both the agent through whom he has become killer of his own children, and also the characterization of his present situation: his enslavement to necessity has made him unable to evade even this final horror.[35] Heracles cannot maintain his position consistently, and indeed claims in 1291–93 — if the text is correct — that suffering is even worse if one has once known happiness.[36] But he insists on the idea that he has lost all autonomy because his great enterprises have lost the name of action. He presents his labors as passive submission to the will of others, and the killing of the children as only the final labor (1279–80). In this respect, the labors of Heracles are like the marriage and parricide of Oedipus: both Heracles and Oedipus claim that they have only "acted" under compulsion. The labors and the child-killings were not Heracles' own choice, and to go on living would be to remain trapped under the same "compulsion." If he lives, Heracles will only become involved in further supposed choices between intolerable evils.

At 1301 Heracles asks, "Why then should I live?" (τί δῆτά με ζῆν δεῖ;).[37] At 1351 he declares that he will remain alive. In the fifty lines between these two moments, Theseus invokes the example of the gods (1313–21) and offers Heracles a place in Athens (1322–39); Heracles replies with his own, quite different, account of the nature of the gods (1340–50) and then announces that he will go on living. Heracles' decision to live must be partly a response to Theseus's kind offer of a welcome in Athens. He cannot remain in the city where he has killed his family, a fact of which he has shown himself desperately aware (1281–84). His question "Why then should I live?" is provoked most immediately by the thought that there is nowhere on earth he could go in his state of pollution (1295–98). Theseus offers him a final place to live, suggesting that in Athens Heracles will be able to wash away his pollution (1324–25). He will receive various presents, and will be honored by the city at his death.

Theseus's offer provides Heracles with an escape from some of his troubles. He will not be destitute, and he will not be entirely an outcast from human society. Theseus assumes that even in his polluted state, Heracles is worthy of honor (1335). It has been argued that after Theseus's offer Heracles no longer has a heroic motive for committing suicide: once Theseus has offered Heracles a place in Athens, Heracles is no longer in a hopeless situation, no longer dishonored by remaining alive — unlike Megara.[38] Perhaps Heracles' decision to live conforms to contemporary ethical norms. Nevertheless, grief for his dead wife and children is not his only problem. Heracles goes on living despite a loss of what had seemed his essential attributes — including his strength and his capacity to benefit the weak. Theseus offers him honor, but he cannot restore Heracles' ability to win honor for himself through his own heroic actions.[39] The murder of the children is not only a cause of grief but also compromises Heracles' heroic character, and continues to do so even after he accepts Theseus's offer of a position in Athens. Heracles' honor is now dependent on the generosity of Theseus; he can never recover his former state of independence. Moreover, the honor that Heracles tried to achieve for his children through his labors (1370) can never be recovered. The children are, and will remain, dead. The weapons are, and will remain, tainted by the killings; they can no longer be simply a source of pride. Theseus may be able partially to restore Heracles' honor, but Heracles can never be "Heracles the victorious" again.

The debate about suicide is associated with a further disagreement between Theseus and Heracles, about the gods. Heracles insists on contrasting his own life with that of the gods. In line 1253 he says that men do not have the power to help him, whereas the goddess Hera has the power to do him harm; men, unlike gods, are powerless to do what they might wish. The difference between himself and the dominant, successful, and powerful goddess Hera is a reason to give up on his own life. He expresses disgust at the behavior of Hera: "She has enacted the plan she planned" (ἔπραξε γὰρ βούλησιν ἣν ἐβούλετο, 1305; the polyptoton emphasizes the ability of the goddess to do exactly what she intends). Heracles, by contrast, has acted only under necessity, under orders from others. He is only a mortal man, not a goddess, and therefore he is enslaved to fate; suicide is not a decision but an acceptance of the inevitable fact that, being mortal and not divine, he can take no more.

Theseus does not challenge Heracles' view that freedom is impossible. But he does challenge the contrast Heracles makes between the powerful gods and vulnerable, weak mankind. Theseus suggests that gods and men are equally weak. The gods have, he argues, done all kinds of terrible things; yet they go on living and put up with their own imperfections:

οὐδεὶς δὲ θνητῶν ταῖς τύχαις ἀκήρατος,
οὐ θεῶν, ἀοιδῶν εἴπερ οὐ ψευδεῖς λόγοι.
οὐ λέκτρ' ἐν ἀλλήλοισιν, ὧν οὐδεὶς νόμος,
συνῆψαν; οὐ δεσμοῖσι διὰ τυραννίδα
πατέρας ἐκηλίδωσαν; ἀλλ' οἰκοῦσ' ὅμως
Ὄλυμπον ἠνέσχοντό θ' ἡμαρτηκότες.

No mortal is untainted by these chances,
nor any god, if the stories are not false.

Have they not shared unlawful beds with one another?

For the sake of sovereignty, have they not bound

their fathers and defiled them? But nevertheless they inhabit

Olympus, and put up with having done wrong.

(1314–19)

Theseus's argument relies on two assumptions: that the gods are flawed, and that the gods ought to be the models for human behavior.[40] He claims that humans should accept their own moral weakness because the gods do so.[41] He tells Heracles that fate is inescapable (1314) and even the gods cannot escape it; therefore they cannot help behaving badly; therefore mortal men also must accept their own weakness; therefore Heracles must allow Theseus to help him. Theseus allows little or no room for free choice on the part of either gods or men.[42] The entire thrust of Theseus's speech is an appeal to Heracles to submit to external authority: that of the gods, of fate, of the law, and of Theseus himself, whom Heracles should follow to Athens.

The subject of the conversation has become not the injustice of the gods but the question of how to respond to past guilt and present vulnerability. How should Heracles react to the fact that he is now brought as low as a man can be? Theseus argues that he must accept both moral and physical weakness as part of the natural course of things. The gods do not try to salvage their dignity by committing suicide or leaving Olympus. It would be reasonable, he implies, for Heracles to kill himself if his suffering were unusual.[43] But, as things stand, suicide would be an attempt to gain an impossible kind of purity or integrity, which is never available either to gods or to men. Heracles need not pretend he could ever be untainted by fortune (ἀκήρατος, 1314). Theseus implies both that there is nothing wrong with life under compulsion and that there is no alternative to it.

Heracles begins his speech by saying that everything Theseus has said is beside the point: "Alas! This is all irrelevant to my sufferings" (οἴμοι· πάρεργα < > τάδ' ἔστ' ἐμῶν κακῶν, 1340). Editors disagree about whether "all this" means the offer of sanctuary in Athens or Theseus's claims about the gods.[44] But there is surely no reason to decide between the two readings: "all this" can refer to both. It is important that the question of the gods and the debate about whether to go on living in Athens are not kept as clearly distinct as one might expect. Heracles does not distinguish between the two issues: he dismisses Theseus's representation of both. Heracles denies, first, that the gods are no different from people —

especially, from vulnerable and polluted people like himself—and, second, that his own position will be no different from what it was before, even if he accepts the offer of sanctuary in Athens (1353–55).

The example of the gods is irrelevant because the analogy between gods and men does not hold. Theseus has said that the gods suffer the same kind of situation as mortals only "if the stories are true" (εἴπερ οὐ ψευδεῖς λόγοι, 1315). Heracles is quick to retort that the stories are not true, being merely the wretched tales of the poets:

ἐγὼ δὲ τούς θεοὺς οὔτε λέκτρ' ἃ μὴ θέμις
στέργειν νομίζω δεσμά τ' ἐξάπτειν χεροῖν
οὔτ' ἠξίωσα πώποτ' οὔτε πείσομαι
οὐδ' ἄλλον ἄλλου δεσπότην πεφυκέναι.
δεῖται γὰρ ὁ θεός, εἴπερ ἔστ' ὀρθῶς θεός,
οὐδενός· ἀοιδῶν οἵδε δύστηνοι λόγοι.

But I do not believe the gods enjoy love affairs that are not right,
and bind chains with their hands,
nor have I ever thought so, nor will I believe it,
nor that one of them is master of another;
for a god, if he is really a god, needs
nothing; but these are the wretched stories of the poets.
(1341–46)

Heracles adopts a rationalist position in relation to mythology.[45] In doing so, of course, Heracles denies certain stories about himself, including stories essential to the plot of the *Heracles*. If the gods do not commit adultery, Heracles cannot be the son of Zeus, and Amphitryon is not the "bed-sharer of Zeus" (*pace* the first line of the *Heracles*); and if the gods do not dominate one another, the domination of Iris over Lyssa that the spectators have just witnessed in this very play and that caused Heracles' madness and downfall must have been a mass delusion.[46] Heracles is denying part of the myth on which the play depends. Moreover, he is also contradicting his own declared beliefs. Heracles declares emphatically that he has always held the same views about the gods and always will (1343). But his new, antimythical description of divinity contradicts his own previous speech, in which he accused Hera of bringing him down in jealousy for the infidelities of Zeus (1263–70, 1303–7); and he will again blame Hera for his troubles at the end of the speech (1392–93).

The clash between Heracles' outburst and the myth does not justify reading his words as an interpolation of Euripides' own beliefs into the mouth of his character.[47] Nor is it clear that Heracles is straightforwardly wrong, even in the terms of the play's own narrative, despite the fact that his declaration seems to be contradicted by the Iris-Lyssa scene and by his own views elsewhere. Rather, we are led to believe at least two incompatible things about Heracles: that he suffers because of the cruel anthropomorphic gods; and that he suffers because he is a man and cannot imitate the independent, unmoved, and inhuman gods. The declaration undoes the coherence of "Heracles" as a dramatic character.[48] The play asks us to believe both that Heracles is the son of Zeus, persecuted by Hera and driven mad by Iris, and also that he is an ordinary man, who doubts, suffers, and weeps. The contradiction undermines the authority of myth: the greatest of heroes thinks his own story is untrue. In the process, it also undermines the audience's expectations of coherent narrative.

Heracles rejects Theseus's analogy between gods and men as a motive for going on living. There is a distinction between the gods and himself because he is in a position where his gods could never be: "in trouble" (ἐν κακοῖσιν, 1347).[49] But despite his deeply pessimistic view both of his own life, and of human life in general, Heracles nevertheless decides to go on living.[50]

> ἐσκεψάμην δὲ καίπερ ἐν κακοῖσιν ὢν
> μὴ δειλίαν ὄφλω τιν' ἐκλιπὼν φάος·
> ταῖς συμφοραῖς γὰρ ὅστις οὐχ ὑφίσταται
> οὐδ' ἀνδρὸς ἂν δύναιθ' ὑποστῆναι βέλος.
> ἐγκαρτερήσω θάνατον· εἶμι δ' ἐς πόλιν
> τὴν σήν, χάριν τε μυρίαν δώρων ἔχω.[51]

> But I have taken thought, although I am in trouble,
> lest I be convicted of some cowardice, if I abandon the light;
> for a man who does not stand up under misfortunes
> would also be unable to withstand a human weapon.
> I shall be strong to death; and I shall come to your city,
> and I have the numberless thanks of gifts.
> (1347–52)

Heracles' decision to live reverses Megara's decision to die (275–311). His immediate motive for avoiding suicide is the fear of being accused of cowardice (δειλία). There is a clear echo here of Amphitryon's declaration that it is cowardice to give up; the best and bravest man is the one who trusts in hopes (105–6). There is also an echo of Theseus's reproach to Heracles — talk of suicide was the language of an "ordinary man" (1248). One might wonder whether there is anything new or surprising about Heracles' decision, if it is based on a principle that has already been articulated at least twice in the play.

But there is an important modification here from the earlier versions of the principle. Amphitryon and Theseus implied a clear distinction between the best kind of man, like "Heracles," and the "ordinary man." They gave an unusual account of heroism, but they assumed that heroic identity itself was a constant. Heracles, on the other hand, emphasizes his own weakness even as he makes his decision to do the supposedly less cowardly thing and live. His denial of the poets' stories about the gods articulates his awareness of his own vulnerability. He marks his own distance from divinity in his claim that "god, if he is really god, needs nothing" (1345). Heracles himself now knows that he needs all the help he can get. However much courage he may have, it will not be enough to preserve either his life or his reputation, unless he is also willing to rely on the material help of Theseus and of his tainted weapons. Human beings cannot be bravest and best all the time.

As soon as he has declared his decision to go on living, Heracles reminds Theseus that his vulnerability is new and unexpected. Theseus argued that weakness was the universal condition of men and of gods. Heracles denies this, showing that he is in a new and unexpected position. He says,

ἀτὰρ πόνων δὴ μυρίων ἐγευσάμην
ὧν οὔτ' ἀπεῖπον οὐδέν' οὔτ' ἀπ' ὀμμάτων
ἔσταξα πηγάς, οὐδ' ἂν ὠιόμην ποτὲ
ἐς τοῦθ' ἱκέσθαι, δάκρυ' ἀπ' ὀμμάτων βαλεῖν.
νῦν δ', ὡς ἔοικε, τῆι τύχηι δουλευτέον.

But I have tasted countless labors,
nor did I refuse any of them, nor from my eyes
did I shed streams, and I never thought
I would come to this, to let tears fall from my eyes.
But now, it seems, one must be enslaved to fate.
(1353–57)

Against Theseus, Heracles insists that to be abject is not inevitable or universal. Even as he acknowledges his own vulnerability, he also remembers that it was not always so. Heracles was not always the kind of man who wept. The reminder movingly emphasizes his present weakness, but it also recalls his former strength. Heracles takes his weakness not as an inevitable result of his humanity but as a particular feature of his present circumstances. Whereas Theseus sees weakness as a permanent component of life, Heracles insists that his experience has been varied and complex. Once he was strong; now, he must be enslaved to fate, and tears fall from his eyes. Heracles rejects Theseus's suggestion that he should live because both people and gods are vulnerable. He decides to live only after he has asserted that enslavement and vulnerability do not constitute the only possible mode of life. His declaration about the falsehood of a certain image of the gods implies a particular view of human beings. People, unlike gods, do sometimes dominate one another and do sometimes need one another. Heracles emphatically connects his decision to live with the assertion that gods are not vulnerable and that he himself has, in the past, been strong. He contrasts his present weakness with his former strength and reminds Theseus that he has not always been the weaker of the two friends.

In declaring that he will live, he says, according to the manuscripts, ἐγκαρτερήσω θάνατον (1351). Most commentators have emended the text of Heracles' most emphatic declaration, usually adopting the conjecture, ἐγκαρτερήσω βίοτον, "I shall be strong to life."[52] Certainly, if the text is correct, the usage of ἐγκαρτερεῖν is unparalleled: it always elsewhere means "stand fast in," whereas Heracles is here declaring his intention to resist death, rather than to endure it.[53] Heracles uses a phrase that sounds as if he is proposing to show courage by dying, when in fact he is showing courage by living.[54] The decisive reason to prefer the manuscript reading is that the phrase parallels Heracles' earlier declaration, which was similarly difficult: οὐκ ἐκπονήσω θάνατον; (581). When he declared his intention to protect his children, he asked, "Shall I not labor away their death?" Now, he will "be strong toward" his own death. The echo reminds us that when Heracles tried to "labor away the death" of his children, he ended up killing them. To be strong toward death involves living as well as dying, just as Heracles' labors against death included both protecting and killing. "Enduring death" has come to mean the same thing as "living" since life happens under the shadow of death but nevertheless must be endured.

Heracles begins to recognize that life does not always follow a consistent trajectory. Many critics have pointed out that Euripides' *Heracles* can be read as a response to Sophocles' *Ajax*.[55] In the *Heracles*, as in the *Ajax*, a hero renowned for his physical strength is driven mad and goes on a misguided killing spree. Euripides' Heracles is tempted by the choice of Ajax — suicide rather than dishonor — but instead, he decides to live. The play can therefore be read as a correction of Ajax's notions of heroism. Euripides, it has been argued, follows or invents a new ethical standard, suggesting that it is more heroic to endure long life, even in pain, grief, weakness, and dishonor, than to commit suicide.[56]

But an alternative, and in some ways closer, Sophoclean model for Euripides' *Heracles* is the *Oedipus Tyrannus*.[57] As I suggested in chapter 1, the final episode of Sophocles' *Oedipus Tyrannus* shows a character who goes on living and who remains on stage, even when it seems impossible either for Oedipus himself or for the audience to make sense of his life story or his character. In the *Heracles*, as in the *Oedipus Tyrannus*, the representation of overliving creates a crisis of dramatic character and specifically, of heroic character. Heracles lives on beyond a point where it is possible to view him unproblematically either as the protector of the weak, since he has slaughtered his family, or as the strongest man in the world, since by the end of the play he is forced to rely, emotionally, materially, and physically, on his friend Theseus. The play suggests that even the greatest hero in the world cannot escape human society (as does Oedipus at Colonus). Even Heracles is not immune from human vulnerability, including the sense of overliving. Tragic overliving in this play is figured as a kind of living death, which human beings must endure together and which binds people to one another.

Theseus remains unable to accept that his friend cannot maintain his glorious character consistently. When Heracles begs to be allowed to see his children once more and embrace his father (1406–8), Theseus implies, as he did at 1250–51, that Heracles' grief is unworthy of him; heroes should be able to withstand suffering without weeping. He says, "Do you have so little memory of your labors?" (1418), suggesting that someone who has acted as Heracles has done in the past has no business grieving for his dead children. Heracles should not need his family, like a woman; instead, he should rely on Theseus himself, his male peer. Men must always act like men, heroes like heroes, women like women. But Heracles answers, "All those sufferings I endured were less than these." He refuses to accept Theseus's suggestion that one who has performed the heroic and masculine feats of the labors could never be overcome by mere domestic suffering. He also implies that Theseus is wrong to think that the various apparently contradictory spheres of action in a man's life are separable. Theseus, who is now strong, has once been weak. No one can maintain his position as a strong man forever. Heracles talks and weeps and suffers like an ordinary man, because he is an ordinary man, among other things. He cannot always be strong, and neither can Theseus.

In Sophocles' Oedipus plays, tragic overliving is associated very strongly with isolation. Oedipus is cut off from normal social interaction, by blindness, by pollution, by the horrors of what he has done. His isolation from human norms becomes, in the *Tyrannus* and still more in the *Coloneus*, a kind of freedom: he is free from the repetitive patterns of normal human lives. In the *Heracles*, by contrast, tragic overliving is associated with a bitter kind of companionship.[58] The decision not to commit suicide means accepting friendship, φιλία, even at a very high cost.[59] Heracles will be a slave to fate, and he will also be bound to other people and even to his own weapons. Heracles, unlike Oedipus, realizes that he is not abnormal and that he is not free, either from his own past or from human society.

Heracles' debate with himself about whether to retain his weapons immediately follows his decision to live and helps to explain what his continued existence will mean.[60] His best friends are the weapons: he describes them as bitter companions (1377).[61] He places his relationship with his weapons next to his relationship with his dead children: "O bitter pleasures of kisses, and bitter companionships of weapons" (ὦ λυγραὶ φιλημάτων / τέρψεις, λυγραὶ δὲ τῶνδ' ὅπλων κοινωνίαι, 1376–77). The oxymoronic "bitter pleasures" and "bitter companionships" define his life from now on. His relationship with his weapons is based on a need that forces him to overcome his abhorrence. He wants to cast them away; but if he does so, he will be killed dishonorably on the way to Athens:

> ἀλλὰ γυμνωθεὶς ὅπλων
> ξὺν οἷς τὰ κάλλιστ' ἐξέπραξ' ἐν Ἑλλάδι,
> ἐχθροῖς ἐμαυτὸν ὑποβαλὼν αἰσχρῶς θάνω;
> οὐ λειπτέον τάδ', ἀθλίως δὲ σωστέον.

> But stripped of my weapons
> with which I performed the most noble deeds in Greece,
> shall I die shamefully, submitting myself to my enemies?
> I must not leave them, but sadly I must keep them.
> (1382–85)

One might think that in choosing to keep the weapons, he is choosing to live as the brave public benefactor who performed the labors, rather than as a private individual.[62] But with those same weapons, he also performed the most shameful deeds in all Greece, namely the slaughter of his wife and children. The weapons cannot readily be identified only with the public Heracles now that they have also been used to kill the children. The weapons, like Heracles himself, have multiple meanings; they are no longer a guide to his identity but a mark of his unreadability.[63]

In choosing to keep the bow, Heracles is acknowledging his own vulnerability — not simply because he needs a weapon for self-defense but also because this weapon is the bow.[64] In the first episode of the play, when Lycus and Amphitryon argued about Heracles' heroism, Lycus accused Heracles of cowardice because he fights with a bow; Amphitryon replied that Heracles is indeed brave, as his fights with the giants testify, and that fighting with a bow is far more sensible than hoplite fighting.[65] Heracles recalls the debate when he declares that he does not want to behave like a coward and desert his post. The gods are able to evade neediness; they achieve their goals from afar and have no need to be enslaved to fate. Gods are like bowmen; men, on the other hand, must fight hand to hand, like hoplites. The image becomes deeply paradoxical, in that Heracles, a mortal man, takes up the bow as a sign that he cannot fight in the protected manner of a divine bowman; carrying the bow shows that he is as vulnerable as a hoplite. It is important that the weapons he carries include not only the bow but also the club, with which he killed his second child at close quarters (984–94).

Heracles cannot stand alone and protect others; he must rely on the support of his weapons and his friends. Tragic overliving becomes associated with the need of one person for another and with Heracles' need even for such terrible instruments as these weapons as his companions. Whereas Oedipus laments his own and his daughters' solitude, Heracles acknowledges that he can no longer be alone. He must rely on the strength of others, even when he does not want to. In Sophocles' *Oedipus Coloneus*, Oedipus finds a new role outside his own family in the foreign *polis* of Athens; similarly, Theseus offers Heracles, who has apparently lost both his family and his capacity for heroic action, a new role in Athens as both hero and friend.[66] But in the *Oedipus Coloneus*, Oedipus helps Theseus: he is more than a dependent. Heracles, on the other hand, is the object of Theseus's generosity of spirit — a difficult position for someone who has once been so strong. However well Theseus behaves, it is clear that Heracles can never recover his former self-sufficiency and glory.

An important reversal takes place in the relationship between Heracles and Theseus in the final lines of the play.[67] Theseus again accuses Heracles of not being true to himself: Heracles reminds him that Theseus, too, has had a time of vulnerability and dependency.

Θη. εἴ σ' ὄψεταί τις θῆλυν ὄντ' οὐκ αἰνέσει.
Ηρ. ζῶ σοι ταπεινός; ἀλλὰ πρόσθεν οὐ δοκῶ.
Θη. ἄγαν γ' · ὁ κλεινὸς Ἡρακλῆς οὐκ εἶ νοσῶν.
Ηρ. σὺ ποῖος ἦσθα νέρθεν ἐν κακοῖσιν ὤν;
Θη. ὡς ἐς τὸ λῆμα παντὸς ἦν ἥσσων ἀνήρ.
Ηρ. πῶς οὖν † ἔτ' εἴπῃς † ὅτι συνέσταλμαι κακοῖς;[68]

Theseus: If anyone sees you being a woman he will not praise you.
Heracles: Do I live humble in your opinion? But before — I think not.
Theseus: Yes, too much. You are not the famous Heracles in your sickness.
Heracles: And what were you like when you were in trouble in the underworld?
Theseus: In terms of spirit I was a man weaker than anyone.
Heracles: Then how would you still say I am reduced by my sufferings?
(1412–17)

Heracles' reminder that Theseus, too, was once weak and dependent shows that he is wrong to insist that the strong must always be strong. Heracles is now no longer "Heracles"; but Theseus, too, was once not "Theseus." Character is unstable because fortune is unstable. The two roles, of strong rescuer and weak dependent, seem to be entirely interchangeable: Heracles has lived long enough to play both parts.

Heracles has switched places with Theseus and also with his own children. As he goes off stage, leaning on his friend, he reenacts the part his children played when he led them off into the palace.[69] Heracles says as he is led off the stage, "And we, utterly destroyed, having destroyed the house by our shameful actions, will follow Theseus as towboats" (1423–24). The fairly rare word "towboats" (ἐφολκίδες) has been used once before in this play. When the children, in their delight at seeing their father again, cling to his clothes and refuse to let go, Heracles jokes with them that it is unnecessary: he has no wings to fly away from his family (628). But since the children will not stop holding on to him, he will take them with him like towboats: "I will lead them, taking these towboats [ἐφολκίδας] by the hands, and like a ship I will drag them. Indeed, I am not ashamed of looking after children: all human things are equal" (631–33). The great Heracles enjoys playing the game of pretending to be a ship for his children. But in the final lines of the play, childlike or boatlike dependency is no longer even partly a joke. Heracles has been reduced to the level of his own little children and must be led away by Theseus, who stands in for the loved ones he has killed (1401).

The children were led away wearing their burial clothes, and although they thought their father would protect them, they were going to their deaths. Heracles is as vulnerable as a child, but he is, unlike his children, aware that his life will consist largely of preparation for death. Heracles and Theseus are going to Athens, but they must also finish the task begun in the underworld, in disposing of Cerberus. Moreover, the final lines of the play emphasize that death is only deferred. Heracles can now, thanks to Theseus, look forward to burial in Athens, and it is the hope of burial, rather than of future life or even final apotheosis, that dominates the end of the play.[70] The children, too, must be buried (1419), and Heracles' father Amphitryon hopes to be buried by his son (1420).

The final lines look forward to a series of burials, of sons by fathers and fathers by sons. The emphasis on burial suggests that Heracles' future life will consist largely in waiting for death. But it also shows that even dying cannot be done alone. Heracles will need Theseus's help in death, just as he does in life; Amphitryon, too, will be as dependent on the help of Heracles, to be buried, as the dead children are dependent on him. The kind of solitary death with dignity that Megara and Heracles hoped for has been shown to be unavailable, either for Megara or for Heracles. Euripides emphasizes human companionship and mutual dependency as the necessary corollary of a life that goes on too long to be consistently heroic.

CHAPTER FOUR

"Let us live"

Seneca's *Epistles* and *Hercules Furens*

Seneca associates anxiety about the proper length of life with a sense of literary and political belatedness. Those who had to live in imperial Rome under Nero and under Domitian were prone to believe that both they themselves and the Roman state had lived too long. In the opening of his *Agricola* (written in AD 97–98), Tacitus argues that his own age is less conducive both to virtue and to the appreciation of virtue than was his father-in-law's generation. Now, Tacitus is careful to remark, happiness is gradually returning under the rule of Nerva and Trajan (*Agricola* 3.1). But the Romans have been damaged so severely by the terrors of Domitian that their spirits and their moral sensibilities will hardly be revived, since they have learned to love even their own sickness. People are so used to keeping silent in order to survive that they no longer know how to respond like living men.

> quid, si per quindecim annos, grande mortalis aevi spatium, multi fortuitis casibus, promptissimus quisque saevitia principis interciderunt, pauci et, ut <*sic*> dixerim, non modo aliorum sed etiam nostri superstites sumus, exemptis e media vita tot annis, quibus iuvenes ad senectutem, senes prope ad ipsos exactae aetatis terminos per silentium venimus?

Although in the course of fifteen years, a long time in the life of mortals, many people died by lucky accident, while the most energetic died through the savagery of the emperor, a few of us are also, so to speak, not only the survivors of others but even of ourselves. So many years have been extracted from the middle of our lives that those who were young men have been brought to old age, and those of us who were already old have come to the brink of our deathbeds, but all in silence. What then? (*Agricola* 3.2)

Tacitus claims that those who have managed to survive the reign of Domitian have overlived themselves: *etiam nostri superstites sumus.* The pressure to keep silent for so many years, and the loss of so many years of life, have left those who remain like walking dead men, who can no longer judge between good and evil, or do anything but wait for their long-delayed deaths.[1]

Seneca never lived to see the rule of Domitian: he killed himself in AD 65, during Nero's tyranny.[2] But Seneca's writings in both prose and drama betray a preoccupation with the problem articulated later by Tacitus, the problem of overliving. Seneca is interested in the proper length of human life because he fears that he and his contemporaries may be merely "survivors of themselves." Seneca, the tutor of Nero, was not prepared to be as explicit as Tacitus about the failings of the political regime under which he served. But his interest in overliving implicitly articulates his political fears.

Seneca's specifically Roman and Neronian concerns and anxieties lead him to seize upon an issue that all Stoic thinkers have to consider. In the Stoic view of the proper length of human life, what matters is not how long one lives but how well. Marcus Aurelius tells us that "the longest life, then, and the shortest, amount to the same, since the present moment is equal for everyone, and what is lost is not our own."[3] Seneca returns again and again to the question of the proper length of a human life and to the problem of what it could mean either to live too long or to die too soon. For Seneca, as for Marcus Aurelius, the chronological length of life is ultimately irrelevant. He discusses the length of life mainly in the context of arguing against the fear of death. People think life is always too short, but in fact even the shortest life may be long enough, if one uses it to be virtuous.

Suicide is a Stoic concern because it is the ultimate gesture by which people demonstrate their freedom from the fear of death—the worst threat to Stoic equanimity.[4] The main principle of all Stoic belief was that one should live in accordance with nature. For a Stoic, to live too long is to go on living when one can no longer live in accordance with nature. Diogenes Laertius cites the motives for killing oneself the Stoics regard as justifiable: "They say that the wise man will make a rational exit from life, either on behalf of his country or for the sake of his friends, or if he suffers intolerable pain or mutilation or incurable disease" (7.130). One should kill oneself rather than live a life contrary to nature and reason. The trouble is, of course, that this thesis generates a paradox. Only the truly wise and rational man, who is living in accordance with nature and reason, will be able to recognize when the moment has come to kill himself. But he should kill himself only if he is no longer able to be a wise and rational man. Only the wise man will kill himself, but he will kill himself only if he is not a wise man.[5] The Stoics seem to have tried to evade the problem by suggesting that those of us who are not wise can kill ourselves at the prompting of a divine sign.[6] In the *Phaedo*, Plato's Socrates drinks the hemlock at the prompting of his *daimon*. Zeno notoriously killed himself on breaking his finger, crying, "I am coming, why do you call me?"[7] presumably because he took the accident as a divine sign that his body was no longer able to function according to nature. But, of course, there is no guarantee that any sign is truly divine.

Suicide figures more prominently in Seneca than in the work of other Stoics.[8] Clearly, Seneca was particularly concerned with suicide because he knew that he might some day have to kill himself. Those who lived in imperial Rome knew that only suicide might preclude torture or a worse death; under an oppressive political system, the ability to die when one chooses may be the only kind of freedom available. Political pressure influenced Seneca's philosophical interests.[9] In Seneca, the difficult question is not when to kill oneself but when not to kill oneself. He presents suicide in a particularly attractive light; the problem is how to imagine how it could ever be good to go on living. Seneca condemns those who kill themselves for trivial reasons,[10] but when the time to die has come, one should kill oneself in the manner and at the moment when one wishes to do so. Seneca often describes suicide as the ultimate act of freedom and the guarantee that the wise man can always be independent of slavery to political or psychological oppression.[11] For Seneca, living too long is different from dying too soon because one can always choose to prevent it. One can die whenever one wishes, so there is no excuse for putting it off too long. Foolish men fail to realize that living too long is always unnecessary: those who live too long do so through their own fault.

Seneca's writing repeatedly generates the rhetorical paradox that, on the one hand, the length of life is irrelevant to its quality but, on the other, inferior lives go on too long. Time both does and does not matter; it both is and is not possible to live too long. The language of temporality ("too short" and "too long") remains even while Seneca is dismissing time as irrelevant. In epistle 93, for example, he asks:

> quid autem interest quam cito exeas unde utique exeundum est? Non ut diu vivamus curandum est, sed ut satis; nam ut diu vivas fato opus est, ut satis, animo. Longa est vita si plena est; impletur autem cum animus sibi bonum suum reddidit et ad se potestatem sui transtulit. Quid illum octoginta anni iuvant per inertiam exacti? non vixit iste sed in vita moratus est, nec sero mortuus est, sed diu. "Octoginta annis vixit." Interest mortem eius ex quo die numeres. "At ille obiit viridis." Sed officia boni civis, boni amici, boni filii executus est; in nulla parte cessavit; licet aetas eius inperfecta sit, vita perfecta est. "Octaginta annis vixit." Immo octoginta annis fuit, nisi forte sic vixisse eum dicis quomodo dicuntur arbores vivere.

But what does it matter how fast you depart from the place from which you must depart some time? We should not worry about living for a long time, but about living enough; for you need luck to live for a long time, but to live enough you need character. Life is long if it is fulfilled; but it is fulfilled only when the mind has given itself its own good, and taken control of itself. What good do eighty years do a man if they have been passed in idleness? That fellow has not lived but delayed in life, and he died not too late but too protractedly. "He lived eighty years!" What matters is from which day you start counting his death. "But this other man died in his green youth!" But he fulfilled the duties of a good citizen, a good friend, and a good son; there was nothing he had failed to do. Even if his age was incomplete, his life was complete. "He lived eighty years!" No, he existed for eighty years, unless you really mean by "he lived" the same as when trees are said to live. (93.2–4)

Here, as often in Seneca's writings on the subject of the length of human life, apparently living too long and apparently dying too soon are not symmetrical opposites. He tells us it is not the quantity but the quality of life that matters, and he applies this principle consistently to those who died young: they died at the right time. But those who lived to the age of eighty really did live too long: they spent eighty years dying.[12] The linguistic oddities bring out the paradox of this view: the adverb *diu* (for a long time, protractedly) is unexpectedly applied to death, not life. Long life is only a slow way to die.

The mode of the *suasoria* would have trained Seneca to construct arguments for or against any proposition, from a collation of possible *dicta* on the given theme. Seneca's own father's *Suasoria* 6 offers a selection of rhetorical responses to the question of whether Cicero should beg Antony for his life. Cestius Pius says,

Si ad desiderium populi respicis, Cicero, quandoque perieris parum vixisti; si ad res gestas, satis vixisti; si ad iniurias Fortunae et praesentem rei publicae statum, nimium diu vixisti; si ad memoriam operum tuorum, semper victurus es.[13]

If you consider the loss the people will feel, Cicero, you will die too soon whenever you perish; if you look at what you achieved, you have lived long enough; if you have regard to the insults of fortune and the present state of the republic, you have lived far too long; if you remember the immortality of your works, you will live for ever. (*Suasoria* 6.4)

This is a witty formulation of the idea that the proper length of human life is not an objective number (such as three score years and ten) but is always relative to some value. Cicero's life is measured not in chronological time but by his achievements, which give inconsistent results about how long he has lived. The passage undermines the possibility of grieving at the premature death of Cicero by suggesting that it is arbitrary to say of any life that it was either too short or too long. One can always find reasons to call life either too short or infinitely long.

The passage in the *suasoria* makes a serious point, but it also functions, perhaps primarily, as a clever debating tactic. The length of life, like anything else, can be described in a multitude of different ways, depending on what one is trying to prove. The younger Seneca's inconsistent attitudes on the proper lengths of human life are informed at least as much by Roman rhetorical traditions as by anything in orthodox Stoicism.[14] In the *Consolatio ad Marciam* he gives an extraordinarily self-contradictory series of arguments, in quick succession, for why his addressee should not mourn her dead son: first, because many people outlive happiness; then, because everyone dies at the right time.[15] Seneca uses as many as possible of the tropes of consolation, without pausing to make them consistent with one another.[16] Living too long both is and is not possible. Seneca ties himself up in knots about time because he refuses to consider the possibility that, if people can live too long, they may also die too soon.[17]

The *Epistles* contain many of Seneca's most intense discussions of the length of life.[18] Two epistles in particular, 77 and 78, together illustrate the rhetorical tensions in Seneca's account of how long one should live. Epistle 77 argues against the fear of death by showing how easy it is to kill oneself. Seneca describes the suicide of one Tullius Marcellinus as an example of an easy and even pleasurable death: "Although he killed himself, nevertheless he departed most gently, and slid away from life" (*quamvis enim mortem sibi consciverit, tamen mollissime excessit et vita elapsus est,* 77.10). As usual, Seneca's rhetorical mode is dialogic: he imagines the reasons people might give for not killing themselves and sets about dispelling them. He argues that the motives people commonly give for not committing suicide are only excuses. He uses the story of a slave boy who killed himself bravely to imply that those who refuse to kill themselves are held back only by a shameful slavish or childish cowardice (77.14–15): "For life, if the courage to die is lacking, is servitude" (*nam vita, si moriendi virtus abest, servitus est,* 77.15). Seneca here slips between two separate propositions. He implies that people are sometimes held back from suicide by fear and moves immediately to conclude, much less plausibly, that all the other reasons people give for not killing themselves are merely masks for cowardice. They pretend they want to live for exalted reasons, such as for their friends or their country, but in fact they postpone dying only in order to have another luxurious fish supper (77.16–18). He mocks those who claim that they cannot die because to do so would be to abandon their duties:

> "Sed ego," inquit, "vivere volo, qui multa honeste facio; invitus relinquo officia vitae, quibus fideliter et industrie fungor." Quid? tu nescis unum esse ex vitae officiis et mori? Nullum officium relinquis; non enim certus numerus quem debeas explere finitur. Nulla vita est non brevis.

> "But I want to live," he says, "because I am doing many important things. I am reluctant to leave the duties of life, which I am performing faithfully and diligently." What? Do you not realize that one of the duties of life is also to die? You are deserting no duty. For there is no fixed number that you have to fulfill. No life is not short. (77.19)

Seneca refuses to allow that one could have a duty to live. He makes the idea seem absurd, by foisting on his fictive interlocutor the silly notion that there could be a duty merely to fulfill a set number of years. The double negative allows Seneca momentarily to acknowledge that all lives end too soon — "no life is not short" (*nulla vita est non brevis*) — but only in order to support his claim that the length of life is irrelevant to its quality. All life is short, and therefore no life can be too short. The concession that life is short — which Seneca often denies, as in the *De Brevitate Vitae* (despite the title) — is revealing of Seneca's rhetorical manner. If it suits the argument of a particular moment, he will declare that life is short; he is quite prepared to say elsewhere that it is neither short nor long, depending on the particular demands of his current argumentative stance.[19]

Epistle 77 suggests that all reasons for not committing suicide are bad. The immediately subsequent epistle, number 78, provides an example of an apparently overwhelmingly good reason. It begins with an anecdote about how Seneca was tempted to commit suicide, but restrained himself because of his duty to his father.

> poterat adhuc adulescentia iniurias ferre et se adversus morbos contumaciter gerere — deinde succubui et eo perductus sum ut ipse destillarem, ad summam maciem deductus. Saepe impetum cepi abrumpendae vitae: patris me indulgentissimi senectus retinuit. Cogitavi enim non quam fortiter ego mori possem, sed quam ille fortiter desiderare non posset. Itaque imperavi mihi, ut viverem; aliquando enim et vivere fortiter facere est.

> When I was a young man I was able to put up with suffering and take a bold stand against sickness. But then I succumbed and reached the point of total emaciation and constant snuffling. Often I entertained the idea of breaking off my life; I was restrained by the old age of my kind old father. For I did not think, "How bravely I could die!" but "How incapable he would be of bearing the loss of me bravely." So I ordered myself to live. Sometimes even living is acting bravely. (78.2)

For Seneca, filial duty to one's father is the only value stronger than the desire for a brave death. The figure of the old father interrupts the intention he had had of "breaking off" his life. The order of the epistles emphasizes the tension between the two attitudes to the proper length of life, allowing Seneca to create a dialogue not only with fictional interlocutors but also with himself.[20] He can argue, in 77, that one has a duty to kill oneself, or at least to be prepared to die, and that there is no excuse for not dying; and in the very next epistle he can argue that one has a duty not to kill oneself, or at least to be prepared to postpone death and live. He suggests in epistle 77 that it is egotistical and probably hypocritical to say, "I want to live, because I have many honorable things to do" (*vivero volo, qui multa honeste facio*, 77.19). In the next epistle, he says that his own capacity to practice philosophy restored his will to live: he wanted to live because he had honorable things to do. "My studies were my salvation. I set it to the credit of philosophy, that I recovered and became well again. I owe my life to philosophy, and that is the least of my debts to her" (*Studia mihi nostra saluti fuerunt. Philosophiae acceptum fero, quod surrexi, quod convalui. Illi vitam debeo, et nihil illi minus debeo*, 78.3).

One can construct a logically coherent position from the two letters. Perhaps most people use their honorable activities merely as excuses for staying alive;

Seneca himself is the exception who proves the rule. The difference is that Seneca has a good motive for resisting suicide, while most people want to go on living merely to feed their appetites for fish or mushrooms, or for foolish forms of self-promotion. By contrast, Seneca presents his own decision not to kill himself as an act of supreme selflessness. He resisted suicide because he thought not of his own courage but of his father's weakness. He lived not for himself but for philosophy, for his father, and for his friends (78.3–4).[21] The letters suggest that one must resist all forms of selfish desire, including both the wish to live and the wish to die.

But Seneca's rhetoric emphasizes the clash between the two perspectives and does not make any attempt to construct a synthetic account of how long one should stay alive. In epistle 77 he implies that one has a duty to die in certain unspecified cases: "Do you not realize that even dying is one of life's duties?" (*tu nescis unum esse ex vitae officiis et mori?* 77.19). In 78 he suggests that one can always fulfill one's duties alive, even in sickness (78.20). Both arguments are concerned to dispel the fear of death, but they attack that fear from opposite flanks.[22] The defiantly contradictory rhetorical poses of epistles 77 and 78 allow Seneca to skirt the issue and give no definite opinion on whether it is possible to outlive the time when one can perform one's proper actions — and, if so, what should be done about it.

At the end of epistle 78 Seneca finally denies the possibility that physical weakness can ever deprive a person of his ability to perform his own proper duties. Lucilius complains that illness removes his capacity to act (78.21); Seneca tells him that even in a sickbed, one can behave well:

> Est, mihi crede, virtuti etiam in lectulo locus. Non tantum arma et acies dant argumenta alacris animi indomitique terroribus: et in vestimentis vir fortis apparet. Habes quod agas: bene luctare cum morbo.

> There is, believe me, a place for virtue even in bed. It is not only arms and battle lines that give proofs of a brave soul and one unconquered by terrors; a brave man is revealed even in his bedclothes. You have something you can do: to struggle well with your sickness. (78.21)

There is therefore no need to long for death, nor is there any reason to think a life could ever be too long to do the only thing that matters: to be good. The length or brevity of life becomes irrelevant, because the wise man "knows that honorable things do not grow with time" (*scit tempore honesta non crescere*, 78.27). He

knows, therefore, that time does not matter.[23] The battle to be good is one that
can be fought and won at any time and in any place, even in bed.

It is not clear whether it matters how long one lives or when one dies. Seneca's
imagery shifts in the course of these two epistles, reflecting an important ambivalence about whether death, the ending of life, contributes in any way to its
meaning. In epistle 77 life is like a journey.[24] The epistle begins with a description
of the arrival of the mail boats in the harbor, which precede the arrival of the main
ships. Seneca declares that he enjoyed taking no share in the desperate bustle
down to the waterfront, since the boats would bring him no material loss or gain.
The literal journey made by the ships into the harbor recalls the metaphorical
journey of life, in which one should try to be as independent as possible of the
storms of fortune. Seneca is particularly delighted at his own immunity from
dependence on fortune because he is an old man, and he will therefore have
enough money left to finish the journey of life: "However little I may have,
nevertheless I have more traveling money left than journey left to go, especially
since that journey we have begun is one that one need not follow to the end"
(*quantulumcumque haberem, tamen plus iam mihi superesset viatici quam viae, prae-
sertim cum eam viam simus ingressi, quam peragere non est necesse*, 77.3). But the
analogy between a literal journey and the journey of life becomes, in the course of
the sentence, a contrast. Unlike literal journeys, life, however short, is never
incomplete: "A journey is incomplete, if you stop in the middle or before the
destination; life is not incomplete, if it is honorable. Wherever you stop, if you
stop well, life is a whole" (*Iter inperfectum erit si in media parte aut citra petitum
locum steteris: vita non est inperfecta si honesta est; ubicumque desines, si bene desines,
tota est*, 77.4).[25] Later in the same epistle, the journey metaphor recurs but is used
very differently: "But did you imagine you would not one day arrive at the place
to which you were always going? There is no journey without an end" (*Tu autem
non putabas te aliquando ad id perventurum ad quod semper ibas? Nullum sine exitu iter
est*, 77.13). Life is a journey whose successful end is guaranteed; there is no way
that we can fail to arrive at our destination. First Seneca distinguishes journeys
from life; now he associates them. At first, therefore, it seems as if the goal of life,
virtue, is to be distinguished from its end, death; but later, the end and the goal
seem to be the same. If death is the end of the journey of life, it might be possible
to arrive at that goal too late.

Seneca relates his attitude to the proper length of life to a particular attitude to
dramatic unity. Epistle 77 ends with a comparison between the proper length for
a life, and the proper length for a play.

Vides aliquem gloriari senectute longa: quis illam ferre potuisset, si contigisset centesimum implere? Quomodo fabula, sic vita: non quam diu, sed quam bene acta sit, refert. Nihil ad rem pertinet quo loco desinas. Quocumque voles desine: tantum bonam clausulam inpone. Vale.

You see someone take pride in living to advanced old age. But who could have borne that old woman [Sattia, a woman whose tombstone boasts that she lived to ninety-nine], if she had reached a hundred? As with a play, so with life: what matters is not how long it is but how well it is performed. It makes no difference where you stop. Stop where you wish; only add a good conclusion. Good-bye. (77.20)

Aristotle would certainly not have approved of Seneca's implicit poetics. Aristotle tells us that,

κεῖται δὴ ἡμῖν τὴν τραγῳδίαν τελείας καὶ ὅλης πράξεως εἶναι μίμησιν ἐχούσης τι μέγεθος· ἔστιν γὰρ ὅλον καὶ μηδὲν ἔχον μέγεθος. ὅλον δέ ἐστιν τὸ ἔχον ἀρχὴν καὶ μέσον καὶ τελευτήν.

We have established that tragedy is the imitation of a complete and whole action, with a certain magnitude. For something can be whole without having magnitude. But "whole" means something which has a beginning, a middle, and an end. (*Poetics* 1450b23–27)

Seneca suggests that, *pace* Aristotle, what matters about a play is not that it should represent a whole single action but that each part of it be well performed — the length or unity of the whole is unimportant. He dismisses the Aristotelian idea that a play needs to be of a certain length in order to have dignity. Even more important, he rejects the notion of dramatic unity. For Seneca, there is no need of a proper beginning, middle, and end. Any time is a good time to end, in either a life or a work of literature, as long as one finishes with a proper closing gesture. Seneca's rhetorical style enacts his theoretical position on closure. He suggests that good writing, like the good life, should be ready to end at any moment: there must be a closing period at the end of every line or every paragraph. As if to prove the point that endings are always available, he immediately ends the letter: "Good-bye" (*Vale*).

But the end of epistle 77 is the end of neither the collection of letters nor Seneca's meditation on the proper lengths of life and of literature. At the beginning of epistle 78, he relates his own decision to go on living specifically to his practice of philosophy and to his *studia* in general. Epistle 78 thus implies an alternative attitude both to the ends of life and to the ends of literature. In 77 Seneca implies that a text, like a life, can end at any point; in 78 he implies that texts, like lives, may have an obligation to keep on going. But in neither case does he suggest that a life, or a text, could have a proper time to end determined by its own internal unity. His Stoic attitude to the ends of life leads him away from Aristotelian poetics. The same process is even more evident in the *Hercules Furens*.

Euripides is certainly the major source for Seneca's version of the story, whether directly or indirectly.[26] Seneca, like Euripides, tells the story of a strong man with a glorious past, who destroys his wife and children in a fit of lunacy. In Seneca, as in Euripides, the hero then decides not to kill himself.

Epistles 77 and 78 are suggestive texts to read beside Seneca's tragedies in general, but they have a particularly close relationship with the *Hercules Furens*. In this play the hero, like Seneca himself at the beginning of epistle 78, is tempted to kill himself and is restrained by the pleas of his old father. Moreover, the *Hercules Furens* reproduces the ambivalence of the *Epistles* between seeing life as too long or too short, or considering time irrelevant to the proper ends of life. The play can be read as an illustration of the poetic mode implied by Seneca's claim at the end of 77, that with both lives and plays "It is irrelevant where you stop. Stop where you want; only put in a good conclusion" (*nihil ad rem pertinet, quo loco desinas. quocumque voles desine; tantum bonam clausulam impone*). Seneca's tragedies despair of Aristotelian unity and substitute a seemingly endless series of *bonae clausulae*. By this I do not mean to suggest that Senecan tragedy is not often very carefully structured. But it is a structure that is not dependent on the representation of a single unified action. It is episodic and thematic, and the end is only one of many closing moments.

Despite similarity of plot, Euripides' and Seneca's versions of the myth are very different. Euripides' Heracles decides to live largely because he realizes that life includes the unexpected. He learns to accept that his story does not follow a consistent trajectory. Seneca's play entirely eliminates the possibility of discovery and of surprise that was central to Euripides. The Roman Hercules seems to learn nothing in the course of the narrative. He entirely refuses to adapt his passionate, aggressive heroic character to his domestic setting. Instead, he goes on trying to find ever more daring, frightening, and innovative labors to perform. Hercules' failure either to change or to die reflects the anxiety of Senecan drama about its own relationship to its literary predecessors and about the excesses of the Roman Empire. Seneca's Hercules has no reason not to commit suicide except the external moral pressure of his father's threat to kill himself too if he does so. He lives on, but his hands will never be clean. His continued existence remains a kind of living death, which is fundamentally no different from any other part of his life.

One might think that the difference between the Senecan and Euripidean texts could be explained entirely by reference to Seneca's Stoicism.[27] A play by a Stoic about Hercules ought to present him as the model of virtue, since Hercules is the Stoic hero, the type for the man who is able to control his passions. But Seneca's dramatic Hercules is precisely the opposite of the Stoic ideal.[28] He is a man who is ruled by his passions and who hopes to use his passions to overcome natural boundaries rather than live in accordance with nature.

The play begins with a prologue delivered by Juno, in which the goddess expresses her hatred of Hercules and struggles with the problem of how to outdo past horrors. Juno is one of a large number of characters in Senecan tragedy who seem to be oppressed by an "anxiety of influence" parallel to that of their creator.[29] Juno has two related grounds of complaint: first, she feels jealous and betrayed because Jupiter has so many concubines and so many illegitimate children, including, most importantly, Hercules; and, second, she can find no way to take revenge and restore her own dignity because Hercules himself has already performed and suffered almost everything she could imagine as punishment for him. Monstrosity, cruelty, and madness, are motivated by a sense of staleness. Language has lost its power. Juno's first words in the play are a complaint that she has lost her status, and therefore only an etiolated form of nomenclature is now applicable to her: "Sister of the Thunderer (for only this name is left to me)" — *Soror Tonantis (hoc enim solum mihi / nomen relictum est)* (1–2). She is no longer entitled to the name *coniunx* because Jupiter has taken up with so many others. But erotic jealousy and erotic disempowerment are expressed as linguistic poverty: she has no name, *nomen*, except that of "sister," *soror*. Moreover, she has nothing new to say. "But my complaints are old and too late" (*Sed vetera sero querimur,* 19): both the injuries to her own pride and the injuries she could hope to inflict on Hercules are passé. Juno's frustrations are parallel to those which impel the Senecan text to struggle against the pressure of a dominating literary tradition, and with the pressure of everyday bloodshed in imperial Rome.

Juno is embittered that Hercules manages so readily to subdue the world of nature. Hercules opens Hades, moving back up again with ease. She says, "It is a minor thing to turn back" (*Parum est reverti*, 49). This is an ironic reversal of one of the most famous passages of the *Aeneid*, where the Sibyl says,

> facilis decensus Averno:
> noctes atque dies patet atri ianua Ditis;
> sed revocare gradum superasque evadere ad auras,
> hoc opus, hic labor est.

> The way down to Avernus is easy:
> both night and day the door of black Dis lies open —
> but to call back one's step and come out into the upper air,
> this is the task, this is the labor.
> (*Aeneid* 6.126–29)

Juno presents Hercules' achievement as a reversal of these lines. For him, the movement up from the underworld is not difficult: Hercules treats it as the most minimal of labors. Rather, the greatest labor is that of returning to Hades after Hercules and after Virgil. Aeneas, in the prayer that precedes the Sibyl's words here, had asked, "Why should I mention great Theseus, why should I mention Hercules?" (*Quid Thesea magnum / quid memorem Alciden? Aeneid* 6.122–21). Seneca answers the question by showing that it is indeed necessary to remember and mention Theseus and Hercules. It is as if Seneca can add to Virgil's description of the underworld only by listing more features of it, making sure he mentions all the heroes Virgil neglected to discuss. Despite Juno's claim, it will prove very difficult for Hercules to find any real way out of Hades; his continued existence will be a living hell. It will prove equally difficult for Seneca's text to move on from *Aeneid* 6.

After Juno's speech comes a choral ode about various human activities (125–201), which advocates a quiet life in the countryside rather than the vain ambitions of moneymaking and political rhetoric. The ode strongly recalls Virgil's *Georgics* and Horace's *Odes*,[30] but toward the end the Chorus gives a surprising twist to the Horatian injunction to seize the day by living quietly in the country. Hercules turns out to be an example of someone who fails to respond properly to the inevitable facts of time and fate.[31]

> durae peragunt pensa sorores
> nec sua retro fila revolvunt.
> At gens hominum fertur rapidis
> obvia fatis incerta sui:

Stygias ultro quaerimus undas.
nimium, Alcide, pectore forti
properas maestos visere manes:
certo veniunt tempore Parcae,
nulli iusso cessare licet,
nulli scriptum proferre diem:
recipit populos urna citatos.

The harsh sisters perform their allotted tasks,
and they do not turn back their threads.
But the human race is carried
in the path of the speeding fates, doubtful of itself:
we seek the Stygian waters of our own accord.
With too brave a heart, Hercules,
you hurry to visit the grim spirits of the dead:
the Parcae come at a fixed time,
nobody may refuse to come when bidden,
nobody may postpone the written day:
the urn receives the summoned peoples.
(*Hercules Furens* 181–91)

Hercules' attempt to bring back Cerberus and Theseus from Hades shows a failure to respect the proper limits set to human life. The ode introduces the central irony of the play: by trying to defeat death, and by bringing back Theseus from the dead, Hercules hastens the death of his own family. He brings the underworld up with him, so that life on earth becomes a kind of hell. The play advances on the Augustan poets only by offering an even more intense meditation on the inevitability of death, even in life.

Amphitryon and Megara have some confidence that Hercules will return from the land of the dead to rescue them (274–83). They characterize him as one who can undertake massive and perhaps excessive acts of strength to prove his own superiority. But they also suggest that without Hercules, the kingdom of Thebes has lost its moral and political order.[32] The tyrant Lycus blusters in (329–31) but does not, like Euripides' tyrant, threaten the family immediately with death. Instead, he suggests that Megara should marry him. This new motif radically changes the terms of Megara's willingness to submit to death. In Euripides, she prefers death by the sword over death by burning, but she does so only when it seems that there is no possibility to remain alive. Death itself seems compulsory and therefore value-neutral; the question is only how to die. In Seneca, death seems a positively good thing in that it offers freedom from oppression for the weak. Seneca's Megara is given a clear option to choose life — if she will marry Lycus. She rejects this choice adamantly; death is her escape from the dishonor of submission to the tyrant. Lycus threatens her, "You will be forced" (*Cogere*, 426), and she replies, within the same line, "One who can be forced does not know how to die" (*Cogi qui potest nescit mori*, 426).

The idea of political tyranny played a relatively minor role in Euripides' version of the Heracles story. In Seneca, it is central. Death is attractive because it liberates everyone, rich and poor, male and female, from the tyrant's rage and proud man's contumely. Megara finds Hercules admirable because he has killed kings (431). She seems at least momentarily to read the Heraclean labors in Stoic terms, as an allegory for the wise man's capacity to withstand the emotional turbulence of the world. The orders or *imperia* of Eurystheus have provided Hercules with an opportunity to prove his manly courage, his *virtus*: Megara asks, "Take away hard orders — what valor will there be?" (*Imperia dura tolle: quid virtus erit?* 433). When Lycus demands "Do you think it valor to oppose wild beasts and monsters?" (*Obici feris monstrisque virtutem putas?* 434), Megara is able to convert the labors into acceptably abstract terms: "It is the task of valor to subdue what everyone fears" (*Virtutis est domare quae cunti pavent*, 435). Seneca's Megara associates *virtus* with the willingness to die. In stark contrast to Euripides' *Heracles*, no one in Seneca's play — including Amphitryon — challenges this assumption. Death is the final mark of courage. Seneca's play struggles to find anything more ultimate, more final, or more heroic, than death — and fails to do so.

When Hercules arrives home and discovers that the tyrant Lycus has seized the throne and is threatening his wife and children, he rushes off promising to kill him (631–40). In his absence, Theseus gives a set-piece description of his own sojourn in Hades (658–829). The description invokes all the poetic clichés of previous descriptions of the underworld. It alludes particularly to Virgil's account of Aeneas's descent in *Aeneid* 6. The portal to Seneca's underworld (*Hercules Furens* 689–96) clearly echoes that of Virgil (*Aeneid* 6.273–81). Both poets set a group of sinister personifications at the edge of Hades.[33] But Seneca eliminates Virgil's emphasis on conflict. It is as if the struggle to make literary war on the *Aeneid* is so great that Seneca's text is physically exhausted by it. Theseus concentrates not on the horrors of the mind but on those of the body. He is reduced to listing corporeal sufferings without suggesting that they might have any moral implications. His Hunger is merely hungry, his Sleep merely weary; even his Wars (which become plural to

Virgil's singular, as if Seneca realizes he has to fight on more than one front here) are *cincta ferro* (695): their very armor restricts them. Most important of all, the final element in Seneca's list is his own addition, and it is to this that Seneca gives the emphasis that in Virgil was accorded to Discord: last comes "weak Old Age," *iners Senectus*. Seneca's hell is aware of the feebleness of its own old age.

Theseus ends by declaring that he can see the crowd of people come to welcome Hercules home:

> Densa sed laeto venit
> clamore turba frontibus laurum gerens
> magnique meritas Herculis laudes canit.

> But the thronging crowd is coming
> with joyful shout, wearing laurel on their brows,
> and is singing the deserved praises of great Hercules.
> (827–29)

The Chorus responds with an ode which describes a different crowd: the crowd (*turba*, 845, 849) of the dead, who are more numerous than any living crowd, larger than the crowd at a dramatic festival or the Olympic games. The comparison is particularly chilling because the various crowds are ultimately all part of the same group—which even includes the audience of the *Hercules Furens*.[34] The theatergoers, and the attendants at the games, and the crowd that comes to welcome Hercules, and Seneca's own contemporaries will all eventually join the crowd of the dead. The Chorus prays,

> Sera nos illo referat senectus:
> nemo ad id sero venit, unde numquam,
> cum semel venit, poterit reverti.
> quid iuvat, durum, properare, fatum?

> May old age carry us there late;
> no one comes to it too late, the place from which he will never
> be able to return when once he comes there.
> Why do we like to hasten cruel fate?
> (864–67)

These lines suggest that it is impossible to live too long. No one comes to death too late (*Nemo ad id sero venit*). *Serus* is used to mean both "late" and "too late."[35]

The play on *sera . . . sero* suggests a shift from momentarily imagining that old age could be a truly "late" death to an immediate realization that even that "late" death is in fact early: no one dies late.

The ode goes on to describe death as the universal human condition, even from birth:

> tibi crescit omne,
> et quod occasus videt et quod ortus.
> parce venturis: tibi, mors, paramur;
> sis licet segnis, properamus ipsi:
> prima quae vitam dedit hora carpit.

> For you, death, everything grows,
> what the dawn sees and what the setting sun.
> Spare those who are to come! — for you, death, we are prepared;
> though you be slow, we ourselves hasten:
> the first hour that gave life plucks it.
> (870–74)

The use of the verb *carpit* suggests a correction of the Horatian *carpe diem* tradition.[36] We can pluck nothing in life, not even a day; rather, we ourselves are plucked by death.[37] After this, the Chorus's declaration of Hercules' victory over the underworld rings hollow: "Now no fear remains; there is nothing beyond the lower world" (*iam nullus superest timor; / nil ultra iacet inferos*, 891–92). It is hard to believe that Hercules really has defeated death, if death is so universal an enemy.[38] Theseus's grim description of the underworld forms the central passage of the play (662–829). But the final scenes show Seneca struggling to find somewhere that might lie beyond the land of Hades, some worse horror for Hercules to confront. He has great difficulty in doing so, and, as a result, the end of the play is oddly jerky and unresolved. Seneca has done to death the land of the dead but has nowhere else to go.

Seneca's Hercules is not, like Euripides' Heracles, a complex character. Euripides' version of the hero is a man who reflects on his own life and who doubts the value of his own acts of strength. Seneca's Hercules never questions the value of his own physical power. The doubt is transferred to other characters.[39] Amphitryon, for instance, enumerates the labors of Hercules (205–78) only to ask, "What good do those things do?" (*Quid ista prosunt?* 249). Hercules has freed the world of monsters but is lost in Hades himself and has left political chaos behind

him in Thebes. When he emerges from the underworld, he hopes to bring down
the unjust ruler, Lycus, and sacrifice him to the gods (920–24). He declares that
he wants to make the world new, to bring universal peace, and to cleanse the
world of tyranny; he offers to take on himself any future monstrosity: "Let it be
mine" (*meum sit*, 939). But immediately after he makes this declaration, madness
begins to descend on him. Even in the middle of a line (939), he shifts from
ambition to paranoid hallucination: "May the monster be mine. But what is
this? Shadows encircle the noonday" (*Monstrum meum sit — Sed quid hoc? medium
diem / cinxere tenebrae*, 939–40). The fact that the promise of a political solution
comes in the middle of Seneca's play, not the end, produces a far bleaker ending
even than that of Euripides.[40]

Seneca moves the slaughter of the children, which Euripides presents in a
messenger speech, into the main action. It becomes an entertainment for the
audience gruesome enough to challenge the gladiatorial displays of imperial
Rome.[41] We actually hear Hercules himself as he suffers his successive hallucina-
tions and dashes out his children's brains.[42] The effect of this is to humiliate the
hero in the eyes or ears of the audience. Hercules launches into a series of the
wildest fantasies, imagining he sees the battle of the Titans and the Furies (976–
86), then that his own children are those of Lycus (987–89), and that his wife is
Juno, his divine enemy (1018–20), and finally that he has destroyed the house of
Eurystheus (1035–38).

When Hercules wakes up after the murders, he is bewildered. He asks a series
of questions, in the course of which he realizes what he has done. His response to
that discovery is very different from that of Euripides' Heracles, who wanted to
hide his head and die. Seneca's Hercules demands recognition from heaven of his
own sinfulness through the noisiest punishment possible: he orders, "Now, father, be angry and thunder from every part" (*nunc parte ab omni, genitor, iratus
tona*, 1202). He asks,

> cur Promethei vacant
> scopuli? vacat cur vertice immenso feras
> volucresque pascens Caucasi abruptum latus
> nudumque silvis?[43]

> Why are the rocks of Prometheus empty?
> Why is the steep side of Caucasus empty,
> feeding the wild beasts and birds on its vast summit,
> and naked of woods? (1207–10)

Prometheus's rocks are empty because Hercules himself has rescued him. Hercules cannot find a monstrous way to die because he has himself destroyed all the monsters. He longs less for death than for punishment, and punishment of the most public and dramatic kind.[44] Hercules can make suicide an adequate punishment only by imagining more and more strange and unusual ways to die. Each time he imagines a new punishment, he then remembers — with a kind of egotistical pleasure and pride — how difficult it will be for "Hercules" to be subdued by any of them. The list of punishments he longs for ends with his own name: "This, this is what must be done — I shall return Hercules to the lower world" (*sic, sic agendum est: inferis reddam Herculem*, 1218).

Amphitryon becomes, in Seneca's version, much more important in the last scene than Theseus. Seneca's final episode is about the relationship between father and son and about Roman patriarchy. It is Amphitryon who tries to persuade Hercules that being "Hercules" will in this instance involve not risking death or confronting monsters but staying alive: "Now there is necessary work for Hercules; endure this weight of suffering" (*Nunc Hercule opus est: perfer hanc molem mali*, 1239). But Hercules will have none of it. He refuses to face the shame of his life. He calls for his arms, which have been wisely confiscated by Amphitryon and Theseus, and declares that in any case, "I shall find a way to die" (*mortis inveniam viam*, 1245). Amphitryon tries to restrain him but not by further appeals to what is appropriate to a hero, or a man of courage and virtue, a "Hercules," like those of Euripides' Theseus. Amphitryon's final appeal is purely selfish: he himself will suffer from the loss of his son (1246–57).

Hercules refuses to listen. He declares that the power to kill himself is his last labor and the only one that is truly his own: "only this is mine" (*hoc unum meum est*, 1268). The line ironically echoes his earlier call for any new monster to be his, *meum* (938–39). But his desire for an action that is his own also recalls Lycus's taunt earlier in the play, that only Hercules' lusts were his own: "This [sc. the defloration of virgins] was ordered by no Juno and no Eurystheus; these actions are his very own" (*hoc nulla Iuno, nullus Eurystheus iubet; / ipsius haec sunt opera*, 479–80). Hercules' desire to kill himself is associated with the ungentlemanly lusts of which Lycus accused him. His longing for death is not presented as a Stoic ideal; rather, it is the result of his excessive *animus*, his egotistical passion. Suicide is a sign of lack of self-restraint; it is yet another way in which Hercules indulges in macho self-promotion. Hercules takes pleasure in exhibitionism. He launches into a virtuoso fantasy about how much it will take to kill himself, since Hercules is the last monstrous opponent worthy of Hercules (1278–94). The hero who once wanted to touch the stars with his head now hopes that the whole universe and sky will be enough to kill him:[45]

> urbe versa condar, et, si fortibus
> leve pondus umeris moenia immissa incident
> septemque opertus non satis portis premar,
> onus omne media parte quod mundi sedet
> dirimitque superos, in meum vertam caput.

> I shall be buried in the overturned city, and if on my strong shoulders
> the walls fall as a light weight
> and I am not sufficiently pressed down by the seven gates,
> then the whole burden that sits in the middle part of the world
> and that divides those above, all that weight I shall turn onto my own head.
> (1290–94)

Amphitryon at first tries to talk Hercules out of killing himself, but at this ultimate masochistic fantasy of suffocation, he is overwhelmed. He has been keeping hold of Hercules' weapons, for his own protection, but at this, he agrees to return them: "I give back your arms" (*reddo arma*, 1295). Amphitryon is overcome not by argument, since Hercules has given none, but by the sheer potency of his rhetoric.

But as Hercules sets his bow to kill himself, Amphitryon at last finds a way to stop him. He tells him that his father's life is in his hands: "Either you live or you kill" (*aut vivis aut occidis*, 1308). This seems merely a figure of speech, until Amphitryon takes up a weapon of his own:

> tam tarde patri
> vitam dat aliquis? non feram ulterius moram,
> letale ferrum pectori impresso induam:
> hic, hic iacebit Herculis sani scelus.[46]

> Does anyone give life so reluctantly
> to a father? I shall not delay further,
> I shall press the lethal weapon to my heart and thrust it in;
> here, here will lie the evil deed of Hercules sane.
> (1310–13)

Hercules cannot resist his father's final threat: he yields, but he does so with heavy emphasis on how difficult it will be.

Iam parce, genitor, parce, iam revoca manum.
succumbe, virtus, perfer imperium patris.
eat ad labores hic quoque Herculeos labor:
vivamus.

Now father, have mercy, have mercy, now call back your hand.
Lie down, manhood, carry out the order of your father.
Let this labor come also to the Herculean labors;
Let us live.
(1314–17)

Megara associated manhood, *virtus*, with the ability to endure *imperia* (433) and to overcome fear (435); through *virtus*, one can always be free, because death offers an escape from any tyranny (424). Hercules now finds that the power of his father overcomes his *virtus*. Patriarchal control conquers even the final possibility of freedom, which is death. Hercules has to negotiate between his *genitor*, his father or begetter, and his own *virtus*, his manhood; he gives orders to his father to "have mercy" (*parce*), and then to his *virtus*: "lie down" (*succumbe*). It is tempting to see the suppression of Hercules' *virtus* as a form of symbolic castration. In deciding to go on living, he entirely represses his own will and his own character. He has been associated exclusively with *virtus* — unlike Euripides' Heracles, he has previously shown no interest in friendship or domestic values — and now he must sacrifice his *virtus* to his father. He has reached no new understanding of himself or of heroism; he will live only out of duty, *pietas*.

The episode obviously recalls the anecdote in epistle 78, in which Seneca himself claims to have resisted the lure of suicide for his father's sake.[47] Hercules' decision is different from Seneca's; for one thing, Hercules responds only when his father actually takes up arms to kill himself, whereas Seneca is restrained even by the thought of his father's suffering.[48] But in both the dramatic and the prose passages, the protagonist is kept back from suicide not by any thought of his own honor or fear of being a coward (like Euripides' Heracles), but by his duty to another family member. The decision in both cases is difficult, and in both cases it is unclear what continuing to live will mean.

Other characters in Senecan tragedy who resist suicide are similarly motivated by duty to other family members. Andromache and Oedipus are both persuaded not to kill themselves because of their responsibility to their children.[49] Both these characters, like Heracles, remain alive on sufferance, and both declare themselves torn between two contradictory duties. The children force them to stay alive, but they are tempted to kill themselves by an alternative set of family obligations. Oedipus asks, "Why, daughter, do you keep me bound with a diseased love? Why do you hold me? My father calls me" (*quid me, nata, pestifero tenes / amore vinctum? quid tenes? genitor vocat*).[50] Andromache says bitterly, "I would already have escaped the Greeks, and be following my husband, if this child did not keep me here" (*Iam erepta Danais coniugem sequerer meum, / nisi hic teneret*).[51] Seneca's tragic characters decide to stay alive, as he himself does in epistle 78, out of duty to their family members. Unlike in Sophocles or Euripides, there is no sense in Seneca that continued existence could contain new and unexpected discoveries.

The *Hercules Furens* ends with unending pain; the play does not provide even the partial emotional resolution achieved in Euripides' version of the story. Unlike in Euripides, there is no sense that Hercules' future life involves participation in a community; there is no companionship here, even the tense and difficult kind of mutual dependence imagined in the Greek play. "Let us live," Hercules declares (*Vivamus*, 1317), but the first-person plural cannot hide the fact that he imagines life as essentially solitary, brutal, and tainted. His final speech is an outcry that no place can now receive him, and no river can ever make him clean.[52]

> Quem locum profugus petam?
> ubi me recondam quave tellure obruar?
> quis Tanais aut quis Nilus aut quis Persica
> violentus unda Tigris aut Rhenus ferox
> Tagusve Hibera turbidus gaza fluens
> abluere dextram poterit? Arctoum licet
> Maeotis in me gelida transfundat mare
> et tota Tethys per meas currat manus,
> haerebit altum facinus.

> What place can I run to in exile?
> Where can I hide myself, where on earth can I be covered in oblivion?
> What Tanais or what Nile or what whirling Tigris
> with its Persian wave, or wild Rhine
> or Spanish Tagus, flowing swollen with treasure,
> could wash my right hand? Let the frozen
> Maeotis pour its arctic sea over me,

and let the whole Tethys run through my hands,
still the deep evil will stick.

(1321–29)

Hercules cannot imagine that his hands will ever be clean. He goes on living but without any hope for the future. The excesses of time in tragic overliving are here figured as excesses of place.[53] The list of rivers translates Hercules' temporal stagnation into geographical terms: he will never be able to find purity, and therefore no place can wash him clean. The list of places traces the borders of the Roman Empire, suggesting that the limits of Rome are the limits of the world. Hecules' excessive guilt and his excessive life are associated with the enormous power of Rome. The Roman Empire, like Hercules, oversteps natural boundaries and pushes its power beyond natural temporal and geographical limits. Neronian Rome may, like Seneca's Hercules, have lived too long, but there is nowhere left for the Romans to go.[54]

Hercules goes on living because he has been prevented, almost forcibly, from killing himself. The ending of the *Hercules Furens* has often been read as redemptive — and, as such, unique in the Senecan tragic corpus.[55] But there is nothing to justify this view in the text. Hercules squeezes a neat little paradox out of the fact that living is a harder task than all the others (1316–17). But his final words in the play are a plea to return to Hades — except that even Hades knows who he is:

> redde me infernis, precor,
> umbris reductum, meque subiectum tuis
> substitue vinclis: ille me abscondet locus —
> sed et ille novit.

> Return me to the underworld, I beg you,
> lead me back into the darkness, and subdue me, with your own
> chains; that place will hide me —
> but even it knows me.
> (1338–41)[56]

Hercules can never go offstage; he will be familiar to the audience everywhere, even in the underworld. This particular anxiety is unparalleled by anything in Euripides' play and reflects a specifically Senecan concern with literary and political belatedness. Only an author disturbed by the oppressive dominance of the Roman Empire could give voice to Hercules' fears about his own celebrity. Like

Juno at the beginning of the play, Hercules can find nothing new to say and nowhere to go. Tragic overliving has become associated with the imperial experience of being unable to escape the power of Rome. The sense of geographical staleness is linked to the feeling of temporal belatedness: there is nothing new, either in time or space, because everything is subject to the same authority.

There is nowhere to go but back. The only possible form of movement available to Hercules is regression. Theseus offers to take him to Athens:

> Nostra te tellus manet.
> illic solutam caede Gradivus manum
> restituit armis: illa te, Alcide, vocat,
> facere innocentes terra quae superos solet.

> Our country remains for you.
> There Mars restored his hand, set free from slaughter,
> to arms; that land, Hercules, calls you,
> the land that is accustomed to make gods innocent.
> (1341–44)

As in Euripides, Theseus and Hercules will go together to Athens. But, unlike in Euripides' version of the story, nothing in Seneca's play up till this point has prepared us for the offer of sanctuary; and Hercules does not reply. The play ends abruptly, so that Hercules' last words remain his despairing, half-funny realization that even Hades knows him all too well. For a fifth-century Athenian dramatist, to end with a journey to Athens was a gesture of hope that the very place where the play was being performed might, in the present or the future, help redeem the past. But a journey to Athens means something very different for Seneca as a Roman. It is a regressive move, back to the past, and even the past can offer no hope.[57] The suggestion that Hercules is like Mars hardly implies that his hands will ever become clean of blood. Rather, in taking Hercules with him to Athens, Theseus is taking the same old bloodshed and violence back to his own city.

In Sophocles' Oedipus plays and in Euripides' *Heracles*, tragic overliving is both the result and the cause of new discoveries. Oedipus finds out who his parents were and that he is not who he thought he was; he lives on after his identity becomes fragmented and his story is no longer readily comprehensible. Euripides' Heracles becomes both the benefactor of mankind, and a madman who kills his family, and a vulnerable, broken man who weeps and needs his friends. For the Greek tragedians, living on after disaster provokes the realization that character may not be stable, and that endings may not come when we expect. In Seneca's play, by contrast, Hercules' decision to live shows the impossibility of achieving any new kind of understanding. Hercules can neither change nor die. He will never cease to be "Hercules," and he will never find any new meaning for that name. His living death will be only more of the same, a revisiting of places that are already far too familiar.

CHAPTER FIVE

"A wheel of fire"

King Lear

In my first four chapters, I discussed the representation of overliving in antiquity. In the second half of the book, I move to a new period in the tragic tradition: seventeenth-century England. The cultural, political, philosophical, religious, and literary developments that separate imperial Rome from early modern Britain are, of course, enormous. But Shakespeare and Milton share with the Greek tragedians and Seneca the fear that life may go on too long. In these writers, as in the ancients, the representation of tragic overliving frustrates the spectator's or reader's expectations of unified character and unified plot. As in the earlier texts, the sense of overliving is countered by alternative visions of time, or by narratives of revenge or escape, that are never entirely successful in repressing the feeling that never to be born is best.

The most obvious new cultural influence is Christianity. In both Shakespeare and Milton, Christian injunctions against suicide and Christian visions of human history and the Apocalypse are invoked against the tragic sense of overliving. There is a new suspicion that the character who feels he has lived too long may be making a terrible mistake, which may be a sign of ignorance or lack of faith in the divine plan. Overliving becomes a more subjective phenomenon, which these texts try, more vigorously than the classical tragedies, to correct. But Christianity may also intensify the horror: perhaps neither body nor soul will ever be able to die. Perhaps, then, all human beings must inevitably suffer the experience of living too long. Death becomes, for all of us, a part of life, not an ending. The sense of the living body as a burden that can never be cast away is much greater in Shakespeare and Milton than in the classical poets. *King Lear* alludes to the Senecan, Stoic vision of suicide as a release from tyranny and torture, but suggests that it may be no longer possible to die by one's own choice. The play links the metaphysical with the physical, binding the abstract problems of existence to the pains and burdens of the material world.

The *Hercules Furens*, one of the most popular plays in early modern Europe, has important affinities with *King Lear*.[1] Lear, like Hercules, goes mad; he causes the death of a beloved child; he goes on living but sees his life as a living hell. But the differences in plot structure are as striking as the thematic similarities. Hercules recovers from madness, whereas Lear moves from one kind of madness to another: he is mad to divide his kingdom and reject Cordelia, and he becomes mad in another way when he begins to realize what he has done, and raves in the storm.[2] Lear, like Oedipus, disintegrates as a dramatic character: "Who is it that can tell me who I am?" (1.4.230).

Shakespeare moves beyond both the Greeks and Seneca in his emphasis on the body in pain.[3] Overliving is linked not only to the mythical and perhaps figurative torments of the underworld, but to the torture of living men; the spectators are made to feel the discomfort of watching pain continue and increase, and still not end. The infliction of physical pain is one of the central subjects of *King Lear*. We see Kent in the stocks, Gloucester's eyes poked out, poor Tom shivering against the storm, and Cordelia's body brought on stage after she has been hanged. Lear himself is subject to a torture that is both physical and metaphysical. He has been "bound / Upon a wheel of fire" and stretched on the "rack" of the world (4.7.45–46, 5.3.315). The play is cruel both to its characters and to its audiences.[4] Not surprisingly, many have found it unwatchable.[5] Nahum Tate notoriously gave the play a happy ending, and Samuel Johnson approved, on the grounds that the death of Cordelia is "contrary to the natural ideas of justice."[6] The spectators of Shakespeare's *King Lear* are confronted by a world that is radically unjust: the worst always leaves room for worse, and all divisions and attempts to balance inequity and excess produce only pain and further imbalance, until death.

The play contains two old men who live too long: Gloucester and Lear himself. I begin with Gloucester, whose story is a simplified version of the main Lear plot.[7] In the Dover Cliff episode (4.6), he has had his eyes poked out and wanders blindly searching for death. He now understands the full horror of the new regime and realizes that he has terribly misjudged his sons, trusting the false Edmund and rejecting Edgar. He asks poor Tom — who is his good son Edgar in disguise — to lead him to the top of Dover Cliff so that he can throw himself off it and die. Edgar pretends to do so (4.6), and Gloucester hurls himself from what he believes is the dizzying verge. "*He falls,*" as the stage direction in the Quarto tells us (4.6.41). But he falls not to his death, but flat on the ground, on the stage; and he has to stand up again.[8]

The sight of an old man falling on his face, imagining himself dead and then getting up again, is liable to make an audience laugh — although the laughter cannot last very long.[9] The Dover Cliff episode is tragedy formed out of what had been a comic trope.[10] The shocking pathos of Gloucester's failure to die arises largely from the fact that an audience expects to find death tragic and survival comic — as in earlier Shakespeare plays where a supposedly dead man revives.[11] In *Midsummer Night's Dream*, for example, when the mechanicals perform the "tedious brief scene of young Pyramus / And his love Thisby; very tragical mirth" (5.1.56–57), Bottom pretends to kill himself as Pyramus. After the play, the main characters all lie supposedly dead on stage, but Bottom leaps up, offering to provide further entertainments: "Will it please you to see the epilogue, or to hear a Bergomask dance between two of our company?" (5.1.353–54). In *1 Henry IV*, Falstaff pretends to be dead on the battlefield but gets to his feet again once it is safe to do so; to be a "counterfeit" of a dead man has allowed him to avoid becoming the real thing. His revival contrasts with Hotspur's heroic awareness of the finality of life, death, and action.[12] Bottom and Falstaff represent comic alternatives to tragic overliving. In *King Lear*, Shakespeare reshapes his audience's expectations about death and living on. The Dover Cliff episode teaches us that the failure to die at the expected time may be not funny but terrible.

In the *Hercules Furens*, Megara declares that "one who can be compelled does not know how to die" (*cogi qui potest nescit mori*).[13] Gloucester, like Megara, sees suicide as the ultimate escape from political tyranny and from a life that no longer seems worth living; but for him, that refuge seems to be no longer available. He asks,

> Is wretchedness depriv'd that benefit,
> To end itself by death? 'Twas yet some comfort,
> When misery could beguile the tyrant's rage,
> And frustrate his proud will.
>
> (4.6.61–64)

The answer to Gloucester's apparently rhetorical question is yes. Even death, the ultimate "benefit" and "comfort," has been taken away. Suicide is not rejected by any conscious decision, as in previous representations of tragic overliving. Gloucester speaks of suicide as freedom after he has tried to die and failed. It is a lost form of liberation for a problem that is both personal and political.

Gloucester's life after torture is associated both with physical pain and with material excess. *King Lear* shows us again and again that society is unjust, that some have too much property and others too little.[14] Gloucester, as he gives his purse to poor Tom, cries to the heavens,

> Let the superfluous and lust-dieted man
> That slaves your ordinance, that will not see
> Because he does not feel, feel your pow'r quickly;
> So distribution should undo excess
> And each man have enough. Dost thou know Dover?
> (4.1.67–71)

By giving the purse away before he dies, he hopes to put right social injustice. But Gloucester has too much life as well as too much money: he wants Tom to help him dispose of both. "Dost thou know Dover?" sounds like a non sequitur; but Dover is the place where Gloucester hopes to "undo excess" of life, now that he has done what he can to counterbalance the economic inequities of the world. Dover is figured as the place where all desires can be satisfied, the place of final justice and truth.[15] But "Dover" becomes the name of an unattainable hope: even there, Gloucester cannot "undo" his "excess" of life. The hope of a just distribution of resources likewise remains unsatisfied.

Edgar tries to reconcile Gloucester to life. Oddly, he does not reveal himself, which might mitigate at least his father's sense of isolation.[16] Instead, he suggests that a false taste of death may cure the desire for the real thing. He claims, "Why I do trifle now with his affliction / Is done to cure it" (4.6.33–34). He offers Gloucester an impermanent and delusory form of closure, in the hope that it will satisfy his desire for a final ending. He tells him that he was led to the top of the cliff not, as he had thought, by "a poor unfortunate beggar" but by "some fiend." He continues.

> Therefore, thou happy father,
> Think that the clearest gods, who make them honors
> Of men's impossibilities, have preserved thee.
> *Gloucester:* I do remember now. Henceforth I'll bear

Affliction till it do cry out itself
"Enough, enough," and die.
(4.6.72–77)

Edgar induces a false memory in Gloucester — "I do remember now" — to persuade him to assimilate his experience of overliving to a traditional temptation narrative.[17] He wants to convince Gloucester that it was a devil who tempted him to try to commit suicide, and that it is the gods who now preserve him. This is what Gloucester ought to "think" or believe; it is not necessarily the truth, but it is a useful fiction.[18]

The problem with Edgar's cure is that its effectiveness is very limited and very short-lived. Once he realizes he has survived what he thought was death, Gloucester says that he will "henceforth bear / Affliction" (75–77). But he has been convinced that he must endure life, not that he deserves the title Edgar gives him, of "happy father" (4.6.72). He still longs to die. Even toward the end of 4.6, he declares, "You ever gentle gods, take my breath from me, / Let not my worser spirit tempt me again / To die before you please!" (4.6.217–19). Gloucester is willing to submit to the gods. But he continues to hope that they will "take my breath from me." He has not lost the feeling that he has lived beyond his time and that his life, even his breath, is now a burden. He remains desperate for oblivion, however bravely he may school himself to wait for death. He goes on living in a state between life and death, waiting for the end. He experiences the state of being alive as essentially excessive: for Gloucester in his despair, all living is overliving.

Later (5.2), Edgar again leads Gloucester onto the stage, and leaves him there as he dashes off to fight, promising that "If ever I return to you again / I'll bring you comfort" (5.2.3–4). The audience is left watching the blind Gloucester sitting in silence, waiting.[19] When Edgar returns, Gloucester reverts to his desire for death, refusing to be led off any further: "No further sir, a man may rot even here" (5.2.8). Edgar's promised "comfort" turns out to be no more than a repetition of his advice to submit: "Men must endure / Their going hence even as their coming hither, / Ripeness is all" (5.2.9–11).[20] Gloucester replies, "And that's true too."[21] Gloucester's remark implies a blasé feeling that any or all of Edgar's *sententiae* may be true and that there is no way of distinguishing between them.[22] Edgar suggests that Gloucester wrongly thinks he is rotten when he is not yet even ripe for death. But there is no special reason to think Edgar is right.

Edgar takes a Christian line against despair and the desire to commit suicide.[23] Some have seen Christian allegory in *King Lear* and specifically in the fall of

Gloucester and his subsequent determination to "bear affliction." Gloucester's fall has been compared with the Fall of Man,[24] and the sense of a "failed apocalypse" has been read as an explicitly Christian scheme of imagery.[25] Gloucester has to bear affliction rather than kill himself because he is living in a Christian world.[26] But the metaphysical and theological background implied by the play is not consistently Christian.[27] Gloucester suffers a perversion of the Resurrection: he rises not to new life but to a continuance of the old suffering, which continues without hope of ending or of change. Although Edgar tells Gloucester, "thy life's a miracle" (4.6.55), the savior of Gloucester is not the gods, but Edgar himself.

The play offers no stable account of the nature of the gods. It includes at least two contradictory theological systems: the just world, in which the gods preserve us, and the world of the storm, in which man is "a worm" (4.1.33), killed in mockery by wanton gods.[28] Gloucester remarks, "As flies to wanton boys are we to the gods / They kill us for their sport" (4.1.36–37). Gloucester knows that killing itself is not the worst torture that can be inflicted on man; the gods enjoy prolonging the agony by killing us slowly. These lines echo the main source for the play, the *True Chronicle of King Leir*, where the king makes a great outburst against his ungrateful daughters: "I care for them / While they like wantons sport in youthfull rage" (3.209–10). What is for the anonymous author of the *True Chronicle* a complaint against the ingratitude of children becomes in *King Lear* an outburst against the indifference of the gods, who behave like cruel children. In Shakespeare's play, both the gods who preserve and the gods who torment are modeled on the different ways human beings behave to one another.

The play makes concrete the notion of divine torturers by showing the audience how human beings inflict pain on one another. Gloucester's pronouncement about the wantonness of the gods is shaped by his own experience of cruelty. Only a little earlier, Cornwall and Regan bound him to a chair, taunted him, and put out both his eyes. The theatrical violence and horror of this scene (3.7) shapes our understanding of the world of *Lear*; after such suffering, it is hard to see how Gloucester — or anyone — could wish to go on living.[29] The torture of Gloucester is both physical and rhetorical; he is broken by a combination of physical bondage, mutilation, and pain, with words designed to reduce him to the status of an animal. Regan calls him an "ingrateful fox" (3.7.28) and a "dog" (3.7.75), and Gloucester himself imagines that he is like a bear tied to the stake (3.7.54). The torturers ignore Gloucester's appeal to nature, which will, he hopes, defend Lear against his unnatural daughters (3.7.56–66); instead of offering any argument in return, Cornwall relies on the power of his own body against Gloucester's. As he tears out the first of Gloucester's eyes, Cornwall makes the mocking promise that "upon these eyes of thine I'll set my foot" (3.7.68), and Gloucester cries, "O cruel! O you gods!" (3.7.70). After Cornwall stabs out his second eye, treating it as a glutinous blob rather than the means of sight ("Out, vile jelly," 3.7.83), Regan tells Gloucester that he is mistaken to call for help to Edmund: "thou call'st on him that hates thee" (3.7.88). Cornwall and Regan have done everything possible to reduce Gloucester to the status of an inhuman object, but he remains a man, conscious of what he has suffered and of what he has done. He must live even after torture, deprived of his eyes, and with the sense both of betrayal and of guilt, knowing that he has been wronged by one son and has himself wronged the other. Gloucester's inability to die prolongs his suffering; he has no hope, except the desire for death.

There are two ways to die in *King Lear:* by violence at the hands of others (as are Cornwall, Oswald, Edmund, Goneril, Regan, and Cordelia); or by heartbreak after long suffering, like Gloucester and Lear. Edgar tells Albany that his father's "flawed heart" "burst smilingly" when he at last revealed himself to him, "'Twixt two extremes of passion, joy and grief" (5.3.195–200). Gloucester's death happens offstage, which allows the full attention of the audience to turn now to Lear. Gloucester's smiling joy is partly his response to finding his good son again and knowing that he may have "good success" (5.3.195) in defeating Edmund. But he is happy also because he is at last able to die. Death in *King Lear* never comes when called.

The play suggests obvious parallels between the literally blind old Gloucester, with his unrecognized good son and his falsely favored bad son, and the metaphorically blind old Lear, with his unrecognized loving daughter and his falsely favored unloving daughters. The two old men both try to conclude their lives prematurely.[30] Lear gives away his kingdom as if making a living will, but he must then find a place to set the "rest" of his life (1.1.124); he fails to realize that the only sure resting place is the grave.

Early modern audiences would have been suspicious of the whole notion of retirement.[31] There are many examples in the period of old men who lose all dignity by abrogating their power, property, and responsibility too soon.[32] *Pasquil's Jests* (1604) contains the following black little anecdote about an old man who bequeaths his belongings to his son before he is yet dead:

> After the deed of gift was made, awhile the olde man sate at the upper end of the table; afterwards, they set him lower, about the middle of the table; next, at the tables end; and then, among the servants; and, last of all, they made him a couch behind the doore and covered him with olde sackcloth, where, with grief and sor-

row, the olde man died. When the olde man was buried, the young mans eldest
childe sayd unto him: I pray you, father, give me this olde sackcloth. What wouldst
thou do with it? sayd his father. Forsooth sayd the boy, it shall serve to cover you, as
it did my olde grandfather.[33]

Part of the joke is against the old man, who is fool enough to hand over his power
and wealth while he is still alive. But the story also serves to remind us that one
generation must necessarily give way to the next. Although it is painful for the old
man to be mistreated and disrespected by his children, the punch line reminds us
that it will be equally painful for his son to be cast out by his children in turn. Old
men must hold onto their property and power right up till the moment of death;
otherwise, they will be treated as if dead while they are still alive.

Lear's desire to give up only the burdens of his life, and yet stay alive, is on one
level foolish; the play gradually reveals a world in which everyone is bound to the
wheel of fortune, bound to pain and to one another. There is no way out of the
burdens of life, except through death. But Lear's wish is also deeply understandable.[34] *King Lear* shows a world that is heavy, unjust, and full of suffering. Lear
wants to go on living precisely because he refuses to recognize what life involves;
his madness or folly is an extreme version of a blindness we must all cultivate, in
order to find life endurable.

King Lear puns on the word "living," which can mean "being alive" but also
"livelihood."[35] The Fool tells Lear he wishes he had two daughters and two
coxcombs, since "If I gave them all my living, I'd keep my coxcombs myself"
(1.4.107–8). There is a connection between the value of "living" (life) and the
value of "living" (wealth). Lear has given away his "living," forgetting that he
must also take care of his life.

Lear thinks he can give away his life and have it too. Like Oedipus, he wants to
control the lives of his children, even when he himself is an outcast from society.
He wants a retinue of knights, the respect of his subjects, and the love of his
daughters, as well as the constant pleasures of feasting, hunting, and making
merry, without any of the burdens of kingship. He gives his kingdom to the
younger generation or "younger strengths," so that he may "unburthen'd crawl
toward death" (1.1.41). The image of "crawling" to death suggests the agonizing
slowness with which he will make his way to the grave. But the line also suggests,
misleadingly, that Lear will cast off everything he owns. In fact, he hopes to keep a
substantial amount, but make other people do the work of bearing it. He tells
Cornwall and Albany that the hundred knights are "by you to be sustain'd"
(1.1.134). He wants to keep for himself only the things that seem to weigh nothing.

He abandons his "power, / Pre-eminence and all the large effects / That troop with majesty" (1.1.130–32), but he retains "the name, and all th' addition to a king" (1.1.136). But even the title, the retinue of knights, the respect of his people, the love of his family — apparently light or immaterial objects — become a kind of burden. Lear remains a weight on his family, on his community, and on himself. In *King Lear*, it is harder than it might seem to reduce oneself to nothing.

The word "addition" (1.1.136) is important in a play that returns obsessively to nonsensical questions of arithmetic, and particularly to the problem of "additions" left over after apparently ultimate divisions. In the first scene of the play, Lear hopes to receive extravagant declarations of love from each of his daughters in return for the division of his kingdom. Cordelia warns her father that her single heart, divided in two, has room for only half her love: "That lord whose hand must take my plight shall carry / Half my love with him, half my care and duty" (1.1.101–2). Cordelia is able to divide her heart and leave nothing over. She breaks her own heart and has no need to wait for a long-delayed heartbreak, as Gloucester and Lear must do. But Cordelia's plain logic does not fit Lear's situation. There are multiple "additions" left over after the division of the kingdom, the division of the family, the division of Lear from himself, and the agonizingly slow cracking of his heart.

Shakespeare adapts the concept of Lear's superfluous life from his sources, which contain early instances of the word "overlive." The primary source for *King Lear* was *The True Chronicle of King Leir* (1605), and in this text, after the king has been brutally rejected by Goneril, he asks,

> Why do I overlive myselfe, to see
> The course of nature quite reverst in me?
> Ah, gentle Death, if ever any wight
> Did wish thy presence with a perfit zeal:
> Then come, I pray thee, even with all my heart,
> And end my sorrowes with thy fatall dart.[36]

The anonymous author of the *True Chronicle* is borrowing from William Warner's *Albion's England* (1589), in which, after Gonorill [*sic*] "openly did hold him in contempt" (23), Leir [*sic*] weeps and says, "O God, who so thou art, that my good hap withstands, / Prolong not life, deferre not death, my selfe I over-live, / When those that owe to me their lives, to me my death would give."[37] In the *True Chronicle* and in *Albion's England*, Leir longs for death because of the cruelty of his elder daughters in rejecting him. These texts imply that a man and his offspring together form a single organism. It makes no sense for the father to go on living when his own flesh and blood has turned against him. Shakespeare's Lear similarly accuses Goneril of being "my flesh, my blood, my daughter — / Or rather a disease that's in my flesh" (2.4.221–22). He is, like the Leir of the sources, a father who loses the love of his children. He is also — like Richard II — a king who goes on living when he is no longer a king.[38]

But whereas in the sources Leir himself recognizes that he overlives himself, Shakespeare's Lear only very gradually begins to acknowledge that his life is a burden both to himself and to others. It is Goneril and Regan who insist that Lear has too many followers, too much wealth, too much life, as they try to free themselves from their father and his hundred riotous knights. What does he need with even fifty, even twenty-five, even "ten, or five?" (2.4.261): "What need one?" asks Regan (2.4.263). Lear answers with a defense of superfluity:

> O, reason not the need! our basest beggars
> Are in the poorest thing superfluous.
> Allow not nature more than nature needs,
> Man's life is cheap as beast's.
> (2.4.264–67)

Lear here assumes that the "superfluous" is desirable, not burdensome. It is what raises man above the level of the beast; superfluity makes us human. When his daughters think he needs nothing, Lear still retains his desires for the super-fluities of clothes, companionship, respect, and other such luxuries. To want what one does not need is an essential feature of being alive — and life itself is unnecessary. Lear, like all of us, will not cease to want unnecessary things until he is dead.

But to be alive and to be human also carries certain responsibilities and burdens. The superfluities of life must be paid for, and this is a lesson that Lear is slow to learn. When he pities the Fool and Poor Tom in the storm, as "poor naked wretches," Lear acknowledges that the demands of justice might outweigh the man's desire for what he does not need. He cries,

> Take physic, pomp,
> Expose thyself to feel what wretches feel,
> That thou mayst shake the superflux to them,
> And show the heavens more just.
> (3.4.33–36)

The lines imagine society as a sick body, which must take "physic" and be purged of its excess humors through enduring further sickness.[39] Lear is beginning to recognize that imbalance and inequality may be associated with pain. The lines have been read as an appeal either for social justice or for Christian charity.[40] But they suggest that it is the responsibility of the "heavens" to be just, not of man, still less of Lear himself. Lear deplores injustice, but he does not imagine he personally could do anything to mitigate it—and perhaps, within the terms of the play, there is nothing that can be done, while life lasts. Lear feels what wretches feel, in the storm; but his attempts at the redistribution of wealth have produced only more suffering.

Lear remains in one sense "superfluous" because he is still alive. He loses kingdom, family, property, servants, dignity—he abandons even his clothes. In the storm he tries to reduce himself to the life "as cheap as beast's," becoming "unaccommodated man," "a poor, bare, fork'd animal," without his "lendings" (3.4.106–8). Almost his last words are, "Pray you undo this button" (5.3.310).[41] But life and time remain when everything else is gone. In the Lear plot, as in the Gloucester subplot, there is a slippage between physical and temporal forms of excess. He tells Regan with heavy irony, "Dear daughter, I confess that I am old; / Age is unnecessary" (2.4.154–55). Life, like all the superfluities of civilization—clothes, money, power, and servants—is something that nobody needs, but for which we can offer no "reason." Lear becomes, like "the poorest beggars," superfluous in living when he has no means to support his life.

Lear gradually begins to realize that he is in the paradoxical position of being both dead and not dead. He speaks of himself as one who has already died. When Gloucester wants to take his hand, Lear says, "Let me wipe it first; it smells of mortality" (4.6.133). The smell of death hangs particularly heavily on Lear, because he has given away or lost all that he owned, except his life. But all mortals smell of mortality; all of us will die. Lear tells Gloucester, "Thou know'st, the first time that we smell the air / We wawl and cry" (4.6.178–79). The exceptional experience of Lear is less unlike our own than we might think. Lear's conversation with Gloucester suggests that these two superfluous old men, one mad and one blind, who are yet not dead, are models for everyone who is still alive and still smells the air.

Like Seneca's Hercules, Lear's hands are tainted. As has been noticed, his rhetoric becomes Senecan as he longs both for his own death and for the dissolution of the universe, crying, "Blow, winds, and crack your cheeks!" (3.2.1).[42] But Lear's sense of the weight of the human bodies that surround him is far greater than in any Senecan play. Lear's winds have "cheeks," which correspond to nothing in Seneca's "Now, father, be angry and thunder from every part" (*nunc parte ab omni, genitor, iratus tona*).[43] Lear's experience is expressed in corporeal terms. He returns obsessively to the female body: the womb or the vagina is a living hell, "there's hell, there's darkness / There is the sulphurous pit, burning, scalding / Stench, consumption. Fie, fie, fie!" (4.6.127–29).[44] Lear tries to distance himself from the hell that is the body: "there's hell," he says, not "here's hell." But he cannot escape from either his own body or those of others; the burdens of physical life implicate everyone in the play.

Lear repeatedly imagines that his end has come, and repeatedly he turns out to be premature in his anticipation of death. It is wishful thinking to imagine that he can escape from the world's pain so easily. On waking from madness, he says,

> You do me wrong to take me out o' th' grave:
> Thou art a soul in bliss, but I am bound
> Upon a wheel of fire, that mine own tears
> Do scald like moulten lead.[45]
>
> (4.7.44–47)

The words imply confusion about where hell is. The "wheel of fire" suggests a torment of the underworld, like Ixion's wheel. But it also represents the pain Lear has discovered in this world, now that he has been removed from the grave. Lear knows that it is not only in the mythical underworld but in this life that people are bound and tortured. Kent has been locked in the stocks, Gloucester has been bound to a chair and mutilated, and Lear's scalding tears recall the agonies of Gloucester's blinding. Lear shares their experience of physical and mental torture. But he still hopes to evade the heaviest burdens of human life. He insists on seeing himself in hell, and Cordelia as a "soul in bliss," a "spirit": "You are a spirit, I know; [when] did you die?" (4.7.48). But Cordelia is a vulnerable human girl, with a body that can suffer physical harm; she is not a "soul in bliss." She is not yet dead, and Lear is not yet free of the burden of responsibility toward her. He is bound not only to a wheel of fire but also to his daughter.

Lear still longs for an easy way to be free of life. He says, on emerging from madness, "If you have poison for me, I will drink it" (4.7.71). But no one has poison for him that could kill him once and for all. The passing of Lear's madness is figured as yet another death:

> Gentleman: Be comforted, good madam, the great rage,
> You see, is kill'd in him.
>
> (4.7.77–78)

But this death is no more lasting than any of the others: the rage that has been "killed" will rise again in response to the death of Cordelia: "Howl, howl, howl!" (5.3.258).[46] Cordelia, unlike Lear, gives up her life and is dead forever.

King Lear ends disastrously not because Lear himself dies, but because Cordelia does. Most previous promised ends have been only images of that horror. Cordelia's death is framed by numerous deaths that should have come and do not. Lear's hope that she may yet live can momentarily be shared by the spectators, since we have become used to the idea that those whose lives seem to be over can return to life. He says, as he carries Cordelia onto the stage in his arms, "I know when one is dead, and when one lives; / She's dead as earth" (5.3.261–62). The full pathos of the end of the play is generated precisely by the fact that it has become so difficult, both for Lear and for the audience, to know when one is dead and when one lives. Lear himself has in a sense already died and yet is still capable of carrying his daughter onto the stage; it is therefore reasonable for him—and the audience—to hope that she will be able to breathe again even after being hanged. The expectation is increased by the fact that none of the sources for *King Lear* make Cordelia die before her father.[47]

> *Lear:* If that her breath will mist or stain the stone,
> Why then she lives.
> *Kent:*　Is this the promised end?
> *Edgar:* Or image of that horror?
> *Albany:*　Fall and cease!
> (5.3.263–65)

In this exchange Albany hopes if he simply says, "Cease!" the horror will cease. But by this stage of the play it is clear that to aspire to an ending is to jinx any hope that things will end right. Every time someone demands that horror "cease," it revives and becomes even worse. Now, the king who has lived too long is confronted by a daughter who has died too soon. There will be no resurrection for Cordelia, and she will never come again.

Cordelia's too early death provides the only alternative to Lear's life that goes on too long.[48]

> And my poor fool is hang'd! No, no, no life!
> Why should a dog, a horse, a rat, have life,
> And thou no breath at all? Thou'lt come no more,
> Never, never, never, never, never.
> (5.3.306–9)

The repetitions of "No, no, no" and "Never, never, never, never, never" are set against the mere listing of things that happen to be alive ("a dog, a horse, a rat"). Lear is protesting that Cordelia has "no, no, no life!" But he is also saying "no, no, no!" to life itself. The finality of Cordelia's death makes all life seem excessive.

Lear's own death comes as a relief. But it is also almost irrelevant.[49] The exact moment of his passing is obscure: the other characters on stage seem puzzled about when Lear dies and wary of saying prematurely that "He is gone indeed."[50] Lear has already practiced death so many times that the moment of his physical death seems unimportant.[51] The surprising thing is not that he dies, but that he did not die as soon as he resigned his throne, at the beginning of the play. Kent urges the others to let Lear die:

> *Kent:* Vex not his ghost. O, let him pass, he hates him
> That would upon the rack of this tough world
> Stretch him out longer.
> *Edgar:*   He is gone indeed.
> *Kent:* The wonder is he hath endur'd so long,
> He but usurp'd his life.
> (5.3.314–18)

The image of the "tough world" as a "rack" on which Lear is stretched extends the notion implied by Lear's own "wheel of fire" (4.7.46). But Kent suggests that the king was not a figure in Hades, but a prisoner punished for an act of usurpation. The lines imply that, paradoxically, in abdicating his throne, Lear "usurp'd" his life, which properly belonged not to himself, but to nature or to death. Overliving becomes analogous to the political problem of finding a ruler who will claim the throne rightfully, not as a usurper. But *King Lear* may make us wonder whether anyone can bear to be the rightful king either of his own life, or of the "gored state" of England.

A play about the division of England and the chaotic aftermath of a long-lived monarch's rule must have resonated for the play's original audience, in 1605 or 1606 — only a couple of years after the death of Elizabeth I and the accession of James of Scotland (1603).[52] This play about lives which go on too long struggles to show that the life of Queen Elizabeth is truly over, by staging both the premature death of Cordelia (who might otherwise have been queen), and the belated death of Lear himself.[53] The survivors at the end of the play hope for a new England, in which lesser, quieter men will take up the weight of the crown and will restore unity to the divided kingdom.

The final lines of the play try to a draw a clean distinction between Lear's experiences, and those of the younger generation left on stage. The three survivors hope that the England of the future will be different. Just as Cordelia expresses her love for Lear by acknowledging that she does not love him infinitely, so the survivors at the end of the play express their love for Lear by admitting that they are glad he is dead.[54] The last lines imply that Lear's world of excess, where men have too much property as well as too much life, has passed away, in favor of a starker and bleaker world, in which people live only as long as they need to.

> *Albany:* Bear them from hence. Our present business
> Is general woe.
> [*To Kent and Edgar.*] Friends of my soul, you twain
> Rule in this realm, and the gor'd state sustain.
> *Kent:* I have a journey, sir, shortly to go:
> My master calls me, I must not say no.
> *Edgar:* The weight of this sad time we must obey,
> Speak what we feel, not what we ought to say:
> The oldest hath borne most; we that are young
> Shall never see so much, nor live so long.[55]
>
> (5.3.319–27)

The state is "gor'd" in that it is covered by gore; life in England is violent and bloody. It is also "gor'd" because it is divided, torn like a body pierced by a bull. England, like the bodies of its citizens, has been tortured. The state must now be "sustained" or kept alive after torture. But it is still unclear — as it was in the case of Gloucester — how such a life can be made bearable.

Albany, who "usurped" Goneril's bed,[56] must now act like a true king and be man enough to heal the wounded country. He seems to divide power between himself, Kent, and Edgar, so that the play ends as it began, with a division of the kingdom.[57] He emphasizes that the duty of government will be a burden that they must "sustain" — a word that recalls Lear's investment of his power to Cornwall and Albany, leaving only the hundred knights "by you to be sustain'd" (1.1.134). The survivors must "bear" not only the bodies of the dead, but also the "weight of this sad time." But Kent and Edgar, like Lear himself, are reluctant to take up their burdens, hoping rather that they may "unburthen'd crawl toward death." Kent, whose heart is already almost broken,[58] insists that he is not long for this world: he has a journey "shortly to go." Edgar and Albany, too, have both spoken as if their hearts are on the point of breaking.[59] These characters long for death and hope it will come soon. Edgar — or Albany, if the last lines are his —

reassures himself and the audience that Lear's life is over and that such long lives will never come again. But one may well suspect that the final pronouncements are partly wishful thinking. Like the Chorus at the end of the *Oedipus Tyrannus*, the last lines insist on the final closure of death. All those who witness tragic overliving, including the spectators of the play, hope that they will not have to share the experience. But here, as in Sophocles' Oedipus plays, there is no guarantee that the hope will be fulfilled. The play has taught us that death may not come at the expected time and that those who remain alive may still suffer more. Lear's long life, like that of Oedipus, is both exceptional and a model for all human life. The survivors, like Lear himself, hope that they will not have too heavy a weight to bear. They desire brevity of life and speedy death. But they do not know that death will come soon. Moreover, it is hard to see how a state, especially a gored one, can be "sustained" by men who are waiting only for their hearts to break. The end of the play concentrates on the desire for ending over any hope of long-term political order, and perhaps suggests that such a thing is impossible. In a world where life is torturous and burdensome, the best men will hope only for death, since as long as life goes on, things can always get worse.

CHAPTER 6

"To-morrow, and to-morrow, and to-morrow"

Macbeth

Lear is an old man, and not obviously mistaken in his belief that his life is over — however unwise he may be in thinking that he can give away his "living" and still go on living. Macbeth's achievements seem to lie before him, yet he treats his life as if it is already in the past. In *Macbeth*, even before the murder of Duncan, it is as if the decisive event has already taken place. The first line — "When shall we three meet again?" — implies that what will happen in the course of the play will be repetition of what has gone before, a meeting again. The witches look forward to the future, through prophecy; for those with second sight, all action, even future action, seems already predetermined and hence, repetitious. Macbeth's sense that he is always too late is partly a response to the witches' ability to predict the future. Macbeth looks at time backward. He tries to look back to the present as if he were already always in the future; he treats the actions he is performing as if they have already taken place.[1] In *Macbeth*, the belief that the proper moment may already have gone by, and the fear that life may have gone on too long, are presented as dangerously mistaken. Gloucester's sense that he has lived too long is challenged by Edgar, but it harms no one but himself. Lear's attempt to give away his living and keep it too leads him not to crime but to madness. Macbeth, on the other hand, is led to kill by his confused attitude to time and premature sense of overliving.

Both the Macbeths treat time precipitately. When Lady Macbeth first meets her husband in the play, after his victory in battle and his acquisition of new titles, she addresses him as

> Great Glamis! worthy Cawdor!
> Greater than both, by the all-hail hereafter!
> Thy letters have transported me beyond
> This ignorant present, and I feel now
> The future in the instant.
> (1.5.54–58)

She refuses to live in the "ignorant present" and instead insists on being "transported" by anticipation into the future. She addresses Macbeth not only by the titles he already has but also by that of his future greatness, in the "all-hail hereafter."

Macbeth wants to "overleap" the present and jump straight into the future. He uses the word "o'erleap" first after Duncan declares Malcolm Prince of Cumberland (and therefore presumed heir to the throne):

> The Prince of Cumberland! that is a step
> On which I must fall down, or else o'erleap,
> For in my way it lies. Stars, hide your fires,
> Let not light see my black and deep desires;
> The eye wink at the hand; yet let that be
> Which the eye fears, when it is done, to see.
> (1.4.48–53)

Duncan had said that "signs of nobleness, like stars, shall shine / On all deservers" (1.4.41–42). Macbeth seems to be expressing the desire to hide his own sin from the light, but his echo of Duncan's words suggests that he actually wants to hide the glory of Malcolm. He leaps over his immediate desires, shrinking from naming them: he wants "that" to be done, without having even to say what "that" may be. Macbeth repeatedly tries to live in the future, when the unnameable present action will already have been done. But he also knows that he cannot leap far enough into the future to evade all consequences for his actions.

> If it were done, when 'tis done, then 'twere well
> It were done quickly. If th' assassination

Could trammel up the consequence, and catch
With his surcease success; that but this blow
Might be the be-all and the end-all — here,
But here, upon this bank and [shoal] of time,
We'ld jump the life to come.
(1.7.1–7)

The tongue-twister quality of the language expresses a confusion about time. The sentence itself fails to end when it seems it should, as further conditional clauses keep being added on ("if th' assassination," "that but this blow"). The word "jump" recalls Macbeth's earlier desire to "o'erleap." One might expect jumping or leaping to be done across a "bank or shoal," but, in fact, the "jump" is the risk of staying merely on one side of the bank, trapped like the souls in Virgil's underworld who are unable to cross over to the other side. Macbeth can "jump" into the future, when "it" will be done; but in making that leap, he will also "jump" or risk stepping so far into the future that he will have no time left for redemption. As the speech goes on, he reminds himself of all the reasons not to kill Duncan (because he may be punished for it, and Duncan is his kinsman and his king, and a good man). He concludes,

I have no spur
To prick the sides of my intent, but only
Vaulting ambition, which o'erleaps itself
And falls on th' other.
(1.7.25–28)

The final "o'erleaps" suggests either a man trying to vault onto a horse, or a horseman who jumps too far and falls over.[2] More literally, ambition is someone trying, nonsensically, to vault over himself — it "o'erleaps itself." Of course, it is impossible to jump over oneself, but in metaphorical terms, this is exactly what Macbeth tries to do. He wants to jump over his own present life and actions, into the future. Even the image leaps ahead too fast: ambition is at first like a "spur," then becomes a rider "vaulting." Macbeth tries to jump forward into the time in which the unspeakable present will have become the past. But the Macbeths become trapped in constantly repeating the past. "What's done, is done," says Lady Macbeth (3.2.12), after the murder; but her husband immediately begins to have doubts, which hinge precisely on the question whether anything is ever really done.[3] Things are never done when they are done; there is always more.[4]

For Macbeth, the trouble with actions in life is that they are inconclusive. He finds himself envying the dead Duncan, who has at last reached the end of "life's fitful fever" (3.2.23). Within life, Macbeth can find no peace. But he sees his life as a living death; it would have been better to have died. His public response to the announcement of Duncan's death acknowledges that in killing the king, he has also robbed his own life and death of significance.

> Had I but died an hour before this chance,
> I had liv'd a blessed time; for from this instant
> There's nothing serious in mortality:
> All is but toys: renown and grace is dead;
> The wine of life is drawn, and the mere lees
> Is left this vault to brag of.
> (2.3.89–96)

On one level, Macbeth is pretending to feel grief at the death of a man he has just himself murdered, in order to divert suspicion. Clearly, it is disingenuous to use the word "chance" for the death of Duncan. But Macbeth is pretending to a grief that he does actually feel. He mourns for himself rather than for the dead king; he describes as "dead" not Duncan, but the qualities that he himself once had and now has lost— "renown and grace." Macbeth is unable to acknowledge the reality of what he has done to Duncan. But he is also right to suspect that he has done terrible damage to himself. *Macbeth* is concerned as much with the "death" of Macbeth's soul as with the deaths of those he murders. It will become more and more clear that Macbeth will never hereafter be able to live a blessed time.

Macbeth uses the imagery of the remains of a night of heavy drinking in his first description of the experience of overliving.[5] The "vault" that is now empty of everything but lees carries a sonic echo of Macbeth's earlier "vaulting ambition, which o'erleaps itself" (1.7.27); because he has vaulted over the lives of others, his own life is now an empty vault. What is left when the party is over and the wine is drunk is only talk: "All is but toys."[6] His life will now be all aftermath, the hangover of the murders he has committed. When Macbeth equates wine with life, he forgets that wine leaves not only lees but also hangovers. Macbeth lives on after apparent pleasure is over and when the sense of potency is gone, but the sickness and headache of its aftermath remain.

One reason why he has lost grace forever is that he refuses to admit the possibility that it might not be too late. He claims to "repent" of killing the grooms: "O, yet I do repent me of my fury / That I did kill them" (2.3.106–7). But he immediately retracts even that public confession, arguing what he did was what any man who loved Duncan would have done: "Who could refrain?" (2.3.116). He insists both in public and in private that, after the first murder, it is too late to turn back; his hands, like those of Seneca's Hercules, can never be clean again.[7]

> What hands are here? Hah! they pluck out mine eyes.
>
> Will all great Neptune's ocean wash this blood
>
> Clean from my hand? No; this my hand will rather
>
> The multitudinous seas incarnadine,
>
> Making the green one red.
>
> (2.2.56–60)

Macbeth, like Hercules, sees his hands as permanently polluted; no water could wash them. But unlike Hercules, he assumes that these bloody hands will also, inevitably, harm anything else they touch. He cannot prevent himself from doing more harm if he goes on living. Macbeth's hands are dangerous as well as dirty. They are a danger even to himself: they pluck out his eyes, as if both to punish him, and to protect him from the knowledge of his deed and of himself.[8]

The premature sense of overliving deprives Macbeth of his capacity for moral choice. The killing of time is connected to the killing of other people. The Second Murderer tells him, "I am one, my liege, / Whom the vile blows and buffets of the world / Hath so incens'd that I am reckless what / I do to spite the world" (3.1.107–10), and the First Murderer declares himself "So weary with disasters, tugg'd with fortune, / That I would set my life on any chance, / To mend it, or be rid on 't" (3.1.111–13). Macbeth himself is "so weary with disasters" that he creates more disasters. Like the Murderers, he transforms his recklessness about his own life into a willingness to kill. The old proverb, "it will have blood, they say; blood will have blood" (3.4.121) ought to mean that the murderer will die; but Macbeth interprets it to mean that the murderer will have to go on killing. He declares, "I am in blood / Stepp'd in so far that, should I wade no more, / Returning were as tedious as go o'er (3.4.135–37). Macbeth refuses to admit that there could be any action that would not involve wading through a glutinous lake of blood; he cannot even imagine innocence. He sees the middle of an action as a kind of excess; it is already too late not to have gone too far.

Macbeth is adapting a familiar quotation from Seneca: "The safe way to crimes is always through crimes" (*per scelera semper sceleribus tutum est iter, Agamemnon* 115).[9] The most important difference is that what is in Seneca an abstraction ("crimes") becomes in Shakespeare concrete and physical — "blood." *Macbeth* offers material images for the fear that life may go on too long. Macbeth himself is horrified by the appearance of Banquo at his dinner table, after he has been killed (3.4). Lady Macbeth assures her husband that the Ghost is merely a delusion, like the "air-drawn dagger" that led Macbeth to Duncan's chamber (2.1.33–61; 3.4.61–62). But the Ghost, unlike the dagger, is visible to the spectators as well as to Macbeth.[10] The delusory dagger suggested Macbeth's diseased state of mind, and his need for supernatural assurance that the murder must be done. The Ghost, by contrast, shows the spectators of the play that actions have consequences, and that murder is not the end of life. When he saw the dagger, Macbeth imagined Murder moving "like a ghost" "towards his design" (2.1.55–56). Now Banquo moves into his chair, not only "like" a ghost but as a ghost.

The appearance of the Ghost is a counterpart to the fall of Gloucester in the Dover Cliff scene in *King Lear*. Banquo's revival, like Gloucester's, is described as a perverted version of the Christian Resurrection. Macbeth, like Gloucester, longs for the old days when the dead were allowed to die and stay dead — although whereas Gloucester hoped only for his own death, Macbeth wishes he could kill other people and make them stay dead.

> The time has been,
> That when the brains were out, the man would die,
> And there an end; but now they rise again,
> With twenty mortal murthers on their crowns,
> And push us from our stools. This is more strange
> Than such a murther is.
> (3.4.77–82)

Macbeth's monosyllables express fury as well as fear, as he tries to make sense of something which seems to make no sense. The dead rise again: death can offer no true closure to life, either for the dead or, more important, for the living. The murder does not even end the line, and it begins a new line of kings. Macbeth pluralizes Banquo as "they," in what is perhaps an attempt to distance himself from the killing of his friend. But the pluralization also works to foreshadow the long line of multiple kings, the ancestors of James VI and I revealed by the Apparition, who will push Macbeth from his crown as well as from his stool.[11]

Macbeth wants to catch up with time, which is speeding ahead of him; time itself becomes his enemy. He is disturbed to hear that Macduff has fled to England, but he addresses not Macduff but time itself:

Time, thou anticipat'st my dread exploits:
The flighty purpose never is o'ertook
Unless the deed go with it. From this moment
The very firstlings of my heart shall be
The firstlings of my hand.
(4.1.144–48)

Macbeth finally responds to his wife's taunt that he lets "I dare not" wait upon "I would" (1.7.44); now he declares, "No boasting like a fool; / This deed I'll do before this purpose cool" (4.1.153–54). He recognizes his own too vivid imagination as a danger and decides not to allow it to evade the control of his hands.[12] He will kill Macduff's firstlings, his beloved pretty chickens, in order to make live the firstlings of his own heart.[13]

But his violence toward the Macduffs results only in a greater and greater split between Macbeth's external brash confidence in his powers of military victory, and his solitary conviction that he has already lost the battle against time. As the English soldiers and Scottish rebels move toward the castle of the "tyrant," Macbeth calls on his servant to interrupt his own inner monologue.

Seyton! — I am sick at heart
When I behold — Seyton, I say! — This push
Will cheer me ever, or [disseat] me now.
I have liv'd long enough: my way of life
Is fall'n into the sear, the yellow leaf,
And that which should accompany old age,
As honor, love, obedience, troops of friends,
I must not look to have; but in their stead,
Curses, not loud, but deep, mouth-honor, breath,
Which the poor heart would fain deny, and dare not.
(5.3.19–28)

There is a stark contrast between the outer Macbeth, the soldier, general, and killer who wants his actions to bear fruit and his orders to be obeyed, and the inner reflective man. On the one hand, "this push" is the critical moment that will "cheer me ever, or disseat me now"; on the other, he is aware that no action, either now or in the future, can make any difference, since he has already "liv'd long enough." The language with which he expresses his desire for companionship makes it quite clear why he is isolated. Macbeth looks at what he "must not look to have" with the eyes of a general. He has troops but no friends, and he imagines that friends, if he had them, would come in "troops"; he wants from his nonexistent friends not only "love" but also "honor" and even "obedience," as if friends were only subordinates of a superior kind, who might be more likely to conform to one's own desires. Macbeth wants to impose his will both on other people and on time, and in both cases, it is clear that he has already failed. The natural, seasonal imagery suggests that there is not a single proper time for action but, rather, that there are proper actions and proper accompaniments for each time of life. Macbeth has lived long enough because the autumn of his days is barren: he has survived a certain amount of time but has nothing to harvest. He is angry that the appropriate forms are not being observed: the things that should accompany a particular time of life do not do so. He thus undermines his own claims to hope for military victory: the language he uses shows that the battle against time has already been lost.[14] No war against leaves or time can ever be won.

Macbeth lives beyond a time when he is able to feel fear, or to feel at all.

> I have almost forgot the taste of fears.
> The time has been, my senses would have cool'd
> To hear a night-shriek, and my fell of hair
> Would at a dismal treatise rouse and stir
> As life were in 't. I have supp'd full with horrors;
> Direness, familiar to my slaughterous thoughts,
> Cannot once start me.
> (5.5.9–15)

Macbeth cannot "start" in both senses: he cannot jump at the apprehension of fear, but he also cannot begin any new action, because he feels his life is already over.[15] The phrase "the time has been" echoes Macbeth's horror at the reappearance of Banquo at the feast: "The time has been / That when the brains were out, the man would die, / And there an end" (3.4.77–79). But times are not what they were, because the present is always haunted by the past. Macbeth's "slaughterous thoughts" have murdered not only other people but also his own hopes and fears for the future.

Macbeth's response to the death of his wife is the culmination of his paradoxical vision of time. He tries to look back on the present even while he is in it. He sees the present from the perspective of the future, and turns tomorrow into yesterday;

in doing so, he deprives the present of any possible significance. All time is like time in the theater, because every moment has been performed already.[16]

> *Seyton:* The Queen, my lord, is dead.
> *Macbeth:* She should have died hereafter;
> There would have been a time for such a word.
> To-morrow, and to-morrow, and to-morrow,
> Creeps in this petty pace from day to day,
> To the last syllable of recorded time;
> And all our yesterdays have lighted fools
> The way to dusty death. Out, out, brief candle!
> Life's but a walking shadow, a poor player,
> That struts and frets his hour upon the stage,
> And then is heard no more. It is a tale
> Told by an idiot, full of sound and fury,
> Signifying nothing.
> (5.5.16–28)

"She should have died hereafter" can be taken in two quite different senses, depending on whether we take it with "there would have been a time" or with what follows.[17] Either it means, "She would have died sometime," "If she had not died now, she would have died later, so it makes no difference that she died today." Or it means, as Dr. Johnson suggested, "Her death should have been deferred to some more peaceable hour; had she lived longer, there would have been a more convenient time for such a word, for such an intelligence." The ambiguity reflects a confusion in the speech about whether we die too late, or too early, or whether time matters at all.[18]

The speech hinges on temporal words: "the time has been," "She should have died hereafter," "time for such a word," "to-morrow, and to-morrow, and to-morrow," "day to day," "recorded time," "yesterdays," "hour." But the temporality of the speech is very odd: it continually suggests that the future has already happened. Even the last syllable is of "recorded" time: the record has been made, we have only to play it out, act out the script already written. The culmination of this backward vision of time comes in the declaration that "all our yesterdays have lighted fools / The way to dusty death." From the perspective of Macbeth's lofty first person plural ("our yesterdays"), present lives are only "yesterdays," already lived through and outworn. The "fools" who are lighted to dusty death are fools of time.[19] They do not realize that they are living only repetitions of days that have already been lived: they live in "yesterdays" and imagine they live in todays.

Macbeth's language is flat, his diction prosaic and unremarkable, in sharp contrast with the flashy imagery and rhetorical flourish he used earlier in the play. Now there is no "pity like a naked new born babe" (1.7.21), no "sleep, that knits up the ravell'd sleeve of care" (2.2.34).[20] It is as if he is exhausted, rhetorically as well as emotionally. Since all days are the same, all words might as well be the same; Macbeth has lost his impetus for linguistic innovation. He repeats the same rhetorical structure three times over. "The way to dusty death." "And then is heard no more." "Signifying nothing." In each case, the first three feet of the line form the end of the sentence, and each describes the bathetic ultimate *telos* of human life. The lines shift from death as temporal end, to death as silence, to silence as end or purpose. Life ends with nothing, with "dusty death"; it therefore has "nothing" as its end: it signifies nothing. Macbeth moves directly from the lack of signifying in the silent grave, "and then is heard no more," to declaring that there is no significance either in the grave or out of it: life is a tale "signifying nothing." The end of life, death, becomes its only meaning or purpose — "nothing."[21] The silence of death extends back to rob the whole of life of its capacity to speak and make sense.[22] Death and life are both the absence of signification: both seem to signify, but in fact do not.

Macbeth's tendency to abstraction and generalization is motivated by the desire to avoid talking about his own situation. He says, "Life's but a walking shadow" in order not to admit that he is only a shadow of himself. The speech is prompted by a single death: "The Queen, my lord, is dead." But it says nothing about her as an individual: now she is not "Lady Macbeth," or "dearest chuck," but "she." Nor does Macbeth mention himself, or use any first-person singulars. Macbeth subsumes both his wife's individuality and his own into the dustiness of life and death. He refuses to see any distinctness either in an individual death, or in a life, or in the various days that make up a person's life.

Macbeth makes all people, like all days, the same: he universalizes his own experience. One could see this as a self-protective move. The name of "Macbeth" has become too closely associated with the word "murder." In denying the validity of any name or role, Macbeth tries to evade responsibility for his crimes. The play repeatedly suggests that Macbeth is dressed in clothes that do not fit him.[23] He has killed his king and his friend to take on the "borrowed robes" of king himself. Macbeth is like a miscast actor dressed up in the costume of a part he cannot play. But now he extends the phenomenon so that all "life," not only his own life, is "a poor player" on the stage. He claims not only that he, Macbeth, inhabits a false role, but also that all men, the nameless hordes of players, all lack names or costumes of their own, and all wear the "borrowed robes" of the theater. In claiming that "life" in general is only a "poor player," he implies that there could be no such thing as a real king, one on whom the title would not sit "like a giant's robe / Upon a dwarfish thief" (5.2.21–22). The poor player is never really any of the roles he plays. The same is true not only of Macbeth himself but of all people, and not only of people but also of "life" in general.

The shifts in imagery make "life" itself repeatedly change costume, like a player. Macbeth offers a quick succession of incompatible images for "life." First it is a candle, then a walking shadow, then a poor player, then a tale told by an idiot. The quick switches are like costume changes in the theater: life is dressed up first in one guise then in another. Each leads to the next: the light implied by the candle is snuffed out by the "shadow"; the implication of mimesis in "shadow" is developed by the "poor player"; the player's performance on stage becomes the "tale told by an idiot." The shifts in imagery are fast enough that one registers them only fleetingly; more important even than the distinctions between the various images is the fact that they seem to come to the same thing. A candle might seem very different from a shadow, or from a player, or from a tale, but Macbeth's speech equates them all, giving no indication that there is a contrast between comparing life to a shadow or a man, a candle, or a tale. Ultimately it makes no difference which of the various rhetorical costumes life wears. All are equally fragile and temporary and lacking in true substance or value.

Like Sophocles' Oedipus and like Euripides' Heracles, Macbeth feels that he has too many different parts to play. He has lived on after he can no longer be simply a soldier or a husband, and therefore, never to be born would have been best. Macbeth suggests that it does not matter what role one plays in life, or on stage, since none of them are one's own, and none last for longer than the "hour upon the stage." The plurality of roles a man can play, in the "catalogue ye go for men" (3.1.91), makes any single role seem meaningless. "All our yesterdays" are lights to nowhere because they are multiple but all the same. Tomorrow repeats tomorrow, and therefore no day means anything. No death is a true ending, because there are always more fools ready to get up on stage and pontificate. But the tomfoolery of life, like that of the theater, can always happen over again. It hardly matters whether the man who plays the part one night is the same as the one who played the night before; it is equally repetitious. In invoking the image of the "poor player" in close succession with that of the "tale told by an idiot," the actor undermines the dramatic illusion that he has created up until this point in the play: the man whom we had been believing to be "Macbeth" is now no more than a "poor player" and an "idiot" spouting nonsense.

Despite being a character on stage, Macbeth adopts the perspective not of the "poor player" but of the audience. After he leaves the stage, the player "is heard no more"; the speech does not consider what might happen to the actor off in the wings, once he is no longer visible to the audience. He goes to dusty death; when the lights are on we see him, when the candle is out and the actor leaves the stage or the candles dim, there is nothing. All actions in the theater happen not once but over and over again; similarly, the speech suggests, all actions in life are repetitions, and therefore all are as meaningless as those of actors on stage.

In the "poor player" speech, life loses its significance because it ends in death, but even death means "nothing." Many of the characters in *Macbeth* view death as the defining moment of life, the time at which even the wicked can redeem their former time.[24] In the beginning of the play, we learn of the traitor Cawdor that "Nothing in his life / Became him like the leaving it" (1.4.7–8). Macbeth appears as substitute for Cawdor: he steps into the title when Cawdor loses his life, and betrays Duncan his king in an even more terrible way than Cawdor had tried to do. In the final scenes of the play, Macbeth becomes able, like Cawdor, to "throw away the dearest thing he ow'd, / As 't were a careless trifle" (1.4.10–11), because he has lived beyond the time when his life, which should have been the dearest thing he owed, is anything more to him than a "careless trifle." When he hears that Birnam wood is indeed moving toward Dunsinane, and that therefore his destruction may be near, his response is a combination of despair and bravado:

> I gin to be a-weary of the sun,
> And wish th' estate o' th' world were now undone.
> Ring the alarum-bell! Blow, wind, come, wrack,
> At least we'll die with harness on our back!
> (5.5.48–51)

Macbeth chooses violence against the world rather than against himself. Because he is weary of the sun, he begins to "wish th' estate o' th' world were now undone." Only a total apocalypse could undo what he has done — or, rather, only by turning his energies to destroying the whole world can he distract attention from the emptiness of his own position. Like Seneca's Hercules, he searches for some kind of ultimate and violent ending, because for him, as for Hercules, it is unclear how any ending could be an adequate conclusion or could undo the feeling that his life went on too long.

Macbeth repeatedly says that he has lived long enough, or too long, or that all life is a tale told by an idiot; and yet he deliberately refuses to kill himself. He asks, "Why should I play the Roman fool, and die / On mine own sword? Whiles I see lives, the gashes / Do better upon them" (5.8.1–3). Refusing suicide is figured as being modern, refusing to play a classical role, "the Roman fool."[25] Macbeth's refusal to commit suicide makes him someone who can perform like a man, like a soldier, even if he can no longer "feel it like a man." Lady Macbeth presumably commits suicide;[26] suicide is figured as a female way to die, while Macbeth dies like a man.[27]

Publicly, Macbeth rejects the awareness he expressed in "to-morrow, and to-morrow" that life is like theater in its trivial failure to reach any true ending. Macbeth wants his own death to matter; he dies insisting on the permanence of his own role as man and soldier, and therefore on his own immunity to the theatrical pointlessness of life. In insisting on his military manliness Macbeth implies that he is not a "poor player," spouting someone else's words, but both the actor and the director of his own end. But he cannot so easily distance himself from the world of the theater. He refuses to "play the Roman fool" and instead tries to choose his own part as a Scottish soldier; but he cannot choose not to play any part at all. Even his own aggressive imperatives in the final scenes of the play are as much like directorial gestures as royal ones: "ring the alarum-bell! Blow, wind, come wrack" (5.5.50). He comforts himself with the thought that he can, by choosing to die on his own terms, die in a costume of his own choosing, that of the soldier: "at least we'll die with harness on our back" (5.5.52).

Macbeth refuses to yield to Macduff, though knowing that he will lose the battle, and in his refusal he dresses himself again in the mask of martial masculinity, which he had apparently lost forever: "[B]efore my body / I throw my warlike shield" (5.8.32–33). "Manliness" of the kind recommended by Lady Macbeth is, for Macbeth, only another assumed role.[28] He tells the lords the morning after the murder, "Let's briefly put on manly readiness" (2.3.133). He cannot "put on manly readiness" for more than brief moments, and he is not allowed to retain his chosen role in death. When he is surrounded in the castle, he becomes no longer even an actor trying to play the part of a man, but an animal in an even more primitive kind of performance: "[T]hey have tied me to the stake; I cannot fly, / But bear-like I must fight the course" (5.7.1–2). He cries, when Macduff tells him the truth, "Accursed be the tongue that tells me so, / For it hath cow'd my better part of man!" (5.8.17–18). The play has shown that "man" includes many different possible parts.[29] To die "like a man" is to die like part of a man.[30] Macbeth's conception of manhood is challenged by the man whom Macbeth assumed could not exist, the man who was "from his mother's womb / Untimely ripp'd" (5.8.15–16). Unlike Euripides' Heracles, Macbeth fails to realize that the life of a strong, brave man may include a whole "catalogue" of different moments.

The final battle between Macbeth and Macduff is between two men who both hope to live beyond the normal rules of time.[31] Macduff, ripped "untimely" from his mother's womb, is able to defeat Macbeth. He threatens, "Then yield thee, coward, / And live to be the show and gaze o' th' time" (5.8.23–24). Macbeth refuses to yield, and Macduff cuts off his head. The head itself will become the "gaze o' th' time." Malcolm uses the head as a prop for the first speech of his reign, to illustrate the liberation of Scotland not only from the "tyrant" Macbeth, but also from the tyranny of false attitudes toward time. Malcolm uses the word "time" no less than three times in his final speech: "we shall not spend a large expense of time . . . What's more to do, / Which would be newly planted with the time . . . We will perform in measure time and place" (5.1.26–38). Malcolm tries to emphasize that he will not try to enslave time or o'erleap it, as Macbeth did; rather, he will defer to time. He will let the time be "free": he will neither waste time nor kill it, but allow an organic growth "newly planted with the time," abiding by "measure time and place."

Malcolm will wait for time to do as it will, and therefore his new regime will, he hopes, be able finally to conclude the reign of Macbeth. He calls the Macbeths, "this dead butcher and his fiendlike queen" (5.9.35), using adjectives that set the Macbeths at a safe distance from himself and his audience. "Fiendlike" obviously suggests that Lady Macbeth is infernal and inhuman, and therefore her life and death need not be seen (as Macbeth saw them) as a model for human life and death in general. But it is equally important that Macbeth is described not only as a butcher but as a "dead" butcher. "Behold, where stands / Th' usurper's cursed head," says Macduff (5.9.20–21). Dead men rise again but only on sticks. Malcolm needs to reassure his audience and himself that Macbeth really is dead. It is a necessary reassurance at the end of a play in which the audience has seen the Ghost of Banquo appear on the stage, and in which Macbeth himself has described life as only a series of tomorrows, and death as a meaningless theatrical pause until the next fool gets up on stage.

Macbeth's precipitate and murderous sense of overliving had become associated with the world of the theater. Malcolm responds by promising both a new relationship with time, and a new model of theatrical spectacle. Macbeth's poor-player speech suggests that both life and theater are empty of value or meaning; Malcolm tries to restore significance to both life and theater. In order to show that his own life and rule will not be like the struttings of a poor player, Malcolm has not only to condemn the Macbeths but also invent for himself and his new rule a different set of theatrical imagery. He implies in his final speech that the theater need not represent insignificance, illusion, and inconclusiveness. The new reign will not be "full of sound and fury." Rather, both Macduff and Malcolm associate the Scotland of the future with a masquelike form of theater that will depend less on action than on spectacle. Macduff had threatened Macbeth that should he live, it would be as "the show and gaze o' th' time" (5.8.24). Macbeth's decapitated head is indeed the "show" of the new time: Macduff declares, "Behold, where stands / Th' usurper's cursed head" (5.9.20–21). Macbeth has become not a moving, speaking, acting player, but an object to be looked at. By reducing theater to spectacle, Macduff and Malcolm try to protect themselves from the threat of time and theatrical repetition.

Malcolm's final words imply a shift from public theaters to court masques, from the public theater, in which the same actions and words are played over and over again, to a court audience, which will assemble less for a story than for a vision performed according to its proper measure. *Macbeth* was performed in the new Blackfriars theater, which allowed for new kinds of special effects (such as the Ghost and the Apparitions). Malcolm's words remind the spectators that they are participating in a transition from one kind of theater (the open-air public theater of the Globe) to another, the indoor, technically spectacular, private theater at Blackfriars, which became heavily influenced by the court masque.[32] Malcolm declares that "what needful else"

> We will perform in measure, time, and place.
> So thanks to all at once, and to each one,
> Whom we invite to see us crown'd at Scone.
> (5.9.39–41)

Malcolm will "perform," but he will do so before a select audience, not before a public crowd; he will do so not in a passion of "sound and fury" but "in measure, time, and place"; and he will do so not over and over again but once and for all, and "at once."

But there is a danger that the audience may not feel entirely satisfied by

Malcolm's promises. His assurance that he will do what "would be planted newly with the time" recalls Duncan's first greeting to Macbeth: "I have begun to plant thee, and will labor / To make thee full of growing" (1.4.28–29). The echo may imply that there will be less difference than one might hope between the old time and the new. The word "Hail"—"Hail, King!" and "Hail, King of Scotland!" (5.9.20 and 25)—likewise suggests a parallel between Malcolm's new honors and Macbeth's. Malcolm, like Macbeth, inherits a title from a disloyal traitor whose head is "fix'd upon our battlements."[33]

At the beginning of the last scene, Old Siward chillingly assumes that his son's death is "worth" only three and a half lines of cheerful relief that he "had his hurts before" (5.9.12). His grief is "measur'd" (5.9.11) at a moment when one would expect a feeling man to be emotionally distraught. Malcolm's insistence on "measure, time, and place" (5.9.39) echoes Siward's belief that public performance must be valued beyond any private emotion.[34] Macbeth's poor-player speech offered us a glimpse behind the curtain, both of his own mind, of the theater, and of life itself. Malcolm resolutely lowers the curtain again, suggesting that we must defer to time and simply cease to ask what it signifies. The spectators of the play are excluded from Malcolm's new performance at Scone. There will be no further discussion of how it feels to live in time, to fear that time may go too slowly or too fast, or that days may be mere repetition of one another. The drama can imply that the problem is over only by ceasing to offer any access to the characters' inner life. In *Macbeth*, as we shall see in *Samson Agonistes*, the sense of overliving is repressed rather than cured.

CHAPTER 7

"A moving grave"

Samson Agonistes

The last two chapters of this book are about Milton, a poet haunted by the fear that time has gone wrong, and that life will either end too soon or go on too long.[1] The representation of overliving acquires a new intensity in Milton because there is a conflict between the attempt to "assert eternal providence" (*Paradise Lost* 1.25) and the feelings of Adam and of Samson that they have lived too long. Milton's poetry often suggests that feelings of belatedness may be corrected by a larger historical or divine perspective, from which the time is too early, not too late. But the emotional and poetic emphasis, in both *Samson Agonistes* and *Paradise Lost*, is on the human sense of overliving.

The fear that life has gone on too long, and the struggle to accept God's timing, recur throughout Milton's poetic career. In an early letter, he writes of "a certain belatednesse" in himself, and offers as an account of his "tardie moving" a sonnet about time, "the subtle thief of youth."[2] Time has stolen the speaker's "three and twentieth year," but he fears that his "late spring no bud or blossom sheweth."[3] He is both too old and too immature to produce the work God demands of him. Both letter and poem suggest that a time that feels too late may in fact be too early. Perhaps Milton has not missed the moment to produce great work; perhaps that work still lies in the future. The sonnet ends with an attempt at reconciliation with time:

> Yet be it less or more, or soon or slow,
>> It shall be still in strictest measure even,
>> To that same lot, however mean or high,
> Toward which time leads me, and the will of heaven;
>> All is, if I have grace to use it so,
>> As ever in my great task-master's eye.
> (Sonnet 7.9–14)

The feeling that twenty-three years have been wasted is corrected by the reminder that it may be still too early to know what God intends. Moreover, the sense of belatedness may itself be caused by earliness. Slow inward development gives the appearance of time lost, but in fact the time to perform life's great work has not yet arrived. The octet ends with a contrast between the speaker's deceitful outward "semblance" and his lack of "inward ripenesse"; the sestet shifts to God's eye, which is not deceived and which can perhaps discern an even more secret pattern of development. For those who can defer to God's pattern, time does not rob or betray but provides "strictest measure," even for people who do not seem "timely-happy" (8), and "leads" the speaker to some mysterious "lot," along with the "will of heaven" (12).

The sonnet moves from the perfect tense ("How soon hath time," 1), to the future ("it shall be still," 10), and finally the present ("all is," 13). Time is first too late, then too early, and finally the last lines suggest that no time is either too late or too early, since at any moment one can serve God. The "strictest measure" of the sonnet itself is a sign that Milton's youth has not been entirely wasted; even as he agonizes about the flight of time, he is led to serve his great taskmaster through poetry. There are, then, two different solutions to the sense of belatedness: the final lines suggest both that it is not too late but too early to serve God, and also that it is neither too early nor too late, neither "soon or slow" (9), in the eyes of eternity.

But the dense syntax of the final lines convey how difficult it is to make peace with God's timing. The poem's attempts at reassurance are strikingly obscure. It is unclear where time leads, what "ripenesse" would involve, and what task the "great task-master" will impose. The word "it" is used three times in lines 9–14, presumably with at least two different referents.[4] The reader is offered a strong assurance that all will be well, and that in God's eyes, all is always well. But we are not able to see with God's eyes, and the poem emphasizes the inaccessibility of the divine perspective. In this sonnet, as in his later poetry, Milton responds to a vividly imagined sense of belatedness with an appeal to something beyond human knowledge or understanding.

Milton's sense of his task as a poet and as a political teacher grew clearer, but his fear of being too late only increased.[5] After the failure of the English republic and the loss of his sight, he was afraid that it was already too late for him to save his people.[6] As in sonnet 7, so in *Paradise Lost* and *Samson Agonistes*, Milton tries to resolve the sense of time gone wrong by deference to the will of God. Both Samson at the beginning of his tragedy and Adam after the Fall feel that they have lost the role for which they were created, and that they can no longer hope to fulfill their proper task in relation to God. Both feel that they are forced to live a kind of living death, enduring repetitive, pointless time in which they are able neither to be their true selves nor to die. In both *Paradise Lost* and *Samson Agonistes*, divine and historical ways of understanding the proper purposes of human life compete with the fear of belatedness and the intense human longing for an ending.

Samson Agonistes and *Paradise Lost* are both, I shall suggest, tragic works; both are centrally concerned with the tragic sense of overliving. Some have suggested that Christian tragedy is impossible, because in a world governed by an omnipotent and benevolent God, all must eventually be for the best; everything, even pain, even sin, can be turned to good by God.[7] But Milton himself certainly thought there could be Christian tragedy. In the preface to *Samson Agonistes*, he defends the genre as "the gravest, moralest, and most profitable of all other poems" and appeals to Paraeus's definition of the book of Revelation as a tragedy: "Paraeus commenting on the Revelation, divides the whole book as a tragedy, into acts distinguished each by a chorus of heavenly harpings and song between."[8] He uses the same example in *Reason of Church Government*: "The Apocalypse of Saint *John* is the majestick image of a stately Tragedy, shutting up and intermingling her solemn Scenes and Acts with a sevenfold *Chorus* of halleluja's and harping symphonies: and this my opinion the grave autority of *Pareus* commenting that book is sufficient to confirm."[9] Milton's explicit definition of the word "tragedy" is purely formal: a tragedy is composed of episodes or acts divided by choral songs.

But he also has thematic reasons for classifying Revelation as tragic. The adjectives give some indication of what these are: "the majestick image of a stately Tragedy." Revelation is tragic because its subject matter is serious, even sublime.

The inclusion of Revelation in the genre of tragedy suggests that tragedy is associated with sin, death, and woe: the ultimate tragic subjects are the suffering of the church as she awaits her redemption at the Apocalypse, and the suffering of the damned.[10] Moreover, those who are forced to wait for so long will inevitably, like Samson and like Adam and Eve, wish that there could be some briefer end. They will believe that they have lived too long but will still be unable to die. "And in those days shall men seek death, and shall not find it; and shall desire to die, and death shall flee from them" (Revelation 9.6). Milton associates the Apocalypse with tragedy because it will involve immense and unending pain for most of the human race. Christian tragedy need not concentrate on the happy ending for the redeemed.[11] It may, rather, emphasize the pain of those who are lost (like the dead Philistines, or Adam's son Cain); or the long period of waiting before the end of time, when everyone may suspect that life has gone on too long. Adam, Eve, and Samson, who live before the Incarnation, must go on living with only faint glimpses of God's final plan. But the same is true, as the last books of *Paradise Lost* make clear, even for those who live after Jesus. All human history, in Milton's view, is a time of expectation, which may at any moment feel too long.

In Milton's poetry, pagan tragic models for overliving are mingled with the book of Job.[12] Job's animals and other property are destroyed, his sons and daughters are killed, and he is left in the mud covered with boils. His wife makes the laconic and sensible suggestion, "Curse God and die" (Job 2.9). But Job refuses either to curse God or to die. He curses the day of his birth, saying "May the day perish when I was born, and the night that told of a boy conceived. May that day be darkness, may God on high have no thought for it, may no light shine on it" (Job 3.2–4). Adam and Samson—like Job, and like Oedipus and Heracles—curse the days of their creation or birth and long for a death that never comes.

The book of Job provides two different narrative models for how the sense of overliving might be cured. There is the external, folkloric solution: Job is given back his property, his boils are finally cured, and he is awarded new sheep and new daughters; he recovers his old role as a righteous, wealthy, and healthy man. But there is also the internal and more metaphysically sophisticated answer: God speaks from the whirlwind and reminds Job that suffering is only one of many mysteries in a world that is largely incomprehensible to man.[13]

Samson Agonistes and *Paradise Lost*, similarly, suggest two distinct kinds of solution to the problem of overliving. There may be an external change: Adam and Samson can commit an ultimate act of revenge and redemption. Samson finally redeems his people by killing the Philistines; at the end of history, at the Apocalypse, the descendants of Adam will finally have their revenge on Satan, and God's chosen people will be saved. There is, in both texts, a fear that this kind of solution will merely substitute one kind of tragedy for another; tragic overliving gives way to revenge tragedy, which perpetuates the feeling that all action is only repetition of suffering. Moreover, as in the book of Job, the external and impersonal solution to the vivid evocation of human despair may seem merely to miss the point or to change the subject. Alternatively, there may be an internal change — such as Samson's discovery of his "rousing motions" or Adam's "paradise within." But at these moments, the reader no longer has access to the characters' interiority; the internal "cure" for the sense of overliving resists literary representation. The emotional center of both *Samson Agonistes* and *Paradise Lost* lies not with the superhuman and impersonal visions of history, or with the inaccessible mysteries of faith, but in the agonized sense that life goes on too long.

Like the book of Job, *Samson Agonistes* illustrates multiple possible strategies to contain or repress the sense of overliving. The character's attitude may change: perhaps Samson can be calmed, assuaged, or cured of his despair by the soothing truisms of the Chorus, or by his encounters with his three visitors, or by the inner workings of God. The situation may change: perhaps the restoration of Samson's strength and his ultimate success in destroying his enemies redeem the time of suffering. Or the text may change the subject. *Samson Agonistes* moves away from its initial concentration on Samson's subjective experience of time as loss and living death. His interiority becomes illegible, and the focus, in the final lines of the play, is on the attempt of those who are left behind to make sense of his life and his death. Samson's own initial sense of confusion about God's purposes is inherited by his father, by the Chorus, and by the reader. *Samson Agonistes* suggests that one can suppress the sense of tragic overliving only at the cost of suppressing all human emotions.

At the beginning of the play, Samson cannot understand why he was marked as a deliverer of Israel and favorite of God, but now lives "a life half dead, a living death, / And buried" (100–101). He has betrayed his divine secret to Dalila and has lost his strength, his eyesight, and his freedom. He no longer believes he will ever be able to liberate his people, the action for which he was born. He has lost his reason for living and yet remains alive. "A little onward lend thy guiding hand," he says in the first line, echoing Oedipus at Colonus.[14] Samson at the beginning of the play is continuing to live, to move "a little onward." But he cannot yet see any way "onward" away from his state of mental stasis and despair.

Samson was known among medieval and Renaissance biblical commentators primarily as a type of Christ—a suffering hero who laid down his own life for the redemption of his people.[15] On one level, then, the meaning of his own story must inevitably remain hidden both from Samson himself and from the other characters in the drama; they live too soon to see what is foreshadowed by Samson's final actions.[16] On another level, as Protestant theologians insisted, Samson and other Old Testament figures did not live too soon, since they, like Christians, were people of the promise, who had the choice whether or not to put their faith in God.[17] But Samson's final relationship with God is inaccessible to the reader, whereas his initial despair and bewilderment are intensely and unforgettably evoked.

Samson sees God as the creator of a story that seems to have a nonsensical plot, one whose ending does not match its initial design. In his opening speech (1–114), he is torn between his sense that he has lived too long and his desire to submit to the divine will. God apparently does not want him to die; and yet Samson is unable to discern any consistent pattern in the course of his life. The speech is structured around the pattern of anguish, then repression. Three times, Samson expresses in different ways his resentment at the fact that he is still alive, and three times he corrects himself or is corrected. First (18–42), Samson shows why he feels he has overlived himself: he depended on a future that never materialized, since he expected to be the liberator of his people. He cannot understand why he was born at all, and apparently destined for greatness, since it was all to come to nothing.

> Why was my breeding ordered and prescribed
> As of a person separate to God,
> Designed for great exploits; if I must die
> Betrayed, captived, and both my eyes put out,
> Made of my enemies the scorn and gaze?
> (30–34)

God's plan for Samson's life seems to have gone wrong. Samson begins with a question ("Why . . . "), but assumes that there can be no explanation, as he turns instead to the horrors of his present condition. He seemed "designed for great exploits," and yet he is "eyeless in Gaza at the mill with slaves" (41), the blind object of the "gaze" of others. He can neither confront his human enemies nor escape from a time scheme that makes no sense. The future Samson was promised has come to nothing, and he seems to have lost the opportunity to do what he was born to do; and yet he has to go on living.

Samson tries hard to avoid direct criticism of God, who has ordered the timing of his life. He does not actually say that he would rather not have been born or that he wishes he were dead. But his questions imply a rebuke to God's design. He asks, "Wherefore was my birth from heaven foretold?" (23) and "Why was my breeding ordered and prescribed?" (30), implying that there was no reason: the promises of heaven were always false; God deceived Samson with the lure of a future that was never going to come. Samson's life seemed to have a plot or a pattern, but it did not. His end does not fulfill the promise of his beginnings. But Samson quickly corrects such blasphemous thoughts and reminds himself it was all his own fault: "Yet stay, let me not rashly call in doubt / Divine prediction" (43–44). God would have kept his word, had it not been for Samson's own folly; he missed the opportunity God would have given him. Samson's own character is the only flaw in God's plan.

But the acknowledgment of his error leads to another set of questions of "divine disposition": "But what is strength, without a double share / Of wisdom?" (53–54). Although Samson acknowledges that he caused his own downfall, which was the result of the inherent weaknesses in his own constitution, this prompts him to wonder why God made his constitution so weak in the first place, and why he was destined for greatness but apparently incapable of achieving it. Samson's failure to be the savior of his people is God's fault, for making him unable to live up to his supposed potential: "God, when he gave me strength, to show withal / How slight the gift was, hung it in my hair" (58–59). Physical strength is as fragile as the weakest part of the body, the hair. God mocked Samson by giving him what was supposedly a gift but was really insultingly useless.

Again, he corrects or suppresses his own complaint: "But peace, I must not quarrel with the will / Of highest dispensation" (60–61). God may have purposes that to Samson remain dark. But the impulse to accept his suffering is followed almost immediately by another outcry at his worst affliction: "O loss of sight, of thee I most complain!" (67). Samson's great outburst on blindness (67–109) is likewise repressed, but not, as in the two previous cases, by an internal check, but by the entrance of the Chorus (110). It is as if this climactic expression of pain is too intense for Samson to be able to discover any response to it within himself.

Scarce half I seem to live, dead more than half.

O dark, dark, dark, amid the blaze of noon,

Irrecoverably dark, total eclipse

Without all hope of day!

O first created beam, and thou great word,

Let there be light, and light was over all;

Why am I thus bereaved thy prime decree?

The sun to me is dark

And silent as the moon,

When she deserts the night

Hid in her vacant interlunar cave.

(79–89)

Samson treats his blindness as both the cause and the sign that he is "dead more than half," a "moving grave" (79, 102). The association between overliving and blindness, which was implicit in *King Lear* and *Oedipus Coloneus*, here becomes explicit. Samson's blindness is, he at first suggests, the worst part of his suffering: "O loss of sight, of thee I most complain!" (67). Samson must live on in a mutilated body, which only half functions. He articulates the terrible cruelty of living without the ability to see, that most basic of all God's gifts. But on another level, his blindness is an appropriate marker of what he has done and suffered — and even, he later suggests, a kind of comfort. Samson later remarks that he is protected by blindness from some of his shame (195–202). Physical blindness is both the worst and the least of his troubles. Far worse, on another level, is his spiritual and psychological blindness: his inability to make sense of his life as a whole, or to understand why God has made him live with such a terrible combination of strength and weakness.

Samson has lost the most important element of his body, his eyes, and he has also lost his spiritual center, his intimacy with God. Indirectly, he again evokes his sense that God has abandoned him: God is like the moon who "deserts the night / Hid in her vacant interlunar cave" (88–89). But the image of the moon in her "vacant interlunar cave" also describes Samson himself. The moon, like Samson, is in an intermediary position. She lies between light and darkness, just as Samson himself lives between life and death. He insists that he is half dead, but forced to carry on living:

As in the land of darkness yet in light,

To live a life half dead, a living death

And buried; but O yet more miserable!
Myself, my sepulchre, a moving grave,
Buried, yet not exempt
By privilege of death and burial
From worst of other evils, pains and wrongs.
(99–104)

The juxtapositions of "life" with "light" suggest that there is a terrible paradox in life without light: light is "almost life itself," just as the word "light" differs from "life" only by one small sound, and yet it is possible to have life but no light. Samson's verbal repetitions do not have the power of God's "great word," to turn "light" into light. Instead, his words evoke the agonies of a life that continues without hope of change. The rhymes and alliterations increase the obsessive insistence on "light," which is echoed by "sight" (67, 93), "night" (88), and "delight" (71). Samson has neither sight, light, nor delight, and yet he has life — or at least, a half life, a life that lacks everything that gave life value. The repetitions of the words "live," "life," and "living" bitterly emphasize the frustration of a life that continues after all that mattered has been lost.

In earlier tragedies, the sense of overliving is often associated with the multiplication of roles for a particular character: Oedipus, for instance, is both a king and an outcast; Heracles is both the protector of the weak and the killer of his own children. Samson, on the other hand, feels he has lived too long because he has lost capacity to perform the single action for which he was born — the redemption of his people. There is nothing else. There is no other light for the body when the eyes are out, no other light for the world without the sun, and no further reason for Samson to live, once he has lost God. His present life is characterized only by darkness, enslavement, pain, and loss.

Samson's problem at the beginning of the play is both intellectual and emotional. He believes that God has abandoned him, that he has done terrible things and lost what mattered most in his life, and that his situation both is and is not his own fault. Like Oedipus in the *Tyrannus*, and like Euripides' Heracles, Samson finds that his identity has been compromised: he is both strong and weak, both the savior and betrayer of his country, both God's favorite and deprived even of light. Samson's emotional agony is largely the result of his intellectual bewilderment. He cannot understand his own contradictory roles, and God's apparently contradictory purposes toward him. The sense of overliving is associated with doubt and puzzlement about God's timing.

Samson cannot believe his light could ever come out again. There is only darkness, "O dark, dark, dark, amid the blaze of noon, / Irrecoverably dark, total eclipse / Without all hope of day!" (80–82). But the comparison of blindness to a natural eclipse might imply that the darkness will be only temporary. Samson's images, even at his moment of greatest despair, suggest a kind of "counterplot," reminding the reader that there may be more reason to hope than Samson is able to believe.[18] Light that is "quenched" (95) can be again illuminated. Those who are "exiled" from light, God's prime decree (98), languishing in the "land of darkness" (99), may once again be brought home to their father's house. Prisoners, even those who can envision only "life in captivity" (108), a "prison within prison" (153), may eventually be released. Christian readers may consider that even those who are dead and "buried," "a moving grave," may not only remain alive but may even emerge again from the sepulcher. The question, then, is how Samson's feeling that he has lived too long might be cured.

Samson Agonistes has often been understood as a drama of regeneration, which shows the hero's gradual movement away from despair, and his final triumph, when his strength is restored and he pulls down the theater of the Philistines. Samson, according to this way of reading, is wrong to think at the beginning of the play that he has lived too long;[19] in fact, God had further plans in store for him and enabled him to become again the destroyer of his enemies and the glorious savior of his people. *Samson Agonistes* is a tragedy of overliving that becomes a revenge tragedy.[20] As in *Paradise Lost,* there is a suggestion that the protagonist's sense of overliving may be dispelled by the opportunity to take violent revenge on his enemies.[21]

Samson's father, Manoa, and the Chorus of Danites certainly understand his death as a glorious triumph, which proves to them that he died, as Manoa says, "with God not parted from him" (1719). The Chorus compares Samson to the phoenix, who "revives" from her own "ashy womb" (1687–1707). Samson, who at the beginning of the drama felt only half alive, has come back from the dead; even at the moment of his death, he has been restored to life. Manoa and the Chorus insist that "nothing is here for tears" (1721) and that "All is best" (1745). The ending of the drama is, they assure us, a happy one, and some critics assume that the reader ought to take them at their word.[22] The destruction of the Philistines may be read as brave, admirable, and a sign of God's final favor toward Samson.[23] Samson's sense of overliving was, then, simply premature; he failed to realize that all would be well in the end. The Chorus's final line, "calm of mind, all passion spent" (1758), alludes to Milton's theory of tragic catharsis and implies that excessive emotions, such as despair, can eventually be purged away.

But there are two difficulties with understanding the end of the play as redemptive in this way, and they are related to one another. First, as many critics have pointed out, Samson's final action is extremely violent.[24] It is figured as a kind of apocalypse, which destroys an entire population.[25] The sound the Chorus hears from the theater is of "blood, death and dreadful deeds" (1513), and the Messenger emphasizes the numbers of those he has killed:

> Lords, ladies, captains, counsellors, or priests,
> Their choice nobility and flower, not only
> Of this, but each Philistian city round
> Met from all parts to solemnize this feast.
>
> (1653–56)

He kills not only those directly responsible for his suffering and that of his people, but the whole mass of those in the building: "[T]he vulgar only scaped, who stood without" (1659). Moreover, Samson kills himself as well as his enemies. The Chorus and Manoa are unsure whether his death should be regarded as suicide — and therefore to be condemned — or as a victory in which Samson died "not willingly, but tangled in the fold, / Of dire necessity" (1665–66).[26] One can see his suicidal destruction of his enemies as an act of terrible violence against both himself and others, an example of precisely how a true Christian ought not to behave.[27]

Second, and even more important, the drama shifts away from the inner emotional state of Samson himself and concentrates instead on the outward events of his final act, and on the struggle of the Chorus and of Manoa to make sense of what has happened. At the beginning, we read his agonized outbursts about the sense of overliving; at the end, we are offered no access at all to his inner state. We know only what he did, not how he felt. Nor do we know anything about Samson's final relationship with God — and hence, we have no way of knowing whether his final action was divinely inspired. In *Samson Agonistes*, the voice of God not only proclaims the many mysteries of the world — as in the book of Job — but also is itself mysterious, since we do not know whether it is heard at all.[28] In Milton's biblical source for the Samson story, the book of Judge, the reader is given access to Samson's thoughts before he kills his enemies: he prays, "Let me die with the Philistines."[29] In *Samson Agonistes*, Milton's messenger cannot even tell us whether he is praying. As he feels the pillars of the temple, he is "As one who prayed, / Or some great matter in his mind revolved" (1637–38). We do not know whether Samson's life was too long, or whether he did in the end not only save his people by violence but also hear again the voice of God. Milton's drama makes Samson's end far more obscure than it is in the book of Judges.

It is also more obscure than the death of Oedipus — one of his central classical models. *Samson Agonistes* echoes both Euripides' *Heracles*, and the *Oedipus Coloneus*.[30] Samson, like Heracles, is a hero who is renowned primarily for his physical strength, who has a divine mission to use that strength in service for the benefit of his people, and who finds himself in a domestic setting where his strength is worse than useless. He is a once powerful man, physically weakened and overcome with shame, who longs for death and feels that it should already have come. But Samson is a Heracles who turns into Oedipus at Colonus, a broken and polluted man summoned by a mysterious divine voice to become a powerful redeemer, elevated to heroic stature. In both Sophocles and Milton, the final transformation scene in which the blind man turns into a savior happens offstage and is reported by a messenger's speech; and both dramatists surround this final transformation with mystery. But the kinds of mystery are very different. Theseus and his heirs are sworn to secrecy about what happened in the Grove of the Eumenides because they have witnessed the first instance of what will be, in Sophocles' time, a cult mystery surrounding Oedipus. There is no explicit secrecy surrounding the last actions of Samson, and indeed they take place in a theater: Milton changes the "house" of Judges to a "spacious theater" (1605). But paradoxically, his performance or "act" in the theater will be his moment of greatest opacity.[31] In the *Oedipus Coloneus* the Messenger announces that everyone heard the voice of the god, calling him to delay no longer (1626–27). Nobody knows whether Samson is really called by God to the theater, or, once there, what impulse moves him to destroy it. The arena of mystery is shifted from the geographical location to the mind of the hero.

Emotions are always a problem in *Samson Agonistes*. The drama suggests that emotional disturbance may always be associated with a suspicion that there is something wrong with God's timing — and especially, with the sense of overliving. The theory of catharsis implied by Milton's preface to *Samson Agonistes* suggests that emotional disturbance can be moderated. But the drama itself suggests a very different account of the emotions. Samson himself seems to become more and more passionate until he is dead, while the end of the play suggests that one can avoid the sense of overliving only if one avoids emotions altogether. I return to this point, and to the interpretation of Samson's final action, at the end of the chapter. I turn now to Milton's theory of catharsis.

In the preface, Milton associates tragedy with the power to "temper and reduce" excessive passions, by homeopathy:[32]

> Tragedy, as it was anciently composed, hath been ever held the gravest, moralest, and most profitable of all other poems: therefore said by Aristotle to be of power by raising pity and fear, or terror, to purge the mind of those and such-like passions, that is to temper and reduce them to just measure with a kind of delight, stirred up by reading or seeing those passions well imitated. Nor is nature wanting in her own effects to make good his assertion: for so in physic things of melancholic hue and quality are used against melancholy, sour against sour, salt to remove salt humours. (in Carey and Fowler 1968, p. 343)

The preface suggests that tragedy always calms or purges excessive emotions in the reader or spectator. The imitation of pity and fear and "such-like passions" moderates the passions of the reader, "with a kind of delight." Our enjoyment in reading about the passions of others helps to regulate our own emotional state.[33] The preface implies that it is possible to develop moderate emotional responses.

The supposed effect of successful tragedy — the purgation of certain passions — is also the subject of *Samson Agonistes*. Unlike Aristotle, Milton suggests that catharsis may happen not only to the spectators but also to the characters within the play.[34] There is an association between the tragic catharsis that the reader of tragedy might experience, and the purgation of Samson's excessive passions within the drama. The reader is led to expect that Samson's purification will follow the model of tragic catharsis outlined in the preface. Perhaps Samson's initially extreme emotional state will be moderated through meetings with characters whose excessive passions reflect his own.[35]

We are reminded of the homeopathic model for the purgation of emotions in Samson's encounters with three figures who mirror his own passions in different ways: Manoa, his father, Dalila, his wife, and Harapha, a gigantic adversary. Samson is able to reject each of his three visitors, and after Harapha has gone, the officer appears to summon him to the public theater. Samson initially refuses but then agrees to go. One might say, then, that Samson's passions have been cured by his three encounters; through them, he has been made ready to do God's work.[36]

However, Samson's passions often seem to be stirred up far more intensely by the passions of those he meets. Johnson was closer to being right when he famously remarked that *Samson Agonistes* "must be avowed to want a middle";[37] the three visits do nothing to explain God's mysterious dealings with Samson, and they do not show how Samson's emotions might be tempered. But it is better to say that Milton's tragedy is all middle. Its main emotional focus is on the pain of middle periods of time, when it is unclear when the end will come and when it seems too late for any kind of redemption. The drama offers no model of how the moderation of emotion might happen. *Samson Agonistes* is a difficult play largely because it raises an emotional and psychological problem — Samson's initial sense of overliving — and provides no solution to it.

When he talks to his father, Manoa, Samson is in the depths of despair. Manoa sympathizes with Samson's despair and shares it to a large extent. His questions about the purposes of God echo Samson's own agonized bewilderment: "For this did the angel twice descend?" asks Manoa (361). Momentarily, Manoa's despair seems to help Samson out of his own. In response to Manoa's grim questioning of God's purposes, Samson is able to proclaim his faith in God more confidently than he has done before: "Appoint not heavenly disposition, father," he says (373).

But Manoa fails to cure Samson's sense that he has lived too long. Samson refuses to believe that there is any reason to postpone death. Manoa wants to ransom him from the Philistines, and reminds him to trust in God's salvation and fear God's "further ire" (520). But Samson rejects his father's attempts to save his life, even in the hope of further serving God: "His pardon I implore; but as for life, / To what end should I seek it?" (521–22). Samson even seems depressed by the offer of help.[38] Life without spiritual regeneration would be no cure at all and would only prolong the agony. He can no longer see any point in even trying to serve his people, or his God; instead, he will wait, until "oft-invocated death / Hasten the welcome end of all my pains" (576–76). By the end of their conversation, it seems that the likeness of Manoa's situation to his own actually increases Samson's despair. He rejects the possibility of a life that would be like Manoa's own present life, as a pitiable, useless old man: were he to be ransomed and lie, he would live a "burdenous drone" — "till length of years / And sedentary numbness craze my limbs / To a contemptible old age obscure" (570–72). Manoa tries to cure Samson by offering to turn him into a version of himself — an ineffective and sad, though benign, old man.[39] But the prospect of bleak and burdensome old age only makes Samson more eager to die. One melancholic does not cure another; instead, he makes him even more depressed. The reflection of his own despair in his father's weakness and mistrust in God increases Samson's sense of "heaven's desertion." Manoa, presumably realizing that he has utterly failed to cheer Samson up, can only turn him back to the "healing words" (605) of the Chorus.

Dalila is also a mirror of Samson, but she reflects not his melancholic desire to die but his ambitious desire for honor, as a savior of his people and servant of God. Dalila claims that she hoped, like Samson, to save her people and serve her God, Dagon. Her prediction of her own funerary glory anticipates that of Samson (982–87). Dalila presents herself as someone who shares Samson's inability to keep a secret: "To what I did thou show'dst me first the way" (781). She suggests that her similarity to Samson should bind them together: "Let weakness then with weakness come to parle / So near related, or the same of kind" (785–86). But Samson utterly rejects his former wife. He will not accept that Dalila and he have anything in common. He refuses to allow the possibility that her motives are anything but the basest, or have ever been.[40] In rejecting Dalila, Samson reverses his earlier sin when he betrayed his secret to her. But his ability to resist the allure of his former wife also seems to inspire him with a renewed self-confidence that equals hers. Her faith in Dagon is answered by a new trust, on Samson's part, in his own God, whose purposes he feels he can read clearly: "God sent her to debase me" (999). Although he speaks as if he has cast off every aspect of Dalila, he will, like her, fight to redeem his people. In this encounter, as with Manoa, Samson himself does not admit that he can learn anything from his visitor. But again, as in the encounter with Manoa, his passions seem to be stirred up in response to the passions of the person he has met.

The third character who confronts Samson is the violent giant, Harapha, who challenges him to fight. Samson declares "Nothing from thy hand / Fear I incurable; bring up thy van, / My heels are fettered, but my fist is free" (1233–35). Samson here denies what he earlier lamented, that his external suffering can affect his mind (cf. 617–22). He suggests that there may, after all, be nothing here, "incurable"—from the violent blustering of the giant, or even from the hand of heaven. Samson allows the violence of the giant to bring out his own violent tendencies. Samson's violence is not dispelled but nurtured by the giant's bluster.

Samson's various passions—including melancholy, ambition, and anger—are aroused to an intense degree by his three encounters. This might suggest that Samson needs to become more passionate, not less so, in order to pull down the theater of the Philistines. Perhaps emotions, even apparently excessive emotions, are necessary after all—despite what the cathartic theory of the preface seems to imply.

But Samson does not immediately agree to accompany the public officer to the Philistine theater, even after the third visitor, Harapha, has left. He tells him repeatedly, "I cannot come" (1321), and "I will not come" (1332, 1342). Eventually, he assures the Chorus,

> Be of good courage, I begin to feel
> Some rousing motions in me which dispose
> To something extraordinary my thoughts.
> I with this messenger will go along.
> (1381–84)

There is no reason to believe that the "rousing motions" have anything to do with the three visits that have been the main action of the play; they seem to appear out of nowhere — perhaps from God, perhaps not. We are offered no explanation for why Samson eventually agrees to go with the officer. At the beginning of the drama, Samson's identity is mysterious to himself. At the end, he becomes increasingly mysterious to the other characters, and to the reader.[41]

Samson's actions tell us nothing about his inner life. The focus of the drama was, at the beginning, on Samson's diseased consciousness; by the end, the Messenger describes him in purely external and inhuman terms, like a natural disaster: he tugs the pillars "as with the force of winds and waters pent, / When mountains tremble" (1647–48). Milton's tragedy moves away from Samson's sense of overliving. The emotional vividness of the opening scene, with its evocation of the strong man's despair, is lost as Samson's interiority becomes more and more opaque to the reader. *Samson Agonistes* is a tragedy about the inaccessibility of any real drama (such as Samson's psychic struggle) to external dramatic representation. It shows the intellectual and emotional struggles of those who try to understand God's mysterious ways, and the reader is forced to participate in those struggles.

We are given no explanation of how Samson's emotional agonies might be cured. His despair and anger are not moderated, as long as we have access to them. In his final decision to go with the officer, and at his death, his emotions become entirely obscure to the reader. At the end of the play, the problem of how to interpret and respond to God's apparently inconsistent dealings with Samson is taken up by those who remain alive after his death: his father, Manoa, and the Chorus.

Manoa and the Chorus are in the position of readers as they try to understand Samson's life and death. They search for a design and try to interpret Samson's death as the key both to his life and to the dealings of God with man. The Chorus insists that he was "with inward eyes illuminated" (1689); Manoa, that he died "with God not parted from him" (1719). God's plan was slow but sure; all is best in the end. But these judgments are based on pure speculation; the Chorus and Manoa have no way of knowing whether Samson made peace at last with God. They, like the reader, are interpreting the Messenger's speech, which leaves Samson's final state of mind entirely opaque. The Chorus assures us that God has dismissed "his servants" "with peace and consolation" (1755, 1757), and one may be tempted to take "his servants" to include Samson himself. But there is no way that either the Chorus or the reader can know whether Samson died consoled. The willingness to insist that "all is best" is not something that the Chorus has learned as a result of Samson's death; its final pronouncement about the ultimate benevolence of "the unsearchable dispose" (1746) is little different from its warning to Samson, "Tax not divine disposal" (210). The Chorus and Manoa, like Job's comforters, are unconsoling because they do not seem to understand the problem which they try to address.

Manoa insists that "Samson hath quit himself / Like Samson" (1709–10). The lines beg the question of what it is to be like Samson. Samson himself did not know; he could make no sense of the strange inconsistency of God's dealings with him, or of the combination of blessings and curses, weakness and strength that he was given. Even Manoa acknowledges that he can still not understand why his son made the marriages he did, and can only ascribe them to bad luck: "only bewailing / His lot unfortunate in nuptial choice, / From whence captivity and loss of eyes" (1742–44). The bizarrely telegraphic style of that final line (1744) suggests a fear of being sucked again into endless speculation about the meaning of Samson's long-drawn-out suffering. The danger of such speculations is that they might overwhelm the bereaved father with the desire to weep for his son, and to mourn not only his death but also the long sufferings of his life. Manoa and the Chorus assume that they must, if possible, feel nothing but "a kind of delight" at the death of Samson. The subject of the drama shifts to the passions of the Chorus and Manoa, away from the passions of Samson himself. It is their minds that are, they assure us repeatedly, with an almost hysterical insistence, calm after all.

One might think that the Chorus and Manoa are like the spectators of tragedy, whose passions have been reduced to "just measure" by their experience of the passions of Samson. The Chorus declares,

All is best, though we oft doubt
What the unsearchable dispose
Of highest wisdom brings about,
And ever best found in the close.
Oft he seems to hide his face,
But unexpectedly returns
And to his faithful champion hath in place
Bore witness gloriously; whence Gaza mourns
And all that band them to resist
His uncontrollable intent,
His servants he with new acquist
Of true experience from this great event
With peace and consolation hath dismissed,
And calm of mind, all passion spent.
(1745–58)

The lines contrast two possible attitudes to the story of Samson: "Gaza mourns" (1752), whereas "His servants" are enlightened and consoled, with "calm of mind all passion spent" (1758). Milton thus includes within his tragedy two alternative ways of reading it. There is the bad — and literally Philistine — way, which is to mourn; and there is the good, holy way of the servants of God, which is to be "Calm of mind all passion spent." The proper response to the tragedy of Samson is to experience the cathartic cure that Milton promised in the preface to his readers.[42] But there is an important disparity between the homeopathic theory of the preface, which suggests that it is possible to experience the passions in "just measure," and the claim implied by the Chorus's phrase, "all passion spent," which suggests that emotions have been tempered only by the radical means of eliminating them entirely.

All passionate emotions must be eliminated, since they might imply criticism of God's plan. Manoa urges the members of the Chorus, who have been glorifying Samson in his moment of triumph, "Come, come; no time for lamentation now, / Nor much more cause" (1708–9). The possibility of lamentation is suppressed even when nobody had shown any sign of wanting to weep. Manoa repeats, "Nothing is here for tears, nothing to wail / Or knock the breast" (1721–22). The insistence on not weeping implies a deep suppressed desire to be allowed to shed tears.

Perhaps, intellectually, the Chorus and Manoa are wrong to think they know the meaning of Samson's death. We might condemn them for succumbing to the "temptation of interpretation."[43] But the emotional problem remains: how are either Manoa or the Chorus, or the reader, to feel about the events of the play? What emotions should we have, or do we have, about a bewildering and mysterious set of events? Samson's outbursts at the beginning of the drama have provided one possible answer: those who feel confused by God's plan and God's timing may, like Samson, acknowledge the intensity of their despair and express the sense of overliving. The alternative is the response of Manoa and the Chorus at the end: they insist that all events are comprehensible and that there is no need of emotions. The mind is calm, and passions are a thing of the past. *Samson Agonistes* associates all intense emotions with the sense of overliving. Emotions are to be suppressed, because they imply doubt of God's purposes. As in previous tragedies of overliving, there is a risk that the apparently exceptional experiences of the protagonist will be shared by all human beings — including the reader. Not only Samson, but everyone who contemplates the mysterious workings of God and responds emotionally to the puzzling discrepancies in human events, risks feeling that life makes no sense and goes on too long. Readers who respond emotionally to *Samson Agonistes* risk sharing Samson's feeling at the beginning of the drama, that God's ways and God's timing make no sense. Only those who suppress all emotions and all questions can avoid the sense of overliving.

The final lines of *Samson Agonistes* (1745–58) are a tetrameter sonnet, which is comparable in theme to sonnet 7. Like that early poem, the Chorus's final words are concerned with the puzzles of God's timing. But whereas sonnet 7 began with a melancholy exclamation ("How soon hath Time!"), the Chorus declares with apparent certainty, "All is best," and repeats that God's work is "ever best found at the close" (1748). The lines are troubling in their refusal to acknowledge the possibility, shown with such intense starkness by the beginning of the tragedy, that all might not always feel best; "we oft doubt" is not an adequate summary of Samson's earlier suffering. The Chorus cannot reduce to just or strict measure the ambiguities of Samson's end and his doubts about God's timing. The end of *Samson Agonistes* achieves a kind of catharsis only at the cost of changing the subject.

CHAPTER 8

"Why do I overlive?"

Paradise Lost

Paradise Lost brings together many of the strands of the tradition I have discussed so far. We see again the now familiar set of tropes and images associated with the representation of overliving: repetition and reduplication, both of individual words, of scenes and of arguments; the sense of unending shame, guilt, and pollution; the desire to be invisible and unseen; images of torture, heaviness, and the body as a burden; the loss of selfhood, order, meaning, and understanding; the presence of multiple, competing ways to understand time; the conflict between human emotions and impersonal, historical responses to them; revenge as a possible solution to overliving; regret at birth and desire for death; depictions of life as living death. It is on this last image that I concentrate in my discussion of *Paradise Lost,* since the poem provides the most extensive development of the idea that life may feel, in various ways, like death, and that death may fail to provide a true ending for life. The fallen Adam begins to realize that "death" means many things but does not mean the end. The final books of the poem are dominated by the tragic human sense of overliving. Only the last lines of book 12 begin to suggest a new possibility: that living death may itself become a kind of freedom — and not only for exceptional characters like Oedipus, but for us all.

Paradise Lost tries to supersede its models and might seem to offer a final answer to the problem of overliving. It is, after all, an epic, not a tragedy; and some critics insist that epic, particularly Christian epic, must have a happy ending.[1] The last two books include the revelation that humanity will finally take revenge on Satan and will finally be redeemed. The Paradise lost by Adam and Eve will be replaced by a new Paradise: God will make a new heaven and a new earth. Some critics find in *Paradise Lost* a suggestion of the idea that the Fall was fortunate after all, a *felix culpa*, in that it gave God the opportunity to turn all to good.[2] The loss of paradise is not the end of Milton's story; *Paradise Lost* looks forward to the Atonement and reminds the reader that human history will eventually be redeemed. From one perspective, then, Adam's question is simply a mistake, and a sinful one at that. The archangel Michael implies that Adam was wrong to be mistrustful of God's plan, and wrong to think that he had lived too long; rather, as Michael's historical revelations make clear, he has not lived long enough. Moreover, the poem reminds the reader that time itself will end; in the eyes of eternity, it makes no sense even to think in terms of "too long" or "too short."

But like earlier tragic texts, *Paradise Lost* does not entirely repress the sense of overliving. Instead, the poem provides alternative, nonhuman ways of thinking about time — through history, or *sub specie aeternatis*. These offer intellectual and moral correctives to Adam's question, but they do not provide an emotional release. Nor do the final books provide a clear endorsement of the view that the Fall led ultimately to good.[3] Rather, they emphasize the misery of postlapsarian human life, the sense of loss, and the feeling that life goes on too long.[4] The subjective experience of history after the Fall, imagined from the point of view of those who have to endure it, will be mostly wretched and will constantly seem too long — even if, from some standpoint beyond humanity, it is not. The reader can escape this feeling only by ignoring the human emotions the poem evokes, and also by ignoring his or her own reading experience.[5] Human history will inevitably seem slow to those who inhabit it, because after the Fall all human action will be merely a repetition of the actions of *Paradise Lost*. All actions will either reenact the first disobedience or correct it through humble prayer, echoing Adam and Eve's repentance, or through staunch refusal to be tempted, echoing Abdiel's stand against the fallen angels in book 6. The reader's desire for narrative rather than mere repetition is frustrated by books 11 and 12. We are made to experience the painful fact that nothing new can happen until the end of time.

Milton alters the traditional representation of overliving in ways that mostly make it seem not less painful but more so. *Paradise Lost*, far more than any previous text discussed in this study, expresses anxiety about the moral and theological implications of tragic overliving. If never to be born is best, perhaps parents are responsible for the suffering of their children and descendants; and perhaps God is responsible for the pain of the human race. Tragic overliving threatens the narrator's attempt to justify the ways of God to man.

The poem implies several alternative ways of understanding its own narrative. The epic or historical visions of Michael and of God are set against Adam's tragic despair. The same subject matter is viewed as either epic or tragic, depending on one's point of view. In the invocation to book 9 we are told,

> I now must change
> Those notes to tragic; foul distrust, and breach
> Disloyal on the part of man, revolt,
> And disobedience: on the part of heaven
> Now alienated, distance and distaste,
> Anger and just rebuke, and judgment given,
> That brought into this world a world of woe,
> Sin and her shadow Death, and Misery
> Death's harbinger: sad task, yet argument
> Not less but more heroic than the wrath
> Of stern Achilles on his foe pursued.
> (9.5–15)[6]

Within the very same sentence in which the narrator declares that his notes will be changed to "tragic," we are also told that his is a "sad task, yet argument / Not less but more heroic than the wrath / Of stern Achilles." "Heroic" (epic) and "tragic" are apparently incompatible generic categories, but as soon as the poet claims that his model is tragedy, he turns to his epic or "heroic" models — the *Iliad*, the *Aeneid*, the *Odyssey* (and then, in 29–41, romance) — and shows how his own work surpasses all of them.[7] The narrator seems to slide away from his tragic pretensions almost as soon as he declares them.[8] But Milton's epic draws heavily on the tragic tradition and includes tragic elements that cast a shadow over the final books. Tragic "notes" are struck in *Paradise Lost* which continue to resonate beyond their proper time.[9]

One could associate the problem of overliving in the poem with the tension between the epic as we have it and the tragedy on the Fall of Man that Milton originally intended to write.[10] Perhaps the dramatic version would have been more closely modeled on *Macbeth* — an obvious tragic model for a narrative about the aftermath of sin.[11] But even the epic narrative contains obvious parallels with classical and Shakespearean tragedy. Once he knows the truth, Oedipus wants never to see his parents or be seen by the world, just as Adam longs to hide himself from the face of his father, God. Adam's decision to go on living is as tragic as the choice of Euripides' Heracles to live on after his fall into a horror deeper than hell.

The two competing genres, tragedy and epic, reflect two distinct ways of understanding the narrative of *Paradise Lost*, which correspond to the different perspectives of the human and the heavenly characters. From God's point of view, Milton's poem is an epic about wrath: "On the part of heaven / Now alienated, distance and distaste, / Anger, and just rebuke, and judgment given." Epic is associated specifically with anger in the invocation to book 9.[12] The Fall of Man is an epic story "on the part of heaven" (9.9) because for heaven, the Fall brings "anger and just rebuke and judgement given" (9.10). But for man, the story is about the origins of suffering, a story that involves death and woe — and is therefore tragic. So there is a generic conflict in the narrative of the poem, which corresponds to a dual temporal scheme, the human and the divine. From God's epic perspective, the ultimate end of human history will not come until the Apocalypse, when time will give way to "ages of endless date" (12.549). But Adam tends to understand his life, and human history in general, as a tragedy in which the proper moment for action and for death has already passed, and in which all that remains is dead time.

God's epic narrative competes with two tragic plots in *Paradise Lost*. As many critics have suggested, *Paradise Lost* conflates multiple different genres, including not only epic but also pastoral, history, romance, and tragedy — of two different kinds.[13] The story of Satan is associated both with pagan epic and with tragedies of damnation and of revenge.[14] The tragedy of Adam and Eve is a tragedy of overliving. Adam's Complaint (10.720–844), which marks him for the first time as a tragic character, invites comparison with Satan's great soliloquy at the beginning of book 4 (32–113). Adam's "sea of passion" (10.718) recalls Satan's "passion" (4.114).[15] Satan finds himself embroiled in contradictions that plunge him deeper and deeper into self-damnation, "and in the lowest deep a lower deep" (4.76), while Adam exclaims at the end of his speech, "O conscience! into what abyss of fears / And horrors hast thou driven me; out of which / I find no way, from deep to deeper plunged!" (10.842–44). The echoes of Satan may suggest that the tragic soliloquy is the linguistic mark of all fallenness.[16] But the story of

Adam's Fall and its aftermath is tragic in a different way from the story of Satan. Adam shows his capacity for redemption by the fact that he ends not, like Satan, with resolutions of revenge but with a moment of *aporia:* "I find no way."[17] He leaves room for an appeal to God, who is "the Way, the Truth and the Light." Satan momentarily imagines acknowledging his own sin and turning to God: "But say I could repent . . ." (4.93). But he immediately dismisses the thought: the original sin would only repeat itself because he could never eliminate his own abhorrence at God's authority.

Satan's soliloquies recall particularly Marlowe's Dr. Faustus and Shakespeare's villains.[18] His tragedy is associated both with damnation and with revenge. Satan's suffering is in a different temporal mode from that of Adam: he wants to undo or frustrate God's original works of Creation and the promotion of the Son. He does not want to put an end to himself, but to give himself a new beginning, of his own making. Even when he comes closest to wanting to unwrite his own story, he dreams not of nonexistence but of a life in a different role, as "some inferior angel":

> O had his powerful destiny ordained
> Me some inferior angel, I had stood
> Then happy; no unbounded hope had raised
> Ambition.
> (4.58–61)

There is an important difference between the desire to have been born as a more lowly creature and the desire never to have lived at all.[19] Satan never imagines that he has lived too long. He has not lost his true role; rather, his true role is itself the source of his sufferings, because in a world ruled by God, it is hell to be Satan. Insofar as God has always held power, Satan has never had access to anything but "eternal woe" (4.70). He resents above all the fact that it was God who made him and not himself. Satan wants, repeatedly, to make a new beginning, first in Hell, and then in the "new world" of earth (4.113); and he will do it by taking revenge. He suffers because he is unable to control his own origins.[20] By contrast, Adam suffers because he is unable to control his own ends. The tragedy of Adam and of his descendants is therefore a tragedy of overliving.[21]

The tragedy of Adam is both more central to the poem than that of Satan and more threatening to the attempt to "justify the ways of God to man."[22] Critics have often suggested that the power, dignity, and emotional intensity of Satan in the early books of the poem steal much of God's thunder. Blake famously declared that "the reason Milton wrote in fetters when he wrote of Angels & God, and at liberty when of Devils & Hell, is because he was a true Poet and of the Devils party without knowing it."[23]

Some critics have reversed Blake's terms, suggesting that Milton can be a true poet only if he is not of the devil's party — as if metaphysical consistency and literary greatness were coextensive.[24] *Paradise Lost* is and remains of interest even to those who do not share Milton's theological beliefs, both because of the beauty of its language and because of its intense and often unresolved struggle with issues that matter, such as freedom, power, love, knowledge, and unhappiness. Many critics since Blake have argued that Milton's sympathy for the devil undermines his attempt to "justify the ways of God to man"; studies of Satan, Eve, Chaos, and Milton's representation of the physical universe have shown that there are elements in the poem that seem to contradict God's order and God's story.[25] Whereas these approaches show the intellectual tensions in Milton's depiction of the universe, my focus on Adam's sense of overliving draws attention to the conflict between the large and impersonal visions of history and the emotional world of the individual — between the story seen from some external perspective and the story as it feels to those who live it. I hope to defend a reading of the poem that is in some ways close to that of Romantic readers such as Blake, not in concentrating on Satan but in taking seriously both the emotions it depicts and those which it arouses in the reader.[26]

The tragic situation of Adam and his descendants is far more threatening to the epic drive of the narrative than that of Satan. Satan's plots become incorporated into God's plans, and Satan himself becomes less and less attractive as the poem goes on. Adam's sense of overliving is not, like Satan's rebellion, based on deliberate denial or rejection of reality. Satan refuses to acknowledge his inferiority to God or the Son and, even after his Fall, refuses to accept defeat and recognize his own responsibility. He is trapped in a cycle of repetition because he cannot acknowledge what he has done or what he is. Adam, by contrast, soon becomes aware of what he has done; but this realization is not a final cure for misery. His unhappiness is a response to reality, to what he gradually learns about death and life after the Fall. *Paradise Lost* suggests that although all will, in the very long run, turn out well, the long time of waiting for the end will feel repetitious, bewildering, and often wretchedly unhappy for those who have to live through it.

Some critics have acknowledged that the story of postlapsarian man is tragic but suggested that it is a "Christian tragedy" that results in a final catharsis, in the manifestation of God's grace at the end of book 10.[27] But this is to neglect the tragic mode of the next two books of the poem, which present Christian history as no less depressing and apparently endless than pagan tragedy. We are assured that there will be a final triumph, the seed of Adam and Eve will bruise the heel of Satan, and humanity will enter eternity. But our feelings are directed toward the repetitive in-between time, after the Fall and before the Second Coming—the timer that we all inhabit, and the time that will feel, for all of us, too long.

My reading of *Paradise Lost* puts at the poem's center the emotions of the human characters, especially those of Adam, and suggests that Adam's feelings shape those of the reader. The debate about whether there are contradictions in the world vision of *Paradise Lost* has concentrated on intellectual issues, such as conflicts between divine omnipotence and human freedom;[28] it has dealt relatively little with the tensions between what we are told to think and how we are led to feel.[29] I argue that the emotional effect of *Paradise Lost* is tragic. The reader's sympathy with the fallen Adam, and sense of gloom at the final books of the poem, cannot be dismissed as simply a mark of his or her own fallenness, or as a conscious strategy on Milton's part to test the reader's moral progress.[30] We cannot choose to reject Adam's emotional responses, except by abandoning or losing our connection with the human characters of the poem. Neither the reader nor the narrator can be free from the implications of Michael's account of human history. Milton himself was often overwhelmed by political and moral disillusionment after the failure of the English republic. Michael's revelations show a world that constantly repeats the pattern of recent English history seen through Miltonic eyes: the people fail to listen to the one just man and lapse again into bondage. Human despair dominates the last books of the poem.

Both characters and readers want true action and final endings. The final books of *Paradise Lost* mourn the impossibility of either.[31] All action after the Fall and before the Apocalypse will be mere repetition; and final closure to human life is impossible within the universe of Milton's God. The poem is haunted by the desire for death as a true ending, which must always remain out of reach. Death appears as an allegorical figure and is constantly mentioned both by God and the Son and by Adam and Eve; the poem presents death in a multitude of different guises. But literal death as the true and total end of human life and human suffering can never come until the end of time. The final lines of the poem suggest that the only way to become reconciled to living death is to imitate the qualities of Death itself—a solution that makes the emotions of Adam and Eve finally inaccessible to the reader.[32]

As soon as he sees what he has done, Adam longs to hide himself and his actions. Tragic overliving is often associated with the desire to be covered or blind. Those who have experienced horrors often feel polluted and want to hide their actions from others — and, if it were possible, from themselves. Oedipus puts out his eyes; Heracles covers himself in his cloak; King Lear sees his own mental blindness in the eyes of Gloucester; Macbeth wants the stars to hide their fires. Samson complains most of loss of sight, but he is also grateful to blindness, for hiding his shame (*Samson Agonistes* 195–202). In all these cases, the desire to be hidden inevitably fails; these characters must go on living without the possibility of complete darkness to hide what they have done. Similarly, after the Fall, Adam longs to hide himself and "in solitude live savage" (9.1085). He movingly appeals to the trees to hide him from the faces "of God or angel" (9.1081): "Cover me ye pines, / Ye cedars, with innumerable boughs / Hide me, where I may never see them more" (9.1088–90). Adam longs to be both unseeing and unseen. His interlocking, incantatory repetitions ("Cover me . . . Hide me," "ye pines / Ye cedars") suggest an attempt to cover himself in language, as if the comfort of words could shield him from the sight of God. The trees of the natural world offer a hope of protection from divine judgment; Adam and Eve "cover round" their "middle parts" (9.1096–97) in the hope of hiding their uncleanness and hide themselves among "the thickest trees" (10.101) to escape the Son's presence when he comes to pass sentence. But these coverings can do nothing to protect them from God's sight, and the fact he knows that he is naked is itself a proof that Adam is fallen (10.121–23). Adam and Eve are covered by the Son's mercy, clothed and protected from the Father's anger (10.211–23), but they cannot hide from God entirely or evade the recognition that they have brought death into the world.

When the Son has passed sentence on fallen humanity, Adam surveys the ruin of his world and wonders why he remains alive. His long Complaint (10.720–844) is one of the most important passages of the poem.[33] He asks,

> Why delays
> His hand to execute what his decree
> Fixed on this day? Why do I overlive,
> Why am I mocked with death, and lengthened out
> To deathless pain? How gladly would I meet
> Mortality my sentence, and be earth
> Insensible, how glad would lay me down

As in my mother's lap? There I should rest
And sleep secure; his dreadful voice no more
Would thunder in my ears, no fear of worse
To me and to my offspring would torment me
With cruel expectation.

(10.771–82)

Adam feels he has lived too long for two reasons: because he no longer wants to live, and because he thinks God promised or threatened that death would be the result of eating the apple. He repeatedly slips between the two, conflating his desires with God's word, and vice versa. Adam is puzzled that he is not already dead. He longs for death as a final ending; only very gradually does he begin to realize that "death" has many different meanings and that he is already experiencing a kind of living death. His sense of overliving arises from a mismatch between his own sense of the proper time for his life to end and God's quite different narrative structure.

Book 10 has shown the effects of the Fall in Heaven, in Hell, and in nature: now we begin to see the full impact of what has happened on humanity.[34] As Adam surveys the environmental and moral damage done to Earth by the Fall, he is dismayed, seeing "the growing miseries" of the world outside him (10.715), "but worse felt within" (10.717). He is in "a sea of passion" (10.718), and his speech fluctuates between complaint against God and self-reproach. Adam clutches at a series of possible endings to his emotional turmoil, but his hopes are frustrated again and again. He begins by asking, "Is this the end?" (10.720). But he continues with a long series of questions. This is not the end "of this new glorious world," though it will now no longer be new or glorious. Adam implies that the lack of ending is the worst thing he has to suffer. Happiness has ended, and yet there is no end to life.

The speech itself can find no resolution. Multiple voices and points of view argue with one another, but none conclusively wins the debate. Adam begins (10.720–25) with an outcry at the contrast between the glorious beginnings of his life and his world, and its present ruin. The bitterness of the question, "Is this the end?" implies that God has betrayed both the world and Adam in letting things come to this. But Adam instantly corrects such an implication, reminding himself (10.726): "I deserved it." Again, after questioning God's purpose in making him in the first place, he answers himself: "[Y]et to say truth, too late, / I thus contest" (10.755–56). Adam addresses himself in the second person, ventriloquizing

God's voice to accuse himself of quarreling unfairly with God's terms: "[T]hou didst accept them" (10.758). He switches to yet another voice to address himself as his own potential son, who asks, "wherefore didst thou beget me?" (10.762). There are more than twenty separate questions in the speech, and no conclusive answers at all.

The multiple shifting perspectives are marked syntactically by a dizzying number of adversative conjunctions and adversative prepositions. As soon as Adam adopts one position, he immediately corrects it with a "yet" or a "but." The end of the world might seem undesirable: "yet well, if here would end / The misery" (10.725–26). Adam wants to take full responsibility for what he has done: "But this will not serve" (10.727), "for what can I increase or multiply / But curses on my head?" (10.731–32). His descendants will curse him sarcastically, "for this we may thank Adam" (10.736). Adam reproaches God for his own creation, but then corrects himself: "[Y]et to say truth, too late / I thus contest" (10.755–56). He makes an analogy with his own putative son, who would be wrong to reproach Adam for his birth; and yet the analogy does not hold: "Yet him not thy election / But natural necessity begot" (10.764–65). Adam submits to God's punishment and longs for death, yet even death may be no true ending: "Yet one doubt / Pursues me still, lest all I cannot die" (10.782–83). "Yet why?" (10.789), he asks; death will surely kill the whole man. But God is infinite; but "be it, man is not so, / But mortal doomed" (10.795–96).

But then he realizes that perhaps the sentence of mortality is to be read not literally but metaphorically: "But say / That death be not one stroke, as I supposed, / Bereaving sense, but endless misery" (10.808–10). Adam shifts the subject again as he realizes all his sons are cursed. The direction changes yet again as he corrects himself, realizing that no son of his could be innocent: "But from me what can proceed, / But all corrupt, both mind and will depraved, / Not to do only, but to will the same / With me?" (10.824–27). The speech seems about to end with an acknowledgment of his own total guilt. He acquits God of all responsibility, in what seems like a final gesture of self-condemnation. "Him after all disputes / Forced I absolve" (10.828–29), he says, and admits that he is solely to blame: "All my evasions vain, / And reasonings, though through mazes, lead me still / But to my own conviction" (10.828–31). Adam tries to end his bewilderment at God's sentence by imposing a final "conviction" on himself.

But "after all disputes" turns out to have been precipitate. Adam is not yet ready to acquiesce in God's will, if that means staying alive. He is still desperate for God to grant proper ending to his life by punishing him with death. He claims that he is the beginning and should therefore be the end of all his suffering: "First and last / On me, me only, as the source and spring / Of all corruption, all the blame lights due; / So might the wrath" (10.831–34). Adam tries to become the Alpha and the Omega, performing the Christ-like task of taking "all corruption" on himself.[35] But he is also aware that the task is beyond him. He reverts to addressing himself in the second person, and asks, "Couldst thou support / That burden heavier than the earth to bear?" (10.834–35). Adam's punishment is greater than he can bear, but—like his son Cain after him—he will not be allowed by God to die.[36] He ends by exclaiming, "O conscience! into what abyss of fears / And horrors hast thou driven me; out of which / I find no way, from deep to deeper plunged!" (10.842–44). The only conclusion Adam can reach is that he can find no conclusion, either to life or to his confusion and dismay.

Adam presents his sense of overliving as a frustrated desire for the fulfillment of God's word: "How gladly would I meet / Mortality my sentence!" (10.775–76). Death, "mortality," ought to be the immediate result of eating the forbidden fruit. The Son has just passed "sentence" on Adam, declaring that "dust thou art, and shalt to dust return" (10.208). Death is due to disobedience in the Genesis story: "And the Lord God took the man, and put him in the Garden of Eden to dress it and to keep it. And the Lord God commanded the man, saying, of every tree of the garden thou mayest freely eat. But of the tree of the knowledge of good and evil, thou shalt not eat of it: for in the day thou eatest thereof, thou shalt surely die" (Genesis 2.15–17). But the judgment passed when Adam and Eve do fall is apparently different from God's initial threat. After the Fall, Adam is told, "cursed is the ground for thy sake; in sorrow shalt thou eat of it all the days of thy life" (Genesis 3.17). Far from dying that very day, Adam is to live on and suffer for many days to come. One might be tempted to describe Adam's sense of overliving simply as a function of the gap between the two incompatible pronouncements about death from God in Genesis. Adam is a character who has to try to live in a story that makes no sense; he feels he has lived too long because he is trying to reconcile God's inconsistent "sentences."

But although Milton is committed to the Genesis narrative, he does his best to make God's story coherent. Milton's God says, when warning Adam against the Tree of Knowledge,

> The day thou eat'st thereof, my sole command
> Transgressed, inevitably thou shalt die;
> From that day mortal, and this happy state

Shalt loose, expelled from hence into a world
Of woe and sorrow.
(8.329–33)

Milton's God carefully glosses "thou shalt die" with "from that day mortal," which is not in Genesis. "Thou shalt die" does not mean that literal death will ensue as soon as Adam and Eve eat the apple, but rather that they will thenceforth be subject to mortality.[37] Adam feels he has lived too long because he takes "thou shalt die" literally, not realizing that God means it in another sense. The Father declares at the beginning of book 10 that man misunderstands the "mortal sentence" (10.48). He tells the angels,

Fallen he is, and now
What rests but that the mortal sentence pass
On his transgression, death denounced that day,
Which he presumes already vain and void,
Because not yet inflicted, as he feared,
By some immediate stroke; but soon shall find
Forbearance no acquittance ere day end.
(10.47–53)

The Father is somewhat unfair to man here, since Adam has no tendency at all to regard the sentence of death as "vain and void."[38] Adam is puzzled precisely because he assumes that death will not be vain and void, and yet there is no sign of the "immediate stroke" of death.

Adam fails to understand that "death" does not necessarily mean instantaneous and total cessation of being. In *De Doctrina Christiana* (1.12, 13, 33) Milton adopts the traditional division of death into four degrees or levels. He notes the problem of the apparently inconsistent Genesis story and proposes that "death" does not mean the same thing in Scripture as it does in ordinary language.[39]

In scripture, every evil, and everything that seems to lead to destruction, is indeed under the name of *death*. For physical death, as it is called, did not follow *on the same day* as Adam's sin, as God had threatened. So four degrees of death may conveniently be distinguished. First, as I said above, come ALL EVILS WHICH TEND TO DEATH, AND WHICH, IT IS AGREED, CAME INTO THE WORLD AS SOON AS MAN FELL.
(1.12, p. 393)

Adam is already suffering the first degree of death. Indeed, Milton explicitly associates the first degree of death with guiltiness and with conscience.[40] When Adam cries out, "O Conscience! into what abyss of fears / And horrors hast thou driven me!" (10.842–43), he is experiencing the first level of death.

Moreover, Adam has also already experienced the second degree of death, and continues to suffer from it even as he complains at the inaccessibility of mortality: "The second degree of death is called SPIRITUAL DEATH. This is the loss of that divine grace and innate righteousness by which, in the beginning, man lived with God" (*De Doctrina Christiana* 1.12, p. 394). The aftermath of the Fall has been a downward cycle into "spiritual death." After Adam and Eve eat the apple in book 9, new horrors enter their world: they flirt and make bad puns (9.1017–33); they make love in the afternoon, and sex and nakedness become, for the first time, sordid and shameful (inspired by "carnal desire," 9.1013, rather than the "wedded love" of their prelapsarian state, 4.750); they become ashamed before heaven and the angels; they begin to squabble with one another in "mutual accusation . . . but neither self-condemning" (9.1134–89). All of these are the marks of human degradation, and of the increasing "distance and distaste" between heaven and earth. Even within his Complaint, Adam is experiencing spiritual death: his inner discord is a sign of his lack of innocence.

Adam's sense of overliving is caused by the fact that he is suffering from the first and second degrees of death, and yet he is not, in any sense that he can understand, "dead." His happiness and innocence are over, but his life is not. In the course of his Complaint, Adam has glimmerings of the truth that God may have meant the pronouncement, "thou shalt surely die," in some peculiar sense. He begins to suspect that "death" may be the name for his suffering, rather than for any possible release from it. Moreover, Adam has a moment of horrible suspicion that even the third degree of death may not constitute a true ending of life. "The third degree of death is what is usually called the DEATH OF THE BODY" (*De Doctrina Christiana* 1.13, p. 399). The third degree is the most problematic, both for Adam and for Milton.

> Yet one doubt
> Pursues me still, lest all I cannot die,
> Lest that pure breath of life, the spirit of man
> Which God inspired, cannot together perish
> With this corporeal clod; then in the grave,
> Or in some other dismal place who knows

But I shall die a living death? O thought
Horrid, if true!
(10.782–89)

Adam wonders whether God could have meant by "thou shalt die" not that the whole man should die but only the body. Perhaps, then, death will be no end to his "deathless pain," "but I shall die a living death" (10.788). Adam immediately represses this "horrid" possibility.

> Yet why? It was but breath
> Of life that sinned; what dies but what had life
> And sin? The body properly hath neither.
> All of me then shall die: let this appease
> The doubt, since human reach no farther knows.
> (10.789–93)

Adam convinces himself that "death" cannot mean simply the death of the body. The whole person sinned, in eating the apple: "All of me then shall die." Adam hopes that the third degree of death, the death of both body and soul, may save him from the first two deaths, of guilt and spiritual degradation. He reasons that overliving ought not to happen, since no part of man should survive after spiritual death.

Adam has arrived by natural reason at a position that apparently anticipates Milton's own view on the third level of death, or "the death which is called the death of the body." Physical death is "called" the death of the body, but in fact, Milton believed, the whole man dies, body, spirit, and soul. He defines the third level of death as "the loss or distinction of life. For the separation of body and soul, which is the usual definition of death, cannot possibly be death at all. What part of man dies when this separation takes place? The soul? Even those who adhere to the usual definition deny that. The body? But how can that be said to die which never had any life of its own?" (*De Doctrina Christiana* 1.13, p. 400). Milton's position on the third level of death identifies him as a Mortalist.[41] The overlap between Adam's theory and Milton's own beliefs might seem disturbing, since Adam is prompted to theological correctness by his un-Christian despair. But Adam's position is not identical with Milton's. Adam has not heard Michael's revelations about the Resurrection of the dead, nor has he had the advantage of reading the Bible—unlike Milton and the reader. He is therefore vulnerable to the extreme and heretical position of annihilationism.[42] He assumes that those who die will remain dead, and there an end: he does not know that they rise again. He asks, "Can he make deathless death?" (10.798), and dismisses the question at once: "That were to make / Strange contradiction, which to God himself / Impossible is held" (10.798–800). This is a moment of dramatic irony, since readers know that God will make an even stranger contradiction and give "Death his death's wound" (3.252).

God's utterances on the subject of death in *Paradise Lost* are always paradoxical, because they play with the idea that Death itself will die, when "death is swallowed up in victory" at the Last Day (1 Corinthians 15.54). The only level of death that will be made "deathless" is the fourth: eternal damnation.[43] All of the first three levels of death can be followed by new rebirths. Adam feels that his life is now, like Samson's, "a life half dead, a living death" (*Samson Agonistes* 100). He longs not for rebirth but for total death; he does not yet even consider the possibility his dead part may be restored to new life.

Toward the end of his Complaint, Adam begins to see that he is already suffering from the first and second levels of death: he is already dying a "living death." Prompted presumably by grace rather than reason — since he gives no reason — he says,

> But say
> That death be not one stroke, as I supposed,
> Bereaving sense, but endless misery
> From this day onward, which I feel begun
> Both in me, and without me, and so last
> To perpetuity; ay me, that fear
> Comes thundering back with dreadful revolution
> On my defenceless head; both death and I
> Am found eternal, and incorporate both.
> (10.808–16)

Death is "incorporate," and it is therefore impossible to "meet mortality" in the way Adam hoped he could. Adam is beginning to acknowledge the empirical fact that "death" does not, in God's world, mean the end of human life. But the realization is no comfort to him. Annihilationism posits a "level" of death that is unavailable within Milton's Christian theology, but Adam still longs for it.

The problem of living death in *Paradise Lost* is made more difficult by the presence of Death as an allegorical character in the poem. Adam longs to "meet / Mortality my sentence," and Satan literally "meets mortality" when he makes his way up from Hell at the end of book 2. But it is a meeting that only increases death's obscurity and intensifies the sense that death is a condition of life, not its end. Death makes his first physical appearance in the poem at line 666, the number of the Beast in Revelation (13.18). But the literal manifestation of Death is a kind of antirevelation. Death evades descriptions and even shape:

> The other shape,
> If shape it might be called that shape had none
> Distinguishable in member, joint or limb,
> Or substance might be called that shadow seemed,
> For each seemed either.
> (2.666–70)

The description is the opposite of a definition: it defines Death only by his indefiniteness. This Death makes impossible even the ordinary usage of descriptive language, since he is a "shape" that cannot properly be "called" either "shape" or "substance," and which has no "distinguishable" features at all. Satan tries to attack this hideous monster, but Sin intervenes, telling him that Death is his own son. The meeting between Satan and Death is thus intercepted, and we are told that "never but once more was either like / To meet so great a foe" (2.721–22). Satan's ultimate meeting with mortality is deferred. The materialization of Death in the poem oddly serves to make our understanding of the concept "death" far less solid than it was before.[44] God uses the words "die" and "Death" to threaten man with an unknown, incomprehensible horror; the more often the words "death" and "die" are repeated, the less clear their meaning becomes.[45] Adam will never be able to "meet" mortality in any final sense.

It has been suggested that Milton deliberately creates multiple allegorical and metaphorical meanings for "death" in *Paradise Lost*, in order to obscure the desirability of literal death as true ending.[46] But if so, the tactic backfires, because if death can be read in all kinds of ways, it can be seen either as something bad or as something good. Satan uses Eve's inability to imagine death to remove her fear of it. He tells her that he has eaten the fruit without fear of death, "whatever thing death be" (9.695). He offers a new interpretation of the threatened "death": "So shall ye die perhaps, by putting off / Human, to put on gods, death to be wished" (9.713–14). Eve uses the illegibility of God's sentence of death as a reason to avoid reading that sentence at all. She concedes the possibility that death may be a good thing, when she asks, "What fear I then, rather, what know to fear / Under this ignorance of good and evil, / Of God or death, of law or penalty?"

(9.773–75). Eve denies that she "knows" even that death is bad and God is good. God's refusal to give a definite sense to the word "death" leaves open the possibility for a sinful reading of the term that removes from it all terror.

Adam is prone to feel that the proper moment for death has already happened, whereas God defers the moment of death indefinitely. Adam's belief after the Fall that he has lived too long is structurally similar to his decision to eat the apple in the first place. In both cases, he has a sense of an overdue ending that is, from God's perspective, premature. Adam believes too soon that the time of death has already arrived. Like Lear and Macbeth, he believes his life is already over before it has actually ended, and thereby precipitates his ruin.[47] As in *Macbeth*, the premature sense of overliving is the cause of sin: Adam, like Macbeth, is inclined to forget that he still has moral choices to make.

When Eve appears after eating the apple, Adam lets fall the bouquet of flowers he had gathered for her: it "down dropped, and all the faded roses shed" (9.893). The alliterative *d*'s of the faded roses mark the first death in Paradise, while the internal rhyme of the line ("faded roses shed") draws attention to the submerged word: "dead." But the death ought to belong to Eve, not her husband. Adam, however, acts as if it is he who is already dead now that Eve has fallen. His reaction is like a death: he "Astonied stood and blank, while horror chill / Ran through his veins, and all his joints relaxed" (9.890–91).[48] In his meditation to himself before he speaks to her (9.896–916) he acknowledges that in choosing to eat the apple with her, he is choosing death: "[F]or with thee / Certain my resolution is to die" (9.906–7). When he speaks to her, he adopts the comforting pretense that death may after all not ensue from fallenness, but his pronouns suggest that he does so only for her sake, not his own: "Perhaps thou shalt not die" (928), he says, not "perhaps we shall not die." But then he again reverts to the idea that "death" may after all be no bad thing, for himself in particular: "If death / Consort with thee, death is to me as life" (9.953–54). Adam is not deceived. He knows that in choosing to eat the apple, he is choosing death (unlike Eve, who "knew not eating death," 9.792). But Adam also knows that he loves Eve, and he chooses to be with his "consort," even if the third party in the marriage is death. He regards his own death as inevitable once Eve has fallen and is therefore condemned to die. Adam feels that he has already in some sense suffered death and therefore he eats the apple, knowing, unlike Eve, that in doing so he is "eating death."[49] Adam feels that he has already tasted death; eating the apple fulfills an action that has already been decided. Like Macbeth, he is led to sin by the feeling that the moment of death has already gone by.

Adam does not share God's perspective on time because he has a different notion of what is most important in his life. Adam feels that his relationship with Eve is a fundamental feature of his character: he declares, "to lose thee were to lose myself" (9.959). He plays the female "part" in deferring to Eve and in feeling his life to be dependent on hers rather than the other way around; God condemns him in these terms after the Fall (10.155–56). From God's point of view, Adam is wrong both about time and about gender, and the two mistakes are related. Because Adam—again like Macbeth—is prepared to defer to his wife, rather than assert his own male authority, he is also unwilling to accept that the proper time for his own death has not already passed, once Eve has fallen.

After the Fall, in his Complaint, Adam is still more convinced that he has already passed the proper time to die, and again his sense that the time to die has already happened is associated with a privileging of feminine over masculine authority. Adam's desire for death is ostensibly a desire for the fulfillment of God's word. But it is also clear that the sense of overliving is incompatible with subjection to God's timing. Even as Adam claims to long for his "sentence," his language shows his desire to escape from God. He asks,

> How gladly would I meet
> Mortality my sentence, and be earth
> Insensible, how glad would lay me down
> As in my mother's lap? There I should rest
> And sleep secure; his dreadful voice no more
> Would thunder in my ears, no fear of worse
> To me and to my offspring would torment me
> With cruel expectation.
> (10.775–82)

Adam says "I" again and again in the course of the Complaint, and "God" never. His avoidance of the name of God is a symptom of his doomed desire to evade his Maker. His desire to "meet mortality" is figured as an alternative to meeting God. Adam tries to make God's "sentence" his own ("my sentence"), in his eagerness to evade God's word in its entirety, to escape "his dreadful voice" (10.779). The dreadful thing about God's voice is that it goes on and on indefinitely. There is always "more." There is an irreconcilable distance between God's "dreadful voice" (10.779), which continues forever, and the human desire for an ending. Adam feels that he has lived too long because his timing does not match that of God. He hopes for endings that are, from God's point of view, premature.

God may "draw out" His sentence (10.801), "extend" it (10.804) "beyond dust and nature's law." In God's world, Adam will remain on death row indefinitely. Adam therefore hopes to align himself instead with "dust and nature's law." If Adam can define himself in terms not of his immortal father but of his mother earth, then a true ending is appropriate and due to him; he ought to revert to dust and nature, dust to dust. The alternative legal system that allows the possibility of a true ending is distinctly feminine. Adam's position, lying on the ground, recalls the Petrarchan starved lover.[50] As at the Fall, he is "fondly overcome with female charm" (9.999). The masculine paternal authority of God and his "dreadful voice" is evaded in favor of "mortality my sentence" and the comforting figure of "my mother's lap."

Adam implies that it is not he who has failed to know himself "aright" but God who has failed to play his proper part. Immediately after his long Complaint, we are given another account of Adam's sense of overliving, which repeats the same unresolved tension between bitter reproach against God for creating him, against Death for failing to appear, and against himself for his own sin:

> On the ground
> Outstretched he lay, on the cold ground, and oft
> Cursed his creation, death as oft accused
> Of tardy execution, since denounced
> The day of his offence. Why comes not death,
> Said he, with one thrice acceptable stroke
> To end me? Shall truth fail to keep her word,
> Justice divine not hasten to be just?
> But death comes not at call, justice divine
> Mends not her slowest pace for prayers or cries.
> O woods, O fountains, hillocks, dales and bowers,
> With other echo late I taught your shades
> To answer, and resound far other song.
> (10.850–62)

Adam lies "on the ground, / On the cold ground," trying to approach the earth, the element associated with melancholy.[51] Like Job, he curses the day of his birth or, rather, of his "creation." But Adam has none of Job's steadfast refusal to abandon his trust in God. He shields himself from accusing God of faithlessness directly; instead he condemns feminized abstractions who stand in for the absent father figure of God: "Shall truth fail to keep her word, / Justice divine not hasten to be just?" (10.856–57). This second passage parallels the Complaint and thereby enacts Adam's failure to discover any way out of his predicament.[52] Adam implies that his pastoral songs of praise could be sung only in a state of innocence. He longs for the lost time when he could "resound far other song." In a fallen world of woe, to which it would have been better never to have been born, no song can justify the ways of God to man.

In books 11 and 12, Michael will reveal to Adam the destiny of his children. But before he is granted the angelic vision, Adam has to decide to live and beget children. He must eliminate or repress his sense that his life has already gone on too long and that it would be better for him never to have been made. He moves away from his intense sense of overliving in the course of an argument with his wife. As he lies on the ground, "thus afflicted" (10.863), Eve appears. Even her presence makes it easier for Adam to resign himself to the sense that he has lived too long.[53] Adam produces a long and irrelevant misogynistic outburst (10.867–908), reformulating his wish that he had never been born into a wish that women had never existed.[54] Eve suggests the solution Adam will finally adopt: repentance and prayer. She declares that she will take all the burden of punishment on herself: she will return to "the place of judgment" and

> There with my cries importune heaven, that all
> The sentence from thy head removed may light
> On me, sole cause to thee of all this woe,
> Me me only just object of his ire.
> (10.934–37)

Eve's declaration that she is "sole cause" and that God's anger should fall only on "me me" echoes Adam's claim in his Complaint that "all the blame lights due" on himself, "on me, me only" (10.832–33). Both these human moments of self-condemnation also echo the Son's declaration that he is willing to sacrifice himself for humanity, in 3.236.[55] The echo may show the egotism of Adam and Eve, in their self-aggrandizing belief that they are capable of shouldering full responsibility for the Fall. But it also shows that both are willing to sacrifice themselves for others, with a generosity parallel to that of the Son. Adam wishes he could take all the punishment on himself and protect his children, and Eve wishes she could take it all and protect both the children and Adam.

But Adam initially sees nothing admirable in Eve's self-sacrificial gesture, despite the fact that it echoes his own. He immediately rejects her proposal, and reproves her as "Unwary, and too desirous, as before, / So now of what thou know'st not, who desir'st / The punishment all on thy self" (19.947–49). Instead, they must accept their shared "woe" and work out how to live commodiously, lightening each other's burden. Adam is, like Samson, emboldened by his rejection of his wife. He becomes confident enough to speak to her as if he has finally resolved the question of what death is. For the first time, he uses not questions but statements and imperatives; for the first time, he presents overliving as a condition that must be accepted as inevitable:

> Since this day's death denounced, if aught I see,
> Will prove no sudden but a slow-paced evil,
> A long day's dying to augment our pain,
> And to our seed (O hapless seed!) derived.
> (10.962–65)

Adam is now prepared to accept the idea of life as a "long day's dying." Living is only dying in slow motion, but it is the inevitable destiny not only for Adam and Eve but also for their "hapless seed." The only possible thing to do, then, is to make the best of a disastrously bad situation.

Eve's speech in reply (10.967–1006) takes up Adam's suggestion that they should consider "how we may lighten / Each other's burden in our share of woe" (10.960–61). Like Dalila, Eve develops the idea that "life yet hath many solaces" (*Samson Agonistes* 915). She accepts Adam's assumptions that he and she have lived too long and that it will be better for all their descendants never to be born. But she is ready also to consider how they may lighten the burden, not only for each other, as Adam had implied, but also for the "hapless seed." Adam and Eve have to confront the possibility that, after the Fall, life will be horrible not only for themselves but also for all their descendants. Eve assumes that the only way these children can escape from "certain woe" is by never being born at all. Her first proposal is therefore that they should practice sexual abstinence. But she acknowledges that this is likely to be too "hard," "with desire to languish without hope / Before the present object languishing / With like desire" (10.995–97). Eve refuses to wait for what she wants, whether that be sex or death, and rather than languish in desire she proposes suicide: "Let us seek death, or he not found, supply / With our own hands his office on ourselves" (10.1001–2). Eve implies that suicide, as the most effective form of family planning, is the only responsible policy for the potential parents of the human race.

Adam in his Complaint raises the possibility that a son might ask, "Wherefore didst thou beget me? I sought it not" (10.762). But he instantly dismisses the question as mere cheek. Eve brings the question up again but from the father's perspective. She argues that Adam has a responsibility to his children not to beget them:

> If care of our descent perplex us most,
> Which must be born to certain woe, devoured
> By death at last, and miserable it is
> To be to others cause of misery,
> Our own begotten, and of our loins to bring
> Into this cursed world a woeful race,
> That after wretched life must be at last
> Food for so foul a monster, in thy power
> It lies, yet ere conception to prevent
> The race unblest, to being yet unbegot.
> (10.979–88)

Eve's refusal to "bring / Into this cursed world a woeful race" echoes the very beginning of the poem, in which we were told that the tree's "mortal taste / Brought death into the world and all our woe" (1.2–3). Her language associates all postlapsarian life with tragedy, since the narrator changed his "notes to tragic" in order to describe the moment "That brought into this world a world of woe / Sin and her shadow death, and Misery / Death's harbinger" (9.11–13).[56]

The invocation to book 9 associates three elements with tragedy, the three things "brought into the world" at the Fall: sin, death, and suffering. But in books 9–12 the relationship between the three elements becomes less and less clear. "Misery" is said in book 9 to be "Death's harbinger" (9.13); but, of course, Adam and Eve's problem after the Fall is that death fails to follow misery. It has become unclear whether death is a punishment for sin or a desirable end to a "world of woe."

Eve's solution to the problem of overliving is Stoic. She thinks it is unnecessary for anyone to live too long, since death is always in our power. She reminds Adam, "in thy power / It lies" (10.986–87).[57] But Eve goes much further than Seneca, since it is not only his own life that Adam holds in his power but also that of the whole future race. Her suggestion conflates the ideas of suicide and sexual abstinence with euthanasia.[58] Eve speaks in the language of a Thyestean banquet: the "woeful race" of future humanity will be "food for so foul a monster" (10.986)—which might make us suspicious that her proposal is associated with a monstrous and tragic paedophagia.[59] But Eve is proposing a way to avoid such a banquet, by avoiding all tragic "woe," either Senecan or Sophoclean. If the human race is never born at all, "death shall be deceived his glut" (10.990). Eve suggests a way of preventing tragedy and also preventing the generation of the poem itself. *Paradise Lost* is an etiological work, which explains how unhappiness entered the world. If Eve's suggestion could be adopted, the world need not become a "world of woe" (9.11); there need be no "woeful race" in the world at all.

Eve's proposal shifts the perspective from which overliving is understood. Up until this point, both in *Paradise Lost* and in the earlier literary tradition, overliving has been represented as a tragic problem only for those who feel that they themselves have lived too long or that they should never have been born. Now, human suffering is seen from the perspective of the father whose responsibility it is to ensure that he brings only good lives into being. She tells Adam, "in thy power it lies," presenting it as entirely Adam's decision whether to produce children and perpetuate the human race. But Eve's emphasis on fatherhood (rather than parenting, including mother and father) also introduces an implicit analogy between Adam and God. If it is doubtful whether Adam should beget children, there also lurks behind in Adam and Eve's debate a still more disturbing thought: perhaps God Himself was wrong to father the human race.

For the time being, Adam represses the question of a father's responsibility to prevent overliving. He refuses even to consider whether he might be wrong to beget children, let alone whether God might have been wrong to produce humanity. The mirror of Eve's despair allows Adam to reject his own. He adopts a vehemently pro-life position. He tells Eve that she is motivated not, as might appear, by "something more sublime" (10.1014), but by "anguish and regret / For loss of life and pleasure overloved" (10.1018–19). The same reproach is leveled repeatedly against Eve: she is "too desirous," or loves life and pleasure too much: even her desire for chastity or death is merely the symptom of "life and pleasure overloved." Eve's solution to the problem of overliving is unacceptable because it implies "overloving," or excessive love of the wrong things. Adam's use of the word "overloved" answers his own previous use of the word "overlive" and explains why it was misguided. Eve imagines that postlapsarian life is overliving, but only because she "overloves" the wrong objects—life and pleasure rather than God. According to Aquinas, despair springs from either sloth or lust: those who despair either give up hope of achieving the good, through sloth, or they are persuaded by excessive desire for other supposed goods not even to try to attain the true good.[60] Adam's desire to lie down and sleep in earth, his "mother's lap," was a slothful version of despair, while Eve's sense of overliving is spurred by overloving and is therefore a lustful form of despair.

Adam reminds Eve of the true ends of human life. There is an enemy still to subdue — and therefore a reason to live, for revenge. He also reminds her that they must remember both God's anger and God's grace. Adam's first argument against suicide is fear: God may prolong or worsen their sense of death-in-life if they defy Him by suicide: "[S]uch acts / Of contumacy will provoke the highest / To make death in us live" (10.1026–28). Then Adam moves to positive inducements, arguing that the contempt of life and pleasure will cut them off from hope of revenge against Satan, since according to the Son's promise, it is their children who are to crush the serpent's head (10.1029–40).[61] Finally he speaks of the goodness and mercy of God, who will "undoubtedly . . . relent" (10.1093) if they repent and humble themselves before him. The last had been Eve's suggestion in the first place.

Eve's second suggestions — that they should either practice sexual abstinence or commit suicide — are the first practical, active proposals for how to deal with life after the Fall. In his Complaint, Adam could imagine no response to postlapsarian life beyond lying on the ground waiting for the slow arrival of death. Now Adam makes a new suggestion that will allow humanity to stay alive on earth without being merely passive. They can, he suggests, improve things themselves, both by hard work and by appeal to God's grace. He says that the tempestuous sky

> bids us seek
> Some better shroud, some better warmth to cherish
> Our limbs benumbed, ere this diurnal star
> Leave cold the night, how we his gathered beams
> Reflected, may with matter sere foment,
> Or by collision of two bodies grind
> The air attrite to fire, as late the clouds
> Justling or pushed with winds rude in their shock
> Tine the slant lightning, whose thwart flame driven down
> Kindles the gummy bark of fir or pine,
> And sends a comfortable heat from far,
> Which might supply the sun: such fire to use,
> And what may else be remedy or cure
> To evils which our own misdeeds have wrought,
> He will instruct us praying, and of grace

Beseeching him, so as we need not fear
To pass commodiously this life, sustained
By him with many comforts, till we end
In dust, our final rest and native home.
(10.1067–85)

Adam here becomes a new Prometheus. He is the savior of mankind from Eve's proposal that they—or rather, we, the implied readers of the poem—not be born at all. He brings fire, not by stealing it from the gods, but by his own labor, combined with God's grace.

Adam conflates three different accounts of how to make fire: by concentrated reflection; by the grinding "collision of two bodies"; and by using fires started by lightning. Fire can be generated by using the "gathered beams" of the sun, or by rubbing bodies together, or by the "comfortable heat" from lightning fires. The three possibilities correspond to three distinct ways in which human labor can relate to heavenly grace. Either man may be entirely dependent on the fire from heaven and simply wait for the spark from heaven to fall—like using the fires started by lightning. Or he may produce what he wants entirely by his own labor, as by the "collision of two bodies." Or there may be a joint enterprise between heaven and earth, by which man "gathers" and "foments" the beams sent down from above. Adam makes no final decision among these three alternatives. He therefore leaves it unclear whether humanity after the Fall will be capable of independent action or will be entirely dependent on the "comfortable heat" of heaven. But the structure of the passage implies a movement from reliance on merely human methods to deference to God. Adam at first is full of his own ideas; he has, extraordinarily, managed to invent fire without having to be informed about it by an angelic teacher. But by the end of the passage, he implies that he will need the instruction of God even to make fire ("he will instruct us praying"), and will certainly need divine teaching to produce any other "remedy or cure" for the sufferings of postlapsarian life.

Adam's willingness to acknowledge dependence on God is important, not least because it is the only respect in which his response to fallenness differs from that of the devils. Adam and Eve's debate about what to do after the human Fall parallels the devils' debate in book 2 about what to do after their own fall from Heaven.[62] Their various proposals map precisely onto those of the different speakers in the infernal conference: Moloc, Belial, Mammon, and Beelzebub. The similarity challenges the reader to distinguish the conversation in book 10 from that in book 2, and to identify the differences between demonic and human responses to fallenness, if any. The challenge for Adam and Eve is to find a solution to the sense of overliving that is different from the various solutions imagined by their infernal counterparts — and, hence, one that will feel like a real solution, not mere repetition.

In the devils' debate, Moloc is the first speaker after Satan. He declares: "My sentence is for open war" (2.51). He assumes that they now have nothing left to lose and are therefore free to attack heaven openly. Moloc's wager imagines only two possible outcomes to a renewed war with heaven. Either God will obliterate the devils, in which case they will exchange eternal misery for extinction; or else they will survive to plague God through eternity, "which if not victory, is yet revenge" (2.105). When Adam has abandoned the hope of death as total extinction, he, too, turns to the possibility of revenge, arguing that they must live and beget children to take revenge on Satan.

The other arguments that Adam gives for staying alive sound strikingly similar to those of other devils in book 2, Belial, Mammon, and Beelzebub. Belial rejects Moloc's proposal on the grounds that it is too dangerous; he fears God's possible retribution. Adam, similarly, rejects Eve's suggestions on the grounds that they are too risky because God may take revenge. He tells her to remember "his vengeful ire" (10.1026) and instead urges "some safer resolution" (10.1029). Adam's emphasis on safety echoes Mammon's suggestion that the devils consider "how in safety best we may / Compose our present evils" (2.280–81). Adam, like Mammon, thinks he must make the best of being in the horrible world in which they now find themselves. He urges Eve to count her blessings and to remember that things might have been worse. He reminds her,

> We expected
> Immediate dissolution, which we thought
> Was meant by death that day, when lo, to thee
> Pains only in child-bearing were foretold,
> And bringing forth, soon recompensed with joy,
> Fruit of thy womb: on me the curse aslope
> Glanced on the ground, with labour I must earn
> My bread; what harm? Idleness had been worse.
> (10.1048–55).

Both Belial and Mammon, too, had reminded the other devils that things could have been worse. Belial asked, "Is this then worse, / Thus sitting, thus consulting, thus in arms?" (2.163–64). He reminded them how much worse it was when they fled "pursued and struck / With heaven's afflicting thunder" (2.165–66), and how much worse things might be, were He to "arm again / His red right hand to plague us" (2.173–74). Mammon suggested that even returning to heaven would be worse—it would be a return to servitude in which they would have to worship God again "and to his Godhead sing / Forced hallelujahs" (2.242–43).

After Belial's speech recommending passivity in relation to heaven, Mammon advocates a positive acceptance of Hell. Adam, similarly, moves from advocating revenge (like Moloc, the first devilish speaker), to urging resignation to their present conditions, which might have been so much worse (like Belial who speaks after Moloc), to suggesting that he and Eve devise technological improvements to their material conditions—which is what Mammon suggests. Mammon proposes that practical innovation can make an apparently unlivable place seem bearable. He says that the devils can "in what place so e'er / Thrive under evil, and work ease out of pain / Through labour and indurance" (2.260–62). Mammon suggests that they try to make the best of postlapsarian life by scientific advances. They can exploit the natural resources of Hell to make light, parallel to the light of Heaven:

> As he our darkness, cannot we his light
> Imitate when we please? This desert soil
> Wants not her hidden lustre, gems and gold;
> Nor want we skill or art, from whence to raise
> Magnificence; and what can heaven show more?
> (2.269–73)

Mammon argues that the devils can make Hell a perfectly acceptable place to live if they exploit its natural resources and their own cleverness to produce light. Adam, similarly, suggests that he and Eve can improve their living conditions themselves, by their own efforts at technological innovation. Mammon wants to install in Hell God's first creation, light; Adam wants to extend the power of His second creation, the sun and moon, by making fire.

Beelzebub, the final speaker in the infernal council of book 2, suggests that rather than risk losing their "titles" as lords of heaven, and rather than risk open war with heaven, they should try "some easier enterprise" (2.345), namely, an attack on earth. Adam's "some safer resolution" (10.1029) echoes Beelzebub's "some easier enterprise" (2.345). The explicit motive for Beelzebub's proposal is revenge: he declares, "This would surpass / Common revenge" (2.370–71). Beelzebub suggests exploiting the "puny habitants" (367) of earth in order to hurt the enemy, God. Adam, too, proposes to use his own children, the yet unborn human race, as part of a long-term strategy by which to take revenge on Satan. He reminds Eve of the prophecy that they will crush the serpent's head, which

> Would be revenge indeed; which will be lost
> By death brought on our selves, or childless days
> Resolved, as thou proposest; so our foe
> Shall scape his punishment ordained, and we
> Instead shall double ours upon our heads.
> (10.1036–40)

He rejects Eve's proposal to avoid perpetuating human life on the grounds that if they do not have children, they will miss the opportunity to take revenge on Satan.

Adam differs from the devils in book 2 only in his attitude to God. He does not, like them, treat Him simply as an enemy. It occurs to none of the devils in the council that they might repent and find God merciful. Nor do any of them seem to notice that their complaints about the tyranny of heaven take place in a group over which Satan sits "High on a throne of a royal state" (2.1). Adam's decision to live and have children is based not on reason but on faith.[63] He is inspired by God's grace within him, which is, we later learn, performing a kind of imperceptible spiritual surgical operation, removing "the stony from their hearts" (11.4). Unlike the devils, Adam acknowledges the possibility that God may do him good, and he is prepared to humble himself before his maker and admit that he has sinned. He trusts that God "will instruct us praying, and of grace / Beseeching him, so as we need not fear / To pass commodiously this life" (10.81–83).

But it is clear to the reader that there are still a lot of unanswered questions. Adam's Polyanna vision of God's mercies relies on a very heavily edited version of events. He skips over the central question, namely whether any postlapsarian life, even one in which he buries himself in his work, will be worth living. Adam has apparently forgotten that only two hundred lines before, he had regarded God's failure to provide "immediate dissolution" as the very worst possible punishment. Now he is humbly grateful for God's small mercies. Moreover, Adam entirely falsifies Eve's position on childbearing. He reassures her that the pain now associated with childbirth will be "soon recompensed with joy, / Fruit of thy womb" (10.1052–53). But Eve had expressed no anxiety at all about the physical pain of labor. Her reason for being reluctant to give birth was that she did not want to produce children for whom life would not be worth living. Adam decides that the children will be born, without knowing what their lives will be like.

Until Michael's final revelations, Adam has very little reason to think it will be good for humanity to be born. All he knows is that the seed of Eve will bruise the serpent's head (10.181), whatever that may mean. The prophecy suggests there may be some kind of ultimate revenge taken by the children of Adam and Eve on Satan; but he does not know when or how that will take place, or what will become of humanity in the meantime. Adam makes the decision to live despite the fact that he knows nothing, at this stage, about the immediate future for his descendants and his world.[64] Adam chooses to live and beget children in almost total ignorance of what it may involve either for himself or for them, trusting only on God. He risks not only his own suffering but also that of his children. Burton lists two possible cures for despair through religious melancholy, one good and one bad: "good hope out of God's Word, to be embraced; perverse security and presumption from the devil's treachery, to be rejected."[65] Adam's rash decision to go on living and to beget children seems very difficult to identify as good hope rather than as perverse security and presumption; at this stage of the poem, it is hard to see how anyone could tell the difference. Moreover, despite his contrition and faith in God's mercy, Adam can still imagine no better ultimate comfort than death. His best hope is only that humanity may find a way to pass the time "commodiously," until they are at last allowed to rest and "sleep secure," "in dust, our final rest and native home" (10.1085).

All implied readers of *Paradise Lost* are descendants of Adam and Eve. Every reader is therefore implicated in the conversations between Adam and Eve and later, Adam and Michael, about whether it would have been better for all Adam's children — us — not to have been born. Milton's poem takes us back to the time at which it was possible for the father of humanity to decide not to beget us. The reader of books 11 and 12 therefore searches with a particular intensity for the reasons Michael might offer Adam to justify his decision to live and have children, because such reasons might justify our own existence. If Adam has no reason to believe that postlapsarian life is worthwhile, we readers have no reason not to regret our own birth. If, on the other hand, there is a possibility of rebirth and regeneration, either in time or at the end of history, then Adam was indeed wrong to think that he had already lived too long.

By the end of book 10, Adam and Eve begin to discover some hope of renewal and rebirth. They are starting to imagine the possibility that their lives may be more than dead time waiting for death. They repent and, "repairing where he judged us" (10.1087), pray to God in "sorrow unfeigned and humiliation meek" (10.1092, 1104). As Addison remarks, the passage recalls Sophocles' *Oedipus Tyrannus*, where Oedipus longs to return to Cithaeron, to die where he should have died as a baby.[66] But Oedipus reproaches Mount Cithaeron because he wishes he really had died (1391–93) before revealing his birth. Adam and Eve, by contrast, go back to the place where it all began because they hope not to undo their own birth but to be born again. They want to make the place where they were sentenced to die into a place of rebirth. They will apply their gardening skills to the earth, "with tears / Watering the ground" (10.1089–90, 1102–3). The fruits are seen at once, in the "new flesh" that God makes grow in their hearts (11.4). After repentance and prayer, their spirits pick up. Adam now remembers again, as if for the first time, that the Son promised that the seed of Eve would bruise the serpent's heel, "Which then not minded in dismay, yet now / Assures me that the bitterness of death / Is past, and we shall live" (11.156–58). Adam has in fact already remembered the Son's prophecy: he used it, as we have seen, to restrain Eve's suicidal tendencies (10.1030–40). It seems as if, in his overexcitement at the renewed sense of doing the right thing and having God on his side, Adam has again forgotten what he learned at the end of book 10, that the "bitterness of death" (11.157) is by no means the same as literal extinction. Actual dissolution of the self may indeed be desired as the only possible end of the "bitterness" of the other levels of death, and Adam himself recognized this in his Complaint. Adam's forgetfulness allows the reader to encounter the sense of overliving again and again in the final books of the poem.

The last two books of the poem have long been a problem for readers of *Paradise Lost*, on both literary and theological grounds.[67] They present human history as almost unremittingly dismal; any brief moment of pleasure or hope is almost immediately squashed.[68] They describe human history as a repetitive cycle of sin, suffering, and temporary hope, followed by more sin and more suffering. There is far more emphasis in books 11 and 12 on the sufferings of the human race than on the final redemption of the just.[69] The gloominess of Michael's predictions has been explained biographically: the books express Milton's despair at the state of postrepublican England.[70] Milton's understanding of God's dealings with the world is informed by his own sense of isolation.[71] Michael often seems to present the whole of human history as dead time, in which humanity will sin, suffer, and wait for the end.

Of course, there should be a difference between this Christian eschatological narrative, and Adam's narrative of overliving. Adam suspected that the proper moment to act and die had already passed, whereas Michael claims that it is still to come. The ultimate moment in human history has not passed; it lies in the future, in the Apocalypse. But it feels terribly similar. The repetitiveness of the narrative tends to confirm the idea that there will be no possibility for new life or action after the Fall. The focus on the final end and on the final felicity of the Fall feels inadequate as a response to the problem of postlapsarian existence.[72] The structure of *Paradise Lost* makes the Fall the central event in human history; everything that happens in books 11 and 12 is either a repetition or a reversal of that first action.

Books 11 and 12 of *Paradise Lost* imply that most of the lives of Adam's descendants will entail unmitigated suffering, corruption, and slavery. Michael has difficulty teaching Adam — or the reader — that it would not have been better for these people never to have been born. It is often said that the generic model shifts in the final books, from tragedy to heroic epic.[73] There are also, of course, epic precedents for revelations of the future.[74] But the final books are also just as close to tragedy, as Milton understood it, as books 9 and 10. Book 11 of *Paradise Lost* fits the pattern of the "tragic" book of Revelation, as described by Milton, if one takes each of the visions as an "act," divided by the conversations and comments of Adam and Michael.[75] Book 12 consists of set-piece narratives by Michael, rather than visions, but it has the same episodic structure: there are five main narrations, interrupted by Adam's comments.[76] The last books are also "tragic" because they, again like Revelation, include the description of enormous human suffering, which will feel endless to those who must experience it.

Michael suggests that human history is worth enduring for the sake of the final end. Books 11 and 12 often imply that the only reason it is good for Adam's children to be born is so that they can be used to produce the ultimate revenge on Satan. Most of human history will be spent in painful waiting through dead time until that revenge can be achieved, when the Son "shall bruise the head of Satan, crush his strength / Defeating Sin and Death" (12.435–36). Things will turn out well at the very end of time, for a very small percentage of the descendants of Adam. The Apocalypse is the final justification of world history and the existence of humanity. But it, too, will be tragic. Even or especially at the end of time, most people will feel that they have lived too long and will wish they had never been born. Michael suggests that God's creation and treatment of these people is justified since they choose to sin. But the poem does not lead us to regard the fact of these lives as any less tragic.

Adam is appalled at what Michael shows him of postlapsarian life. He repeatedly sees the lives of his descendants as tragic and repeatedly fails to understand why it would not have been better for these people never to have been born. Adam's responses are constantly corrected by Michael, who often sounds suspiciously like the comforters of Job.[77] Michael ascribes the murder of the innocent as well as physical suffering and disease to human sinfulness: suffering should not be taken by Adam or the reader to be signs of God's neglect. But the archangel offers no response to the sense of overliving on the part of Adam and his children. He responds to Adam's horror at the distortion of the "image of God in man created once / So goodly and erect" (11.508–9) by telling him that it is man's own fault (11.515–25). Michael seems to leave unchallenged the understanding of postlapsarian life that Adam had at the end of book 10. The best we can hope for is to live "commodiously" until we are reunited with our mother earth.

Michael tells Adam he is sent to teach him, through the visions, "true patience, and to temper joy with fear / And pious sorrow" (11.361–62). His purpose, bizarrely, is to prevent Adam being too optimistic about his descendants' lives — which does not seem a very pressing danger. Michael concentrates on the most upsetting moments of biblical history and thereby confirms Adam's initial suspicions that death cannot come too soon. But Michael also proves to Adam that even death will give humanity no release from suffering. The first vision Michael shows Adam is the murder of Abel by Cain. Adam is horrified, first, at the injustice of a world in which the wicked kill the good ("Is piety thus and pure devotion paid?" he asks at 11.452) and, second, at the idea that death is not the restful union with mother earth for which he had longed. He cries out,

> Alas both for the deed and for the cause!
> But have I now seen death? Is this the way
> I must return to native dust? O sight
> Of terror, foul and ugly to behold,
> Horrid to think, how horrible to feel!
> (11.461–65)

Adam's vision of how his son will "return to native dust" is far less comforting than the peaceful return to "dust, our final rest and native home" for which he hoped at the end of book 10 (1085). Michael's next vision only makes things worse. He shows him a lazar house, "wherein were laid / Numbers of all diseased" (11.479–80).

The conversation between Michael and Adam (11.465–555) over the lazar house closely echoes Adam's Complaint. The Complaint was an internal debate; in the second passage, the debate is literal. It is now Michael, rather than voices in his own head, who tries to repress Adam's fears. In book 10, Adam himself was afflicted by "moping melancholy" and accused death of "tardy execution" (10.853). Now he sees his children experiencing a far worse version of the same horror. They, too, will long for death, but death will come too late:

> Dire was the tossing, deep the groans, despair
> Tended the sick busiest from couch to couch;
> And over them triumphant death his dart
> Shook, but delayed to strike, though oft invoked
> With vows, as their chief good, and final hope.
> (11.489–93)

Death comes slow to the sufferers in the lazar house, though "oft invoked," just as he seemed slow to Adam after the Fall, when he "oft / Cursed his creation, death as oft accused / Of tardy execution" (10.851–53).[78] Now he sees his descendants in the same position, only worse. He is tempted to curse their creation, or regret their begetting. Adam is overcome with grief at his children's suffering, and "though not of woman born" (11.496), he bursts into tears: "Compassion quelled / His best of man, and gave him up to tears / A space, till firmer thoughts restrained excess" (11.496–98). The phrases "of woman born" and "best of man" invite comparison with *Macbeth*.[79] But Adam's "firmer thoughts" (whatever they may be) do not impel him, like Macbeth, to "try the last" and fight unyieldingly to the death. Rather, Adam feels that human life is given on false terms, and he wants to give up on life as soon as possible.

> O miserable mankind, to what fall
> Degraded, to what wretched state reserved!
> Better end here unborn. Why is life given
> To be thus wrested from us? Rather why
> Obtruded on us thus? Who if we knew
> what we receive, would either not accept
> Life offered, or soon beg to lay it down,
> Glad to be so dismissed in peace.
> (11.500–507)

Adam here echoes the maxim from Sophocles' ode in *Oedipus Coloneus*, that never to be born is best, μὴ φῦναι τὸν ἅπαντα νι- / κᾷ λόγον.[80] Adam says, "Better end here unborn" (11.502): the second best, again as in the Sophoclean ode, is to die quickly, "glad to be so dismissed in peace." His outburst recalls Eve's argument that life should not be given to children who would rather not have had it. In the conversation with Eve, Adam insisted on the father's right to make decisions on behalf of his son, including the choice to give him life. Now, Adam recognizes the unfairness of forcing the unwelcome gift of life on the human race. Once he knows what the life of his descendants will involve, he feels that it is not worth having. The echo of Eve's argument may make the reader wonder whether Eve was not also right to suggest that it would be better for the potential father of the human race not to beget them at all. Implicitly, the tragic Sophoclean maxim becomes an indictment both of Adam himself as a father and of God.

Michael responds by telling Adam that the sufferers were sinners. Overliving, he suggests, is not the necessary condition of all postlapsarian human life. When Adam asks if there is any other way to death, besides "these painful passages" by which we may "come / To death, and mix with our connatural dust" (11.528–29), Michael tells him that if he follows "the rule of not too much," there is indeed another way to die:

> So mayst thou live, till like ripe fruit thou drop
> Into thy mother's lap, or be with ease
> Gathered, not harshly plucked, for death mature:
> This is old age.
> (11.535–38)

Milton himself was devoted to the ideal of physical moderation. The best kind of life Michael can recommend to postlapsarian humanity is one of temperance in all things. This is a new way of passing the time "commodiously" until the end. Adam's invention of fire suggested that the way for postlapsarian humanity to live was by using the resources of the fallen world as actively as possible, with the help of God. Michael now suggests that the ideal is to cultivate temperance, which is here figured as an extreme passivity. The image of dying "like ripe fruit" suggests that the temperate human being is not the sinful apple gatherer but the passive fruit itself. By living moderately, humanity can reverse Eve's original sin. Those who die of old age will be "not harshly plucked" (11.537) but "gathered" — unlike the apple that Eve "plucked."[81] To die of old age is to encounter death in the most desirable way possible. Eve "knew not eating death" (9.792), whereas those who are "gathered" to earth in old age know death and quietly drop into it.

Michael offers Adam no alternative to the goal he desired in book 10, namely to "meet / Mortality" (10.775–76). The ultimate reward for temperate living is to receive what Adam longed for in his Complaint: to fall "into thy mother's lap" (11.536, echoing 10.778). Even this most desirable path to death is not readily attainable. Michael establishes here a pattern that will be repeated over and over again in the final books of *Paradise Lost*. He proffers hope of a comforting ending, only to backtrack and explain how long and how bitterly humanity must suffer before that end could ever be achieved. Even if Adam lives as temperately as possible, abstains from rich food and drink, and governs all his appetites, he will not immediately be gathered to earth. Rather, he will postpone that happy end even further and extend his "long day's dying" (10.964). He will live on to see all his physical powers decay and suffer greater and greater degrees of spiritual and psychological degradation.

> Thou must outlive
> Thy youth, thy strength, thy beauty, which will change
> To withered weak and gray; thy senses then
> Obtuse, all taste of pleasure must forego,
> To what thou hast, and for the air of youth
> Hopeful and cheerful, in thy blood will reign
> A melancholy damp of cold and dry
> To weigh thy spirits down, and last consume
> The balm of life.
> (11.538–46)

The tendency to despair will only increase: Michael follows the traditional association between old age and melancholy. Physical, senescent overliving is a curse that will afflict even and especially the best and most moderate of people. The promise that it is possible to "outlive" one's strength and "all taste of pleasure" is hardly comforting; this kind of "outliving" seems indistinguishable from senescent overliving. Even those like Milton himself who follow the rule of not too much may find themselves subject to "melancholy damp" (11.536), similar to the sense of belatedness that the Miltonic narrator feared might "damp my intended wing" (9.45). In the invocation to book 9, Milton had raised but dismissed the specter of being overwhelmed by an "age too late, or cold / Climate" (9.44–45). Now Michael implies that all ages are too late, all climes too cold. Even if one avoids all other excess, no postlapsarian man will be able to avoid the feeling that he has lived too long.

The choice for future humanity is between death by violence, death by disease, or becoming a Struldbrugg.[82] The question Adam asked was whether there is any way, apart from the "painful passages" of disease, by which we may come "to death, and mix with our connatural dust" (11.528–29). Michael's account of the temperate life is presented at first as the "fairest and easiest" (11.549) way to pass the time until the longed-for end. But the subsequent description of old age suggests that it may be impossible to find any way to live that qualifies as either fair or easy. Even temperance cannot make postlapsarian life attractive. Michael shifts his terms, and advocates a temperate attitude toward life itself. "Nor love thy life nor hate; but what thou livest / Live well, how long or short permit to heaven" (11.553–54). The advice is Senecan: "We need to be warned and strengthened in both directions: both not to love life too much, and not to hate it too much" (*in utrumque enim monendi ac firmandi sumus, et ne nimis amemus vitam et ne nimis oderimus, Epistles* 24.24). Michael, like Seneca, warns against the excessive lust for death, *libido moriendi* (*Epistles* 24.25). He tells Adam to relinquish any control over how "long or short" his life may be. But he has not yet given him any reason not to hope it will be as short as possible.

The last books suggest that world history will be a long series of failed endings. Repeatedly, Michael urges Adam to look forward to the end, only to return to the painful time of waiting.[83] Each anticipation of the apocalyptic end is followed immediately by a reversion to the long period of suffering that must precede any such ending. Adam brings the angel back to the suffering of the followers of Christ, asking "will they not deal / Worse with his followers than with him they dealt?" (12.483–84). The question is puzzling, because it seems to be prompted by nothing in Michael's speech immediately before. But it is a sign that Adam has, at last, begun to understand what postlapsarian life will be like. Michael has been showing him all along that "so shall the world go on, / To good malignant, to bad men benign" (12.537–38). The whole of history will be merely dead time, like Macbeth's "to-morrow, and to-morrow, and to-morrow."[84] Nothing will change, except that things will get progressively worse; the world will "still tend from bad to worse" (12.106). The only new event to which mankind can look forward is the Second Coming; before that, the world will simply "go on," and on and on, the same as always, only worse. All human history will be mere repetition.

Even the ultimate assurance that the world will be made new is not new in the terms of the poem, and therefore it is hard to see how it can solve old problems.

Michael's revelation of the future apocalypse and future redemption of the faithful is inevitably anticlimactic for the reader, because we already know the ending of the story. We know it even from the poem itself: the Father and the Son discussed the final "dissolution" of the world, when Christ will come again and reward the just (3.321–41). There is a strong sense of closure at the end of book 10, achieved largely through the repetition of lines 1086–92 as lines 1098–1104.[85] But the poem goes on. There is a strong sense of closure again at the end of book 11.[86] But again, the poem goes on.

Moreover, it is not only the reader who has already heard the true ending of the story before the final revelation of book 12; Adam, too, has already heard Michael's final revelation, both implied in the prophecy that the seed of man will bruise the serpent's head and also explicitly revealed at the end of book 11, when Michael told him that the world will endure and the seasons hold their place, "till fire purge all things new, / Both heaven and earth, wherein the just shall dwell" (11.900–901). At the end of book 11, Noah's ark is saved from the Flood, and God gives humanity the rainbow. Adam is overjoyed:

> I revive
> At this last sight, assured that man shall live
> With all the creatures, and their seed preserve.
> Far less I now lament for one whole world
> Of wicked sons destroyed, than I rejoice
> For one man found so perfect and so just,
> That God vouchsafes to raise another world
> From him, and all his anger to forget.
> (11.871–78)

Adam begins to realize that there will be a reason to have been born, although only for the minority of his descendants. Everything Adam will learn in the final book is implicit in the story of Noah's Flood in book 11: the world will become steadily more corrupt; one just man will save his people; God will make the world anew. After this, book 12 is bound to feel repetitious, since the main themes have all been articulated: suffering, wickedness, the work of one good man, redemption. But we have to go on reading and encounter the same pattern again and again.

Even Michael's account of the ultimate defeat of Satan, which ought to be a climactic moment in the poem, is itself oddly repetitious. The death of the Son will be the last death in the poem, when he

Shall bruise the head of Satan, crush his strength
Defeating Sin and Death, his two main arms,
And fix far deeper in his head their stings
Then temporal death shall bruise the victor's heel,
Or theirs whom he redeems, a death like sleep,
A gentle wafting to eternal life.
(12.430–35)

The passage describes the same event several times over, in minimally different terms, as if Michael struggles to find the right language for what will happen. The Son will "bruise the head of Satan," and likewise he will "crush his strength," which are presumably synonymous. Physical death, again, is described three times over, as "temporal death," as "a death like sleep," and as "a gentle wafting to eternal life."

In a pattern familiar from sonnet 7 and from *Samson Agonistes*, Michael tries to transform the sense of belated overliving into a sense of earliness.[87] He reassures Adam that postlapsarian life is not hopeless: Adam and his descendants should not feel that they live too long but rather that they have not yet arrived at the "happy end": they live not too late but too soon. They will live,

Which will be many days,
Both in one faith unanimous though sad,
With cause for evils past, yet much more cheered
With meditation on the happy end.
(12.602–5)

The true end is deferred, until the Last Days. From God's eternal perspective, the true ends of human lives are deferred beyond life on earth, to the Apocalypse, when man will inherit God's eternity, in which there shall be time no more.[88] The proper moment for human happiness is in the future, not at some lost time in the past.

Paradise Lost looks forward to eternity, and therefore cannot end.[89] But Michael continues to imply that there will be an end and that the thing to do is wait for it. He promises that at last the Son will come again,

When this world's dissolution shall be ripe,
With glory and power to judge both quick and dead,
To judge the unfaithful dead, but to reward
His faithful, and receive them into bliss,

Whether in heaven or earth, for then the earth
Shall all be paradise, far happier place
Than this of Eden, and far happier days.
(12.459–65)

Here at last Michael reveals to Adam what ought to be the final answer to his doubts. The final "dissolution" (12.459) of the world at the Last Day substitutes for the "immediate dissolution" that Adam looked for in his Complaint (10.1049). Here, Michael implies that happiness must be deferred until the end of time, when earth "shall" be Paradise.

But Michael also suggests that it is possible to be happy and to find Paradise even now, in the apparently empty period between the Fall and the Apocalypse. He tells Adam that if only he can cultivate the right mental attitude, adding to his knowledge of the promised end not only deeds but also virtue, "then wilt thou not be loath / To leave this Paradise, but shalt possess / A paradise within thee, happier far" (12.585–87). It is for Adam and Eve themselves to breathe life into the dead time of waiting. They can do so only on their own terms, not by reference to any external good or external ending. The "paradise within" is the closest Adam will get to the final dissolution he longed for in his Complaint. Michael's phrase, "a paradise within thee, happier far," echoes the debate of the devils in book 2. Moloc had argued that the worst that could happen, should the devils choose to make war on heaven, would be extinction, which would hardly be worse than eternal torment: God's anger may "quite consume us, and reduce / To nothing this essential, happier far / Then miserable to have eternal being" (2.96–98). Moloc regards total extinction as "happier far / Than miserable to have eternal being." He associates happiness with extinction, misery with "eternal being" (compare 12.465–66). Michael's echo of Moloc's phrase corrects the devilish vision, suggesting that happiness is not extinction but rather some kind of internal, invisible intimacy with God. The ultimate solution to Adam's fear of living on in wretchedness, "miserable to have eternal being," is not a promise of death, or even the various promises of ultimate revenge on Satan, but a promise of the possibility of inner transformation in the present. Even the slow time between the Fall and the Second Coming can be imbued with intense meaning. The apparently empty middle time contains endless moments of inner vision, and of individual choices between good and evil. Living death may even feel like being alive.

Adam learns to abandon his hope of an imminent literal ending in the external world. Michael has foretold "ages of endless date" (12.549), and Adam does not now, as he has to each of the previous predictions in book 12, ask what will happen next. He now acknowledges that the end of eternity is unattainable and unknowable:

> How soon hath thy prediction, seer blest,
> Measured this transient world, the race of time,
> Till time stand fixed: beyond is all abyss,
> Eternity, whose end no eye can reach.
> (12.553–56)

Adam has seen the end of the "race of time," in what Michael has told him about the Apocalypse. He at last admits that his eyes cannot reach eternity, and he ceases even to look toward it. He will no longer try to reach an end. Endings exist only within time, and in time every end is followed by something else. There can be no end in or of eternity. Once he has realized the impossibility of a final end, in the eye of eternity, Adam repeats or parrots Michael's words about what death is: "and to the faithful, death the gate of life" (12.571). Adam now realizes that death is only a "gate," not an ending. Moreover, even understanding reaches no end. Each of Adam's supposedly ultimate realizations turns out to need more and yet more supplementation. Michael urges Adam to "add" to the "sum / Of wisdom," but the final score is never reached; the only end point is not in the outside world at all but in the "paradise within" (12.587). As Adam and Michael descend the hill, the narrator repeats the word and the sound "end" again and again, only to reinforce the fact that none of these "ends" are the ultimate ending:[90] " ' . . . With meditation on the happy end'. / He ended, and they both descend the hill; / Descended . . . " (12.605–7). The repetition of the word "descended" reminds the reader that Adam's story does not end here; when he has descended the hill, he will beget a whole line of descendants. What happens after the end of *Paradise Lost* is human history, including the lives of the readers of the poem.

Eve is excluded from Michael's revelations. While Adam is being instructed by the archangel, she has a dream that seems to teach her both about future redemption and, even more important, about life in the present. The most significant change in Eve is not her hope for the future but her understanding that she can live independent of time or place. When Adam rejoins Eve, she says to him:

> In me is no delay; with thee to go,
> Is to stay here; without thee here to stay,
> Is to go hence unwilling; thou to me

Art all things under heaven, all places thou,
Who for my wilful crime art banished hence.
(12.615–19)

She has also been told that "such favour I unworthy am vouchsafed, / By me the promised seed shall all restore" (12.622–23), but she mentions this only secondly, as a "further consolation." Indeed, the "further consolation" is hardly news to her, since even before she went to sleep, she already knew that, "I who first brought death on all, am graced / The source of life" (9.168–69). The emphasis is on Eve's new ability to find in Adam "all places."[91] It recalls her earlier declaration of love to Adam, who was associated with each time of day: "[W]ith thee conversing I forget all time, / All seasons and their change, all please alike" (4.639–40). Now Eve's love for Adam can compress both time and place. Her love is a version of Michael's primary ingredient for the possession of the "paradise within," namely Charity (12.584–85). Love for Adam allows Eve to live not in the lost happiness of the past or even in the hope for future release or future revenge, but in the present.

One of the major images for tragic overliving, both in the tradition before Milton, and in *Paradise Lost*, is that of living death: life is seen as a version of the underworld, and those who overlive are, as it were, half dead, "a moving grave" (*Samson Agonistes* 102). Eve's final lines pick up and transform this image: she becomes not the victim of living death but herself a new and human version of Death, taking upon herself the power of Death the character, both to accept and to transform the world. Her "in me is no delay" implies an answer to Adam's frustration at the endless postponement of death. She becomes similar to Death himself in her undifferentiated acceptance of all places and all times. Death said, "To me, who with eternal famine pine, / Alike is hell, or Paradise or heaven, / There best, where most with ravine I may meet" (10.597–99). Eve escapes not only from the fear of death but also from the desire for it, by becoming like Death herself. She now has Death's capacity to evade definition and to redefine both place and time.

The poem ends on a note of neither definite triumph nor unadulterated tragic gloom. The book of Revelation ends with a vision of the City of God: the new Jerusalem comes down from heaven as a bride, and the faithful dwell with the Lord: "And God shall wipe away all tears from their eyes; and there shall be no more death, neither sorrow, nor crying, neither shall there be any more pain: for the former things are passed away" (21.4). Adam and Eve have to wipe away their own tears:

Some natural tears they dropped, but wiped them soon;

The world was all before them, where to choose

Their place of rest, and providence their guide:

They hand in hand with wandering steps and slow,

Through Eden took their solitary way.

(12.645–49)

The last lines of *Paradise Lost* create a final gulf between Adam and Eve and their children — the readers of the poem. Like Oedipus at the end of the *Oedipus Tyrannus*, Adam and Eve live on when they no longer have a clearly defined role to play.[92]

It is important that the last word of the poem is "way." *Paradise Lost* ends with the beginning of the long journey.[93] Michael has offered Adam a task: to wait for the Apocalypse in which God's chosen will finally take their revenge on Satan. But in the final lines of the poem, the end-directed lessons of the Second Education are momentarily set aside. Adam and Eve must now find a way to live through the long, slow time ahead, after their terrible loss, and through the long generations until the end of time. The "wandering" of the final lines has often been read as a sign that *Paradise Lost* moves away from strictly epic form, toward romance or the novel.[94] But as I hope my study has shown, "wandering" may be as much a feature of tragedy as of these later genres, where the main focus is not on the end but the middle of the journey. Adam and Eve's steps are both wandering and slow; they wander not for the romantic love of wandering but because they can neither end nor undo what they have done.

They will have many more choices to make, but none that are known to the reader. As we have seen in earlier tragic texts, the story of those who live on after terrible loss becomes opaque to the reader or spectator. We become increasingly unable to understand characters whose stories seem to go on after the climactic moment. This phenomenon may make us feel bewilderment or dismay. But it may also generate a sense that the characters are like real people. The feelings of Adam and Eve are no more accessible to us than those of anyone else. The characters are liberated; they seem to evade our scrutiny, and pass out of the limits of their own story. When Adam and Eve go out into the world, they become "solitary" not only because they have lost their angelic companions but also because there is a new distance between man and woman even when they hold hands, and between the characters and the reader. Paradise is now "within" each of them; it is not subject to external representation. It is when Adam and Eve are most like us that they are most difficult for us to read. Adam and Eve become inaccessible to the reader because they live on even when we no longer know what they will do or where they will go to find their "place of rest."

Tragic overliving, for Adam and Eve as for Oedipus, becomes a kind of liberation. But in *Paradise Lost*, both the tragic sense of all life as living death and the possibility of indeterminacy, privacy, and freedom become entirely universal. Oedipus is an exceptional figure whose terrible story becomes representative of all our lives; but he escapes the fate of his children and of the rest of humanity, to repeat forever the pains of a life better left unlived. Adam and Eve are exceptional human beings only because they are the first. Their experiences will form the pattern for those of all their children, all the readers of the poem.

Notes

Introduction

1. *Oxford English Dictionary*, ed. J. A. Simpson and E. S. C. Weiner, 2nd ed. (Oxford: Clarendon Press, 1989), hereafter *OED*.

2. The idea that there is a right time to die, determined by nature or biology, often runs aground on the possibility that people may not want to die at the appropriate time. Admetus in the *Alcestis* offers one of many examples in ancient and early modern literature of the man who clings to life longer than those around him think he should, because he has already reached the "right" natural time to die. Another is the old man in Lucretius's "diatribe against death," who protests that he wants to go on living, even though his body is decrepit and it is, supposedly, time for him to die. He is reproved by Natura herself, who condemns him for refusing to accept that his life is over (*De Rerum Natura* 3.955–62). In the *Republic*, Socrates argues vehemently against the use of medicine to treat anything other than wounds and some seasonal diseases (*Republic* 405a–409e). Advanced medicine, he claims, prolongs life beyond its proper time by keeping people alive when they can no longer perform their proper function; this rule seems to apply particularly to the lower classes, whose proper function is likely to be limited to their capacity for physical labor. Socrates' recommendation on this issue, as on many others, is adopted by the inhabitants of More's Utopia: "If the disease is not only incurable, but also troubles and torments him perpetually, then the priests and magistrates urge the man that, since he is unequal to all the duties of life, and is both annoying to others and a burden to himself, he has now overlived his own death" (*ceterum si non immedicabilis modo morbus sit, verumetiam perpetuo vexet atque discruciet, tum sacerdotes ac magistratus hortantur hominem, quandoquidem omnibus vitae muniis impar, aliis molestus ac sibi gravis, morti iam suae supervivat*; More 1995, p. 186; my translation). The word *supervivat* is translated "outlived" in More 1995, p. 187, but "overliving" in More 1909–14, and the latter is a closer translation, since it retains the physical metaphor of *super*. There are heated contemporary debates among both moral philosophers and lawyers about whether individuals have a right to determine their own time of death; see Dworkin 1993.

3. The locus classicus for the myth is the Homeric *Hymn to Aphrodite*, 218–38; it is also referred to in Horace, *Odes* 1.27 and 2.16, and Propertius 2.18. Tennyson's poem on the subject evokes the horror of physical overliving: *Tithonus*, 1–10 (Ricks 1969, p. 1114). On the Tithonus myth, see King 1986 who argues (against Segal 1981), that Tithonus's long life puts him not between immortal gods and mortal men but lower even than the beasts; the "eternity of old age" is "not desirable but terrifying" (p. 81).

4. See especially *Iliad* 23.626–50, and discussion of Nestor in Falkner 1989, pp. 21–38.

Cf. also *Heraclidae* 740–41 (and see Falkner 1989, pp. 114–31), and Aristophanes' *Acharnians* 210.

5. *Gulliver's Travels, III: A Voyage to Laputa* (Swift 1941, pp. 191–202). Swift mocks those who imagine that human beings would be capable of living happily for any longer than their natural life-spans. Gulliver is disabused of his naive belief that it would be delightful to be immortal when he goes to Luggnugg, where a minority of the population are born with a mark on their foreheads that signals the curse of immortal life. The mark is obviously an echo of the mark of Cain (Genesis 4.13–15), which God puts on his forehead to prevent him from being killed — although in the case of Cain, immunity from violent death seems to be a mercy, not a further punishment. There is another tradition, discussed by Midrash commentators on Genesis 64.8, of a whole city in which there was no death, the city of Luz (Freedman 1983, 2:634–35). The legend is represented in an engraving by Rosso Fiorentino, which shows a winged and skeletal figure of Death presiding over the interment of a human skeleton outside the city walls, while a group of old people look on in fascination; see Ciardi 1997.

6. See especially chapter 5, on *King Lear,* and chapter 7, on *Samson Agonistes.* Senescent overliving may also be used as an image for the continuance not of an individual but of a curse or a pattern of events, as in Aeschylus's *Agamemnon.* In the beginning of the play, the Chorus describes the situation in Argos: some are too young to fight, while others, like the Chorus members themselves, are old men who live on when strength and power are lost (*Agamemnon* 79–82). The cycle of human life has become stuck, since the young do not grow, and the old do not die. They are out of their proper time, like a withered leaf or a dream in the daytime. As the play continues, the emphasis on individuals who have lived too long makes way for a broader concern with the ways the past haunts the present. Senescent overliving is used here as a synecdochal image for a stale temporal pattern in which the past repeats itself from one generation to another. See below for more discussion of the relationship between tragic overliving and revenge tragedy.

7. Questions of social history, about the situation of the aged in ancient and early modern societies, are of only incidental relevance to my study. For the representation of old age in antiquity, see Richardson 1933, Falkner 1989 and 1995, and the annotated bibliography by Emiel Eyben, in Falkner 1989, pp. 230–51. On old age in early modern England, see Thomas 1976. For more bibliography on the representation of aging in literature, see Polisar et al. 1989.

8. See chapter 4.

9. My use of the word "traumatic" invites comparison with contemporary trauma studies. My discussion of possible solutions to overliving in tragic texts concentrates on the difficulty of reconstructing or constructing a narrative of one's life in response to an event or action that seems incomprehensible — a difficulty comparable with the problems of trauma discussed in Caruth 1996. There are two obvious and important differences between my study and the work of most trauma theorists: I discuss ancient and early modern texts rather than those of the twentieth century; and, still more important, I am not concerned with these texts as evidence or testimony of a literal event but in the exploration of a problem in narrative.

10. On the ancient sources of the Silenus story, see Hubbard 1975.

11. Nietzsche 1967, p. 42.

12. See below for more discussion of the term "tragic" applied to nondramatic genres. The maxim is also found in early lyric writers (Theognis and Baccylides) and was presum-

ably a commonplace. Theognis 425, Bacchylides 5.160; see also *Oedipus Coloneus* 1225. See chapter 2 for more analysis. For discussion of the idea in ancient writers, see also Hubbard 1975.

13. It may or may not be historically true that the origins of tragedy had something to do with Dionysus. For recent discussions of the issue, see Friedrich 1996.

14. Wittgenstein 1953, 66–67 (pp. 31–32).

15. The cognitive psychologist Eleanor Rosch, drawing heavily on Wittgenstein, showed in a series of experiments in the 1970s (see Rosch 1978 for summary of her findings) that subjects tended to treat some members of a category as more "prototypical" than others: for instance, a robin was considered a better example of the category "bird" than chicken or ostrich.

16. I share this view with Williams 1966, who uses subgenres such as "secular tragedy" and "social tragedy." See below for some of the ways tragic overliving interacts with other tragic subgenres, such as revenge tragedy.

17. There are those who would resist any attempt to give a transhistorical definition of tragedy, or to link ancient with early modern or modern tragedy. Raymond Williams (1966) has argued powerfully against the idea that tragedy is a "single and permanent kind of fact." He criticizes the "universalist character of most tragic theory," which depends on an assumption of unchanging human nature, unmodified by changes in the social and material conditions of human life (against essentialist tragic critics like George Steiner 1961). For Williams (1966), tragedy is "a series of experiences and conventions and institutions" (pp. 45–46). Williams's pragmatism seems to leave little room for cross-cultural analysis. But paradoxically, he emphasizes discontinuity in the tragic tradition only in order to allow room for a greater continuity. He defines tragedy in terms of different responses to differing social conditions in order to link modern revolutionary thought to the tragic traditions of the past. Terry Eagleton (2003), whose recent book on tragedy is deeply indebted to Williams, makes a similar point apropos of Williams's work, noting that we need to explain why we use the same term for "*Medea* and *Macbeth*, the murder of a teenager and a mining disaster" (p. 3). Eagleton's own definition — "tragic" means "very sad," or sometimes "very *very* sad" (pp. 2 and 3, emphasis in original) — is highly unsatisfactory; it is hard to think of a less apt adjective to apply to the *Medea*. But as Eagleton convincingly suggests, the Western tragic tradition is continuous from the Greeks to the twenty-first century, *pace* those, such as Steiner 1961, who have proclaimed the "death of tragedy" in the twentieth century. See also Braden 1993, on the continuities between Greek, Senecan, and Shakespearean tragedy. For a more extended defense of cross-cultural tragic comparison, see Silk 1996, general introduction (pp. 1–11).

18. See Genette 1992, among many others (p. 19: "[T]he tragic can exist apart from tragedy"). See also Unamuno 1954.

19. George Steiner claims that "any realistic notion of tragic drama must start from the fact of catastrophe. Tragedies end badly" (1961, p. 8). Eagleton 2003 is right to correct Steiner on this question; see especially pp. 57–58.

20. See especially Langer 1953, who argues that "tragedy is a cadental form. Its crisis is always the turn towards an absolute close" (p. 351).

21. *King Lear* 4.7.45. For further discussion of Euripides' *Heracles*, see chapter 3; for *King Lear*, see chapter 5. The passages are linked by Braden 1993.

22. Tragic overliving is analogous to damnation but not identical with it. The key difference between those who overlive and the damned, such as Milton's Satan or the

inhabitants of Dante's *Inferno*, is that the latter have not lost their proper roles. The damned do not live past their proper moment; rather, they relive their proper moment again and again, constantly repeating themselves to the point of self-parody. I would contrast tragedies of damnation — like Marlowe's *Doctor Faustus* — with tragedies of overliving. Faustus, at the end of the play, famously longs to hold back time, hoping uselessly to slow down the horses of night: *O lente lente currite noctis equi!* (*Doctor Faustus* 13.70). He feels not that he has lived too long but that he has not lived long enough; he would rather defer infinitely the moment of reckoning. In *Paradise Lost*, as I argue in chapter 8, there is a contrast between the "tragedy of Satan," which is a tragedy of damnation, and the "tragedy of Adam," which is a tragedy of overliving. On tragedies of damnation, see Gardner 1948.

23. The diatribe (*De Rerum Natura* 3.830–1094) suggests that all the torments of the underworld are present in this life (977–1034); death is the only end to "deathly life" (*mortalem vitam*, 869).

24. On the ways female characters in Greek tragedy die, see especially Loraux 1985 on "tragic ways of killing a woman." Whereas Loraux studies the deaths of female characters, I am interested in how and why male tragic characters fail to die. Loraux argues that suicide was for the Greeks "a woman's solution, and not, as has sometimes been claimed, a heroic act" (p. 8). She reads Euripides' *Heracles* as evidence for this view. Her reading is suggestive, although it underplays the possibility that Euripides was innovating in his representation of the rejection of suicide. See further discussion in chapter 3. On the gendering of suicide in Greek culture, see also *Laws* 873c–d where Plato argues that suicide shows a lack of manliness and therefore should have an unmarked grave.

25. I say "not exclusively" because there are instances of female characters who overlive; one obvious example is the Duchess of Malfi, who replies to Bosola's injunction, "Come, you must live," "That's the greatest torture souls feel in hell, / In hell: that they must live, and cannot die" (4.1.69–71). Webster reworks the tropes of tragic overliving from Shakespeare, especially *King Lear* and *Macbeth*. Bosola, like Edgar with Gloucester in *King Lear*, tries to persuade the Duchess that she must live by pretending that she is already dead (4.2); as in *King Lear*, the strategy does not work, and the Duchess becomes another Cordelia, whose lips give no breath and whose death comes too soon (4.2.327–67). But the Duchess is, in this respect as in many, an exceptional woman; far more frequently, characters who live too long, in classical and early modern texts, are male.

26. One reason for the association between masculinity and overliving is that all these texts assume a much more limited social role for women than for men. In Athenian tragedy and Old Comedy, however, old women sometimes have very assertive roles — a reversal of their actual social status. On the portrayal of vengeful old women in Greek tragedy (especially in Euripides' *Heraclidae*), see Falkner 1995, pp. 167–210; cf. also Mossman 1995 on the *Hecuba*. On aging women in Roman poetry, see Ancona 1994. Middleton's play *The Old Law* ([165b] 1964, vol. 2), illustrates the centrality of gender in early modern representations of overliving. The play imagines the hilarious consequences that would ensue from a law that condemned all men to die at age eighty, and women at sixty. Middleton's women overlive only in an organic and senescent way, in that they live past the age at which they are sexually or biologically viable (sixty); in this play, the female equivalent of a man's public activities is her fertility. Another reason it is female characters who propose suicide is that there is felt to be a particular perversity about a woman who rejects fertility and argues that life is not worth having. Eve recommends sexual abstinence or suicide in almost the same breath; the rejection of children is a natural consequence of the denial that

life is worth living, and it is presented in Milton's poem as a distortion of femininity. See chapter 8 for further discussion of Eve's proposals. The connection between contemporary debates on euthanasia and on abortion is discussed in Dworkin 1993, introduction. Myrrha in the *Metamorphoses* is one of very few female characters in the classical tradition who are described as living too long, but she is the exception who proves the rule. For her, the sense of overliving is intimately connected to the curse of her fertility. She conceives by her own father and can therefore endure neither life nor death.

27. Diogenes Laertius, *Lives of the Philosophers* 1.35. Stevie Smith made a similar remark: "I actually thought of suicide for the first time when I was eight. The thought cheered me up wonderfully and quite saved my life. For if one can remove oneself at any time from the world, why particularly now?" (in an interview in the *Guardian*, 7 June 1967; cited in Spalding 1988, p. 17).

28. See chapter 1.

29. See chapter 4.

30. See Augustine, *De Civitate Dei* 1.17–27, who argues that suicide is never justifiable, even to avoid sin; it is wrong, he suggests, to admire famous pagan suicides, such as Cato and Lucretia.

31. See my discussion in chapter 5 of *King Lear*, and chapter 8, on *Paradise Lost*.

32. See chapter 5.

33. Cf. the texts cited in note 2.

34. *Oedipus Tyrannus* 1391–93. See chapter 1.

35. See especially chapter 2, on *Oedipus Coloneus*.

36. As Poole 1987 remarks, in the theater "the audience and the performers are acutely conscious of time, and of their own and each other's physical limits. The audience knows that the performance has to end, and this knowledge cannot but powerfully underwrite the representation in tragedy of the way in which people meet their ends, the way things have to end" (p. 4). By contrast, Storm 1998 argues that tragedy concentrates on moments "beyond wordly chronology" (p. 35). I would say that tragedy concentrates on the conflict between various different modes of temporality.

37. Cf. Zeitlin 1990, pp. 152–55, who characterizes Thebes — the usual setting for tragic action — as a place that obeys "the law of the Eternal Return in contrast to one where history can unfold into differential narrative for the future" (p. 153).

38. As Gertrude tells him: *Hamlet* 1.2.72–73.

39. See chapter 6.

40. Frank Kermode has written suggestively about how apocalyptic thinking modifies the "sense of an ending" within this worldly life (Kermode 1967).

41. For further discussion of *Paradise Lost*, see chapter 8.

42. On this terminology, see Sipiora and Baulin, 2002, especially Smith (pp. 46–57), and Smith 1969. For further discussion of concepts of time in Greek tragedy, see Romilly 1968, especially pp. 3–49.

43. καιρός means, first, "due measure, proportion, fitness" and, second, most commonly, "exact or critical time, season, opportunity"; see H. G. Liddell, R. Scott, and H. S. Jones, *A Greek English Lexicon* (Oxford: Clarendon Press, 1968), s.v. (hereafter LSJ).

44. LSJ, s.v.: "time; a definite time, period."

45. LSJ, αἰών: "lifetime, life; age, generation," or "long space of time." In the plural, the word came to mean "eternity."

46. See chapter 4.

47. *Paradise Lost* 12.557; see chapter 8.

48. See chapter 7.

49. For helpful discussion of the various interpretations of catharsis, see Halliwell 1986, pp. 168–201 and 350–56.

50. See Halliwell 1986, especially pp. 331–36.

51. Eagleton 2003 scores some of his most resounding hits against those who assume that tragedy must be ultimately purifying; see especially pp. 23–40.

52. See Steiner 1961, and, for a view opposed to that of Steiner, Williams 1966. See also Krieger 1960, who argues that classical tragedy absorbs the destructive element, whereas modern (post-nineteenth-century) tragedy denies any moral order.

53. Eagleton 2003 rightly objects to the claim that tragedy as an art form is necessarily uplifting, consoling, or orderly; events in tragedy may be presented not as fate but as accident (see especially pp. 101–52).

54. Steiner 1961 insists that tragedy represents "man's" [*sic*] encounter with blind, irrational, amoral necessity. Steiner is not alone; many critics have seen inevitability as the "kernel of the definition" of tragedy (Mandel 1961, p. 24).

55. One of the few critics to recognize this in relation to Shakespeare is Booth 1983.

56. On conflict in tragedy and tragic theory, see Gellrich 1988. Storm 1998 sees rupture as a key characteristic of tragedy. I resist using the term *sparagmos*, or "Dionysus," as a metaphor for tragic rupture, as Storm does (although he restricts his attention to synchronic conflicts within tragic characters, or "personalities"). For a critique of the use of "Dionysus" as a metaphor for various different readings of tragedy, see Friedrich in Silk 1996. Storm is open to the same objection, namely that he dresses up a critical reading in the guise of ritual language, for which he has no historical support.

57. Derrida discusses the representation of "living on," or *la demeure*, in the work of Maurice Blanchot, suggesting that it draws attention to the difficulties of delimiting clear boundaries around any text (Derrida 1979 and 2000). The word *demeure*, like the phrase "living on" in English, implies both "habitation," living in a particular place, especially on the land, or on a particular border, and "continuing to exist," living on in time. Derrida's terms, unlike "overliving," emphasize a slippage between borderlines in place and time. Derrida's central interests are in translation and in criticism or commentary: the "living on" of Blanchot's narrator reflects Derrida's own intermediate or borderline position, as a writer in a foreign or not-quite-native language, and as a commentator on other texts, including his own. Living on, for Derrida, is associated with the ways a text can move beyond its apparently fixed boundaries.

58. "It has been established by us that tragedy is an imitation of a complete and whole action, of a certain size" (κεῖται δὴ ἡμῖν τὴν τραγῳδίαν τελείας καὶ ὅλης πράξεως εἶναι μίμησιν ἐχούσης τι μέγεθος, *Poetics* 1450b23–25).

59. See chapter 1.

60. See chapter 5.

61. See chapter 7.

62. See further, on the Oedipus plays, chapters 1 and 2, and on the *Heracles*, chapter 3.

63. The distinction is similar to, but not identical with, the *fabula-sjuzet* distinction. There is a good account of the *fabula-sjuzet* distinction in Brooks 1984, pp. 3–36. *Fabula* or *histoire* is usually taken to mean the order and individuation of events referred to by the narrative—for instance, the *fabula* of the *Oedipus Tyrannus* would perhaps begin with the oracle to Laius. *Sjuzet* or *récit* means the order of events as they are presented by the

narrative — for instance, the *sjuzet* or *récit* of the *Oedipus Tyrannus* begins with the plague in Thebes.

64. As in 8.729–31, where he lifts up his shield and the future of his people, without understanding it: "Not knowing the events, he rejoices in the image, lifting on his back the glory and fortunes of his descendants" (*rerumque ignarus imagine gaudet / attollens umero famamque et fata nepotum*).

65. For further comparison between the two figures, see King 1989, pp. 72–77, who stresses the weakness of both Tithonus and the Sibyl in myth. The fullest account of the Sibyl is in *Metamorphoses* 14.101–53. In Ovid's reworking of Virgil's Sibyl, the emphasis shifts away from war and death, to the survival of the Sibyl's voice, which croaks on even when she herself becomes a shriveled speck. For Ovid, the Sibyl becomes an image of the feeble but persistent survival of Virgil's poetry; the aged voice of the Sibyl is to be contrasted with the ever vibrant survival of Ovid's own name at the end of book 15 (871–74).

66. Prophetic powers are in some ways comparable with living too long: through prophecy, human knowledge extends beyond ordinary human life-spans, and prophecy, like overliving, emphasizes human dependence on time. Cf. the presentation of Cassandra in the *Agamemnon*.

67. Trimalchio in Petronius's *Satyricon* claims to have seen the Sibyl, hanging in a bottle, *in ampulla*. He reports the legend that when asked, "Sibyl, what do you want?" the Sibyl would reply, "I want to die" (*Satyricon* 48e: *nam Sibyllam quidem Cumis ego ipse oculis meis vidi in ampulla pendere, et cum illi pueri dicerent*, Σίβυλλα, τί θέλεις; *respondebat illa:* ἀποθανεῖν θέλω). The Petronius passage is used as the epigraph to T. S. Eliot's *The Waste Land*, and in that poem the Sibyl's unsatisfied and perhaps unsatisfiable longing for death becomes an image for a cultural tradition that has lingered on too long. But Eliot only reiterates a trope that is already central in Petronius; Trimalchio's little anecdote about the Sibyl is a brief, metonymic introduction to the whole of the *Cena Trimalchionis*. Trimalchio's own gastronomic excesses are anticipated by the Sibyl's "bottle," and Trimalchio himself is, like the Sibyl, suffering from the painful postponement of a longed-for death. If Eliot is anticipated by Petronius, Petronius himself is anticipated by Virgil, in that the Sibyl of the *Aeneid* is already suffering from a desire for a death that has been too long delayed. The figure of the Sibyl who longs to die returns in a powerfully Virgilian recent novel, *The Last Samurai* (Dewitt 2000), in which the depression and despair of Sibylla is set against her son's search for both a father and an escape from tragic repetition.

68. On revenge tragedy in *Paradise Lost*, see chapter 8.

69. Cf. chapter 6.

70. See chapter 8.

71. Cf. chapters 2 and 8. In at least two other Greek tragedies, tragic overliving is combined both with final escape and with the possibility of revenge: Sophocles' *Philoctetes*, and Aeschylus's *Prometheus Bound*. Philoctetes calls for death when his agony comes upon him (797–98, 819–20), and he speaks of his life as a long death (310–14). Once his bow has been taken from him, he calls on the wild beasts to come and kill him, since he no longer has any means of supporting himself (1155–62); with this passage compare the presentation of the same bow in Euripides' *Heracles*, discussed in chapter 3. But Philoctetes much more frequently declares not that he himself has lived too long but that his enemies should have died long ago (see, e.g., *Philoctetes* 416–18, 429–30, 446–50). In *Prometheus Bound*, the hero suffers agonies but never doubts that he will ultimately be restored through his secret power.

72. For an excellent discussion of revenge tragedy, see Kerrigan 1996.

73. See chapter 1 for more discussion of how *Oedipus Tyrannus* alludes to but differs from an Aeschylean tragedy of revenge or ancestral curse.

74. See chapter 7.

75. See chapters 5 and 6. It has been argued that Shakespeare had read at least Euripides in Latin translation (Jones 1977), but although this is possible, the case is not compelling.

76. See chapter 4.

77. See especially chapter 6, on *Macbeth*.

78. Similarly, in Tennyson's poem *Tithonus*, the sense of senescent overliving echoes a larger sense of nineteenth-century cultural belatedness, in a time of an aging population, an aging queen, and an aging empire. Tennyson's *Tithonus* was kept back from publication, perhaps because it was too timely, too obviously relevant to its political context. Tennyson's first draft of what was to become *Tithonus* (*Tithon*) was written immediately after Arthur Hallam's death, but *Tithonus* was not published until 1860. See Ricks 1969, pp. 566 and 1112–18.

79. My selection of texts is partly anticipated by Braden 1993, who discusses, briefly, Sophocles' two Oedipus plays as well as Euripides' *Heracles*, Seneca's *Hercules Furens*, and *King Lear*. I encountered Braden's article at a very late stage of my work; I am pleased to find independent confirmation of the connections I see between these texts.

80. See Garner 1990 for general discussion of the relationship between Greek tragedy and the Homeric poems.

81. See Falkner 1989, pp. 21–67: "Ἐπὶ γήραος οὐδῷ: Homeric heroism, old age and the end of the *Odyssey*."

82. See especially Macleod 1982, pp. 1–11.

83. Devereux 1978 argues that Achilles' killing of Hector is "a kind of vicarious suicide" (p. 14).

84. See Wofford 1992.

85. Chekhov 1954, p. 237.

86. Chekhov 1954, p. 238.

87. Chapter 16.

88. See Tolstoy 1993, pp. 723–24.

89. See especially chapter 29 (Tolstoy 1993, pp. 742–46).

90. Tolstoy 1993, p. 892.

91. Eagleton 2003 suggests that the common experience of human suffering transcends historical diversity. He uses Williams's awareness of the importance of suffering against Williams's desire for cultural specificity, reiterating Williams's complaint that "right-wing" theorists have neglected the key fact about tragedy, which is, Eagleton argues, that people suffer, both on stage and in real life. Eagleton phrases this point as an objection to the "predictable culturalist or historicist riposte that . . . suffering is always culturally specific" (p. xii). As Simpson 2003 says, it is a pity that Eagleton did not develop in more depth the question, "Is there a common quantum of suffering that can be posited as the foundation of a common humanity?" (p. 19).

92. As do both Williams 1966 and Eagleton 2003. Williams 1966 argues that the word "tragic" in everyday life is not used in a radically different sense from its literary usage, in such sentences as "it was a tragic accident"; to deny this is, he claims, snobbery. Eagleton develops the point at length (see pp. 1–40, especially pp. 34–35 on the Crucifixion, which

Eagleton seems to read as a tragic historical event). I suspect that there is a kind of inverted snobbery in Williams's and, especially, Eagleton's eagerness to associate themselves with the language of common men or, rather, the language of journalists. But human casualties should not be treated as literature. For this reason, I do not agree with the claim, made by both Williams 1966 and Eagleton 2003, that it is politically progressive to link the literary and the journalistic uses of the word "tragic."

CHAPTER I : "O darkness": Sophocles' *Oedipus Tyrannus*

1. The *Oedipus Tyrannus* began to assume canonical preeminence in the late Renaissance. See Segal 1993, pp. 16–35, for a survey of the critical reception of the play. Segal remarks that "from the sixteenth century on . . . *Oedipus Tyrannus* becomes established as *the* classical tragedy" (p. 22, emphasis in original). Rudnytsky 1987, pp. 93–250, offers an intellectual history of the reception of the play from Schiller to Nietzsche: he argues that it was the German Romantics who read in it for the first time not the rationalism of the neoclassicists but "their own obsession with self-consciousness" (p. x). See also Dawe 1996 for more discussion of the reception of Sophocles. The reception of the plays in the twentieth century was, of course, shaped by Freud's theory of the Oedipus complex (see particularly Freud 1953, 1: 263–66; 4: 260–64; 6: 177–78; 9: 134–37).

2. Hermeneutic critics have shown how the ways these plays have been read have been shaped by the preoccupations of their readers: see Lear 1998 and Winter 1999.

3. *Odyssey* 11.271–80. Cf. also Antiphanes frag. 189 (Kassel and Austin 1983), which I discuss in more detail in chapter 2.

4. Seale 1982, pp. 226–28, points out that the Teiresias scene functions to ensure that the whole audience knows the truth before Oedipus does.

5. Compare *Ajax* 856–65, where Ajax addresses the light for the last time because he is about to commit suicide.

6. Very little is known about Aeschylus's Theban trilogy, beyond the titles. Most critics assume that the Theban trilogy would have followed the curse on the house of the Labdacids tracing the ancestral curse on the family, but this is based only on induction from the *Oresteia*. In *Odyssey* 11 (271–80) Odysseus sees Epicaste, the wife of Oedipus, who married her own son and then hanged herself; "But he, suffering woes, rules over the Cadmeans in lovely Thebes, through the terrible designs of the gods" (ἀλλ' ὁ μὲν ἐν Θήβῃ πολυηράτῳ ἄλγεα πάσχων / Καδμείων ἤνασσε θεῶν ὀλοὰς διὰ βουλάς, *Odyssey* 11.275–76). This passage includes no mention of an ancestral curse on the house of the Labdacids. Epicaste and her husband are brought down by the gods, but there is no mention of Laius. The passage is also interesting in that it includes no mention of Oedipus's self-blinding or of his exile from Thebes, both of which were probably later additions to the myth. On the myth of Oedipus before Sophocles, see Robert 1915, Delacourt 1944, de Kock 1961, and Edmunds 1985.

7. My point here is not historical or evolutionary: I do not suggest that Sophocles replaced the Aeschylean tragedy of ancestral curse with the tragedy of overliving, once and for all. Both tragic subgenres have continued side by side, throughout the tragic tradition. But within the *Oedipus Tyrannus*, the tragedy of overliving supplants the tragedy of ancestral curse; the text alludes to inherited guilt as a suppressed alternative to the narrative pattern it actually adopts.

8. The Chorus comments immediately that he is terrible to look at (1297–98). We do

not know exactly how the blindness of Oedipus was represented. There are few cases in extant tragedy where the text suggests a change in the appearance of the mask for a single character. Perhaps the only real parallel to the blinded Oedipus is *Hecuba* 1056, where Polymestor emerges blinded. In both cases, probably some alteration was made to the existing mask in order to suggest blindness (such as adding red paint or a stained cloth tied over the eyes), which seems the simplest and therefore most likely solution. Alternatively, there may have been a special blind mask; this is the solution adopted by Webster 1956, p. 50. For interesting discussion of the mask, see Calome 1996.

9. *Seven against Thebes* 772–91. On the development of the Oedipus myth, see Robert 1915; Delacourt 1944.

10. Budelmann 2000, pp. 172–73, argues that τάδε must refer in the first place to the self-blinding. But the vagueness of Oedipus's language creates an ambiguity about which set of sufferings he is referring to; it could be simply the self-blinding, but it could also be his whole past.

11. The first way of reading the self-blinding has often been taken to be the only possible one. Buxton 1980 is typical in taking this reading as self-evident. A reductive explanation for the proliferation of motives would be that it allows Sophocles to reiterate the horrors of Oedipus's life and whip the audience up into an ever greater emotional frenzy. But this account is inadequate because it stops short of explaining precisely what emotions are aroused by the reiterations, or why they compete with one another. Because Oedipus's expressed motives are overdetermined, Freudian critics have suggested his underlying, unconscious reason for mutilating his eyes is the desire for self-castration (Devereux 1973). For a more complex Freudian reading, see Pucci 1992. The castration reading in itself only defers the question of how Oedipus's self-blinding functions as a response to his past. For further discussion of the self-blinding and bibliography, see Calome 1996.

12. Vernant 1988, p. 138. Vernant rightly draws attention to the combination in Oedipus of two opposite but complementary figures, the *tyrannos* and the *pharmakos*—who both stand outside the normal range of human life. On the *pharmakos* in Greek religion, see also Parker 1983, pp. 258–71.

13. Aeschylus's Electra cries out, on recognizing her brother, "O dearest darling to the house of our father!" (ὦ φίλτατον μέλημα δώμασιν πατρός, *Choephoroi* 235); Orestes replies with a vocative address to Zeus, who bears witness (246–49). Sophocles' Electra, when she at last recognizes her brother, addresses first the witnesses, the light that has revealed her brother to her: "O dearest light!" (ὦ φίλτατον φῶς, *Electra* 1224) and the Chorus women who see her joy (1227–29); finally, launching into lyric, she addresses her brother himself: "O child, child born of the bodies I love best" (ἰὼ γοναί, / γοναὶ σωμάτων ἐμοὶ φιλτάτων, 1231–32). Euripides' very curtailed and satirical version of the recognition of Orestes by Electra cuts short the vocative exclamations, allowing his Electra to address Orestes only once before they move on to business: "O you who appear in time," (ὦ χρόνῳ φανείς, *Electra* 578)—the mode of address itself suggests that the post-Aeschylean spectators are likely to be impatient with yet another version of this scene. When Euripides' Ion finally recognizes Creousa as his mother, he exclaims, "O my dearest mother" (ὦ φιλτάτη μοι μῆτερ, *Ion* 1437). Euripides' Orestes, in the *Iphigenia in Tauris*, cries out, "O gods" (ὦ θεοί, 780) when he learns who his sister is, and addresses her as "O my own sister, born of the same father" (ὦ συγκασιγνήτη τε κἀκ ταὐτοῦ πατρὸς, 800); when he convinces her of

the truth, Iphigenia, like Electra, switches to lyric and exclaims, "O my dearest, nothing else, for you are dearest" (ὦ φίλτατ', οὐδὲν ἄλλο, φίλτατος γὰρ εἶ, 827).

14. It has been claimed that Sophocles presents Oedipus as the victim of conspiracy or of his own paranoia or arrogance, and that he is not really the son of Jocasta and Laius at all, or the killer of Laius. This is the major premise of Ahl 1991. Goodhart 1978 argues that "Oedipus may not have killed Laius" (p. 56). The reading is ingenious but perverse, since there is no textual justification for inferring that Oedipus is wrong in believing in his own parricide and incest: the fact that no one ever doubted them previously is perhaps sufficient evidence that the audience is never led to question the facts of the past. Their interpretation is a different matter.

15. On the number of killers, see Goodhart 1978.

16. See Dawe 1982.

17. If this is so, it would contradict the claim of Bers 1997 that "there is no *oratio recta* in the *Oedipus Tyrannus*" (p. 45). However, my main argument does not stand or fall by this claim. It is true that the word "Oedipus" interrupts the Messenger's account of Jocasta's death, whether or not the name is spoken by Oedipus as well as by the Messenger.

18. Moorhouse 1982 notes (p. 7) the use of the plural in Sophocles to generalize and thereby express reverse.

19. Line 1411 was deleted by Meineke, because it is, of course, inconsistent; Oedipus begins the speech by justifying his decision not to kill himself but stay alive, and ends by urging his countrymen to kill him. Reinhardt 1979 claims that the self-contradiction is "characteristic of tragic pathos" (p. 132). I would go further in defending the line: the contradiction is entirely in keeping with the tension in Oedipus's attitude to his own existence after his discovery.

20. See note 13.

21. The author of the *De Sublimitate* comments on this use of plural for singular: he quotes *Oedipus Tyrannus* 1403–8, and comments: "all these are a single name, for Oedipus on the one hand, and Jocasta on the other; but by mixing the number into the plural he has pluralized also the misfortunes" (πάντα γὰρ ταῦτα ἓν ὄνομά ἐστιν, Οἰδίπους, ἐπὶ δὲ θατέρου Ἰοκάστη, ἀλλ' ὅμως χυθεὶς εἰς τὰ πληθυντικὰ ὁ ἀριθμὸς συνεπλήθυσε καὶ τὰς ἀτυχίας, 23.3). The use of plural for singular in tragedy to denote a relative is discussed by Bers 1984 as his type 7; Bers discusses the plural γάμοι for a singular marriage in detail on pp. 28–34. Plurals are used for singular elsewhere in tragedy, but nowhere else, to my knowledge, is there a passage so dense in the device. I would argue, therefore, that the audience would have heard a hint of literal plurality in these lines.

22. See Dawe 1982, pp. 14–15.

23. The cult of Oedipus at Colonus would have been familiar to Sophocles' audience. For evidence of the cult, see Pausanias 1.30.4.

24. LSJ, s.v. B. 2. b. In *Oedipus Coloneus* Oedipus uses the same verb to describe his own birth at 974, and the chorus uses it to describe the birth of any human child at 1225. See chapter 2 for further discussion.

25. Oedipus's desire to control the lives of his children is still more striking in the *Oedipus Coloneus*; see chapter 2. On *King Lear*, see chapter 5.

26. "The months born with me make me little and big" (οἱ δέ συγγενεῖς / μῆνές με μικρὸν καὶ μέγαν διώρισαν, 1082–83).

27. The authenticity of the final lines has been much disputed. Many have argued for

the authenticity at least of 1524–25: Calder 1970; Arkins 1988; Hester 1973; Olson 1989. For discussion of the debate surrounding final lines in Greek tragedy in general, see Roberts 1982. For arguments against authenticity, see Dawe 1982. It is not, strictly speaking, relevant to my argument whether it was Sophocles or someone else who wrote the final lines. My reading makes the case that the last lines form a coherent part of the text as it now stands.

28. Pindar's *Olympian* 2 uses Oedipus as an example of the mystery of life and the reversals of fortune; the story of Oedipus continues in the lives of his children.

29. The final lines are linguistically problematic and may well be textually corrupt. But there is, I think, no compelling reason to doubt that words along these lines formed the end of Sophocles' play. See Roberts 1982 on the literary preconceptions that tempt scholars to delete the final lines of Greek tragedies; for more textual discussion, see Dawe 1974, 1: 1266–73. Dawe 1982, p. 247, pours scorn on the lines' "demented balbutience." This is surely going too far; the general sentiment is no more "demented" than any other piece of gnomic wisdom.

30. That the sentiment was old and hackneyed can be seen from the opening of the *Trachiniae*, where Deinaira says, "There is an ancient saying, that you could not learn whether someone's life is good or bad until the person dies. But I know well, even before going to Hades, that the life I have is unfortunate and burdensome" (Λόγος μὲν ἔστ᾽ ἀρχαῖος ἀνθρώπων φανεὶς / ὡς οὐκ ἂν αἰῶν᾽ ἐκμάθοις βροτῶν, πρὶν ἂν / θάνῃ τις, οὔτ᾽ εἰ χρηστὸς οὔτ᾽ εἴ τῳ κακός· / ἐγὼ δὲ τὸν ἐμόν, καὶ πρὶν εἰς ῞Αιδου μολεῖν, / ἔξοιδ᾽ ἔχουσα δυστυχῆ τε καὶ βαρύν, 1–5). Deinaira defiantly claims the right to judge her life unhappy even before she is dead, despite the popular wisdom that no life can be judged happy or unhappy before it ends.

31. For discussion of the ironies in the Herodotus passage and its relation to (Euripidean) tragic closure, see Dunn 1996, introduction.

CHAPTER 2 : "Never to have lived is best": *Oedipus Coloneus*

1. I discuss the choral ode from which these lines come in more detail at the end of the chapter.

2. Theognis 425–28, Bacchylides 5.160–62.

3. Sophocles died in 406–5; the play was not performed until 401.

4. Sophocles himself was said to have used the *Oedipus Coloneus* as evidence that he was old but not senile: see Lefkowitz 1981, p. 162. The biographical legend may well be an extrapolation from the play itself; see Lefkowitz, pp. 84–85.

5. Stoessl 1966, pp. 5–26, sees Oedipus as a saint called to higher things and held back by a series of this-worldly temptations. Segal 1981 also reads the ending of the play as redemptive (pp. 362–408).

6. The continuing aggression of Oedipus is emphasized by Rosenmeyer 1952, pp. 92–113. On the importance of Oedipus's relationship with Polyneices in the play, see Easterling 1967, pp. 1–13, and Burian 1974. For Burian, it is in the course of the encounter with Polyneices that Oedipus "becomes a hero before our eyes."

7. There was an active hero cult of Oedipus at Colonus when the play was composed. Sophocles' play provides a kind of etiology for the cult, showing how the human Oedipus is transformed into a "hero" in the technical sense — a being intermediate between gods and men, who was worshiped and believed to have special powers to help or harm the city.

Knox 1964 argues (pp. 143–61) that the play plots the gradual dehumanization of Oedipus, as he becomes less and less human. For Knox, even the curse of Polyneices is the expression not of human bitterness, but of "daemonic, superhuman wrath" (p. 159). Knox underplays the extent to which Oedipus's dehumanization is disturbing, both for the other characters and for the audience. Reinhardt 1979 notes the opposition between human and divine perspectives in the *Oedipus Coloneus*, remarking that "the opposing parties are, on the one side, the individual human life, narrow and limited, uncommonly self-centered in its affirmations and denials, and on the other side its involvement with the fate of the locality, the power to bless or curse for all time, the obligation to guard and protect" (p. 195). He glosses over the fact that Oedipus takes up his "obligation to guard and protect" Athens only at the cost of reneging entirely on his obligation to guard and protect his children.

8. See especially Murnaghan 1987 on the importance of Oedipus's body.

9. On Oedipus's pollution, see Parker 1983 (especially pp. 318–21, on the *Oedipus Coloneus*). Parker is sensitive to how Oedipus's "polluting demon" lives on forever, not in Athens but in Thebes, and affects the lives of his children (see p. 320).

10. Kassel and Austin 1983, 2: 418, frag. 189.

11. Aristotle takes a different view, in one of his most interesting references to the Oedipus story (*Poetics* 1453b3–7). The Aristotelian passage suggests that people shudder only when they are told the whole the story of Oedipus. Exactly what Aristotle means by μῦθος here, and thus how he imagines the audience encountering the story without ὄψις, is unclear. Scholars argue about whether Aristotle is talking about the story-myth of Oedipus (Rostagni 1945), the plot of Sophocles' *Oedipus* (Else 1957), or the play itself read rather than acted (Gudeman 1934). What is clear from the context is that this is a version of the story without the visual element; it is less clear that Lucas 1968, p. 150, is right that μῦθος cannot mean the "story" here, as opposed to Sophocles' shaping of the story—*pace* Antiphanes, the name alone would not be enough. But the important point is not the difference between Antiphanes and Aristotle but what they share. Both are imagining a response either to Oedipus's name and thereby his story, or just to his story, which is triggered purely verbally, without any visual element. It is the story and not the sight of the actor appearing on stage in the mask of a blinded man that, Aristotle argues, can alone make one shiver, φρίττειν, or like the Chorus in Colonus, shriek ἰὼ ὤ, even without a full dramatic rendition.

12. Antigone's intervention on behalf of her father was rejected by some ancient critics, on the grounds that it interrupts the main debate between Oedipus and Chorus: it would be better, they argue, for Oedipus to offer his own self-justification immediately. The scholiast on 237 claims that the whole exchange between Antigone and the Chorus (237–57) is out of place. The excision of the lines is rightly rejected by modern editors (and, as the scholiast admits, also by Didymos). Editors defend it on grounds of its inherent beauty, rather than its appropriateness in its structural context: see Jebb 1899, p. 47, and Kamerbeek 1984, who argues that without 237–53 "the play would lose one of its most moving lyric passages" (p. 54). This does not precisely address the objection of the scholiast, that the lines are inappropriate in their immediate context. It is important to notice that Antigone's arguments are significantly different from those of Oedipus, in their emphasis on mercy rather than justice, and we therefore need both.

13. Slatkin 1986 discusses these lines, and rightly remarks that "Oedipus offers the Athenians the opportunity to make real their values by accepting him" (p. 217). On the

reputation of Athens as protectress of suppliants who are rejected elsewhere, cf. *Heraclidae*, 189–201, and see Mills 1997.

14. The debate about whether names relate to things naturally or conventionally, νόμῳ or φύσει, was current when this play was written and performed. For discussion of Sophocles' relationship to sophistic thought, and further bibliography, see Rose 1976. Cf. *Oedipus Tyrannus* 397–98, where Oedipus describes himself, punningly, as ὃ μηδὲν εἰδώς Οἰδίπους ("The know-nothing Oedipus"). There, unlike in this passage, he seems to be suggesting that his name does in fact define who he is: the apparent presence of the verb οἶδα within his name is used to suggest that he is intrinsically knowledgeable, and hence his success with the Sphinx, despite Teiresias's insinuations that he is in fact μηδὲν εἰδώς. On the multiple readings of the name Oedipus, see Pucci 1992, chap. 5, and Goldhill 1986, pp. 217–18. Perhaps Oedipus at Colonus has realized the falsehood of the etymologies he tried to create for his own name and the folly of trying to read his name as an oracle that could reveal his identity. For modern philosophical discussion of names, see Kripke 1980 and Linsky 1977.

15. Eliot 1967, p. 333.

16. Eliot rewrites Sophocles to conform to his own model of Christianity. Another attempt to Christianize the *Oedipus Coloneus* is Lee Breuer's *Gospel at Colonus* (1989), where the suffering, persecuted, broken Oedipus becomes a type for Christ: the scapegoat savior who redeems his people. Breuer's powerful adaptation both reminds one of the ceremonial and religious elements of the play, and reinforces Oedipus's refusal to turn the other cheek. Polyneices' testimony and public confession result not in public absolution but in damnation.

17. See Stoessl 1966.

18. Later, he will himself admit that he has no right to touch Theseus and does therefore seem to acknowledge that he is still polluted (1130–38). See below for more discussion of this apparent inconsistency.

19. Compare the use of the verb παίω in the *Oedipus Tyrannus* for the killing of Laius and the self-blinding (807, 1270, 1331) — discussed in chapter 1.

20. See Murnaghan 1987.

21. Pluralization ("these marriages," "those parricides," 989–90) may be another device by which Oedipus distances himself from what he has done. Cf. Moorhouse 1982, p. 7.

22. On the contrast between the body and speech in the *Oedipus Coloneus*, see Murnaghan 1987, pp. 37–41, especially pp. 39–40, on the impropriety of Creon's speech.

23. The word ἀνόσιον ("unholy," "impure," 981), was first used by Creon himself to describe Oedipus's marriage (946); Oedipus seems to be claiming that the pollution lies not in the fact of his marriage with his mother but in Creon's verbal allusions to it.

24. Segal 1981 argues that the scene is "absolutely necessary to Oedipus' growth and his return to a place of power in a civilized community," which "provides a visual review in small compass of Oedipus' life" (pp. 384–85).

25. See Burian 1974, p. 423.

26. The association between Oedipus and the Furies is discussed by Festugière 1973.

27. Polyneices uses the word at 1269, to refer to his former behavior to his father; Oedipus uses the same word for his parricide and incest at *Oedipus Coloneus* 439. On the concept of ἁμαρτία in Aristotle and in Greek tragedy, see Bremer 1969 and Saïd 1978.

28. This is the suggestion of Easterling 1967; see especially pp. 8–9.

29. See Blundell 1989, chap. 7.

30. I borrow this point from Charles Segal, who argues that "at the price of giving up his *oikos*, he becomes the hero of a *polis* alone, his grave known only to the male ruler of a city to which he has no ties of blood" (Segal 1981, p. 403).

31. Note Oedipus's repetitions of the verb φύω (to beget) and its compounds: see especially lines 427, 448, 445, 1365, 1369, 1377, 1379.

32. Burian 1974, p. 427.

33. On this topic, see especially the discussion in Parker 1983, pp. 318–20.

34. Parker 1983 finds this "a contrast of beautiful plausibility" (p. 320).

35. Jebb identifies those who are experienced, who must suffer together with Oedipus (τοῖς γὰρ ἐμπείροις βροτῶν), as his daughters (1899, 2:181); but the phrase is vague enough to cover Oedipus's whole household.

36. See Murnaghan 1987, pp. 40–41.

37. Cf. *Ajax* 646–49, where Ajax claims that time has the power not only to change physical things, but also human attitudes. Ajax's claim is just as dubious as Oedipus's as a description of his own response to time: Ajax will go on to kill himself—and perhaps he always meant to do so. On attitudes to time in Sophocles, see Romilly 1967. Budelmann 2000, pp. 78–79, comments on *Oedipus Coloneus* 607–15 that Oedipus's generalizations about time are linked specifically to his own character and situation and to this particular play, in which time has been a "key player."

38. As argued, though without specific reference to the *Oedipus Coloneus*, by Zeitlin 1990. Thebes, she argues, "provides the negative model to Athens' manifest image of itself with regard to its notions of the proper management of city, society and self" (p. 131).

39. For discussion of dating, see Edmunds 1996, pp. 87–88.

40. Edmunds 1996 offers a historical reading of the play, arguing that it is an apology for the Knights and appeal for reconciliation in an atmosphere of recrimination after the collapse of the Four Hundred (pp. 67–149).

41. Edmunds 1996, pp. 30–83, emphasizes the fact that the space of the grove is nondramatic, nonvisual. For Edmunds, Oedipus himself, because of his blindness, inhabits "negative dramatic space" (p. 64); his offer to Athens is also nonphysical, nonvisual, non-demonstrable; his withdrawal into the grove is the final culmination of this exclusion of any spectator, the "predicament of a non-dramatizable, non-theatrical action" (p. 57).

42. Yeats 1957, p. 459. The poem was written for Yeats's version of the whole *Oedipus Coloneus* (*Oedipus at Colonus*, performed 12 September 1927); it was first published in *October Blast* (1927) but then became the culminating lyric of *A Man Young and Old* (in the collection *The Tower*, 1928). Yeats lifts the lyric from the play, relating it to an unnamed "man young and old" rather than to Oedipus. Even in the context of his version of the whole play, he offers no translation of the epode, which connects what has been said before to the particular figure of Oedipus. On the writing of Yeats's versions of Sophocles' Oedipus plays, see Clark 1983 and Clark and McGuire 1989.

43. "This be the verse," line 10 (Larkin 1988, p. 180)—a poem that has great affinity with the Sophoclean ode, in terms of both imagery and sentiment.

44. Oedipus repeats the word φύω, insisting that he is the begetter of his sons and therefore they have natural obligations to him; he plays on the link between φύω and φύσις (see previous discussion, and line numbers cited in note 26). The recurrence of the word here may reinforce the connection between Oedipus's apparently exceptional family and the general human condition.

45. See Kamerbeek 1984 ad loc.

46. See note 1.

47. Ellendt 1872, pp. 416–18, divides the sense of the word into two main categories, *oratio* and *ratio*, and *oratio* outstrips *ratio* in Sophocles by four columns to one; which perhaps makes it possible that even when the less common sense is the dominant meaning, as here, the more common sense of *oratio* might still be heard in the word. Ellendt puts this instance under *ratio*; he glosses the word here, *existimatio, locus, quo quid censetur, momentum, pretium rei* (p. 418), and cites also *Oedipus Coloneus* 1163 and *Ajax* 264 and 477. The *Ajax* passage is particularly relevant, in that it comes in the speech where Ajax is declaring the shamefulness of wanting to go on living after dishonor (473–80); see chapter 3 for further discussion of this passage.

48. See chapter 1.

CHAPTER 3 : "Enslaved to fate": Euripides' *Heracles*

1. As Braden 1993 notes (p. 246); he suggests that Sophocles' "sequel" may have been inspired by Euripides. As he says, both heroes manage to "confront and outlive a guilt that somehow both is and is not theirs" (p. 247), and both plots hinge on the heroes' "lethal failure to recognise kinship" (p. 249).

2. *Poetics* 1452a, 1452b–1454a (chs. 10, 13, and 14). Notoriously, Aristotle says in chapter 13 that the best kind of plot structure is that from good fortune to bad, while in chapter 14 he says that it is best of all when, as in the *Cresphontes*, a terrible action is threatened but not performed, due to a discovery (1454a). Aristotle does not even consider the possibility that a tragic plot structure might include more than one reversal, one after another. The closest he comes is in noting the double ending of the *Odyssey*, which ends "in opposite ways for the good and bad characters" (1452a). On Euripides' "plays of mixed reversal," see Burnett 1971. For further discussion of double plot structure, see Empson 1974, pp. 27–88. Empson's main interest is in the interrelationship between main plot and subplot, rather than in the possibility of multiple episodes or reversals.

3. Achilles movingly reminds Priam — as if he might have forgotten — "You too, old man, we hear that you once were happy" (καὶ σέ, γέρον, τὸ πρὶν μὲν ἀκούομεν ὄλβιον εἶναι, *Iliad* 24.543).

4. Herodotus 1.32. Compare the end of the *Oedipus Tyrannus*, and discussion in chapter 1.

5. See especially Arrowsmith 1956: he suggests that the juxtaposition of two autonomous actions produces a tragic contradiction between "world as it is said to be" and "world as it is." On Euripides' love of surprising his audience — without discussion of the *Heracles* — see Arnott 1973. Foley 1985 discusses the Arrowsmith reading, arguing that it is unconvincing because "the last action is in many ways more idealized than the first" (p. 203). Arrowsmith's reading is developed by Barlow 1981, who argues that the technique produces three separate levels of "realism." There are those who dismiss the whole attempt to find literary unity in the play, and explain the jarring plot entirely in terms of the myth Euripides had inherited; see especially Heath 1987, who argues that the reversals of the plot are the result of "a familiar mythological datum" (p. 108). Heath's reductive reading makes no attempt to explain why Euripides chose this particular myth, or why he dealt with it as he did, or what his play meant or means (to the Athenians or to the modern reader).

6. Later retellings of the myth make Heracles kill his family first and then perform the

labors; the rejection of the Euripidean version is most readily explained by the thory that later writers are following pre-Euripidean order (see Bond 1981, pp. xxvi–xxx). The main sources for the story of Heracles' madness are Apollodorus 2.4.11 and Diodorus Siculus 4.10 and 11.

7. The shocking, confusing diversity of the *Heracles* has been attacked by many critics. The structure was condemned by Murray 1946 as "broken-backed" (p. 112), and more recently by Stinton 1975. Kitto 1939 notes that the structure of the play is tripartite, and objects that "a play has no business to be a triptych." There have been many attempts to find thematic unity. Burnett 1971 defends the play's unity by seeing in it the work of poetic justice: Megara is punished for her blasphemy. Burnett's moralizing reading is entirely unconvincing, although she has many good individual observations. Sheppard 1916 sees the tension between wealth versus friendship as a structuring principle of the play. Gregory 1977 emphasizes the theme of double parentage. Strohm 1957 finds in the play the theme of self-sacrifice. Bond 1981, pp. xxi–xxii, views the failure of theodicy as the central theme of the play: "*Heracles* is a miracle play where the miracle turns sour" (p. xxi). Shelton 1979 uses a structural analysis to argue that the play is about the nobility of man in a cruel universe.

8. Schwinge 1972 discusses in detail the parallelism between the first and final episodes.

9. The key terms, repeated in the discussion, are δειλία, δυσγένεια, and κακία, which are opposed to ἀνὴρ ἄριστος, εὔκλεια, and εὐγένεια.

10. On the bow, see Hamilton 1985, George 1994, and discussion below.

11. On the ambivalence about the value of the labors in the Heracles myth, see Silk 1993 and Galinsky 1972.

12. See especially lines 290–94. Michelini 1987, p. 247, shows how Megara takes on the role she sees as that of Heracles.

13. The contradictions in the nature of Heracles were already present in myth. He was sometimes seen as a civilizer of mankind (as in, for example, Pindar, *Isthmian* 4.57); sometimes, as in Homer, as a mindless destroyer. He was the son of Zeus by a mortal woman (Alcmene). Silk 1993 notes that "Heracles is unique in his combination of human and divine properties" (p. 120) and suggests that this "peculiar status" is the reason both for the rarity of tragedies about him, and for the strange character of the two tragedies on the subject which we have. Heracles' primary characteristic was his strength. But he is both strong and weak because he is human as well as heroic. In Homer, Heracles is the prime example of human mortality. He is the strongest man in the world, but he still dies (*Iliad* 18.117–19, discussed by Cropp 1986, p. 189). It became more and more difficult for the Athenians, in particular, to know what to make of him. Euripides' *Heracles*, and Sophocles' *Trachiniae* both present the hero's primitivism as a problem. Both plays show Heracles in a domestic setting, in which his presence causes disaster. Both are about how to integrate force into a civilized society. Comparative readings of *Trachiniae* and *Heracles* are given by Silk 1993, Galinsky 1972, and Ehrenberg 1946. Ehrenberg argues that "the tragedy of Heracles is the tragedy of human strength and fate" (p. 164); he suggests that Sophocles and Euripides give contrasting responses to the same tragic theme: "[T]he Sophoclean superman perishes, while the greatness of the Euripidean man finally triumphs over the fiercest onslaught of fate" (p. 164). See also Romilly 1980, p. 7, for another comparison of the two plays.

14. Amphitryon's primary concern is for the children, not himself, and this, he claims,

distinguishes his refusal to die from cowardice (316–18). Similarly, Lycus is, for Amphitryon, marked by cowardice (δειλία, 210) because of his willingness to kill the weak children of Heracles, rather than protect them (209–12). See Bond 1981, pp. xxvi–xxviii, for the presentation of Heracles' labors as a civilizing force in this play; for more extended discussion of Heracles as symbol of civilization, see Galinsky 1972, chs. 1–3.

15. Heracles has used the same adjective a few lines earlier, to desecribe his club: "I shall defeat with this nobly victorious weapon all the Cadmeans I have found bad under my good treatment" (Καδμείων δ' ὅσους / κακοὺς ἐφηῦρον εὖ παθόντας ἐξ ἐμοῦ / τῶι καλλινίκωι τωιδ' ὅπλωι χειρώσομαι, 568–70). Shelton 1979, pp. 109–10, emphasizes the importance of the word καλλίνικος in the play. The word is repeated at 49, 570, 582, 681, 789, 961, 1046.

16. The cognate noun πόνος is commonly used for Heracles' labors in the play — most obviously, in this very speech only a few lines earlier, line 575. Amphitryon also uses the word for his son's labors, 22; the Chorus uses the word in its celebration of the labors, at 357, 388, 427; Heracles himself uses the word of his own labors at 1275 and 1353.

17. Bremer 1972 argues that this is the first meaning the audience would catch.

18. ἐκπονήσω θάνατον is taken by most editors and translators to mean, "I shall labor to protect my children from death." Bond 1981 rejects this interpretation but then is forced to deny the literal meaning of θάνατον as "death"; he renders the question, "Will I not exert myself over my children's mortal danger?" (p. 210). On the use of the verb here, see Bremer 1972, who argues that Euripides deliberately uses the word in an unexpected sense, to reinforce the irony that in laboring to prevent the death of his children, Heracles finishes the labor of killing them. Bond 1981 acknowledges that Bremer's suggestion "should be taken seriously in view of unintended 'Sophoclean' ambiguities, like S. OT 60–61, and Bacchae 970" (p. 211).

19. The irony might be felt all the more strongly in the light of the legend that the purpose of Heracles' labors was to gain immortality. There is, however, no obvious trace of this tradition in the play, and it is probably a postclassical mystic interpretation of the myth — found in Apollodorus 2.4.12, and Theocritus 24.82.

20. Some critics have argued that Euripides' Heracles is mad all along. See especially Wilamowitz 1895, who makes the implausible case that Heracles' madness is anticipated from the beginning of the play by his mental instability. Wilamowitz's description of Euripides' play makes it sound more like Seneca's; I agree here with Braden 1993, p. 251. The psychological realism of the play has been discussed in more measured tones by Chalk 1962 and by Kamerbeek 1966. Others have argued that the labors cause the domestic murders — Heracles is driven mad by blood (Pohlenz 1930, p. 299). Modern critics are perhaps if anything too scornful of these readings; Michelini 1987, for instance, argues that there is no link between Heracles' character and his downfall (p. 234). This is true; but it is not the end of the story.

21. On the comparison with Lear, see chapter 6, and discussion in Braden 1993.

22. Cf. Bacchae 1259–1300, where Cadmus cross-questions Agave as she emerges from her bacchic trance; in doing so, he makes her realize that the head she is holding is that of her own son.

23. For discussion of revenge as a motive for suicide, see Delacourt 1939.

24. His words recall the exchanges at the beginning of the play between Amphitryon, Megara, and Heracles about friendship in misfortune. See 55–59, where Amphitryon laments the fact that few friends are friends in need; 228–30, where he regrets his own

inability to protect the land of Cadmus like a true friend; 267, where the Chorus does the same; 339–47, where Amphitryon accuses Zeus of failing to protect his friends. Heracles is welcomed by both Amphitryon and Megara specifically as φίλτατε (514, 531–32), not only because he is beloved, but also because he is a true friend who protects his friends.

25. It is not technically an *agon* — see Lloyd 1992, p. 11, who classifies it as an epideixis scene. Collard 1975 discusses the scene as a "formal debate."

26. Theseus is central to the final episode of the play, structurally and dramatically. When Heracles wakes up, he makes a speech about his bewilderment (1089–1108), talks with Amphitryon about what he has done (1111–45), and makes another speech, about his despair (1146–52). The same pattern is followed in Amphitryon's conversation with Theseus, where Theseus speaks (1163–77), then talks to Amphitryon about what has happened (1178–1213), then addresses Heracles (1214–28). Two passages of stichomythic dialogue between Theseus and Heracles (1129–1254, 1395–1420) surround the central discussion of the play, in which Heracles explains why his life is not worth living, Theseus tries to persuade him otherwise, and Heracles gives his response. It is clear from this skeletal account that the relationship between Theseus and Heracles is central to the episode, with the third actor, Amphitryon, very much in third place.

27. Of course, there may also be a political motive for the centrality of the Athenian hero; see Mills 1997. But the element of Athenian propaganda should not be overstated. Theseus's presence makes sense in literary terms, even without any appeal to Athenian nationalism. Moreover, my reading of the final scene suggests that Theseus is not presented in quite such glowing terms as Mills suggests; he is generous and a good friend, but Heracles ultimately gets the better of him in argument.

28. See Bond 1981, pp. 359–60, with bibliography, on the pollution of Heracles; and p. 376 on Theseus's "new rationalist spirit." Parker 1983 emphasizes that Theseus "is not concerned to deny the need for purification" (p. 310). See also his discussion of the play on pp. 316–18.

29. In line 1251, I follow Hermann's emendation, defended by Bond 1981, p. 381.

30. Amphitryon uses the verb when he says at the beginning of the play that his son has completed the labors: ἐξεμόχθησεν πόνους (22). Heracles here echoes Megara's declaration that it is stupid to try to labor against the fates of the gods (309–10, using the same verb: ἐκμοχθεῖ).

31. The colloquialism of the phrase γέμω κακῶν struck the author of *De Sublimitate* (40.2–3). He quotes the line and comments, "The remark is very colloquial, but it has become sublime because it fits with the fiction" (σφόδρα δημῶδες τὸ λεγόμενον, ἀλλὰ γέγονεν ὑψηλὸν τῇ πλάσει ἀναλογοῦν). This line is not discussed by Stevens 1976 in his monograph on colloquialism in Euripides.

32. See Nagy 1979, pp. 303, 318–19, on the name of Heracles. As Nagy says, "the themes of beneficence / maleficence constitute the traditional epic theme embodied in the very name of *Heraklees*, 'he who has the *kleos* of *Hera*'" (p. 303).

33. Heracles' review of the sufferings of his own life is comparable with those of Euripides' Oedipus (*Phoenissae* 1595–1616) and Medea (*Medea* 475–95).

34. Bond 1981 notes the fact that Euripides "makes little use of inherited guilt in his extant plays" (pp. 382–83); this is a rare exception.

35. The line is echoed a little later by "I think I will one day reach this point of misfortune" (ἐς τοῦτο δ᾽ ἥξειν συμφορᾶς οἶμαί ποτε, 1294). Because of the parallel, it is less plausible to take συμφορᾶς as accusative plural, as does Kovacs 1998.

36. The apparent inconsistency has led many editors, from Wilamowitz 1895 on, to delete the lines. Romilly 1980 defends them and suggests that there is no real inconsistency.

37. As Bond 1981 notes (p. 390), "Why then should I live?" (τί δῆτά με ζῆν δεῖ;) is a "tragic formula," found also in *Hecuba* 349, *Medea* 145, *Helen* 56, *Prometheus Bound* 747.

38. See Yoshitake 1994, who distinguishes three distinct motives for suicide — loss of hope, desire to preserve honor, and grief — and argues that only the first two are ever, traditionally, seen as heroic justifications for killing oneself. Heracles' only remaining motive for suicide, Yoshitake argues, is grief for his dead wife and children, and grief is never seen in Greek tragedy as a sufficiently dignified motive for a man to commit suicide.

39. I think Yoshitake 1994 exaggerates the extent to which Theseus's offer can restore Heracles to his former position of honor in the Greek world.

40. Both premises are questionable, as Mills 1997 remarks (p. 154). She argues that we are led to notice Theseus's goodwill beyond the weakness of his arguments.

41. The Nurse makes a similar argument in the *Hippolytus* (433–58), where she urges Phaedra not to die because of her love for her stepson; love, after all, is common to gods and men, and the gods who have had love affairs do not for that reason exile themselves from Olympus (451–58). They accept their passions as "fortune": "But they are acquiescent, I think, since they are conquered by fate" (στέργουσι δ', οἶμαι, ξυμφορᾶι νικώμενοι, 458). The slippage between divine immorality and divine weakness can be seen also in *De Sublimitate* 9.7. The writer is upset by the conflation of human and immortal qualities in the *Iliad* (specifically 21.388), and points out that divine weakness and suffering sit awkwardly with divine immortality, since if gods suffer, they must suffer, as they live, forever.

42. I take it that 1338–39 should be excised as irrelevant; for discussion of the excision, see Bond 1981, p. 397. The lines suggest that gods, unlike men, do have some autonomy and power for free decision, which goes against the previous characterization of the gods in the speech.

43. He may even have said so explicitly: there is clearly a lacuna between 1312 and 1313. See Bond 1981, pp. 392–93.

44. Most editors, following Wilamowitz 1895, think that the line must refer to Theseus's analogy between Heracles' position and that of the gods, since that is what Heracles goes on to challenge. But Bond 1981 insists that the line "can hardly refer some twenty lines back to Theseus' arguments about the gods" (Bond 1981, p. 398); the exclamation must, he thinks, refer to Theseus's offer of sanctuary in Athens. Yoshitake 1994 defends Bond's reading, explaining that Theseus's offer is irrelevant insofar as it cannot eliminate Heracles' grief and sense of loss.

45. Heracles' position echoes that of Xenophanes and probably of many contemporary philosophers. Cf. Xenophanes A 32.23–25 (Diels and Kranz 1934, 1: 122): "He says also concerning the gods that there is no mastery among them: for [he says that] it is not holy for any of the gods to be dominated, and that none of them need anything at all" (ἀποφαίνεται δὲ καὶ περὶ θεῶν ὡς οὐδεμιᾶς ἡγεμονίας ἐν αὐτοῖς οὔσης· οὐ γὰρ ὅσιον δεσπόζεσθαί τινα τῶν θεῶν· ἐπιδεῖσθαί τε μηδενὸς αὐτῶν μηδένα μηδ' ὅλως). Heracles' speech, as has often been noted, is paralleled by other outbursts against popular theology elsewhere in Euripides: cf. *Troades* 969–90; *Iphigenia in Tauris* 380–91; *Electra* 737–46; *Iphigenia in Aulis* 793–800.

46. This problem was seized upon by Verrall 1905 as evidence for his theory that the play is designed to prove that the Olympian gods do not exist (pp. 134–98). For refutation of Verrall, see Greenwood 1953, who argues (p. 91) that the lines express the opinions of

Euripides, not Heracles. Many critics have seen the lines as an expression of Euripides' own theological beliefs, which he was unable to resist including in the play despite (e.g., Grube 1941, pp. 57–59) or because of (Brown 1978) the fact that they do not fit in with its fictive world; so too Conacher 1967, p. 79. Halleran 1986 stresses the fact that the undermining of myth has happened before in the play (p. 179); he argues that the play tends toward an increase of dramatic irony. Arrowsmith 1968, pp. 56–57, sees here a denial of the gods' existence: "[T]he gods are first rendered incredible and then transformed into a collective symbol for all the random senseless operations of necessity in human life"; but Shelton 1979, p. 109, argues that "Heracles is not denying divinity, simply the stories which attribute human behaviour to the divinity," and others, including Bond 1981, pp. 399–400, have argued that the contradiction is only apparent, in that Heracles protests only at adultery between gods, rather than between gods and human beings (e.g., Zeus and Alcmene). This is ingenious but unconvincing, because it does not solve the problem that Iris has been seen on stage dominating Lyssa.

47. As many have maintained (see, e.g., Brown 1978). Critics tend, unjustifiably, to equate "Heracles" with "Euripides," a temptation to which almost all those who discuss the passage succumb; see previous note. An important exception is Lefkowitz 1989, who argues convincingly that the expressions of religious skepticism in Euripides are signs not of the poet's own atheism or rationalism but of his literary realism: she argues that Euripidean characters are spurred to outbursts against the gods by the provocations of their immediate dramatic situations.

48. Some critics have objected to the outburst on the grounds that it violates psychological realism: Grube 1941 complains that "Heracles is not the *kind of person* who would indulge in these religious speculations" (p. 57, emphasis in original). It has been suggested more generally that we should not look for psychological consistency in the characters of Greek tragedy: they are to be judged scene by scene, by situations not in play as a whole: see Dale 1969 and Heath 1987, especially pp. 90–123. Conacher 1981 rightly challenges this view (although without reference to the *Heracles*). The violations of consistency in the character of Heracles go against the norms of Greek tragedy and are startling within the conventions and expectations of the genre.

49. Heracles does not even allow that, as in Homer, the gods may be in trouble in the short term and then be rescued and healed, as when Aphrodite is wounded in the *Iliad* 5.334–417. Heracles, like Xenophanes (see note 45), has no time for such wretched tales of the poets.

50. Gregory 1977 accuses Heracles of inconsistency: she says his "actions do not accord with his pessimistic conclusions" (p. 275). My argument here is that Heracles' actions are entirely consistent with his pessimistic view of life.

51. Most editions (including the Oxford Classical Text) print βίοτον for θάνατον. See below for my reasons for not adopting this conjecture.

52. The conjecture was first proposed by Wecklein 1877. It is adopted by Bond 1981: see pp. 402–3 for his discussion. Wilamowitz makes the peculiar argument (ad loc.) that the text we have is the result not of a copying error but of an emendation in antiquity in response to a conceptual shift on the ethical status of suicide. But the argument seems unnecessary; Romilly 1980 rightly asks, "pourquoi, alors, ne pas admettre que celle-ci se fait, précisément dans l' *Heracles?*" (p. 6, n. 2).

53. In the *Andromache* Hermione asks Andromache whether she will indeed remain fixed in her willingness to die, using the same phrasing that Heracles uses to declare his

willingness to live: "Will you stand fast toward death?" (ἐγκαρτερεῖς δὴ θάνατον; 262). The meaning "stand fast in resistance to" is proposed for ἐγκαρτερήσω in the *Heracles* by Kranz 1927, p. 138.

54. As argued by Romilly 1980, p. 6.

55. See especially Romilly 1980: "ce qui, chez Sophocle, mène au suicide mène, chez Euripide, au refus du suicide" (p. 3). She suggests convincingly that the play is "une reponse combinée à l'*Ajax* de Sophocle et à ses *Trachiniennes*" (p. 7). See also Barlow 1981, and Furley 1986.

56. On Heracles' decision to live compared with Ajax's decision to die, see Hamilton 1985, pp. 21 and 25; Burnett 1971, p. 163, n. 9; Gregory 1977, p. 262. Chalk 1962 was the first to suggest that Heracles discovers a new, humanistic kind of ἀρετή, the sign of a cultural shift away from traditional Greek tolerance or admiration for suicide at least in certain circumstances, toward a general condemnation of suicide. Chalk was savagely attacked by Adkins 1966 on the grounds that Chalk has misused and misunderstood the word ἀρετή. But something approximating to Chalk's reading has become the critical norm. See, for example, Galinsky 1972, and Conacher 1967, pp. 78–90, who reads the play as "humanistic." Dover 1974 argues that the refusal of suicide in the *Heracles* is just what Euripides is committed to from legend, not the result of any real ideological objection to suicide on the part of the Greeks: "Euripides may have felt obliged to treat the matter this way, since he had shown Heracles in a situation to which suicide would have been an appropriate response, but could not turn upside-down a well-established complex of legend" (p. 168). This account is highly unsatisfactory because it implies that Euripides had no choice either about which part of a huge body of legend he used or about how he dealt with it. The problem is created by Euripides' own play; he did not have to show Heracles in a situation to which suicide would have been an appropriate response. There is little evidence for a general tendency to condemn suicide at this date, beyond the internal evidence of the play itself. Dover argues that the Greeks did not, in general, disapprove of suicide; in many circumstances, it was seen as the brave thing to do. Compare Euripides' *Orestes* 1060–64, where Orestes declares he will display εὐγένεια by proposing to stab himself. Plato's Socrates, however, condemns suicide if it is not commanded by a god (*Phaedo* 61–64). In the *Laws* Plato condemns some suicides as a form of self-murder (*Laws* 873c). The difficulties of the *Heracles* are partly a result of its originality: the play challenges expectations about heroic suicide. It includes the notion that living may be more heroic than dying, and also questions that (presumably fairly unexpected) idea.

57. The *Oedipus Tyrannus* is certainly earlier than the *Heracles;* some have seen 425 BC as the terminus ante quem for the *Oedipus Tyrannus* (based on a possible parody of line 629 in Aristophanes' *Acharnians* 27), although Dawe 1982, p. 245, scorns this alleged echo. The date of the *Heracles* is uncertain, although metrical evidence suggests that it was composed relatively late in Euripides' career. Dates of 416 and 414 BC have been proposed, although it may be even later; see Bond 1981, pp. xxx–xxxii.

58. Most critics discussing the end of the play have taken the relationship between Heracles and Theseus to be heartwarming in a simple human way: Heracles, destroyed by the gods, is helped by his human friend. Theseus is often praised for his tact in how he helps Heracles, who has never before needed help. See Mills 1997, p. 142.

59. Garrison 1995 (pp. 36–43) compares the Greek terms φιλία and δίκη with Durkheim's terms, "integration" and "regulation." She remarks that Heracles rejects a form of suicide that would have been, in Durkheimian terms, egotistic and anomic (p. 41).

60. On the significance of Heracles' bow, see Hamilton 1985, Grube 1941, and Vellacott 1975. One of the crucial changes Euripides makes from what was probably the traditional legend is to make the bow the instrument he uses both to perform his labors and to kill his children; in Apollodorus (2.4.11) he burns them.

61. Euripides is at his most Sophoclean in making Heracles form a personal relationship with his bow. Compare Sophocles' Heracles, who addresses his own hands and back and shoulders and arms (*Trachiniae* 1089–90). Cf. also Philoctetes, who forms a personal relationship with his own foot (786), as well as, Caliban-like, with the island caves that were his home (*Philoctetes* 1461–68).

62. So Walsh 1979, who argues that "by choosing to live and to retain his weapons, Heracles accepts his public role as a hero" (p. 308), although Walsh also rightly acknowledges the huge personal cost of the decision.

63. As Michelini 1987 argues, "the sign is packed with multiple, contradictory meanings; it is overloaded with the many different roles the hero might want to adopt. So Heracles remains poised at a remarkable moment: armed with a sign that might mean hero or coward, tragic lesson or constant shame, there is no way to know what or who he is" (p. 125).

64. The play makes relatively little of Heracles' other weapon, his club. His second son plays with it (470–71) and is killed with it (992–94).

65. On this earlier debate about the bow, see Hamilton 1985, who defends it against those who see it as irrelevant or undramatic.

66. For general discussion of Theseus as a character in Greek tragedy, see Mills 1997.

67. Bond 1981 is troubled by this passage (1410–7): "This dialogue seems intended to exhibit Heracles smartly getting the better of an unsympathetic Theseus. After what has preceded, it may seem petty" (p. 411). He tries to resolve the apparent problem by transposing the lines; see his appendix 1.

68. Line 1417 is certainly corrupt (since the subjunctive εἴπης cannot be right), and various emendations have been proposed (see Bond 1981, p. 414); but the general sense is clear enough.

69. There are three moments in the play when one stronger figure leads dependents away from the altar of Zeus in the orchestra, toward a kind living death. Megara takes the children inside, to dress them in burial clothes, at 347. At line 636, Heracles leads the children in, like towboats, to the house where he will kill them all. And at the end, Theseus leads Heracles himself away. On the staging, see Rehm 1988, especially pp. 302–3.

70. Dunn 1996, pp. 115–29, makes much of the problem of Heracles' burial in the play, and argues that at the end "the familiar closing gestures seem to be present until we look more closely and find that they have been emptied of force." The assumption, on the part of Amphitryon, Theseus, and Heracles himself, that he will die and be buried, is in direct contradiction to the myth that his body will be consumed by fire on the top of Mount Oeta, the myth on which hero cults of Heracles depended. This Heracles seems entirely mortal and can hope only for ordinary human death and burial.

CHAPTER 4: "Let us live": Seneca's *Epistles* and *Hercules Furens*

1. On the Tacitus passage in its cultural and historical context, see the detailed discussion of Seel 1972, pp. 111–277.

2. The most detailed and vivid account of Seneca's suicide is in Tacitus, *Annals* 15.62–

64; see also the hostile account of Cassius Dio, 62.65. Griffin 1976, pp. 367–88, discusses both the historical accounts of Seneca's suicide and the ways his own death might be related to his philosophical writing. The theatricality of Seneca's death in Tacitus's account is striking; as Rudich 1993 remarks, "clearly in death as well as in life, Senecan philosophy required an audience if it was to work" (p. 111).

3. *Meditations* 2.14. The thought is a commonplace of Stoic injunctions against the fear of death: compare, for example, Antoninus 2.14. Similar sentiments can also be found in Epicurean writing: see Lucretius, *De Rerum Natura* 3.1087–94. Augustine adopts the motif, in *De Civitate Dei* 1.11: "[T]he end of life puts the longest life on a par with the shortest. For of two things which have alike ceased to be, the one is not better, the other worse — the one greater, the other less." Augustine goes on to attack Stoic attitudes to suicide in 1.17–25.

4. So Griffin 1976 who argues, *pace* Rist 1969, that Seneca's presentation of suicide as an act of freedom is not incompatible with orthodox Stoic thought.

5. Rist 1969 discusses the problem (pp. 239–44) and remarks that "it is not quite clear how far the Stoics are aware of problems of this kind" (p. 239).

6. Rist 1969, pp. 242–44.

7. Diogenes Laertius 7.28.

8. There is a useful survey of modern critical opinions of Seneca's attitude to suicide in Tadic-Gilloteaux 1963, pp. 541–42. Some have been Seneca's preoccupation with suicide as a departure from orthodox Stoicism. For example, Rist 1969 argues that Seneca advocates suicide more vehemently than other Stoics, such as Epictetus, and that he favors it even for trivial reasons. Griffin 1976, pp. 367–88, contests Rist's view, and argues that Seneca, both in his writings and in his own real-life suicide, followed Stoic doctrine, and supported suicide only for good reasons: in case of intolerable deprivation, for the sake of friends or family, or to avoid disgrace. "As for the notion that Seneca exalted suicide, the truth is more that he exalted martyrdom, i.e. the willingness to face death rather than do what one thinks is wrong" (Griffin, p. 386). I think Griffin overstates her case. Seneca's attitude to suicide is perhaps logically reconcilable with Stoic doctrine, but it remains true that his rhetoric, at least in the letters to Lucilius, supports Rist's claim that "fundamentally Seneca's wise man is in love with death" (p. 249).

9. Griffin 1976, p. 391: "The degree of emphasis Seneca lays on suicide and the circumstances in which he recommends it reflect the political terrors of the governing classes in the early Empire. Men could learn to die well, even if they could not live as they chose."

10. See especially epistle 24.

11. See later in the chapter for further discussion of the *Hercules Furens*.

12. Seneca's confused rhetoric on the proper length of human life — in epistle 93, in particular — inspired Jonson's *Ode on Cary and Morison*; on this see Peterson 1981, pp. 195–232. Seneca's *De Brevitate Vitae* (*Dial. 10, Ad Paulinum*) produces similar paradoxes about the length of life. The piece argues that people are quite wrong to believe that life is too short. Life is made too short by the fact that we waste our lives, but for those who live well any life, however brief in years, is quite long enough. "It is not that we have little time, but that we waste a lot of it . . . if you know how to use it, life is long" (*Non exiguum temporis habemus, sed multum perdimus . . . vita, si uti scias, longa est*, 1.3, 2.1). Seneca cites the commonplace of the old man who is reluctant to renounce life, and like Lucretius, he

associates the sense that one's life has been too brief with the failure to make the most of life while alive (3.4–5). See introduction, note 2, for further instances of this trope.

13. The text used here is Winterbottom 1974.

14. On Seneca's specifically Roman reading of Stoicism, see Wilson 1997.

15. *Consolatio ad Marciam* 20–21: "Think what benefit timely death has, and think how many people have been harmed by living too long" (*cogita quantum boni opportuna mors habeat, quam multis diutius vixisse nocuerit,* 20.4); "The end is fixed for everyone" (*fixus est cuique terminus,* 21.4).

16. On this technique of rhetorical excess in *consolationes,* see Braund 1997a. On the *consolatio* in general, see Fern 1948.

17. On Seneca's rhetorical use of contradictory attitudes, see Wilson 1997.

18. As Tadic-Gilloteaux 1963 notes, Seneca's philosophical focus shifts in different works, depending on his addressee. "C'est a Lucilius Junior, chevalier procurateur de Sicile, poète à l'esprit curieux, ayant du gout pour la philosophie, que Sénèque a réservé l'exposé le plus complet de ses idées sur le suicide" (pp. 543–44). It is also to Lucilius that Seneca writes his most complete account of when and why one should avoid suicide.

19. On the conventions of the Roman *consolatio* in general, and in Seneca in particular, see Wilson 1997, Braund 1997a.

20. Seneca gets many of his most striking rhetorical effects through the juxtaposition of one epistle with another. On the ordering of the collection, see Cancik 1967 and Wilson 1987.

21. Wilson 1997, pp. 62–65, emphasizes the specifically Roman concerns and language that Seneca brings to his discussion of Stoic issues.

22. The technique of juxtaposing two apparently contradictory ways of looking at a question is clearly influenced by the Roman educational practice of the *suasoria;* it is a common feature of Seneca's style. Wilson 1997 analyzes the tensions in Seneca's attitudes to grief in the *Epistles.*

23. This is a common sentiment in Senecan prose: compare, for example, epistle 61, in which Seneca responds to the problem of the proper length of life by saying, "If we have lived enough, it is thanks to character, not years or days. My dear Lucilius, I have lived the right amount; satisfied, I wait for death" (*ut satis vixerimus, nec anni nec dies faciunt, sed animus. Vixi, Lucili carissime, quantum satis erat; mortem plenus exspecto,* 61.4).

24. For discussion of some other instances of this metaphor in Seneca, see Lavery 1980.

25. Cf. epistle 12.6.

26. Critics who discuss the relationship between Euripides' *Heracles* and Seneca's version of the myth concentrate on the question of how closely Seneca follows Euripides. Opinions range from those who see Seneca as a slavish imitator, to those who regard the play as a Stoic reworking of the Greek text, to those who claim little or no connection between Senecan and Greek tragedy. There is a useful survey of critical literature on this question in Paratore 1965. It is certainly true that Seneca uses the framework of the Euripidean play, but he does so with important alterations. On Seneca's alterations from Euripides, see Haywood 1941. Seneca also takes a great many elements from the Augustan poets (Ovid, Horace, Virgil), as well as probably using lost post-Augustan sources; see Fitch 1987, pp. 44–49. On the sources for Senecan tragedy, see also Tarrant 1978.

27. See Auvray-Assayas 1987. The Stoicism of Seneca's tragedies in general has

aroused huge critical controversy. The characters in Senecan tragedy tend to live entirely out of accordance with nature (which constantly threatens to be overturned or destroyed), and people are ruled by their most horribly destructive passions. Few characters in Senecan tragedy behave like good Stoics. Some explain the discrepancy between the ideology of Seneca's prose and the behavior of his tragic characters by arguing that the tragedies show what horrors happen when people fail to act on Stoic principles. The unity of outlook between Seneca's prose and dramatic works is vigorously defended by Pohlenz 1959. Lawall 1982 finds in Heracles a "tempered, humane version of Stoicism" (p. 26). For a more nuanced view, see Schiesaro 1997 and now Schiesaro 2003.

28. See Fitch 1987, pp. 15–43. Dingel 1974 rightly rejects the idea that Hercules trusts his own power and is therefore Stoic, as "absurd" (p. 114).

29. See the excellent discussion of Senecan anxiety of influence in Boyle 1997, pp. 112–37.

30. See Fitch 1987 ad loc.: *secura quies* "clearly carries Epicurean overtones" (p. 176), while the contrast of countryside and urban activities recalls both Horace (*Ode* 1.1) and Virgil (the *Laudes Ruris, Georgics* 2.458–540).

31. Fitch 1987 remarks that the "ode is integrated, to a degree that is unusual in Senecan tragedy, into its dramatic context . . . only at the end of this section does the audience realise, surely with a considerable shock, that these generalities are extremely pertinent to the judgement of the play" (pp. 161–62).

32. See especially Amphitryon's speech, 249–67.

33. Seneca was very struck by the Virgilian passage and quotes it more than once in his *Epistles* (e.g., 107.3; 108.29).

34. The point holds whether the play was performed, or read, or recited dramatically. Those who attend select dramatic recitations are no less vulnerable to death than theater audiences.

35. As Davis 1993 remarks, "on the face of it the wish *sera nos illo referat senectus* is pointless, if it is absolutely true that *nemo ad id sero venit*. To extract sense we have to take the adjective *sera* to mean 'late' and the adverb *sero* to mean 'too late'" (p. 241).

36. Horace, *Odes* 1.11.8, *carpe diem*.

37. Compare the uses of the word "plucked" in *Paradise Lost*, discussed in chapter 8.

38. Henry and Henry 1985 rightly ask, "if death has been conquered, why does the lengthy narrative of [Hercules'] visit to Hades dwell on its unchanging desolation, with no actual achievement by Hercules apart from the dragging of Cerberus into daylight?" (p. 108).

39. The difference between Seneca's play and Euripides' is often seen as a shift toward greater interiorization. Seneca's tragedies have been described as "Greek subjects recollected in tranquillity" (Frye 1967, pp. 11–12). Frye distinguishes Euripides' *Heracles* from Seneca's version of the story by saying that "the source of the conflict, to use Greek terms, is *praxis* in Euripides, a conflict in the dramatic action; it is *theoria* in Seneca, a conflict of mental attitudes" (p. 11). I think this is rather misleading, in that there is very little tranquillity in Seneca. Internal conflicts in the minds of Euripides' characters become, in Seneca, external conflicts between the various characters, which can be resolved only by the destruction of one or other of the warring sides.

40. As Braden 1993 suggests (p. 250).

41. Hadas 1939 thinks the scene shows a specifically Roman brutality that echoes the spectacles of the amphitheater.

42. He may even kill the first child on stage, although Fitch (1987, pp. 351–52) argues against this view. My point is independent of any particular view on the staging of Senecan drama. However, I agree with Herington 1966 that Seneca's tragedies must have been written for at least dramatic recitation, using a number of different voices. Boyle 1997 defends the idea that Senecan tragedy was "spectacular" and even "theatrical" (pp. 7–12).

43. Here I follow the text of Fitch 1987. The Oxford Classical Text prints *paretur* for *vacat cur,* and a period, not a question mark, in line 1210.

44. Similarly, Seneca's Oedipus considers suicide and even draws his sword; but he immediately realizes how inadequate such a punishment would be for all his sins (*Oedipus* 935–57).

45. Braden 1993 calls this "a fantasy of destructiveness not so different from that of his madness" (p. 254).

46. The manuscript reading of 1312 is *letale ferro pectus impresso,* which cannot be right because "*letale* is senseless qualifying *pectus,*" as Fitch 1987 argues, ad loc. I follow his emendation here; the Oxford Classical Text prints *senile* for *letale.*

47. The parallel has often been noted, and many try to explain the Hercules passage by citing the epistle (see, e.g., Edert 1909, p. 31). Motto and Clark 1981 suggest that the parallel shows Hercules' ethical responsibility; they argue that he emerges as a "piquant, remarkable and triumphant figure" (p. 116).

48. Dingel 1974 argues that Hercules does not, unlike Seneca, resist suicide out of *pietas:* "Nicht als einem Akt der *pietas* versteht Hercules seine Selbstuberwindung, sondern als Absage an die *virtus*" (p. 111). He claims that "Senecas Krankheit und das Bewusstsein des Hercules, die eigene Families erschlagen zu haben, sind eben nicht kommensurabel" (p. 112).

49. *Troades* 418–25, *Phoenissae* 38–50, 306–19.

50. *Phoenissae* 38–39.

51. *Troades* 418–19.

52. The passage recalls a similar outcry from Theseus in the *Phaedra,* 715–18. The *Phaedra* passage was probably written first, because, as Fitch 1987 notes, "the Amazon theme of that play explains the choice of Tanais and Maeotis" (p. 457). The conceit of the crime no water can cleanse is almost a literary cliché: compare *Choephoroi* 72–74; *OT* 1227–28; *Anthologia Palatina* 14.71.3, *De Rerum Natura* 6.1075–77. But the speech is also particularly appropriate to the *Hercules Furens* because Hercules' polluted hands are the culmination of an emphasis on his hands running through the play. On the theme of hands in the *Hercules Furens,* see Boyle 1997, p. 106, n. 40. There is emphasis on Hercules' hands at, for example, 58, 114, 122, 247, 254, 566, 882.

53. One could compare Bakhtin's concept of the chronotope (Bakhtin 1981). The confusion of excessive time with excessive place will play a prominent part in later representations of tragic overliving, in Shakespeare and in Milton; see especially chapter 6, on *Macbeth.*

54. Seneca was not the first Roman to feel trapped by the spread of the Roman Empire. Cicero (*Ad familiares* 4.7) warns Marcellus, "Wherever you are, remember that you are equally within the power of the emperor." Gibbon 1932 quotes and develops Cicero's observation: "[T]he empire of the Romans filled the world, and when that empire fell into the hands of a single person, the world became a safe and dreary prison for his enemies" (p. 73).

55. The redemptive reading is dominant among commentators; see, for instance,

Henry and Henry 1985 who see a "sense of reconciliation — of self-acceptance — at the conclusion of this play, [which] implies a new beginning and the possibility of a new identity for the fallen Hercules" (p. 112). Boyle 1997 sees "in one play" (*Hercules Furens*) the possibility of human redemption" (p. 33). Motto and Clark 1981 perhaps go furthest, finding in the play "an ultimate active transcendence of disorder and a consciously willed resolution to terminate upheaval" (p. 103). See also Lawall 1982, who, like Motto and Clark, puts a great deal of weight on the fact that the madness is sent by Juno (and is therefore not Hercules' fault). But I am not convinced that Hercules is presented as entirely admirable, even before the madness. I am mainly in agreement with Fitch, who argues (1987, pp. 35–38) that the final act of the play is like other Senecan tragedies in withholding any full sense of resolution: "[I]t is the continuing harshness of Hercules' character, and the conflict and pain which result from it, that remain dominant throughout the Act" (p. 36); and with Braden 1993, who says that "Seneca's play moves not toward transvalued heroism but toward the stifling sense of a dead end" (p. 252).

56. Theseus himself, at the end of Seneca's *Phaedra*, similarly despairs of ever finding a place that could be unknown to him: he says, "I have filled the stars and hell and the waves with my wickedness; there is no further estate; all three realms know me" (*sidera et manes et undas scelere complevi meo; / amplius sors nulla restat; regna me novunt tria*, 1211–12).

57. Compare the ending of the *Thebaid*, where, as here, Theseus is dominant. Braund 1997b reads the final victory of Theseus in that poem as an optimistic ending; but Lovatt 1999 more convincingly emphasizes the multiple endings of the *Thebaid*, and suggests that "Statius denies closure by setting his endings and his models against one another" (p. 147).

CHAPTER 5: "A wheel of fire": *King Lear*

1. See especially Braden 1993 and Miola 1992, pp. 159–74. Hunter 1967 argues that Shakespeare may have known only *sententiae* from Seneca and few whole plays. But there is strong evidence that, *pace* Hunter, Shakespeare had read whole plays of Seneca (see Jones 1977, pp. 267–72, and bibliography); and it seems likely that he had read or seen the whole of the *Hercules Furens*. See Waith 1962 on the influence of this play on early modern drama, including Shakespeare. The wooing scene in *Richard III* is closely modeled on the wooing of Megara by Lycus (see Jones, p. 218), and of course the use of a whole scene, rather than single lines, is unlikely to come from acquaintance only with quotations from commonplace books. Shakespeare also shows signs of close knowledge of certain passages of the play: Hercules' lament that his hands will never be clean seems a likely model for Macbeth's lament at the uselessness of "all great Neptune's ocean" (see chapter 6); and, as I suggest here, Gloucester seems to quote Megara. See also Miola 1992 for a detailed and interesting account of Shakespeare's use of Seneca.

2. Braden 1993 argues that Shakespeare reverses Seneca's plot structure, putting the madness after the destruction of the child. This is a little misleading, because even in the first scene, Lear is called "mad" by Kent ("be Kent unmannerly / When Lear is mad", 1.1.146–47). From the perspective of Kent or the Fool, Lear's later "madness" is less insane than his earlier apparent sanity. Braden suggests that Shakespeare restores some of what Seneca left out of Euripides — the sense of human solidarity and of new possibilities — but then provides an ending bleaker than anything in the Greeks or Shakespeare, with the death of Cordelia.

3. This is noticed by Shuger 1996, who associates with Christianity the "profoundly

unclassical" emphasis on the vulnerability of the flesh as an essential feature of humanity (p. 50).

4. The cruelty of *King Lear* is emphasized by many critics — perhaps most influentially, Kott 1964, who argues that the play practices a "philosophical cruelty" (p. 104) and that it moves from tragedy to the grotesque. I would argue, against Kott, that philosophical — and physical — cruelty is, and has always been, a feature of the tragic mode.

5. Charles Lamb argued that "the Lear of Shakespeare cannot be acted"; in the theater, he writes, the storm scene "has nothing in it but what is painful and disgusting" (Lamb 1912, p. 124).

6. Johnson 1968, p. 704.

7. Lyons 1974 argues persuasively that the subplot of *King Lear* is a simplistic version of the main plot, acting as a naive misreading of the play that brings home to the audience the actual complexity and even unintelligibility of the central story. She describes Gloucester's death as a simplified version of Lear's: Edgar's account of Gloucester's death is "understandable in the way Bradley wanted Lear's to be" (p. 24). See below for more detailed discussion of the connections and differences between Gloucester and Lear.

8. On the Dover Cliff scene, see Bratton 1987, p. 175, and Foakes 1997, pp. 62–63. Hunter 1972 reads Edgar's trick as successful: "Gloucester through his despair is brought to accept his lot." Foakes observes, as I emphasize here, that it is nothing of the kind, because he keeps reverting to thoughts of death (pp. 226–27).

9. As Rosenberg 1972 notes, arguing that the scene manages to escape actual comedy: "If Gloucester's is an absurd world, his ruined suicide is not, as Kott 1964 would have it, an absurdity. This is a stage of fools, not of clowns" (p. 265). In fact, it is largely up to the director to decide whether to allow the audience to laugh at Gloucester. The 2001 Globe Theatre production played the scene partly for laughs — assisted in this by the physical vigor both of Gloucester and of Lear himself — although the production also brought out the disturbing religious mania of Poor Tom/Edgar.

10. As noted by Foakes 1997, p. 62.

11. Compare also Antony's failed suicide in *Antony and Cleopatra*, which is both comic and tragic; see Barton 1994. The comedy of Antony's failed suicide is also discussed by Snyder 1979, who shows how comic structures operate in tragedy: "[L]iterary convention can operate to shape and enrich a work that is moving in a direction opposite to that convention" (p. 16). Rozett 1985 sees comic elements both in the suicides of Antony and of Romeo and Juliet. It can be almost funny that Juliet is still alive and wakes up after the death of Romeo; but it very quickly stops being funny. Desdemona also manages to squeak out more and more nothings after being strangled, but her failure to die at once only increases the pathos of her death.

12. For Hotspur, as for Seneca, life will always be too long if one fails to use it rightly, for the pursuit of virtue or honor (see especially *1 Henry IV,* 5.2.80–85). But Hotspur dies and loses not only his life but also his youth, his image, his status, and even his wild, desperate, self-promoting rhetoric. Even his last words, his epitaph, are stolen from his lips by Hal, who finishes his final sentence for him (*1 Henry IV,* 5.4.85–86). The death of Hotspur represents in Shakespeare the end of the Senecan conception of how long a life should be, and also of a Marlovian or Senecan kind of tragic hero. *1 Henry IV* associates the revival of Falstaff with the rejection of a tragic account of history. Hal kills Hotspur, and ultimately casts off Falstaff, as if identifying history as a sphere that is neither fully tragic nor fully comic. The lives of kings happen in real time, not in Hotspur's intense "short-

ness," which makes every moment the moment of choice between honor and dishonor, nor in Falstaff's sybaritic time, which has nothing to do with the time of day.

13. *Hercules Furens* 426; see chapter 4. The parallel with Seneca is noted by Hunter 1972.

14. See Patterson 1989.

15. See Goldberg 1984.

16. Edgar's failure to reveal his identity to Gloucester is one of the notorious critical problems of *King Lear*. In the main source for the scene, Sidney's *Old Arcadia* 2.10, the son, Leonatus, never conceals his identity from his father, and he openly refuses to lead him to the top of the cliff (see Bullough 1978, pp. 402–8). Edgar's deceitfulness is Shakespeare's most important and puzzling addition to his source. In describing his father's death, Edgar says that he "Never — O fault! — revealed myself unto him" (5.3.191), which hardly explains the motive for the fault. It is, of course, necessary for the plot that he remain in disguise until the end. But it also suggests an element of sadism in Edgar's character, in his willingness to prolong his father's hopeless pain. Cavell 1987 suggests that Edgar shrinks from recognition because he cannot bear to reveal either his own shame or his father's weakness (pp. 54–57). Cavell underplays the desire to dominate, which is common to both Edgar and Lear himself; the disguise allows Edgar to remain fully in control of the situation.

17. The tradition of diabolic temptation to despair and suicide is discussed by Macdonald and Murphy 1990: see especially pp. 38, 50. Cf. also Marlowe's Dr. Faustus, who is tempted to kill himself by being offered the weapons to do it with (*Doctor Faustus* 2.3.21–22); and Redcrosse's encounter with Despayre in *Faerie Queene* 1.9.

18. Goldberg 1984 discusses Edgar's deception as an image of dramatic illusion, emphasizing that at least from one perspective, Gloucester's life "is no 'miracle' (line 55), but a cheat" (p. 543). The extent to which the audience is led to share Gloucester's deception has been much debated. Some, like Foakes 1997, p. 329, argue that "from the opening lines onwards [4.6] makes the audience aware that Edgar is hoaxing his father with conscious deception, and contriving to have him 'die' in order to bring him to life again"; he claims that "it is arguable that the point of the whole incident would be lost unless the audience is fully aware all the time that there is no cliff" (p. 62). Others (Dessen 1975; Peat 1980) suggest that the audience does at least temporarily share the illusion. This is partly a question of staging. Peter Brook made Gloucester faint as he fell and regain consciousness as if after near death experience, which brought out that for Gloucester the subjective experience is like death. On the staging of the scene, see Rosenberg 1972 and Foakes 1997.

19. Kermode 2000 rightly describes the scene as "amazingly bold": it consists, as he says, of "Eleven lines, and a silence probably much longer than either — a silence at the very heart of Shakespeare" (p. 11).

20. Heilman 1948 comments on "ripeness is all," "a man may ripen into fullness of being which means, among other things, that one part of him does not rule all the rest and that one moment's mood does not close off all the perspectives available to him" (p. 112). Cunningham 1960 argues that Heilman is misled by modern sensibility to read the phrase "ripeness is all" in psychological terms; in fact it is an affirmation of Christian resignation to the proper time of death. The inadequacies of a purely Christian interpretation of the phrase are well discussed by Elton 1968, pp. 100–107, who argues that Edgar leads Gloucester to a position that is "both quasi-pagan and quasi-Christian" (p. 104), melding Stoicism with Christianity. Sypher 1976, pp. 165–66, comments on the inappropriateness

of Edgar's comment in the context of *King Lear*. Contrast *Hamlet* 5.2.230–33; Hamlet succeeds in adopting the attitude of passive deference to time, which Gloucester and Lear consistently resist.

21. One oddity here is that Edgar's claim does not seem to fit the situation at all: it is not his going hence which Gloucester is reluctant to endure, nor his coming hither, but rather the inability to stop: "No further, sir," he says. Gloucester longs for immediate death and is unwilling to go on deferring the moment of release. But Edgar replies as if he had expressed a fear of death.

22. On the line, "And that's true too" as informing principle of the play, see Booth 1983 and Kermode 2000.

23. Wymer 1986, pp. 1–15, emphasizes the double nature of suicide as both heroic and damnable, and analyzes the differences between Christian and pagan attitudes to suicide.

24. Levin 1959 argues that Gloucester must, like all of us, try to rise again after a sinful fall into apparently insurmountable depths.

25. The phrase is Frank Kermode's (1967). Laschelles 1973 relates the images of Doomsday in the play to pictorial representations of the Last Judgment. Wittreich 1984 rightly insists that "the Christian analogy provided by the Apocalypse, while a clue to interpretation, does not proclaim the play to be Christian" (p. 123).

26. Wymer 1986, pp. 67–72, argues that the scene is a version of the Christian morality play.

27. Some would disagree; for extended discussion, see Elton 1968. See also Barnet 1955 for a broader argument against finding Christian doctrine in Shakespeare's plays.

28. This is admirably discussed by Elton 1968, who argues that the main characters divide into four quite distinct religious attitudes: the *prisca theologia* of Edgar and Cordelia; the atheism of Goneril, Regan, and Edmund; the superstition of Gloucester; and the "polytheistic-naturalist" paganism of Lear himself.

29. See Foakes 1997, p. 300, on the staging of "a deed so violent as to seem for generations of critics and actors too appalling to enact in view of the audience."

30. Foakes 1997 notes that, "dramatically, Gloucester's passage through a kind of death and restoration to life may be seen as a parallel to Lear's obliviousness in the loss of his wits and subsequent return to sanity" (p. 63).

31. See Thomas 1976. He argues that, although there was probably more respect generally accorded to the old than there is now, their status was dependent on continuing to maintain an active social role.

32. In life as well as art: the strange parallels have often been noticed between *King Lear* and the case of Sir Brian Annesely and his daughter Cordel. See Bullough 1969.

33. Hazlitt 1964, 3: 61, "Pasquils Jests and Mother Bunches Merriments."

34. Cavell 1987 (in "The avoidance of love: A reading of *King Lear*," pp. 39–123, an essay first published in 1969) proposed an influential and appealing account of Lear's motivation in the opening scene. He criticizes the "usual interpretations," that "Lear is senile; Lear is puerile; Lear is not to be understood in natural terms" (p. 57), and proposes instead that Lear is led by "the attempt to avoid recognition, the shame of exposure, the threat of self-revelation" (p. 58). Cavell understands what Lear is avoiding as "love"; I think the burdens of family responsibility are only one of the weights that he mistakenly imagines he can escape.

35. *Oxford English Dictionary*, s.v.: 1. a., "the fact of being alive" (1325); 3. b., "the means of living; livelihood, maintenance, support" (1330). The play on "living" and "liv-

ing" overlaps with the use of another crucial pun, between "loving" and "loving." Hawkes 1964 has shown that the first scene of *Lear* puns on and plays with two etymologically distinct senses of the word "love": "to feel affection for" and "to value" (in material terms). Lear goes wrong because he confuses the two senses of the verb: he thinks that love can be translated into material value.

36. *True Chronicle History of King Leir*, 10.860–65; Bullough 1978, p. 358. The question seems close enough to Adam's "Why do I overlive?" (*Paradise Lost* 10.773) to suggest that Milton had read the *True Chronicle*. For further discussion of Adam's question, see chapter 8.

37. *Albion's England* 25–27, in Bullough 1978, p. 335.

38. Richard II goes on living after he has lost one of the king's two bodies. When he is deposed from his kingdom, he knows that he has lost part of himself: "Alack the heavy day! / That I have worn so many winters out, / And know not now what name to call myself" (*Richard II* 4.1.256–58). He calls for a mirror and searches in the "shadow" of his face for the marks of his loss; but the physical body remains, even when the kingly body is gone. On the concept of "the king's two bodies," see Kantorowicz 1997.

39. Foakes 1997, p. 273, notes the suggestion of "flux"—a discharge from the bowels—in "superflux."

40. Patterson 1989 thinks the passage is a critique of social inequity. Shuger 1996 argues, against Patterson, that it remains within the Christian tradition of the obligation of the rich toward the poor: "[I]n his painful epiphany, the pagan king for a moment grasps the nature of Christian *caritas*" (p. 53).

41. The button is probably his own; this is a final request to be set free from the "lendings" of life. Compare Gloucester's desire that "distribution should undo excess." It is also possible that Lear wants to undo a button on Cordelia's clothing (see Foakes 1997, p. 390), but I think this is less likely, given Lear's desire to remove his own clothes earlier in the play (cf. 3.4.108–9, 4.6.173).

42. See Miola 1992, pp. 143–67, on this and other Senecan features of the play.

43. *Hercules Furens* 1202.

44. See Adelman 1992 for further discussion of this passage.

45. One reason his tears scald him, and are for him the torture of the damned, is that they make him less than a man: he railed at his own tears at 1.4.296–99: "I am asham'd / That thou has power to shake my manhood thus, / That these hot tears, which break from me perforce, / Should make thee worth them". At 2.4, after their refusal to give him any retinue reveals to him at last the nature of Goneril and Regan, he cries to the gods, "touch me with noble anger, / And let not women's weapons, water-drops, / Stain my man's cheeks! . . . No, I'll not weep. / I have full cause of weeping, but this heart / Shall break into a hundred thousand flaws / Or ere I'll weep" (2.1.276–78, 283–86). The storm, which begins to break just as Lear says these words, is the substitute the gods or nature offer for the tears Lear will not weep himself.

46. Braden 1993 notes a return to Senecan rhetoric here—after the un-Senecan possibility of redemption implied by the temporary reconciliation of father and daughter—which is modified only by being "painfully contrary to fact: heaven's vault will not crack, however much Lear might want it to" (p. 261).

47. In all the known sources for the play, Cordelia (or Cordilla) outlives her father. The king and his youngest daughter are reconciled and go on living happily for a few years,

if not ever after. The manner of her death in Shakespeare is also unparalleled by anything in earlier versions of the legend. The historical sources suggest that Cordelia committed suicide. So Geoffrey of Monmouth (Bullough 1978, p. 316); Holinshed (Bullough, p. 319). In the *Mirror for Magistrates* (1574) Cordilla is imprisoned and tempted by a female Despair to kill herself (1.1–371). She yields to the temptation and, after death, reproaches herself for her un-Christian "follye" (363). In *King Lear*, Edmund explains the origin of the legend of her suicide, as a vicious rumor spread by his own servants (5.3.250–53).

48. Freud, in "The theme of the three caskets" (Freud 1953, 12: 291–301), plausibly identifies Cordelia, the "dumb" third daughter of folktale, with death: "Cordelia is Death," he pronounces (p. 301).

49. The final scene (5.3) notoriously casts doubt on the state of mind in which Lear dies: optimists believe that his heart, like Gloucester's, "burst smilingly" in the belief that she lives, and therefore that all sorrow is redeemed, while the less sanguine argue that he dies knowing the worst, that she'll come no more. Those who see Christian redemption at the end include O. Campbell 1948. Mack 1965, pp. 114–17, condemns both redemptive and despairing readings as different kinds of sentimentality and argues that "the victory and the defeat are simultaneous and inseparable" (p. 117). I see less victory than Mack does, but I think it is important not to see Lear's suffering as inevitable or as a reflection of the universal course of human life. The defeat is shocking because we are led to believe that it could so nearly have been victory.

50. He may be still alive until Edgar says, "He is gone indeed" (316), and he may even speak the words ascribed to him by the Quarto, "Break, heart, I prithee break" (313). Or one could follow the Folio's stage direction at 312, and say that after "Look there, look there!" "*He dies.*"

51. Foreman 1978 observes that "death catches Lear by surprise, as it does no other tragic figure, so much so that he never even realises he is dying" (p. 3).

52. *King Lear* has often been read as a play about a transition to a new social order. Colie 1974 gives a sensitive account of Lear and his knights, against Goneril, Regan, and Cornwall, as representatives of old and new styles of aristocracy, suggesting that both are shown to be unsatisfactory: "[T]here is a crisis of values, and neither ethos will do" (p. 215).

53. Patterson 1989, pp. 106–9, suggests a rather different historicist reading, arguing that Lear is "a fictional portrait of the king himself." For criticism of this position, see Foakes 1997, pp. 15–17 and 89–91: Foakes emphasizes that Lear acts in a way that is directly opposite to that recommended by King James in *Basilikon Doron*, where he warns against dividing the kingdom.

54. Barton 1994 observes of *Antony and Cleopatra*, that "in a way for which there is no parallel in any other Shakespearean tragedy, we want Cleopatra to die" (p. 131). In fact, there is a parallel in our relief at the death of Lear.

55. The Quarto assigns the last lines of the play to Albany, the Folio to Edgar. For discussion of the difference this makes to the characterization of the two characters, see Warren 1976, who suggests that in the Quarto Albany is presented as strong and morally upright while Edgar is "an immature young man," whereas in the Folio "Edgar grows into a potential ruler, a well-intentioned, resolute man in a harsh world, while Albany, a weaker man, abdicates his responsibilities" (p. 105). For more discussion of the textual difficulties of the play, see Urkowitz 1980 and Taylor and Warren 1983.

56. See 4.2.28. It is disturbing that the only uses of the word "usurp" in the play are

Kent's description of Lear ("He but usurped his life") and Goneril's of Albany ("A fool usurps my bed"). Lear is a king who fails to fulfill the duties of kingship; the verbal connection may suggest that Albany will do the same.

57. Alternatively, if Albany has the last lines, as in the Quarto, he will presumably be the monarch. In that case, the lines "you twain / Rule in this realm" could be taken as a restoration of Edgar and Kent to their status as nobles, who will help keep order for the new government.

58. Cf. Edgar's account of how Kent's "strings of life / Began to crack" (5.3.217–18) when he found Edgar himself and the dead Gloucester, and told the story of Lear. In the Folio, Kent says, "Break, heart, I prithee break" (5.3.313), speaking both of Lear's heart and his own; in the Quarto, the line is ascribed to Lear himself.

59. Albany says to Edgar, "Let sorrow split my heart, if ever I / Did hate thee or thy father" (5.3.178–79); after hearing of Gloucester's death he says, "If there be more, more woeful, hold it in, / For I am almost ready to dissolve, / Hearing of this" (5.3.203–5). Albany, here and at the very end of the play, emphasizes the duty to refrain from heartbreak, even when it seems almost impossible. Edgar wishes his heart would "burst," like his father's, when he has told the story of his father's life and death (5.3.183); he is surprised "that we the pain of death would hourly die / Rather than die at once" (186–87). He says, or perhaps only hopes, that we choose to stay alive, for "our lives' sweetness" (5.3.185); but the emphasis on heartbreak undermines the idea that it is love of life that makes us keep living, rather than simply the inability to die.

CHAPTER 6: "To-morrow, and to-morrow, and to-morrow": *Macbeth*

1. Mahood 1957, pp. 131–41, sees "the play's major dramatic conflict" in the "confrontation" of different notions of time.

2. The image has been read in both ways; see Muir 1962, ad loc.

3. He answers, "We have scotched the snake, not killed it" (3.2.13). The characters of the Scottish play are able only to scotch, rather than kill. "Scotch'd" is Theobald's emendation for the Folio "scorch'd," and tempting because of the pun, though perhaps (as Muir 1951, p. 81, says fiercely), "unnecessary."

4. Mahood 1957, pp. 136–38, has a good account of the recurrence of the word "done" in the play. Compare Donne's *Hymn to God the Father*, which seems to echo the temporal paradoxes surrounding the word "done" in *Macbeth*, as well as of course playing on Donne's own name. "When thou hast done, thou hast not done, / For I have more" (5–6, 11–12).

5. Compare the Porter scene (2.3.1–40), where the hungover Porter complains of drink the great equivocator, which "provokes the desire, but it takes away the performance." The connections between the Porter scene and the rest of the play are well discussed by Muir 1951, pp. xxiii–xxix.

6. The syntax of "the mere lees / Is left this vault to brag of" is difficult, because it is unclear whether "is left" means "remains in the possession of," so that the vault retains the lees, or whether it means "remains behind," so that the lees remain behind in the vault. The first is probably more likely: "Now this vault can brag only of the lees, not the wine"; but it would also be possible to take it to mean, "Now only these lees, not the wine, can brag of their vault." The ambiguity matters only insofar as it is another sign of Macbeth's

desire to "o'erleap" the present, even to the extent that he describes time in language and imagery that is confused or ambiguous.

7. Cf. *Hercules Furens* 1321–29, and discussion in chapter 4. For extended discussion of the blood-stained hand motif in *Macbeth* and the *Hercules Furens*, see Miola 1992, pp. 111–18.

8. Compare Oedipus's motives for blinding himself, discussed in chapter 1. Line 56 may recall Matthew 18.9, "And if thine eye cause thee to offend, pluck it out and cast it from thee"; it also anticipates Macbeth's remark at the end of the scene: "To know my deed 'twere best not know myself" (2.2.70). See discussion in Muir 1962, pp. xxvii and 55–56.

9. The echo has often been noticed; see discussion in Miola 1992, p. 93.

10. This is an important distinction, which is undermined by productions that make the Ghost invisible — or, like the Roman Polanski film version (1971), make the dagger visible.

11. The importance of the Macbeths' lack of children, and the imagery of children and barrenness in the play, has been widely discussed; see, for example, Brooks 1947.

12. Chaudhuri 1981 sees in Macbeth after the murder a hardening that appears "less as a deliberate and unconscious degeneration than as deliberate control of certain aspects of his being, like an evil parallel to moral discipline" (p. 182).

13. The fact that "firstlings" "can mean 'firstborn young' as well as the 'first results of anything, or first-fruits'" is remarked by Mahood 1957, who links the word with the recurrent theme of children in the play.

14. He seems even to associate himself with those who serve and hate him, who would deny him the "breath" of "mouth-honour" if they dared. His servants have "poor hearts" while he himself is "sick at heart."

15. Compare the *Countess of Pembroke's Arcadia*, 3.10, where Cecropia tries to persuade Pamela to yield her virtue to lust by arguing: "Yesterday was but as to day and to morrow will tread the same footsteps of his foregoers: so as it is manifest inough, that all things follow but the course of their own nature, saving only Man, who while by the pregnancie of his imagination he strives to things supernaturall, meane-while he looseth his owned naturall felicitie" (Bullough 1978, p. 412). The connection with *Macbeth* is noted by Bullough.

16. On Shakespeare's use of the image of life as theater in general, see Barton 1962, especially pp. 130–32, on *Macbeth*.

17. See Muir 1972, p. 159.

18. Cf. Murry 1936: "'Hereafter,' I think, is purposely vague. It does not mean 'later,' but in a different mode of time from that in which Macbeth is imprisoned now" (p. 335).

19. The phrase "time's fool" occurs in sonnet 116 ("Love's not time's fool," 9), and in *1 Henry IV* where the dying Hotspur says that "life, time's fool / Must have a stop" (*1 Henry IV* 5.4.81–82). See also Frye 1967 for full discussion of the concept of "time's fool" in Shakespeare's tragedies and histories.

20. Jorgensen 1971 comments on the restrained style of "tomorrow and tomorrow" (pp. 212–13): he remarks that the speech is "slow and terribly quiet in its rhythms."

21. Neil 1997 argues that "the horror of Macbeth's fate lies precisely in the sense of desperate narrative incoherence produced by the contemplation of his own death" (p. 205).

22. I think it possible that the diction of "struts and frets" is suggested by musical

terminology: there is a submerged image of the struts and frets of a musical instrument that will be "heard no more." "Fret" is attested in a musical sense in C16; see the *Oxford English Dictionary*, s.v. "fret" sb. 3.

23. The central importance of ill-fitting clothes as a theme in the play was first noticed by Spurgeon 1935, pp. 325–27. See especially *Macbeth* 1.3.108 (on the title of Cawdor as "borrowed robes"); and 1.3.145–47, where Banquo remarks that Macbeth's new honors "like our strange garments, cleave not to their mould / But with the aid of use." Barroll 1974 sees Macbeth as a manly soldier who tries unsuccessfully to play the false part of king (see especially pp. 90–91, 256–57).

24. See Stein 1986, pp. 14–16, and Neil 1997, who stresses the shamefulness of death in the early modern period, because it obliterates social distinction.

25. The actor who played Macbeth may well have played Shakespeare's Brutus or Antony in *Julius Caesar*; now the same actor is refusing his own former roles.

26. The Doctor was afraid she would kill herself, in 5.1.72–74, and Macduff claims that she "as 'tis thought, by self and violent hands / Took off her life" (5.9.36–37). The "as 'tis thought" maintains a certain level of doubt about the manner of the queen's death. The play leads us, I think, to see Lady Macbeth's death as the inevitable consequence of the murder of Duncan; whether she dies by suicide or some other means is obscure and relatively unimportant. Lady Macbeth's last words on stage are, "Come, come, come, come, give me your hand. What's done cannot be undone. To bed, to bed, to bed." (5.1.67–68). The retirement "to bed" is equivalent to a withdrawal into the grave, and it comes immediately after her final reenactment of the night of Duncan's murder, as if from that moment on, she has been dead. Similarly, Ophelia is last seen on stage bidding goodnight—"Goodnight, ladies, good night. Sweet ladies, good night, good night" (*Hamlet* 4.4.72–73) and "God buy you" (4.5.201). Gertrude's description of Ophelia's death makes the question, "Was it suicide?" less prominent than the idea that it was the inevitable consequence of her social position: she is drowned not by her own decision, but by her dress, which "pulled the poor wretch from her melodious lay / To muddy death" (*Hamlet* 4.7.182–83).

27. *Pace* Wymer 1986, who claims that "Suicide would, in two separate ways, reconstruct Macbeth as a man, allow us to feel more positive about him than suits the play's purpose. A Roman death would have heroic, 'manly' implications that Shakespeare wished to avoid, and even if considered as an act of despair, would emblematise the workings of a conscience which no longer exists. Macbeth has reached a state beyond even the remorse of Judas" (p. 56). In fact, Macbeth's death in battle is presented as much more "manly" than suicide would have been — at least according to one version of masculinity offered by the play.

28. Lady Macbeth provoked Macbeth to the murder of Duncan by suggesting that failure to kill is unmanly: "When you durst do it, then you were a man; / And, to be more than what you were, you would / Be so much more the man" (1.7.49–51). She repeatedly mocks him for a sensitivity to horror that she regards as incompatible with his status as a man and a soldier (2.2.43, 3.4.57, 3.4.72, and finally, in the sleepwalking scene, 5.1.34).

29. On the concept of manliness in *Macbeth*, see Adelman 1992, pp. 130–46. The equation between physical courage and manhood has been questioned or denied by the entirely different model suggested by Macduff's grief for his family: "I must also feel it like a man" (4.3.221).

30. Old Siward horribly expresses no grief at all for the death of his son, since he

"parted well," and "like a man he died" (5.9.9). He refuses to allow either to himself or to his child the multiple meanings and value of a man's life. Crane 1953 discusses the analogy between the deaths of Macbeth and of Young Siward.

31. For detailed discussion of the parallels and contrasts between Macbeth and Macduff, see Bradshaw 1987, pp. 236–43.

32. For further discussion of the the influence of court masques on Jacobean tragedy, see Sutherland 1983, who links the popularity of the masque form in tragedy both to the court masque and to the opening of Blackfriars.

33. Cf. the Thane of Cawdor, 1.2.23. Roman Polanski's film of *Macbeth* ends with Malcolm visiting the witches, suggesting that he is no different from the tyrant he has deposed. I think this ending goes too far in associating Malcolm with Macbeth: it offers an insight into Malcolm's psyche, which in Shakespeare is kept entirely opaque — unlike Macbeth's.

34. Likewise, the scene in which Malcolm assures Macduff of his own villainy (4.3), only to retract everything and claim that he was only testing him, may leave the audience doubtful of his motivation; it reminds us how little access we have to Malcolm's mind.

CHAPTER 7: "A moving grave": *Samson Agonistes*

1. The 1645 *Poems* contain an extraordinary number of premature deaths and sudden endings. The collection suggests an association in the mind of the early Milton between premature death and premature endings of a literary work. Milton's interest in premature death is discussed by Guilfoyle 1979, pp. 40–44. Quint 1999 discusses the early Milton's fear of premature endings. On the concept of the proper time for action in the early Milton, see Pecheux 1978.

2. Letter 38, "Letter to a friend," in F. A. Patterson 1931, 12: 320–25. Sonnet 7, "How soon hath time" (Carey 1968, p. 146).

3. Sonnet 7.2 and 7.4.

4. Two possible readings are, "All that matters is whether I have grace to use my ripeness in accordance with the will of God as one ever in His sight" (Svendsen 1949b), or "All time is, if I have grace to use it so, as eternity in God's sight" (Dorian 1949). There is a masterful discussion of the ambiguities of the last couplet, and of the whole poem, in Booth and Flyer 1982.

5. See Nohrnberg 1983, who gives a psychological reading of the development of Milton's poetic ego, based on the fact that Milton's major poems almost all move toward the "two poles" of the "the end of youthful maturation . . . and the end of full participation, which anticipates the concluding of existence" (p. 86). My claim here is that those "two poles" "turn askance" (10.668) in *Paradise Lost*, through the representation of overliving. They are perhaps set right again in *Paradise Regained*, which is, as Nohrnberg shows, in many ways a retrospective on Milton's own poetic career, standing as a companion piece to the *Nativity Ode*.

6. Samson's fear that he and his country have been abandoned by God is clearly reminiscent of Milton's own situation in the 1670s, although Milton should not, of course, be identified with his character. The affinity between Samson's situation and Milton's has often been noticed; see, for instance, Lewalski 2000, p. 524, who remarks that *Samson Agonistes* "is not a point-by-point allegory, but it invites application to the post-Restoration ethos and the situation of the Puritan dissenters" (p. 525).

7. For instance, Bowra 1955, pp. 112–29. Ellis-Fermor 1945 argues that *Samson Agonistes* is not tragic because of Samson's final triumph. A new reading of the Christian story as essentially tragic is given by Eagleton 2003; see especially pp. 34–40, where Eagleton reads the Crucifixion as an essentially tragic narrative (or, rather, event; Eagleton's tenses imply that the New Testament is for him a historical document).

8. Carey 1968, p. 342.

9. *Reason of Church Government*, book 2, preface; Wolfe and others 1953, 1: 815.

10. Fixler 1969 argues that *Paradise Lost* is "an elaborate systematic transformation of the revelation or apocalypse of St John the divine" (p. 151). See chapter 8 for further discussion of *Paradise Lost* as a tragic work.

11. Here I disagree with several critics; for instance, Lewalski 1999, p. 121, argues that the end of *Paradise Lost* marks a "turn from classical to Christian tragedy," through God's grace: the "catharsis" is defined, she says, by God's instruction to Michael to send Adam and Eve out of the garden "not disconsolate" (*Paradise Lost* 11.113). See chapter 8, for more discussion of the final books of *Paradise Lost*.

12. Job has often been seen as a model of tragedy, for instance, by Sewall 1959.

13. The beginning and end of the book of Job—containing the folklore story of the agreement between God and Satan to test a virtuous man, and the restoration ending—are probably much older than the rest of the book. Modern scholars mostly agree that the speeches of the first three comforters are also older than the speeches of Elihu and the voice of God from the whirlwind, which represent a more sophisticated and later conception of the story. See Dhorme 1967. Many early modern commentators on the book concentrated not on the central debate but on the folkloric frame narrative, and were thus able to read the story not as tragic drama but as a "brief epic," a heroic story about an extraordinary man who overcomes adversity and emerges victorious; see Lewalski 1966, pp. 10–36. *Paradise Regained* certainly makes use of this traditional interpretation of the book of Job. But Milton would also have encountered tragic readings of the story in Protestant biblical exegesis; see Lewalski, pp. 19–20. Early modern commentators were apparently not aware of the different dates of the various strands of the book; the whole work was thought to be extremely ancient—even, according to J. F. Senault, "the first Booke in the World" (cited by Lewalski 1966, p. 13).

14. Cf. *Oedipus Coloneus* 1–21, where Oedipus is led forward by Antigone; and also compare Euripides' *Phoenissae*, 834–35. The comparison of Milton's drama with the *Oedipus Coloneus* was first made by Epps 1916. Brewer 1927 argued that *Samson Agonistes* is based "almost entirely" on the *Oedipus Coloneus* and Aeschylus's *Prometheus Bound;* this is disputed by W. Parker 1937, pp. 168–85, who sees in Milton a more diffuse echoing of the "spirit" of Greek tragedy. Arnold 1983 discusses Milton's use of contemporary commentaries on Greek tragedy and finds specific parallels between Samson and several classical tragic heroes, especially Heracles, Oedipus, and Philoctetes.

15. On the commentary tradition, see Krouse 1949.

16. For discussion of Samson as a type who does not understand what his actions prefigure, see Low 1974.

17. See Christopher 1975, who discusses Calvinist and Lutheran views of the various promises made to the people of Israel before Jesus and emphasizes that within both these strands of Protestant theology, the central choice of Adam and the other patriarchs and the choices of Christians are exactly the same: to believe or not.

18. Hartman 1958 coins the term "Milton's counterplot" to describe the anticipations

of final redemption in the similes of the early books of *Paradise Lost*. I here extend Hartman's idea to cover *Samson Agonistes* as well.

19. In Christian terms, his sickness may be the sin of despair. See Allen 1954, pp. 82–94, who argues that the drama "includes in its circular scope all of the theological dicta on the genesis and cure of despair." But Radzinowicz 1977 argues that the presentation of despair in *Samson Agonistes* marks a bridge between Renaissance views of despair as sin, and Restoration views of despair as mental illness.

20. On links with Elizabethan revenge tragedy, see Andrews 1979.

21. See further discussion in chapter 8.

22. Spiller 1995, for example, thinks the final conversation between Manoa and the Chorus "directs" the reader in his or her response to the events of the play.

23. Some critics argue that Milton's portrayal of Samson and of his final action is positive—for instance, Mulryan 1983.

24. Some critics argue that seventeenth-century readers would have admired Samson's final action; Krouse 1949 documents the tradition by which Samson is a forerunner and type of Christ. But others have noticed that it was also traditional to criticize Samson's violence. Madsen 1968, pp. 95–114, corrects Krouse in arguing that Milton's Samson retains his limited status as an Old Testament figure. See Samuel 1971, and especially Wittreich 1986, for arguments against the view of *Samson Agonistes* as a drama of regeneration and against seeing Samson's killing of the Philistines in an entirely positive light.

25. On apocalyptic imagery in *Samson Agonistes*, see Low 1974.

26. See lines 1584–86, 1590–95, and 1660–68.

27. It is so read by Wittreich 1986.

28. The incomprehensibility of the drama thus goes beyond even that evoked by Fish (1989 and 2001).

29. Judges 16.30.

30. See W. Parker 1937. Kessner 1974 rightly argues that there are strong connections between *Samson Agonistes* and Euripides' *Heracles*. Kessner sees human friendship or love as the central theme in both plays, arguing about Samson that in his "gradually accumulating wisdom he comes to understand, like Heracles, the power of love" (p. 255). My reservations about this way of reading the *Heracles* are made clear in chapter 3.

31. *Samson Agonistes* is a Restoration drama that shows the reader how little theater can show, and therefore how little those who go to the reopened theaters will see, even if they have their eyesight. Milton shared to some extent the conventional Puritan suspicion of theater-going. He expresses a love of drama in the *Elegia Prima* (26–47), but the passage may refer to the reading of classical plays; it does not necessarily imply theatrical performance (see Howard-Hill 1995, pp. 112–13). In the *Apology for Smectymnus*, Milton defends himself against the charge of being a theatergoer who spends his afternoons "in playhouses and the bordelloes." He admits that he did see plays as a Cambridge undergraduate, but only through necessity, and with all the proper sense of moral, intellectual, and aesthetic outrage at the baseness of the performances. Milton primarily experienced tragedy—and, specifically, the Greek tragedians—from the page rather than the theater; on this, again, see Howard-Hill 1995, who argues that there is no evidence that Milton attended any contemporary theater productions. *Samson Agonistes* is designed to be read rather than performed: Milton tells us in the preface, "Division into act and scene referring chiefly to the stage (to which this work never was intended) is here omitted."

32. Waddington 1971 makes the association of melancholy with Manoa, sour with

Dalila, and salt with Harapha; he sees all three as simply "variant descriptions of melancholia" (p. 269; see also Babb 1951, p. 22), but also speculates that the triad may be influenced by the Paracelsian triad of chemical elements: mercury, sulfur, and salt. J. Hill 1970 argues that the poem deals with the "spiritual education of a Christian 'hero,'" through purgation of his three sins of pride, presumption, and doubt, through three antidote virtues — humility, patience, and faith.

33. Milton's "kind of delight" is based on Aristotle's remark that we enjoy the imitation even of things that are in real life horrible (*Poetics* 1448b); but Aristotle makes no connection between this pleasure and the particular effect of tragedy — see Mueller 1964.

34. Goethe (*On Aristotle's* Poetics) proudly claims to be the first to have discovered the truth about catharsis, namely, that those purged of pity and fear by the end of a tragedy are not the spectators or readers, but the characters in the play. Goethe's reading is, of course, difficult or impossible to defend as an interpretation of Aristotle. Milton's anticipation of Goethe has been noted by Mueller 1964.

35. Hawkins 1970 reads the play in precisely this way; he argues that Samson's emotions are indeed "reduced to just measure" by his three visitors.

36. This reading is common among modern commentators. See, for example, Hawkins 1970 and J. Hill 1970.

37. Johnson claims that "nothing passes between the first act and the last, that either hastens or delays the death of Samson" (*Rambler* 139; Shawcross 1972, pp. 217–20). Most modern critics have disputed Johnson's reading, arguing that Samson's final change of mind is prepared for by the three confrontations with Manoa, Dalila, and Harapha.

38. Allen 1954 argues that Manoa's "well meant attempts to alleviate the suffering of his son have invariably an effect of contrary intent" (p. 57).

39. For extended discussion of Manon's character and role in the drama, see Hoffman 1970.

40. See, for instance, 829–31.

41. On the opacity of Samson's end, see especially Fish 1989, and Fish 2001, pp. 391–473 (a revised version of the 1989 article). Fish argues that *Samson Agonistes* offers the reader the "temptation of understanding" and the "temptation of intelligibility": we, like Manoa, the Chorus, and Samson himself, want to make sense of God's purposes and are disturbed to find that we cannot. Fish's argument is compelling, up to a point, but he is less than convincing on Samson's decision to go with the Officer to the theater of the Philistines. Fish claims that Samson here shows precisely the attitude toward God's purposes to which we should all aspire: he trusts God's power without trying to interpret, showing "a belief in a benevolence whose kind is *not* always known and the evidence of which is *not* always seen or understood" (Fish 2001, p. 418, emphasis in original). Despite his sensitivity to ambiguity in *Samson Agonistes*, Fish here cuts off interpretation too early. It is not clear — since Samson does not say — that his decision is based on a newfound trust in an unknown God. As Fish's own reading shows, we do not know why he goes, and we do not know what it means — and we also do not know how to feel about it.

42. See Mueller 1964.

43. Fish 1989. A similar point is made by Haskin 1994, who argues that Manoa is an interpreter who is "overly intent on establishing meanings" (p. 144), but also that the drama encourages us to see the multiplicity of possible readings of the Bible; Haskin sees freedom where Fish sees temptation. I am sympathetic to these critics, but neither, in my view, pays enough attention to the emotional effects of the drama.

CHAPTER 8: "Why do I overlive?": *Paradise Lost*

1. The generic implications of reading the Fall as ultimately happy have been discussed by Shawcross 1965 and 1969. Shawcross argues that *Paradise Lost* "cannot be considered tragic of effect but hopeful, inspirational and glorious"; the poem is to be classified as epic because "it is a kind of praise: a praise of God rather than of hero and nation" (Shawcross 1969, p. 17). See also Steadman 1976. The discussion of *felix culpa* as dominant theme of the poem was begun by Lovejoy 1937. The *felix culpa* reading of the poem is also favored by Lewalski 1963 and Barker 1949. Many since Lovejoy have challenged the idea that the Fall produces a happier world than the one that would have developed from an unfallen Eden: see Mollenkott 1972. Quint 1993 plausibly suggests that the Fall is "fortunate" only in the sense that it is a "fall into fortune" (pp. 268–324, especially pp. 281–308).

2. Allen 1954 claims that Milton includes the last two books as the final proof of God's justice and mercy: "[T]o prove his unquestioned assertion of providence, Milton invents the vision of consolation" (p. xx). But his ability to find consolation in the misery of books 11 and 12 is a measure only of how deeply Allen wants and expects to find it. Erskine 1917 is unique in objecting to the end of the poem on the grounds that it is too cheerful; his bizarre reading is challenged by Moore 1921.

3. See Mollenkott 1972, and previous notes.

4. The point has been made most forcefully by Kermode 1962. My reading is partly a development of Kermode's insight that the "tragedy" of *Paradise Lost* is "a matter of *fact*, of life as we feel it; the hope of restoration is a matter of faith, and faith is 'the substance of things hoped for, the evidence of things unseen' — a matter altogether less simple, sensuous and passionate, and thus less the stuff of poetry" (p. 103, emphasis in original).

5. The "humanist" strain in *Paradise Lost* is discussed by Belsey 1988. I am less committed than Belsey to the "primacy of textuality itself" (p. 42), but I welcome her resistance to pure historicism: her deconstructive reading has the great virtue of taking seriously the emotions of the characters in the poem and of understanding that they must to a large extent guide those of the (human) reader of the poem.

6. Citations in text are to *Paradise Lost* unless otherwise noted.

7. Milton never cites a specific tragic model in the way that he cites Homer here. This is not because he has no tragic models: as Martz 1964 notes, the "implications of the generic form of Greek tragedy underlie the action of Book 9" (p. 133).

8. Lewalski 1985 makes a valiant attempt to reconcile the two competing genres: she takes it that Milton means books 9 and 10 will be tragic, and 11 and 12, heroic (p. 220). But "tragic" and "heroic" elements, as defined by this passage, often seem to happen simultaneously in the poem: books 9 and 10 have plenty about God's anger, and books 11 and 12 have a great deal about man's suffering and woe.

9. The point has been made by several critics. The plot of *Paradise Lost* was seen as tragic by Addison, who objected that "this kind of fable, which is the most perfect in tragedy, is not so proper for an heroic poem" (*Spectator* 297; Addison 1905, p. 49). See also Kermode 1962, who claims definitively that "the poem is tragic" (p. 102), and Hanford 1917. Fowler (Carey and Fowler 1968) concedes the survival of tragic formal elements: "The final part of the poem, after Milton changes his notes to tragic at the beginning of Book IX follows the neo-classical unities of time and place (if we exclude Michael's visions). There are multiple *peripeteias* interspersed with partial discoveries, as in *Oedipus Tyrannus*" (p. 421). He adds that "the visions Michael shows to Adam in Book XI are like

brief tragedies, some of them with subjects that figure among the 53 Old Testament tragedies projected in the Trinity MS" (p. 421). Frye 1957 notes the special place of tragedy even within a poem as polygeneric as *Paradise Lost*, because "*Paradise Lost* is not simply an attempt to write one more tragedy, but to expound what Milton believed to be the archetypal myth of tragedy," namely, the Fall of Man (p. 211). The influence of Elizabethan tragedy on the poem has been much discussed, as has Milton's use of dramatic technique. Hanford 1917 began modern discussion of the subject, arguing that Milton's debt to Elizabethan dramatists continued throughout his career. Theatricality in the sense of scenic structure and the use of masquelike spectacle is discussed by Demaray 1980. Burden 1967 discusses books 10, 11, and 12 as a lesson in "the poem's demonstration of literary kinds" (p. 187): Michael teaches Adam how to respond to tragedy, and shows him how tragedy is finally superseded. The two categories, "tragic" and "dramatic," have usually been assumed to be coextensive; an exception is Rollin 1973. Some have suggested that Milton chose epic rather than tragedy because it was (according to theorists of the time, such as Tasso) the more inclusive form: in writing epic, Milton was able also to write tragedy. See Shaw 1975. A cohesive reading of the poem's various generic sources is given by Lewalski 1979. Lewalski argues that in ancient and Renaissance theory epic is always thought of as a polygeneric form.

10. The Trinity manuscript preserves four drafts for the tragedy of "Adam Unparadized": these are reproduced in Carey and Fowler 1968, pp. 419–21. See Gilbert 1947, who discusses the survival of formal and structural elements from the proposed tragedy: "[T]he epic differs from other epics in that it is still at heart a tragedy" (p. 26). Woodhull 1907 suggests that the reason for change of genre is Milton's faith in the domination of Christ over Satan (p. 123); see earlier discussion and note 1 for my reservations with this kind of reading.

11. In the Trinity manuscript, Milton has notes for tragedies on various Scottish themes, immediately opposite the drafts of "Adam Unparadized." Howard-Hill 1995 deduces that Milton did not have Shakespeare in mind, from the fact that he does not mention *Macbeth* explicitly here: "Milton made no indication that he knew of Shakespeare's tragedy on the same subject" (p. 117). I am unconvinced; it seems to me that Milton might well have been thinking about *Macbeth* a great deal in the early stages of the project but without wanting to spell out the name of his poetic predecessor and rival. Howard-Hill establishes convincingly that there is little evidence Milton attended many productions of English tragedy; but he does not have a compelling case when he suggests that Milton had not *read* much Shakespeare. One of his earliest poems is addressed to Shakespeare ("On Shakespeare," 1630), and Milton had a copy of his complete works in his library.

12. Milton's account of the Homeric and Virgilian epics emphasizes, above all, wrath. To do so, it resorts to a great deal of distortion, particularly in its implicit reading of the *Aeneid*, a poem whose main subject is certainly not the wrath of Turnus. The second part of the *Aeneid* uses the wrath of Turnus to allude to the wrath of Achilles but also suggests that it may be possible that the old-style heroics of wrath could be replaced by a "better fortitude," which is dangerously close to Milton's own ideal, "the better fortitude / Of patience and heroic martyrdom" (9.31–32). If Milton included a good-faith account of the *Aeneid* here, he would risk jeopardizing his neat contrast between pagan and Christian morality. See Braden 1989 on the association between epic and anger.

13. See Lewalski 1999 and Rollin 1973 for more discussion of the mixed genres of *Paradise Lost*.

14. See Lewalski 1999, pp. 120–21. Most critics equate the Satanic and the tragic: see, for example, Quinones 1972, who says that there are alternative modes of responding to unhappiness in the poem, and Satan's "mode is tragic" (p. 474).

15. Belsey 1988 suggests that the pattern is the same in both Adam's and Satan's soliloquies: Adam "in desperation pushes further and further into the infinite regress of his own subjectivity, only to find there the same absence that Satan too encountered" (p. 88).

16. So Gardner 1948. Broadbent 1960 argues that "the characters of *Paradise Lost* do not soliloquize until they have fallen" (p. 80). Robertson 1995 rightly corrects Broadbent's view; Adam and Eve both soliloquize before falling, and the soliloquy in Milton is not necessarily a fallen mode.

17. Rajan 1947, 44–45, notes the verbal echoes of the Fall of the angels in the human Fall. Tillyard 1951 views Adam and Eve's realization of their own powerlessness, and their humble turn to God, as the ultimate crisis of the poem.

18. Echoes of Marlovian and Shakespearean villains in Satan are discussed by Gardner 1948.

19. Samson's desire to have been born as an "inferior angel" echoes the moment in *Odyssey* 11 where the dead Achilles tells Odysseus that he would rather be the serf of a poor man but alive than king over all the dead (489–91). The *Odyssey* poet reverses the choice of Achilles in the *Iliad*; the desire on the part of the great hero to be alive becomes greater than his desire for glory — although Odysseus himself manages to have heroic courage and go home too; he is not forced to confront Achilles' choice.

20. See Quint 1983, pp. 207–20, on Satan's fantasies about origins.

21. I borrow the phrase "tragedy of Adam" from Shaw 1985.

22. Most readers have felt that they must choose definitively between viewing Satan as the hero and viewing Adam as the hero, not recognizing that they may be alternative kinds of tragic protagonist. Hugh Blair (1784, pp. 30–31) is ahead of his time in recognizing the centrality of Adam to the plot of the poem, and also in recognizing that the story of Adam and Eve is in some ways more truly "tragic" than that of Satan: "It has been asked, Who then is the hero of *Paradise Lost?* The Devil, it has been answered by some Critics; and in consequence of this idea, much ridicule and censure has been thrown upon Milton. But they have mistaken that Author's intention, by proceeding upon a supposition, that, in the conclusion of the Poem, the hero must needs be triumphant. Whereas Milton followed a different plan, and has given a tragic conclusion to a Poem, otherwise Epic in its form. For Adam is undoubtedly his hero, that is, the capital and most interesting figure in his Poem."

23. Blake 1982, p. 35.

24. Discussion of the last two books, in particular, has tended to imply that any defense of Milton's writing, on more than the minutely stylistic level, must rest on proving that it is philosophically coherent; see, for example, Burden 1967. The method has been popular as a way of dealing with the difficulties of the last two books of the poem: see, for example, the almost convincing final chapter of Summers 1962. The most developed account of a monistic Milton is that of Fish 1967 and 2001.

25. For the Satanic perspective on *Paradise Lost*, see most recently Forsyth 2003, who makes a valiant effort to revive the Romantic Milton and to show the attractiveness of Satan, at least in the early books. On Eve, see especially P. Parker 1979a. Several critics

have tried to read the character of Eve as a protofeminist element within *Paradise Lost;* for an approach that draws on both feminist and deconstructive theory, see Belsey 1988, who argues that *Paradise Lost* marks a transition in the development of modern humanism; she thinks that the poem is "two texts in one, an absolutist poem, which struggles to justify the ways of an authoritative God, and a humanist narrative, which recounts how human beings become free subjects, knowing the difference between good and evil in a world of choice" (p. 60). Versions of Belsey's argument have been popular among feminist critics, although Nyquist 1988 argues against the attempt to find feminist discourse within Milton's poem. On Chaos, see Schwartz 1988, and especially Rumrich 1995. Rogers 1996 shows that Milton's vitalism makes way for liberalism, since it suggests that the created world can evade the control of an "authoritarian" God.

26. On Romantic readings of *Paradise Lost,* see Newlyn 1993.

27. Lewalski 1999, especially p. 121.

28. Rogers 1996, for example, finds a conflict in the final books between a sternly authoritarian image of God and a vitalist vision of created matter as capable of freedom.

29. Kermode 1962 is an important exception (and see also Kermode 1967); he rightly emphasizes the tragic emotional burden of time that feels too long, in the final books of the poem.

30. Stanley Fish (1967 and 2001) argues that the purpose of the poem is the moral education of the reader, through a series of interpretative choices or tests: Milton tempts us to sympathize with Satan, say, in order to remind us of our fallenness and to confront us again with the choice between good and evil. Fish's approach takes for granted that the goodness of God is not a question in Milton's poem — hardly a valid assumption. Nuttall 2001, in a review of Fish 2001 (*How Milton Works*), rightly calls it "absurd" to see Milton as a static thinker.

31. P. Parker 1979a argues that *Paradise Lost* contains an antiteleological strain, and that often, "the desire within the poem for resolution or end appears as a form of temptation or reduction" (p. 335).

32. I develop my reading of the very end of the poem in more detail at the end of the chapter.

33. Kermode 1962 remarks that Adam is here "for the first time true kindred to the reader" (p. 118). The speech is most extensively discussed by Svendsen 1949a, who argues convincingly that "in many ways this is the most significant single passage in the poem" (rpt. 1965, p. 328). Svendsen points out that Adam repeatedly "clutches at evasions only to correct himself"; the dialogue begun within Adam continues, in the subsequent conversations between Adam and Eve, and between Adam and Michael. My main departure from Svendsen is that I do not think the conflicts first articulated in this speech are ever satisfactorily resolved.

34. Addison rightly says that "The Tenth Book of *Paradise Lost* has a greater variety of persons in it than any other in the whole poem. The author, upon the winding up of his action, introduces all those who had any concern in it, and shows with great beauty the influence which it had upon each of them. It is like the last act of a well-written tragedy, in which all who had a part in it are generally drawn up before the audience, and represented under those Circumstances in which the Determination of the Action places them" (*Spectator* 357; Addison 1905, p. 157).

35. Martz 1964 remarks that "his rigorous self-examination, utterly different from

Satan's self-deception, leads to an emphasis on 'me' that shows the signs of a regenerated will" (pp. 139–40).

36. "That burden heavier than the earth to bear" echoes the cry of Cain, "My punishment is greater than I can bear"; Cain is also forced to wander the earth, and no one will be allowed to kill him. See Genesis 4.13–16, and discussion in the introduction. But the image also recalls the association between overliving and weight or "burden" in previous tragedies in the tradition, especially *King Lear* — discussed in chapter 5.

37. God's gloss on "thou shalt surely die" is that adopted by Milton himself, in *De Doctrina Christiana* 1.12–14. Milton was following Jerome's solution to a traditional theological dilemma. This and all subsequent references to *De Doctrina Christiana* are taken from the Yale edition, edited by Wolfe 1953–82, vol. 6.

38. Gilbert 1947 notes the problem (pp. 47–49), and suggests that the apparent inconsistency shows the survival of an earlier draft in which Adam did believe God's sentence "vain and void." "Adam does not, then, express any certainty that the 'immediate stroak' of death will be postponed, though if he had done so he would have been right. Nor does he or Eve think the denunciation of the penalty 'vain and void' because postponed. Eve does think it void for other reasons, and Adam with doubt echoes her words. If Adam's presumption, as set forth by the Almighty, is to be connected with other parts of the poem, it is not consistent. We may then suppose that in one stage of his work Milton had Adam utter the sentiments attributed to him by God. The tragedy according to Draft Four would have given a place for such conduct; at least Adam is 'stubborn in his offence' and is warned against impenitence. Though deciding, as he worked further, to omit Adam's bold assumption, Milton failed to delete the Almighty's charge against him" (p. 49). I am not entirely convinced that the inconsistency can be resolved by reference to a putative earlier version.

39. Milton himself appropriates the scriptural use of "mortal" in his prose writing: "How happy were it for this frail, and as it may be truly call'd, mortall life of man, since all earthly things which have the name of good and convenient in our daily use, are withall so cumbersome and full of trouble if knowledge yet which is the best and lightsomest possession of the mind, were as the comon saying is, no burden" (*Reason of Church Government*, book 2, preface; Wolfe and others, 1953, 1: 801). Milton here suggests not only that "mortality" followed upon Adam's original descent into knowledge, but also that our subsequent forms of secular knowledge add to our mortality.

40. *De Doctrina Christiana* 1.12, pp. 394–95.

41. Mortalism is a term that conflates three distinct branches of theological opinion about what happens when we die. The "soul-sleepers" claimed, as their name implies, that the soul sleeps until the final General Resurrection. The "thnetopsychists," like Milton, believed that the soul and body die together, to rise again on the Last Day. By far the most radical were the "annihilationists," who denied the literal truth of the Resurrection altogether and believed that the soul and body simply die. Mortalism had been attacked by Calvin, in *Psychopannychia* (1542), but the soul-sleepers and thnetopsychists maintained that their belief had strong scriptural authority, and it offered a way to explain what becomes of the soul between physical death and the Last Judgment without resorting to the Romish doctrine of Purgatory (see Burns 1972, pp. 13–41). Opponents of mortalism, such as Alexander Ross, tended to conflate the soul-sleepers with the annihilationists and associated both groups with a pagan or Epicurean lack of faith in divine providence (see Williamson 1935, pp. 554–56). But R. Overton, author of *Mans Mortalitie* (1643), one of

the most influential mortalist tracts, makes his belief in thnetopsychism the precondition for his faith in the General Resurrection. There has been hot debate among modern scholars about whether mortalism was a "radical" or "heretical" position for a seventeenth-century English Protestant. Saurat 1925 associates Milton's mortalism with his dynamic engagement with contemporary controversy. Kelley 1941 finds many traces of mortalism in *Paradise Lost.* Williamson 1935 traces the influence of pagan philosophy (particularly Epicureanism) on writers such as Sir Thomas Browne who were sympathetic to the idea of soul-sleeping. He is vigorously and somewhat unfairly attacked by N. Henry 1951, who reminds us that mortalists grounded their ideas in Scripture and retained belief in the General Resurrection (which Williamson did not deny). Henry argues that Milton was quite right to say that his mortalism was "a thing indifferent" in terms of ordinary Protestant belief of the time: the removal of two of the Forty Two Articles of Edward from Elizabeth's Articles of Religion, in 1563, had left "soul sleeping" outside the official doctrines of the Anglican Church. But C. Hill 1977 emphasizes that Milton was certainly in the minority in his belief in mortalism, and argues that he shared it with the most radical religious thinkers of the time (ch. 25, "Mortalism"). As Kerrigan 1975 argues, each of Milton's "major heresies," such as mortalism, fulfills an emotional or psychological need for him: they are " 'necessary' and 'coherent' in other than strictly logical ways" (p. 127).

42. I use the word "heretical" in a sense that I think Milton himself would support. He justifies his own unorthodox positions, such as thnetopsychism, on the grounds that they are compatible with Scripture: "[S]ince the compilation of the *New Testament,* nothing can correctly be called heresy unless it contradicts that" (epistle to *De Doctrina Christiana,* p. 123). Annihilationism does contradict the New Testament, at least as read by Milton. See previous note.

43. "There is a fourth and last degree of death, namely, eternal death, or the punishment of the damned" (*De Doctrina Christiana* 1.33, p. 627).

44. Burke takes Milton's use of the word "death" as his primary example for the sublime, precisely because the more we are told about death in *Paradise Lost,* the less we understand it. Sublimity is a function of incomprehensibility (Burke 1756, p. 41). See Kahn 1992 for more discussion of Burke's reading of Milton. Because of the complexity and — often — opacity of Milton's presentation of death, it is highly misleading to write, as does Daniel 1994, of "the poet's simple insistence that death, both spiritual and physical, is caused by sin" (p. 7).

45. God the Father uses the word "death" interchangeably to each of the four "levels" of death, and also the character, Death. Capital letters are used erratically: often the Son personifies his adversary ("on me let Death wreak all his rage," 3.241), but switches between allegorical and literal when he promises to give "Death his death's wound" (3.252). God the Father and the Son both confuse death as event or punishment with the allegorical figure of Death (7.543–47).

46. Erskine 1917.

47. See chapters 5 and 6.

48. The closest parallel is Sappho (31.9–16), who figures her love symptoms as anticipations of death. Compare also the reactions of Aeneas and others to the events that portend the fall of Troy: "Their hearts were aghast, and cold trembling rang through their bones" (*obstipuere animi gelidusque per ima cucurrit / ossa tremor, Aeneid* 2.120–21); also compare, for example, the death of Turnus, "but his joints were relaxed in cold" (*ast illi solvuntur frigore membra, Aeneid* 12.951).

49. Cf. 9.792.

50. Allen 1954, p. 79.

51. See Babb 1951, pp. 6–7. Adam is surrounded by all the elements associated with melancholy: the night is "black" and "accompanied with damps and dreadful gloom" and the ground is "cold" (10.848–51). But this landscape is not only symbolic of Adam's internal state, as the cave of Despayre symbolizes the emotion in *Fairie Queene*, book 1; natural corruption is also caused by human sin.

52. Adam's second outburst has as its primary generic models not tragedy, but romance and pastoral. But Adam invokes these alternative forms only to cry out at their failure to save him from his own tragic situation. He now feels unable to behave either like a pastoral singer, or a Spenserian knight. To overlive is to survive in a world where pastoral is only a form of nostalgia. Adam slips into the mode of pastoral when he cries out to the woods and fountains, hillocks, dales, and bowers, "With other echo late I taught your shades / To answer, and resound far other song" (10.861–62). He echoes the beginning of Virgil's first *Eclogue*, where Meliboeus tells Tityrus, "We are in exile from our native land; you, Tityrus, relaxing in the shade, teach the woods to resound the lovely Amaryllis" (*nos patriam fugimus; tu, Tityre, lentus in umbra / formosam resonare doces Amaryllida silvas, Eclogue* 1.4–5). Meliboeus's contrast between his own life of exile and Tityrus's pastoral bliss has become a contrast between postlapsarian exile from happiness and the inaccessible pastoral dream of life before the Fall. Rollin 1973 argues that the human plot of *Paradise Lost* is a pastoral tragicomedy. But this reading ignores Adam's insistence on a specifically tragic reading of human life and his failure to find solace, after the Fall, in other generic modes.

53. Here I disagree with Christopher 1975, who argues that Adam remembers God's promise of final revenge with no help at all from Eve, through the workings of grace.

54. This rant resembles Samson's reaction to the arrival of Dalila, and Samson and Adam both begin with animal insults: "Out of my sight, thou serpent!" (*Paradise Lost* 10.877); "Out, out, Hyena!" (*Samson Agonistes* 748). Like Dalila, Eve humbles herself before her husband's feet (*Paradise Lost* 10.914–17). Dalila too is apparently overcome by tears (*Samson Agonistes* 727–29), and asks Samson's pardon (771–72), pleading that he should forgive her for love's sake (811–18). Adam, like Samson, encounters in his wife a mirror of himself.

55. See Broadbent 1960, pp. 151–52, and Summers 1962, p. 183. Christopher 1975 denies that there is anything admirable in Eve's approach to Adam, claiming that she is motivated entirely by the fear of being alone (pp. 74–75). But this neglects the fact that Eve thinks not only of herself but also of her unborn children.

56. Ricks 1963 points out that "brought into this world a world of woe" echoes the beginning of the poem, "the world, and all our woe" (p. 72); he uses the echo as an instance of significant sonic patterning.

57. See chapter 4 on Seneca's suicidal response to overliving. Eve echoes, specifically, Megara in the *Hercules Furens*. The Stoicism of Eve's proposal has been widely noted; see Braden 1989, who elegantly says that Eve "proposes, in grave sincerity, a Senecan apocalypse in which sage and madman merge perhaps more distinctly than anywhere else in the poem" (p. 33). D. Henry and Henry 1985, p. 84, develop the comparison between Seneca's *Thyestes* and Milton's account of the Fall. Eve is also comparable with Job's wife, who advised him, "Curse God, and die"; see Allen 1954, p. 79.

58. Compare Tolstoy's *The Kreuzer Sonata*, where the central character sees in sex and the reproduction of the human species the root of all evil: only sexual abstinence can save

us from the horrors of modern life, and since abstinence may prove impossible, suicide may be the only solution. Compare also modern debates about abortion and euthanasia, and the connections between them (see, e.g., the discussion in Dworkin 1993, pp. 3–29). Eve's proposal is different from most contemporary debates and closer to that of the mad Tolstoian of *The Kreuzer Sonata*, in that she proposes preventing live births on the grounds that it is in the interests both of herself and Adam (who will otherwise incur even more guilt) and, above all, of those who would otherwise be born. Eve defends contraceptive sexual abstinence on grounds normally applied to euthanasia.

59. So Braden 1989, p. 33.

60. *Summa Theologica* 2.2.20.

61. The promise in Genesis 3.15 is called the *protevangelium* and was important in both Lutheran and Calvinist theology, because it suggests that even before Jesus, human beings had the choice to believe in God's plan: see Christopher 1975. Christopher argues that Adam's reference to the *protevangelium* is the essential turning point, "the grand moment in *Paradise Lost*" (p. 75), when man discovers in God's word the possibility of redemption. But as Christopher herself acknowledges, the poem makes very little of this moment; and I am not convinced by her suggestion that it is "deliberately underplayed" to show that it is "designed for the inner ear and eye" (p. 74).

62. The various devils' speeches in book 2 are discussed by Lewis 1942, pp. 101–4.

63. The point is emphasized by Christopher 1975.

64. He is not, like Una in the *Faerie Queene*, an allegorical representation of Christian truth. Una gives what is presumably the last word on Despayre, at least "Till he should die his last, that is eternally" (1.9.54.9). Adam's reasons to live are less obviously authoritative.

65. Burton 1932, 3:410.

66. "Where Oedipus, after having put out his own eyes, instead of breaking his neck from the palace battlements, which furnishes so elegant an entertainment for our English audience, desires that he may be conducted to Mount Cithaeron, in order to end his life in that very place where he was exposed in his infancy, and where he should then have died had the will of his parents been executed" (*Spectator* 363; Addison 1905, pp. 170–71). Addison is contrasting Sophocles' *Oedipus Tyrannus* with Dryden's *Oedipus* (1679), which ends with Oedipus jumping off the palace battlements to his death.

67. C. S. Lewis 1942 notoriously called books 11 and 12 an "untransmuted lump of futurity" (p. 125). Some have defended the books against the charge that they are boring or unpoetic, by drawing attention to the developing relationship between Adam and Michael. Prince 1958 defends them because, he argues, the interrelation between Michael and Adam sustains the reader's interest. Others have emphasized that the ending is structurally necessary for the poem as a whole. The best such reading is by Summers 1962, ch. 8, "The final vision." He also defends the formal shift to narrative rather than visions in book 12: he argues that Michael switches to narrative in order to give Adam the same experience of redemption as we have. See also Thompson 1957, who defends the books as a necessary part of the poem, intellectually and also emotionally; Madsen 1958, who defends them as an "integral part of the poetic and intellectual structure" since they create "a deadly parallel between fallen angel and fallen man, carrying us back to the first two books of the epic" (p. 368); and Radzinowicz 1968, who argues that the last books are not "harsh and pessimistic"; rather, she suggests, they show Adam's education, and reveal how God's plan works out "in the two dimensions of successive time and the immediate present" (p. 33). The theological and literary difficulties overlap: early critics of the poem were bothered by

the gloom of the ending because it was seen as both unepic and un-Christian. For further relevant bibliography, see notes 1, 2, 9, and 10.

68. "The history of mankind, though varied and sometimes thought cheerful by Adam (590), is explained by the angel to be monotonously horrible, and all the result of eating the apple." Empson 1961, p. 190.

69. As Martz 1964 says, "The sad question remains: in poetry, can a hundred lines of hopeful doctrine outweigh six hundred lines of visionary woe?" (p. 163).

70. Tillyard 1930 argues that Milton himself had altered during the writing of the poem; he turns inward and pessimistic in the last books, because of the Restoration (pp. 293–94). C. Hill 1977 says that "in *Paradise Lost* Milton appears to envisage the possibility that mankind is entering a new dark age, in which all that God's servants can do is, like the Waldensians, to keep the truth pure and hand it on" (p. 412). Haller 1955 argues that Milton sees history as tragedy because of the failure of the English republic. He rightly says that the emotional weight, at the end of the poem, is not on Michael's assurance of final victory, but on "Adam and his wife leaving their lost innocence behind them and entering upon the tragic process of human history" (p. 209).

71. The gloom is certainly not simply a reflection of seventeenth-century attitudes to human history, *pace* Rajan 1947, pp. 78–92, who fails to distinguish clearly the various contradictory readings of the book of Revelation available to seventeenth-century thinkers. The last books of *Paradise Lost* are traditionally Augustinian in their understanding of Revelation, but the Augustinian position was not one Milton himself had always held; he had been much more optimistic in the 1640s. By the time he wrote the last books of *Paradise Lost*, Milton had rejected the positions of both the Chiliasts, who believed their own age to be a time of the outpouring of the spirit, and of the Calvinists, whose position he had leaned toward in the 1640s, who believed human history would see a gradual progress toward the Second Coming, hastened by theocratic government like the one in Geneva — or, in Milton's version, hastened by individual spiritual growth. *The Ready and Easy Way* shows his abandonment of hopes for general personal growth toward the Second Coming; the last books of *Paradise Lost* show a position much closer to that of Augustine and Luther. On the intellectual history, applied not to *Paradise Lost* but *Samson Agonistes*, see Lewalski 1970.

72. Kerrigan 1983, pp. 270–98, discusses the problem: "If our situation in this world is endurable in the name of justice solely because of the blissful eschaton, Christianity becomes vulnerable to the sort of attack one finds in Nietzsche, who argued, also with excruciating lucidity, that the postulate of a transcendent world debases and devalues this world. In its concern for reforming our institutions, its passion for liberty and its spiritual materialism, Milton's Christianity eludes this critique triumphantly — but not in the final books of the epic" (p. 279).

73. See Lewalski 1985. Other generic models have been found, especially in masque or spectacle; see Rollin 1973; see also Chambers 1995 on the possible impact of visual art on book 12.

74. These include the shield of Achilles in the *Iliad*, the shield of Aeneas in *Aeneid* 8, and also, most important, the revelations of Anchises to Aeneas in *Aeneid* 6. *Aeneid* 6 shares with *Paradise Lost* 11 and 12 the general structure of visions of the future, related to the man who will father the present race (the Romans in Virgil's case, humanity in Milton's). Aeneas, like Adam, notices the tragic details and has pity where his teacher hopes for glory: he sees Marcellus (6.863). Also common to both is the idea of the one just man who saves

the nation when it lapses into impiety. There is a particularly close echo of Virgil in Michael's account of the relations between the luxurious children of Cain and the sober children of Seth (11.607–12), which resembles Virgil's account of the two future races, the seductive and artistic Greeks and the militaristic Romans, moral legislators to the world (*Aeneid* 6.863–71). Virgil's account of the difference between the Greeks and the Romans has become an account of the two branches of Adam's descendants, who have started to look very much like the two sides in the English Civil War.

75. See Martz 1964.

76. The story of Nimrod and the Tower of Babel (12.6–62); Abraham and the plagues of Egypt (12.79–269); the house of David culminating in the birth of Christ (12.285–374); the final revenge on Satan in the Crucifixion, Resurrection, and Apocalypse (12.386–466); the grim history of the church (12.485–551).

77. So Burden 1967.

78. Compare also Samson, who reproaches "oft-invocated death" (*Samson Agonistes* 575).

79. Compare *Macbeth* 5.7.42–47: Macduff reveals that he is not of woman born, and Macbeth first cries, "Accursed be that tongue that tells me so, / For it hath cow'd my better part of man"; but he recovers and says, "yet I will try the last. Before my body / I throw my warlike shield. Lay on, Macduff / And damn'd be him that first cries, 'Hold, enough.'" Adam's "firmer thoughts" produce no such resolution. See chapter 6 for further discussion of Macbeth's death.

80. *Oedipus Coloneus* 1224–25; see discussion in chapter 2.

81. Compare 9.780–81: "Her rash hand in evil hour / Forth reaching to the fruit, she plucked, she ate."

82. See introduction. Milton's account of old age may well have influenced Swift's Struldbruggs.

83. Compare Augustine, *De Civitate Dei* 22.30, on the six ages of human history. Milton's story in books 11 and 12 is roughly the same as Augustine's, but to attempt to map Augustine directly onto Michael's narrative (as does Fowler 1968) obscures the way Michael constantly breaks up the strict chronological scheme. Michael's structure is thematic as well as chronological, so that he skips back and forth in time: in particular, he repeatedly mentions the final redemption of the faithful (as at 12.458–65) only to retreat back into the gloomy history of the church until that time.

84. As Kerrigan 1983 remarks, this passage suggests that the whole of human history will be dead time. "This period includes *all unlived time*, and those who read the poem now and hereafter will always be living in its dead time: Milton will allow for no future experience but his own, and only for the darkest side of that" (p. 276).

85. See Tillyard 1951.

86. In the 1667 ten-book version of *Paradise Lost*, books 11 and 12 were a single book. The division of the books for the 1674 edition increases the sense that the end of the poem consists of a series of false endings.

87. See chapter 7.

88. Revelation 10.5–6: "And the angel which I saw stand upon the sea, and upon the earth, lift up his hand to heaven, / And sware by him that liveth for evermore, which created heaven, and the things that therein are, and the earth, and the things that therein are, and the sea, and the things that therein are, that time should be no more." Milton's *On*

Time ends with the declaration that "Attired with stars, we shall for ever sit, / Triumphing over Death, and Chance, and thee O Time" (21–22).

89. On the paradoxes generated by eternity in *Paradise Lost*, see Colie 1966, ch. 5: "[T]he story simply stops, but it does not end" (p. 179). Schwartz 1988 develops Colie's insight.

90. See Schwartz 1988.

91. Here I follow the reading of Schwartz 1988.

92. Kerrigan 1983, pp. 393–94, makes the comparison with the *Oedipus Tyrannus*, arguing that the *catharsis* at end of that play depends on the spectators' lack of identification with Oedipus: knowledge produces distance, whereas at the end of *Paradise Lost*, shared knowledge produces identification: we are led for the first time to see Adam and Eve both as our parents and our equals, or rather, as "our parents as our equals" (p. 397). I do not think the distinction is as sharp as Kerrigan makes out. There is, surprisingly, as much distance on the part of the reader from Adam and Eve at the end of the poem as there is on the part of the spectators of *Oedipus Tyrannus* at the end of that play.

93. The point is made by Kerrigan 1983.

94. See P. Parker 1979a, b; Belsey 1988; Quint 1993; Burrow 1993.

Works Cited

Note: All translations of classical authors are my own. I use the most recent Oxford Classical Texts for all quotations from classical authors, except where noted. All biblical quotations are taken from the Authorized King James Version, 1611 (reprinted by World's Classics; Oxford University Press, 1997).

Introduction

Ancona, Ronnie. 1994. *Time and the Erotic in Horace's* Odes. Durham, NC: Duke UP.

Booth, Stephen. 1983. King Lear, Macbeth, *Indefinition, and Tragedy*. New Haven: Yale UP.

Braden, Gordon. 1993. "Herakles and Hercules: Survival in Greek and Roman tragedy (with a coda on *King Lear*)." In *Theater and Society in the Classical World*, edited by Ruth Scodel, pp. 245–64. Ann Arbor: U of Michigan P.

Bronte, Emily. 1976. *Wuthering Heights*. Edited by Hilda Marsden and Ian Jack. Oxford: Clarendon.

Brooks, Peter. 1984. *Reading for the Plot: Design and intention in narrative*. Cambridge: Harvard UP.

Caruth, Cathy. 1996. *Unclaimed Experience: Narrative and history*. Baltimore: Johns Hopkins UP.

Chekhov, Anton. 1954. *Plays*. Translated by Elisaveta Fen. London: Penguin.

Ciardi, Roberto Paolo. 1997. "*Respice Finem:* Per l'interpretazione dell' *Allegoria macabra* del Rosso Fiorentino." In *Scritti per l'Instituto Germanico di Storia dell' Arte Firenze*, edited by Cristina Acidini and others, pp. 269–74. Florence: Casa Editrice le Lettere.

Derrida, Jacques. 2000. *The Instant of My Death*. With Maurice Blanchot, translated by Elizabeth Rottenberg. Stanford UP.

———. 1979. "Living On: Border lines." In *Deconstruction and Criticism*, edited by Harold Bloom, pp. 75–176. New York: Seabury.

Devereux, George. 1978. "Achilles' 'suicide' in the *Iliad*." Helios 6: 3–15.

Dewitt, Helen. 2000. *The Last Samurai*. New York: Hyperion.

Dworkin, R. 1993. *Life's Dominion: An argument about abortion, euthanasia, and individual freedom*. New York: Knopf.

Eagleton, Terry. 2003. *Sweet Violence: The idea of the tragic*. Oxford: Blackwell.

Falkner, Thomas M., and Judith Luce. 1995. *The Poetics of Old Age in Greek Epic, Lyric and Tragedy*. Norman: U of Oklahoma P.

———, eds. 1989. *Old Age in Greek and Latin Literature*. Albany: SUNY P.

Freedman, H., ed. and trans. 1983. *Midrash Rabbah Genesis*. New York: Soncino.

Friedrich, Rainer. 1996. "Everything to do with Dionysus? Ritualism, the Dionysiac, and the tragic." In *Tragedy and the Tragic: Greek theatre and beyond,* edited by M. S. Silk, pp. 257–83. Oxford: Clarendon.

Frye, Northrope. 1957. *Anatomy of Criticism.* Princeton UP.

Gardner, Helen. 1948. "Milton's Satan and the theme of damnation." *English Studies,* n.s., 1: 46–66.

Garner, Richard. 1990. *From Homer to Tragedy: The art of allusion in Greek poetry.* London: Routledge.

Gellrich, Michelle. 1988. *Tragedy and Theory: The problem of conflict since Aristotle.* Princeton UP.

Genette, Gérard. 1992. *Introduction à l' architexte.* Berkeley: U of California P.

Halliwell, Stephen. 1986. *Aristotle's* Poetics. Chapel Hill: U of North Carolina P.

Hubbard, Margaret. 1975. "The capture of Silenus." *Proceedings of the Cambridge Philological Society,* n.s., 201: 53–62.

Jones, Emrys. 1977. *The Origins of Shakespeare.* Oxford: Clarendon.

Kermode, Frank. 1967. *The Sense of an Ending: Studies in the theory of fiction.* Oxford UP.

Kerrigan, John. 1996. *Revenge Tragedy: From Aeschylus to Armageddon.* Oxford: Clarendon.

King, Helen. 1986. "Tithonus and the *tettix."* *Aretheusa* 19: 15–36. Reprinted in *Old Age in Greek and Latin Literature,* edited by Thomas Falkner and Judith Luce, pp. 68–89. Albany: SUNY P, 1989.

Krieger, Murray. 1960. *The Tragic Vision: Variations on a theme in literary interpretation.* New York: Holt.

Langer, Susanne. 1953. *Feeling and Form: A theory of art.* New York: Scribners.

Loraux, Nicole. 1985. *Façons tragiques de tuer une femme.* Paris: Hachette.

Macleod, Colin, ed. 1982. Iliad *Book 24.* Cambridge UP.

Mandel, Oscar. 1961. *A Definition of Tragedy.* New York UP.

Middleton, Thomas. 1964. *The Works of Thomas Middleton.* Edited by A. H. Bullen. New York: AMS.

More, Thomas. 1995. *Utopia.* Latin text and English translation. Edited by George Logan, Robert Adams, and Clarence Miller. Cambridge UP.

———. 1909–14. *Utopia.* Edited by Charles Eliot, translated by Ralph Robinson. Harvard Classics, vol. 36. New York: Collier.

Mossman, Judith. 1995. *Wild Justice: A study of Euripides'* Hecuba. Oxford: Clarendon.

Nietzsche, Friedrich. 1967. *The Birth of Tragedy and The Case of Wagner.* Translated with commentary by Walter Kaufman. New York: Random House.

Polisar, Donna, Larry Wyant, Thomas Cole, and Cielo Perdomo, eds. 1989. *Where Do We Come From? What Are We? Where Are We Going? An annotated bibliography of aging and the humanities.* Washington, DC: Gerontological Society of America.

Poole, Adrian. 1987. *Tragedy: Shakespeare and the Greek example.* Oxford: Blackwell.

Richardson, Bessie Ellen. 1933. *Old Age among the Ancient Greeks: The Greek portrayal of old age in literature, art and inscriptions.* Baltimore: Johns Hopkins UP.

Ricks, Christopher, ed. 1969. *The Poems of Tennyson.* London: Longman.

Romilly, Jacqueline de. 1968. *Time in Greek Tragedy.* Ithaca: Cornell UP.

Rosch, Eleanor, and Barbara B. Lloyd, eds. 1978. *Cognition and Categorization.* New York: Halsted.

Segal, Charles. 1981. *Tragedy and Civilization: An interpretation of Sophocles.* Norman: U of Oklahoma P.

Silk, M. S., ed. 1996. *Tragedy and the Tragic: Greek theatre and beyond.* Oxford: Clarendon.

Simpson, David. 2003. "It's not about cheering us up." Review of *Sweet Violence*, by Terry Eagleton. *London Review of Books*, 3 April, pp. 17–19.

Sipiora, Phillip, and James S. Baumlin, eds. 2002. *Rhetoric and Kairos: Essays in history, theory and praxis*. Albany: SUNY P.

Smith, John E. 2002. "Time and qualitative time." In *Rhetoric and Kairos: Essays in history, theory and praxis*, edited by Phillip Sipiora and James S. Baumlin, pp. 46–57. Albany: SUNY P.

———. 1969. "Time, times and the right time." *Monist* 53: 1–13.

Spalding, Frances. 1988. *Stevie Smith: A critical biography*. London: Faber.

Steiner, George. 1961. *The Death of Tragedy*. Rev. ed. New Haven: Yale UP, 1996.

Storm, William. 1998. *After Dionysus: A theory of the tragic*. Ithaca: Cornell UP.

Swift, Jonathan. 1941. *Gulliver's Travels*. 1726. Edited by Harold Williams. Oxford: Blackwell.

Thomas, Keith. 1976. "Age and authority in early modern England." *Publications of the British Academy* 62: 205–48.

Tolstoy, Leo. 1993. *Anna Karenina*. Translated by Constance Garnet, edited and revised by Leonard J. Kent and Nina Berberova. New York: Modern Library.

Unamuno, Miguel de. 1954. *The Tragic Sense of Life*. Translated by J. E. Crawford Flitch. New York: Dover.

Williams, Raymond. 1966. *Modern Tragedy*. London: Chatto.

Wittgenstein, Ludwig. 1953. *Philosophical Investigations*. Trans. G. E. Anscombe. Oxford: Blackwell.

Wofford, Susanne. 1992. *The Choice of Achilles: The ideology of figure in the epic*. Stanford UP.

Zeitlin, Froma I. 1990. "Thebes: Theater of self and society in Athenian drama." In *Nothing to Do with Dionysus? Athenian drama in its social context*, edited by John J. Winkler and Froma I. Zeitlin. Princeton UP.

CHAPTERS 1 AND 2 : Sophocles

Ahl, Frederick. 1991. *Sophocles' Oedipus: Evidence and self-conviction*. Ithaca: Cornell UP.

Arkins, Brian. 1988. "The final lines of Sophocles' *King Oedipus*, 1524–30." *Classical Quarterly* 38: 555–58.

Bers, Victor. 1997. *Speech in Speech*. Lanham, MD: Rowman.

———. 1984. *Greek Poetic Syntax in the Classical Age*. New Haven: Yale UP.

Bremer, J. M. 1969. *Hamartia: Tragic error in the* Poetics *of Aristotle and in Greek tragedy*. Amsterdam: Hakket.

Breuer, Lee. 1989. *The Gospel at Colonus*. New York: Theatre Communications Group.

Budelmann, Felix. 2000. *The Language of Sophocles: Communality, communication and involvement*. Cambridge UP.

Burian, Peter. 1974. "Suppliant and saviour: *Oedipus at Colonus*." *Phoenix* 28: 408–29.

Buxton, R. G. A. 1980. "Blindness and limits: Sophokles and the logic of myth." *Journal of Hellenic Studies* 100: 22–37.

Calder, W. M. 1970. "*OT* 1524–30." *Emerita* 38: 149–61.

Calome, Claude. 1966. "Vision, blindness and mask: The radicalization of the emotions in Sophocles' *Oedipus Rex*." In *Tragedy and the Tragic: Greek theatre and beyond*, edited by Michael Silk, pp. 17–37. Oxford: Clarendon.

Clark, David R. 1983. *Yeats at Songs and Choruses*. Amherst: U of Massachusetts P.

Clark, David R., and James B. McGuire. 1989. *W. B. Yeats: The writing of* Sophocles' King Oedipus. Philadelphia: American Philosophical Society.

Dawe, R. D., ed. 1982. *Oedipus Rex.* Cambridge Greek and Latin Classics. Cambridge UP.

———. 1974, 1978. *Studies on the Text of Sophocles.* 3 vols. Leiden: Brill.

de Kock, E. L. 1961. "The Sophoclean *Oidipous* and its antecedents." *Acta Classica* 4: 7–28.

———, ed. 1996. *Sophocles: The classical heritage.* New York: Garland.

Delacourt, Marie. 1944. *Oedipe: La legende du conquerant.* Paris: Belles Lettres.

Devereux, G. 1973. "The self-blinding of Oedipus in Sophocles' *Oedipus Tyrannus.*" *Journal of Hellenic Studies* 93: 36–49.

Dunn, Francis M. 1996. *Tragedy's End: Closure and innovation in Euripidean drama.* Oxford UP.

Easterling, P. 1967. "Oedipus and Polyneices." *Proceedings of the Cambridge Philological Society,* n.s., 13: 1–13.

Edmunds, Lowell. 1996. *Theatrical Space and Historical Place in Sophocles'* Oedipus at Colonus. Lanham, MD: Rowman.

———. 1985. *Oedipus: The ancient legend and its later analogues.* Baltimore: Johns Hopkins UP.

Eliot, T. S. 1967. *The Complete Plays.* New York: Harcourt.

Ellendt, F. 1872. *Lexicon Sophocleum.* Hildesheim: Olms.

Else, Gerald. 1957. *Aristotle's Poetics: The argument.* Cambridge: Harvard UP.

Festugière, A. J. 1973. "Tragédie et tombes sacrées." *Revue de l'Histoire des Religions* 184: 3–24.

Freud, Sigmund. 1953. *The Standard Edition of the Complete Psychological Works of Sigmund Freud.* Translated by James Strachey. London: Hogarth.

Goldhill, Simon. 1986. *Reading Greek Tragedy.* Cambridge UP.

Goodhart, Sandor. 1978. "Ληστὰς ἔφασκε: Oedipus and Laius' many murderers." *Diacritics* 2: 55–71.

Gudeman, A. Alfred, ed. 1934. Peri Poietikes. Berlin: Gruyter.

Hester, D. A. 1973. "Very much the safest plan: Last words in Sophocles." *Antichthon* 7: 8–13.

Jebb, R. C. 1899. *Sophocles: The plays and fragments.* Vol. 1, *Oedipus Tyrannus.* Vol. 2, *Oedipus Coloneus.* Cambridge UP.

Kamerbeek, J. C. 1984. *The Plays of Sophocles.* 7 vols. Leiden: Brill.

Kassel, R., and C. Austin, eds. 1983. *Poetae Comic Graeci.* Berlin: Gruyter.

Knox, Bernard. 1964. *The Heroic Temper: Studies in Sophoclean tragedy.* Cambridge UP.

———. 1957. *Oedipus at Thebes: Sophocles' tragic hero and his time.* New Haven: Yale UP.

Kripke, Saul. 1980. *Naming and Necessity.* Cambridge: Harvard UP.

Larkin, Philip. 1988. *Collected Poems.* London: Faber.

Lear, Jonathan. 1998. *Open Minded: Working out the logic of the soul.* Cambridge: Harvard UP.

Lefkowitz, Mary. 1981. *The Lives of the Greek Poets.* Baltimore: Johns Hopkins UP.

Linsky, Leonard. *Names and Descriptions.* U of Chicago P.

Mills, Sophie. 1997. *Theseus, Tragedy and the Athenian Empire.* Oxford Classical Monographs. Oxford: Clarendon.

Moorhouse, A. C. 1982. *The Syntax of Sophocles.* Leiden: Brill.

Murnaghan, Sheila. 1987. "Body and voice in Greek tragedy." *Yale Journal of Criticism* 1: 23–43.

Olson, S. Douglas. 1989. "On the text of Sophocles' *Oedipus Tyrannus*, 1524–30." *Phoenix* 43: 189–95.

Parker, Robert. 1983. *Miasma: Pollution and purification in early Greek religion.* Oxford: Clarendon.

Pucci, Pietro. 1992. *Oedipus and the Fabrication of the Father.* Baltimore: Johns Hopkins UP.

Reinhardt, Karl. 1979. *Sophocles.* Translated by Hazel Harvey and David Harvey. Oxford: Blackwell.

Robert, Carl. 1915. *Oidipus.* Berlin: Weidmann.

Roberts, Deborah. 1982. "Parting words: Final lines in Sophocles and Euripides." *Classical Quarterly* 76: 51–64.

———. 1967. *Time in Greek Tragedy.* Ithaca: Cornell UP.

Rose, Peter. 1976. "Sophocles' *Philoctetes* and the teachings of the sophists." *Harvard Studies in Classical Philology* 80: 49–105.

Rosenmeyer, T. G. 1952. "The Wrath of Oedipus." *Phoenix* 6: 92–113.

Rostagni, A., ed. 1945. *Poetica.* Turin: Chiantore.

Rudnytsky, Peter L. 1987. *Freud and Oedipus.* New York: Columbia UP.

Saïd, Suzanne. 1978. *La faute tragique.* Paris: Maspero.

Segal, Charles. 1993. Oedipus Tyrannus: *Tragic heroism and the limits of knowledge.* New York: Twayne.

———. 1981. *Tragedy and Civilization: An interpretation of Sophocles.* Cambridge: Harvard UP.

Seale, David. 1982. *Vision and Stagecraft in Sophocles.* U of Chicago P.

Seidensticker, Bernd. 1972. "Die Wahl des Todes bei Sophokles." In *Sophocle,* edited by Jacqueline de Romilly, pp. 105–44. Geneva: Fondation Hardt Entretiens 29. Geneva.

Slatkin, Laura. 1986. "Oedipus at Colonus." In *Greek Tragedy and Political Theory,* edited by J. Peter Euben, pp. 210–21. Berkeley: U of California P.

Stoessl, Franz. 1966. "Der Oidipus auf Kolonos des Sophokles." *Dioniso* 40: 5–26.

Vernant, Jean Pierre. 1988. "Ambiguity and reversal: On the enigmatic structure of *Oedipus Rex.*" In *Myth and Tragedy in Ancient Greece,* by Pierre Vidal Naquet and Jean Pierre Vernant, translated by Janet Lloyd, pp. 113–40. New York: Zone Books.

Waldock, A.J.A. 1951. *Sophocles the Dramatist.* Cambridge UP.

Webster, T.B.L. 1956. *Greek Theatre Production.* London: Methuen.

Winter, Sarah. 1999. *Freud and the Institution of Psychoanalytic Knowledge.* Stanford UP.

Yeats, W. B. 1957. *Variorum Edition of the Poems of W. B. Yeats.* Edited by Peter Allt and Russell K. Alspach. New York: Macmillan.

Zeitlin, Froma I. 1990. "Thebes: Theater of self and society in Athenian drama." In *Nothing to Do with Dionysus? Athenian drama in its social context,* edited by John J. Winkler and Froma I. Zeitlin. Princeton UP.

CHAPTER 3 : Euripides

Adkins, A.W.H. 1966. "Basic Greek values in Euripides' *Hecuba* and *Heracles Furens.*" *Classical Quarterly* 16: 193–219.

Arnott, Geoffrey. 1973. "Euripides and the unexpected." *Greece and Rome* 20: 49–64.

Arrowsmith, William. 1968. "Euripides' theater of ideas." In *Euripides: A collection of critical essays,* edited by E. Segal, pp. 13–33. Englewood Cliffs, NJ: Prentice-Hall.

———. 1956. "Introduction to *Heracles*." In *Euripides II*, translated by William Arrowsmith and others. U of Chicago P.

Barlow, Shirley A. 1981. "Sophocles' *Ajax* and Euripides' *Herakles*." *Ramus* 10: 112–28.

Bond, Geoffrey, ed. 1981. *Heracles*. Oxford: Clarendon.

Braden, Gordon. 1993. "Herakles and Hercules: Survival in Greek and Roman tragedy (with a coda on *King Lear*)." In *Theater and Society in the Classical World*, edited by Ruth Scodel, pp. 245–64. Ann Arbor: U of Michigan P.

Bremer, J. C. 1972. "Euripides' *Heracles* 581." *Classical Quarterly*, n.s., 22: 236–40.

Brown, A. L. 1978. "Wretched tales of the poets: Euripides, *Heracles* 1340–6." *Proceedings of the Cambridge Philological Society* 204: 22–30.

Burnett, A. P. 1971. *Catastrophe Survived: Euripides' plays of mixed reversal*. Oxford: Clarendon.

Chalk, H.H.O. 1962. "Αρετή and βία in Euripides' *Herakles*." *Journal of Hellenic Studies* 82: 7–18.

Collard, C. 1975. "Formal debates in Euripides' drama." *Greece and Rome* 22: 58–71.

Conacher, D. J. 1967. *Euripidean Drama: Myth, theme and structure*. U of Toronto P.

Cropp, Martin. 1986. "*Heracles, Electra* and the *Odyssey*." In *Greek Tragedy and Its Legacy: Essays presented to D. J. Conacher*, pp. 187–97. U of Calgary P.

Dale, A. M. 1969. "The creation of dramatic characters." In *Collected Papers*, pp. 272–80. Cambridge UP.

Dawe, R. D., ed. 1982. *Oedipus Rex*. Cambridge Greek and Latin Classics. Cambridge UP.

Delacourt, M. 1939. "Le suicide par vengeance dans la Grèce ancienne." *Revue de l' Histoire des Religions* 119: 154–71.

Diels, Hermann, and Walther Kranz. 1934. *Die Fragmente der Vorsokratiker*. 3 vols. Berlin: Weidmannsche.

Dover, Kenneth. 1974. *Greek Popular Morality*. Oxford: Blackwell.

Dunn, Francis M. 1996. *Tragedy's End: Closure and innovation in Euripidean drama*. Oxford UP.

Ehrenberg, Victor. 1946. "Tragic Heracles." In *Aspects of the Ancient World: Essays and reviews*, by Victor Ehrenberg, pp. 144–66. New York: Salloch.

Empson, William. 1974. *Some Versions of Pastoral*. 1935. Reprint, New York: New Directions.

Foley, Helene P. 1985. *Ritual Irony: Poetry and sacrifice in Euripides*. Ithaca: Cornell UP.

Furley, David. 1986. "Euripides on the sanity of Herakles." In *Studies in Honour of T. B. Webster*, edited by J. H. Betts, J. T. Hooker, and J. R. Green, 1:102–13. Bristol Classical Press.

Galinsky, G. Karl. 1972. *The Herakles Theme: The adaptations of the hero in literature from Homer to the twentieth century*. Totowa, NJ: Rowman and Littlefield.

Garrison, Elise P. 1995. *Groaning Tears: Ethical and dramatic aspects of suicide in Greek tragedy*. Memnosyne suppl. 47. Leiden: Brill.

George, David B. 1994. "Euripides' *Heracles* 140–235: Staging and the stage iconography of Heracles' bow." *Greek, Roman and Byzantine Studies* 35: 145–57.

Greenwood, L.H.G. 1953. *Aspects of Euripidean Tragedy*. Cambridge UP.

Gregory, Justina. 1977. "Euripides' *Heracles*." *Yale Classical Studies* 25: 259–75.

Grube, G.M.A. 1941. *The Drama of Euripides*. New York: Barnes and Noble.

Halleran, Michael R. 1986. "Rhetoric, irony and the ending of Euripides' *Herakles.*" *Classical Antiquity* 5: 171–81.

Hamilton, Richard. 1985. "Slings and arrows: The debate with Lycus in the *Heracles.*" *Transactions of the American Philological Society* 115: 19–25.

Heath, Malcolm. 1987. *The Poetics of Greek Tragedy.* Stanford UP.

Kamerbeek, J. C. 1966. "The unity and meaning of Euripides' *Heracles.*" *Mnemosyne* 19: 1–16.

Kitto, H.D.F. 1939. *Greek Tragedy.* London: Methuen.

Kovacs, David, ed. and trans. 1998. Euripides, *Suppliant Women, Electra, Heracles.* Loeb Classical Library. Cambridge, MA: Harvard UP.

Lefkowitz, M. R. 1989. " 'Impiety' and 'atheism' in Euripides' dramas." *Classical Quarterly* 39: 70–82.

Lloyd, Michael. 1992. *The Agon in Euripides.* Oxford: Clarendon.

Michelini, A. 1987. *Euripides and Tragic Tradition.* Madison: U of Wisconsin P.

Mills, Sophie. 1997. *Theseus, Tragedy and the Athenian Empire.* Oxford Classical Monographs. Oxford: Clarendon.

Murray, Gilbert. 1946. *Greek Studies.* Oxford: Clarendon.

Nagy, Gregory. 1979. *The Best of the Achaeans: Concepts of the hero in Archaic Greek poetry.* Baltimore: Johns Hopkins UP.

Parker, Robert. 1983. *Miasma: Pollution and purification in early Greek religion.* Oxford: Clarendon.

Pohlenz, Max. 1930. *Die griechische Tragödie.* Berlin: Teubner.

Rehm, Rush. 1988. "The staging of suppliant plays." *Greek, Roman and Byzantine Studies* 29: 263–307.

Romilly, J. de. 1980. "Le refus du suicide dans l'*Héraclès* d'Euripide." *Archaiognosia* 1: 1–10.

Schwinge, Monika. 1972. "Die Funktion der zweiteiligen komposition im Herakles des Euripides." Ph.D. diss., Tubingen.

Shelton, Jo-Ann. 1979. "Structural unity and the meaning of Euripides' *Heracles.*" *Eranos* 77: 101–10.

Sheppard, J. H. 1916. "The formal beauty of the *Hercules Furens.*" *Classical Quarterly* 10: 72–79.

Silk, Michael. 1993. "Heracles and tragedy." In *Greek Tragedy*, edited by I. McAuslan and P. Walcot, pp. 116–37. Greek & Roman Studies. Oxford UP.

Stevens, P. T. 1976. *Colloquial Expressions in Euripides.* Wiesbaden: Steiner Verlag.

Stinton, T. W. 1975. "*Hamartia* in Aristotle and Greek Tragedy." *Classical Quarterly* 69: 221–54.

Vellacott, Philip. 1975. *Ironic Drama: A Study of Euripides' method and meaning.* Cambridge UP.

Verrall, A. W. 1905. *Essays on Four Plays of Euripides.* Cambridge UP.

Walsh, George. 1979. "Public and private in three plays of Euripides." *Classical Philology* 74: 294–309.

Wecklein, N., and A. J. Pflugk, eds. 1877. *Heracles.* Leipzig.

Wilamowitz-Moellendorf, U. von. 1895. *Euripides' Heracles.* Berlin: Weidemann.

Yoshitake, Sumio. 1994. "Disgrace, grief and other ills: Herakles' rejection of suicide." *Journal of Hellenic Studies* 14: 135–53.

CHAPTER 4: Seneca

Auvray-Assayas, C. E. 1987. "La conclusion de l'*Hercule Furieux* de Sénèque: Tradition grecque et clémence stöicienne." *Revue des Études Latines* 65: 156–66.

Bakhtin, M. M. 1981. "Forms of time and chronotope in the novel." In *The Dialogic Imagination: Four essays*, edited by Michael Holquist, pp. 84–258. Austin: U of Texas P.

Boyle, A. J. 1997. *Tragic Seneca: An essay in the theatrical tradition*. London: Routledge.

Braden, Gordon. 1993. "Herakles and Hercules: Survival in Greek and Roman tragedy (with a coda on *King Lear*)." In *Theater and Society in the Classical World*, edited by Ruth Scodel, pp. 245–64. Ann Arbor: U of Michigan P.

Braund, Susanna Morton, and Christopher Gill, eds. 1997a. *The Passions in Roman Thought and Literature*. Cambridge UP.

———. 1997b. "Ending epic: Statius, Theseus and a merciful release." *Proceedings of the Cambridge Philological Society* 43: 1–23.

Cancik, H. 1967. *Untersuchungen zu Senecas* Epistulae Morales. Hildesheim: Olms.

Davis, P. J. 1993. *Shifting Song: The chorus in Seneca's tragedies*. Hildesheim: Olms/Weidmann.

Dingel, Joachim. 1974. *Seneca und die Dichtung*. Heidelberg: Winter.

Edert, Otto. 1909. *Uber Senecas* Herakles und den Herakles auf dem Oeta. Inaugural Dissertation: Kiel: Fiencke.

Fern, Mary Edmond. 1948. *The Latin Consolatio as Literary Type*. St. Louis UP.

Fitch, John G. 1987. *Seneca's* Hercules Furens. Ithaca: Cornell UP.

Frye, Northrop. 1967. *Fools of Time: Studies in Shakespearean tragedy*. U of Toronto P.

Gibbon, Edward. 1932. *The Decline and Fall of the Roman Empire*. New York: Modern Library.

Griffin, Miriam T. 1976. *Seneca: A philosopher in politics*. Oxford: Clarendon.

Hadas, Moses. 1939. "The Roman stamp of Seneca's *Tragedies.*" *American Journal of Philology* 60: 220–31.

Haywood, R. 1941. "Note on Seneca's *Hercules Furens.*" *Classical Journal* 37: 421–24.

Henry, D., and E. Henry. 1985. *The Mask of Power: Seneca's tragedies and Imperial Rome*. Chicago: Bolchazy-Carducci.

Herington, C. J. 1966. "Senecan tragedy." *Arion* 5: 422–71.

Lavery, Gerard B. 1980. "Metaphors of war and travel in Seneca's prose works." *Greece and Rome* 27: 147–57.

Lawall, Gilbert. 1982. "*Virtus* and *pietas* in Seneca's *Hercules Furens.*" *Ramus* 12: 6–26.

Lovatt, Helen. 1999. "Competing endings: Re-reading the end of the *Thebaid* through Lucan." *Ramus* 28: 126–51.

Motto, Anna Lydia, and John R. Clark. 1981. "*Maxima Virtus* in Seneca's *Hercules Furens.*" *Classical Philology* 76: 100–117.

Paratore, E. 1965. "Il prologo dello *Hercules furens* di Seneca e l'*Eracle* di Euripide." *Annali Liceo Classico G. Garibaldi di Paltermo* 2: 277–308.

Peterson, Richard S. 1981. *Imitation and Praise in the Poems of Ben Jonson*. New Haven: Yale UP.

Pohlenz, M. 1959. *Die Stoa*. 2 vols. Göttingen: Vandenhoeck and Ruprecht.

Rist, J. M. 1969. *Stoic Philosophy*. Cambridge UP.

Rudich, Vasily. 1993. *Political Dissidence under Nero*. London: Routledge.

Schiesaro, Alessandro. 2003. *The Passions in Play:* Thyestes *and the dynamics of Senecan drama.* Cambridge UP.

———. 1997. "Passion, reason and knowledge in Seneca's tragedies." In *The Passions in Roman Thought and Literature,* edited by Susanna Morton Braund and Christopher Gill, pp. 89–111. Cambridge UP.

Seel, Otto. 1972. *Verschlüsselte Gegenwart: Drei Interpretationen antiker Texte.* Stuttgart: Klett, Verlag.

Tadic-Gilloteaux, N. 1963. "Sénèque face au suicide." *L'Antiquité Classique* 32: 541–55.

Tarrant, R. J. 1978. "Senecan drama and its antecedents." *Harvard Studies in Classical Philology* 82: 213–63.

Wilson, Marcus. 1997. "The subjugation of grief in Seneca's *Epistles.*" In *The Passions in Roman Thought and Literature,* edited by Susanna Morton Braund and Christopher Gill, pp. 48–67. Cambridge UP.

———. 1987. "Seneca's *Epistles to Lucilius:* A revaluation." *Ramus* 16:102–21.

Winterbottom, M. 1974. *The Elder Seneca: Declarations.* 2 vol. Loeb Classical Library. Cambridge, MA: Harvard UP.

CHAPTERS 5 AND 6: Shakespeare

The Shakespeare text I use is the Riverside edition, edited by G. Blakemore and others (Boston: Houghton Mifflin, 1997).

Adelman, Janet. 1992. *Suffocating Mothers: Fantasies of maternal origin in Shakespeare's plays,* Hamlet *to* The Tempest. New York: Routledge.

Barnet, Sylvan. 1955. "Some limitations of a Christian approach to Shakespeare." *English Literary History* 22: 81–92.

Barroll, J. Leeds. 1974. *Artificial Persons: The formation of character in the tragedies of Shakespeare.* Columbia: U of South Carolina P.

Barton, Anne. 1994. "Nature's piece 'gainst fancy: The divided catastrophe in *Antony and Cleopatra.*" Inaugural lecture at Bedford College, London, 1973. In *Essays, Mainly Shakespearean,* by Anne Barton, pp. 113–35. Cambridge UP.

———. 1962. *Shakespeare and the Idea of the Play.* London: Chatto.

Booth, Stephen. 1983. King Lear, Macbeth, *Indefinition and Tragedy.* New Haven: Yale UP.

Braden, Gordon. 1993. "Herakles and Hercules: Survival in Greek and Roman tragedy (with a coda on *King Lear*)." In *Theater and Society in the Classical World,* edited by Ruth Scodel, pp. 245–64. Ann Arbor: U of Michigan P.

Bradshaw, Graham. 1987. *Shakespeare's Scepticism.* Sussex: Harvester.

Bratton, J. S., ed. 1987. *King Lear.* Bristol Classical Press.

Brooks, Cleanth. 1947. *The Well-Wrought Urn.* New York: Harcourt.

Bullough, Geoffrey. 1978. *Narrative and Dramatic Sources for Shakespeare.* Vol. 7. London: Routledge.

———. 1969. "King Lear and the Annesley Case." In *Festschrift Rudolf Stamm,* edited by H. von Eduard Kolb and Jörg Hasler, pp. 43–50. Munich: Bern.

Campbell, O. J. 1948. "The salvation of Lear." *English Literary History* 15: 93–109.

Cavell, Stanley. 1987. *Disowning Knowledge in Six Plays of Shakespeare.* Cambridge UP.

Chaudhuri, Sukanta. 1981. *Infirm Glory: Shakespeare and the Renaissance image of man.* Oxford: Clarendon.

Colie, Rosalie. 1974. "Reason and need: *King Lear* and the 'crisis' of aristocracy." In *Some Facets of* King Lear: *Essays in prismatic criticism*, edited by Rosalie Colie and F. T. Flahiff, pp. 185–219. U of Toronto P.

Crane, R. S. 1953. *The Languages of Criticism and the Structure of Poetry*. U of Toronto P.

Cunningham, J. V. 1960. *Tradition and Poetic Structure*. Denver: Swallow.

Dessen, Alan. 1985. "Two falls and a trap." *English Literary Renaissance* 5:291–307.

Elton, W. R. 1968. King Lear *and the Gods*. San Marino, CA: Huntington Library.

Foakes, R. A., ed. 1997. *King Lear.* Arden. London: Nelson.

———. 1993. Hamlet *versus* Lear: *Cultural politics and Shakespeare's art*. Cambridge UP.

Foreman, Walter C. 1978. *The Music of the Close: The final scenes of Shakespeare's tragedies*. Lexington: UP of Kentucky.

Freud, Sigmund. 1953. *The Standard Edition of the Complete Psychological Works of Sigmund Freud*. Translated by James Strachey. London: Hogarth.

Frye, Northrop. 1967. *Fools of Time: Studies in Shakespearean tragedy*. U of Toronto P.

Goldberg, Jonathan. 1984. "Dover Cliff and the conditions of representation: *King Lear* IV.6 in perspective." *Poetics Today* 5: 537–47.

Hawkes, Terence. 1964. *Shakespeare and the Reason: A study of the tragedies and the problem plays*. New York: Humanities.

Hazlitt, W. C., ed. 1964. *Shakespeare Jest-Books: Reprints of the early and very rare jest-books supposed to have been used by Shakespeare*. 3 vols. New York: Franklin.

Heilman, Robert B. 1948. *This Great Stage: Image and structure in* King Lear. Baton Rouge: Louisiana State UP.

Hunter, G. K., ed. 1972. *King Lear.* London: Penguin.

———. 1967. "Seneca and the Elizabethans: A case-study in 'influence.' " *Shakespeare Survey* 20: 17–26.

Johnson, Samuel. 1968. *The Yale Edition of the Works of Samuel Johnson*. Vol. 8, *Johnson and Shakespeare*. Edited by Arthur Sherbo. New Haven: Yale UP.

Jones, Emrys. 1977. *The Origins of Shakespeare*. Oxford: Clarendon.

Jorgensen, P. A. 1971. *Our Naked Frailties: Sensational art and meaning in* Macbeth. Berkeley: U of California P.

———. 1967. *Lear's Self-Discovery*. Berkeley: U of California P.

Kantorwicz, Ernst Hartwig. 1997. *The King's Two Bodies: A study in medieval political theology*. Princeton UP.

Kermode, Frank. 2000. *Shakespeare's Language*. London: Penguin.

———. 1967. *The Sense of an Ending: Studies in the theory of fiction*. Oxford UP.

Kott, Jan. 1964. *Shakespeare, Our Contemporary*. New York: Doubleday.

Lamb, Charles. 1912. *The Works of Charles and Mary Lamb*. Vol. 6, *Miscellaneous Prose*. Edited by E. V. Lucas. London: Methuen.

Laschelles, Mary. 1973. "*King Lear* and Doomsday." *Shakespeare Survey* 26: 69–79.

Levin, Harry. 1959. "The heights and the depths: A scene from *King Lear.*" In *More Talking of Shakespeare*, edited by John Garrett, pp. 87–103. London: Longman.

Lyons, Bridget Gellert. 1974. "The subplot as simplification in *King Lear.*" In *Some Facets of* King Lear: *Essays in prismatic reading*, edited by Rosalie Colie, pp. 23–38. U of Toronto P.

MacDonald, Michael, and Terence R. Murphy. 1993. *Sleepless Souls: Suicide in early modern England*. Oxford Studies in Social History. Oxford: Clarendon.

Mack, Maynard. 1965. King Lear *in Our Time*. Berkeley: U of California P.

Mahood, M. M. 1957. *Shakespeare's Wordplay*. London: Methuen.

Miola, Robert S. 1992. *Shakespeare and Classical Tragedy: The influence of Seneca*. Oxford: Clarendon.

Muir, Kenneth. ed. 1972. *King Lear*. Arden. London: Methuen.

———. 1966. "Image and Symbol in *Macbeth*." *Shakespeare Survey* 19: 45–54.

———, ed. 1962. *Macbeth*. Arden. London: Methuen.

Murry, J. M. 1936. *Shakespeare*. London: Cape.

Neil, Michael. 1997. *Issues of Death: Mortality and identity in English Renaissance tragedy*. Oxford: Clarendon.

Patterson, Annabel. 1989. *Shakespeare and the Popular Voice*. Oxford: Blackwell.

Peat, Derek. 1980. "*King Lear* and the tension of uncertainty." *Shakespeare Survey* 33: 47–49.

The Riverside Shakespeare. 1997. Edited by G. Blakemore and others. Boston: Houghton Mifflin.

Roche, Thomas P. 1981. "Nothing almost sees miracles: Tragic knowledge in *King Lear*." In *On* King Lear, edited by Lawrence Danson, pp. 136–62. Princeton UP.

Rosenberg, Martin. 1972. *The Masks of* King Lear. Berkeley: U of California P.

Rozett, Martha Tuck. 1985. "The comic structures of tragic endings: The suicide scenes in *Romeo and Juliet* and *Antony and Cleopatra*." *Shakespeare Quarterly* 36: 152–64.

Shuger, Debora K. 1996. "Subversive fathers and suffering subjects: Shakespeare and Christianity." In *Religion, Literature and Politics in Post-Reformation England, 1540–1688*, edited by Richard Strier and Donna Hamilton, pp. 46–69. Cambridge UP.

Snyder, Susan. 1979. *The Comic Matrix of Shakespeare's Tragedies*. Princeton UP.

Spurgeon, Carol. 1935. *Shakespeare's Imagery and What It Tells Us*. Cambridge UP.

Stein, Arnold. 1986. *The House of Death: Messages from the English Renaissance*. Baltimore: Johns Hopkins UP.

Sutherland, Sarah. 1983. *Masques in Jacobean Tragedy*. New York: AMS.

Sypher, Wylie. 1976. *The Ethic of Time: Structures of experience in Shakespeare*. New York: Seabury.

Taylor, Gary, and Michael Warren, eds. 1983. *The Division of the Kingdoms: Shakespeare's revision of* King Lear. Oxford: Clarendon.

Thomas, Keith. 1976. "Age and authority in early modern England." *Proceedings of the British Academy* 62: 205–48.

Urkowitz, Steven. 1980. *Shakespeare's Revision of* King Lear. Princeton UP.

Waith, E. M. 1962. *The Herculean Hero in Marlowe, Chapman, Shakespeare and Dryden*. New York: Columbia UP.

Walker, Roy. 1949. "*The time is free*": *A study of* Macbeth. London: Arden.

Warren, Michael. 1976. "Quarto and folio *King Lear* and the interpretation of Albany and Edgar." In *Shakespeare, Pattern of Excelling Nature*, edited by David Bevington and Jay Halio, pp. 95–107. Newark: U of Delaware P.

Wittreich, Joseph. 1984. *Image of that Horror: History, prophecy and apocalypse in* King Lear. San Marino, CA: Huntington Library.

Wymer, Rowland. 1986. *Suicide and Despair in Jacobean Drama*. London: Harvester.

CHAPTERS 7 AND 8 : Milton

Quotations are from the Longman edition, edited by John Carey and Alistair Fowler (London: Longman, 1968).

Addison, Joseph. 1905. *Criticisms on Milton.* Introduced by Henry Morley. London: Cassell.

Allen, D. C. 1954. *The Harmonious Vision.* Baltimore: Johns Hopkins UP.

Andrews, John F. 1979. "Dearly bought revenge: *Samson Agonistes, Hamlet* and Elizabethan revenge tragedy." *Milton Studies* 13: 81–107.

Arnold, Margaret J. 1983. "*Graeci Christiani:* Milton's Samson and the Renaissance editors of Greek tragedy." *Milton Studies* 17: 235–54.

Babb, Lawrence. 1951. *The Elizabethan Malady: A study of melancholia in English literature from 1580 to 1642.* East Lansing: Michigan State College Press.

Barker, A. 1949. "Structural pattern in *Paradise Lost.*" *Philological Quarterly* 28: 17–30.

Belsey, Catherine. 1988. *John Milton: Language, gender and power.* Oxford: Blackwell.

Blair, Hugh. 1784. *Lectures on Rhetoric and Belles Lettres.* Philadelphia: Aitken.

Blake, William. 1982. *The Marriage of Heaven and Hell.* In *The Complete Poetry and Prose,* edited by David V. Erdman and Harold Bloom. Berkeley: U of California P.

Booth, Stephen, and Jordan Flyer. 1982. "Milton's 'How soon hath time': A colossus in a cherrystone." *English Literary History* 49: 449–67.

Bowra, C. M. 1955. *Inspiration and Poetry.* London: Macmillan.

Braden, Gordon. 1989. "Epic anger." *Milton Quarterly* 23: 28–34.

Brewer, W. 1927. "Two Athenian models for *Samson Agonistes.*" *Publications of the Modern Languages Association* 42: 910–20.

Broadbent, John B. 1960. *Some Graver Subject: An essay on* Paradise Lost. London: Chatto.

Burden, Denis. 1967. *The Logical Epic: A study of the argument of* Paradise Lost. Cambridge: Harvard UP.

Burke, Edmund. 1756. *A Philosophical Inquiry into the Origin of Our Ideas of the Sublime and Beautiful.* London: Dodsley.

Burns, Norman T. 1972. *Christian Mortalism from Tyndale to Milton.* Cambridge: Harvard UP.

Burrow, Colin. 1993. *Epic Romance.* Oxford: Clarendon.

Burton, Robert. 1932. *The Anatomy of Melancholy.* 3 vols. Everyman. London: Dent.

Carey, John, and Alistair Fowler, eds. 1968. *The Poems of John Milton.* London: Longman.

Chambers, Douglas. 1995. "Improved by tract of time: Art's synopticon in *Paradise Lost* Book 12." In *Of Poetry and Politics: New essays on Milton and his world,* edited by P. G. Stanwood, pp. 79–93. Binghamton, NY: SUNY P.

Christopher, Georgia B. 1975. "The verbal gate to Paradise: Adam's 'literary experience' in Book X of *Paradise Lost.*" *Publications of the Modern Languages Association* 90: 69–76.

Colie, Rosalie. 1966. *Paradoxica Epidemica.* Princeton UP.

Daniel, Clay. 1994. *Death in Milton's Poetry.* Lewisburg: Bucknell UP; London: Associated UP.

Demaray, John G. 1980. *Milton's Theatrical Epic: The invention and design of* Paradise Lost. Cambridge: Harvard UP.

Dhorme, E. 1967. *A Commentary on the Book of Job.* 1926. Translated by Harold Knight. London: Nelson.

Dorian, D. C. 1949. "Note." *Explicator* 7: 10.

Dworkin, R. 1993. *Life's Dominion: An argument about abortion, euthanasia, and individual freedom*. New York: Knopf.

Eagleton, Terry. 2003. *Sweet Violence: The idea of the tragic*. Oxford: Blackwell.

Ellis-Fermor, Una. 1945. *Frontiers of Drama*. London: Methuen.

Empson, William. 1961. *Milton's God*. London: Chatto.

Erskine, John. 1917. "The theme of death in *Paradise Lost*." *Publications of the Modern Languages Association* 32: 573–82.

Fish, Stanley, 2001. *How Milton Works*. Cambridge: Harvard UP.

———. 1989. "Spectacle and evidence in *Samson Agonistes*." *Critical Inquiry* 15: 556–86.

———. 1967. *Surprised by Sin: The reader in* Paradise Lost. New York: St. Martin's. Rev. ed, 1997.

Fixler, Michael. 1969. "The Apocalypse within *Paradise Lost*." In *New Essays on* Paradise Lost, edited by Thomas Kranidas, pp. 131–78. Berkeley: California UP.

Forsyth, Neil. 2003. *The Satanic Epic*. Princeton UP.

Fowler, Alistair, ed. 1968. *Paradise Lost*. London: Longman.

Frye, Northrop. 1957. *Anatomy of Criticism: Four essays*. Princeton UP.

Gardner, Helen. 1948. "Milton's Satan and the theme of damnation." *English Studies*, n.s., 1: 46–66.

Gilbert, Allan H. 1947. *On the Composition of* Paradise Lost: *A study of the order and insertion of material*. Chapel Hill: U of North Carolina P.

Guilfoyle, Cherrell. 1979. "'If shape it might be called that shape had none': Aspects of death in Milton." *Milton Studies* 13: 35–57.

Haller, William. 1955. *Liberty and Reformation in the Puritan Revolution*. New York: Columbia UP.

Hanford, James Holly. 1917. "The dramatic element in *Paradise Lost*." *Studies in Philology* 14: 178–95.

Hartman, Geoffrey. 1958. "Milton's counterplot." *English Literary History* 25: 1–12.

Haskin, Dayton. 1994. *Milton's Burden of Interpretation*. Philadelphia: U of Pennsylvania P.

Hawkins, Sherman. 1970. "Samson's Catharsis." *Milton Studies* 2: 211–30.

Henry, D., and E. Henry. 1985. *The Mask of Power: Seneca's tragedies and imperial Rome*. Chicago: Bolchazy-Carducci.

Henry, Nathaniel H. 1951. "Milton and Hobbes: Mortalism and the intermediate state." *Studies in Philology* 48: 234–249.

Hill, Christopher. 1970. *Milton and the English Revolution*. London: Faber.

Hill, John S. 1970. "Vocation and spiritual renovation in *Samson Agonistes*." *Milton Studies* 2: 149–74.

Hoffman, Nancy. 1970. "Samson's other father: The character of Manoa in *Samson Agonistes*." *Milton Studies* 2: 195–210.

Howard-Hill, T. H. 1995. "Milton and 'the rounded theatre's pomp.'" In *Of Poetry and Politics: New essays on Milton and his world*, edited by P. G. Stanwood, pp. 95–120. Binghamton: SUNY P.

Kahn, Victoria. 1992. "Allegory and the sublime in *Paradise Lost*." In *John Milton: A collection of critical essays*, edited by Annabel Patterson, pp. 185–201. London: Longman.

Kelley, Maurice. 1941. *This Great Argument: A study of Milton's* De Doctrina Christiana *as a gloss upon* Paradise Lost. Princeton UP.

Kermode, Frank. 1967. *The Sense of an Ending: Studies in the theory of fiction*. Oxford UP.

———. 1962. "Adam unparadised." In *The Living Milton: Essays by various hands*, edited by Frank Kermode, pp. 85–123. London: Routledge.

Kerrigan, William. 1983. *The Sacred Complex: On the psychogenesis of* Paradise Lost. Cambridge: Harvard UP.

———. 1975. "The Heretical Milton: From assumption to mortalism." *English Literary Renaissance* 5: 125–66.

Kessner, Carole S. 1974. "Milton's Hebraic Herculean hero." *Milton Studies* 6: 243–58.

Krouse, F. M. 1949. *Milton's* Samson *and the Christian Tradition.* Princeton UP.

Lewalski, Barbara. 2000. *The Life of John Milton: A critical biography.* Oxford: Blackwell.

———. 1999. "The genres of *Paradise Lost.*" In *The Cambridge Companion to Milton*, edited by Dennis Danielson, pp. 113–29. 2nd ed. Cambridge UP.

———. 1985. Paradise Lost *and the Rhetoric of Literary Forms.* Princeton UP.

———. 1970. "*Samson Agonistes* and the 'tragedy' of the Apocalypse." *Proceedings of the Modern Languages Association* 85: 1050–62.

———. 1966. *Milton's Brief Epic: The genre, meaning and art of* Paradise Regained. Providence: Brown UP; London: Methuen.

———. 1963. "Structure and the symbolism of vision in Michael's prophecy, *Paradise Lost*, books XI–XII." *PQ* 42: 25–35.

Lewis, C. S. 1942. *A Preface to* Paradise Lost. Oxford UP.

Lovejoy, A. J. 1937. "Milton and the paradox of the fortunate fall." *English Literary History* 4: 161–79.

Low, Antony. 1974. *The Blaze of Noon: A reading of* Samson Agonistes. New York: Columbia UP.

Madsen, W. 1968. *From Shadowy Types to Truth.* New Haven: Yale UP.

———. 1958. *Three Studies in the Renaissance: Sidney, Jonson, Milton.* New Haven: Yale UP.

Martz, Louis. 1964. *The Paradise Within: Studies in Vaughan, Traherne and Milton.* New Haven: Yale UP.

McColley, Diane. 1983. *Milton's Eve.* Urbana: U of Illinois P.

Mollenkott, Virginia R. 1972. "Milton's rejection of the fortunate Fall." *Milton Studies* 6: 1–5.

Moore, C. A. 1921. "The conclusion of *Paradise Lost.*" *Publications of the Modern Languages Association* 36: 1–34.

Mueller, Martin. 1964. "Pathos and katharsis in *Samson Agonistes.*" *English Literary History* 31: 156–74.

Mulryan, John. 1983. "The heroic tradition of Milton's *Samson Agonistes.*" *Milton Studies* 17: 217–34.

Newlyn, Lucy. 1993. Paradise Lost *and the Romantic Reader.* Oxford: Clarendon.

Nohrnberg, James. 1983. "*Paradise Regained* by one greater man: Milton's wisdom epic as a 'fable of identity.'" In *Centre and Labyrinth: Essays in Honour of Northrop Frye*, edited by Eleanor Cook and others, pp. 83–114. U of Toronto P.

Nuttall, A. D. 2001. "Everything is over before it begins." Review of *How Milton Works* by Stanley Fish (Harvard UP, 2001). *London Review of Books*, (21 July, p. 23).

Nyquist, Mary. 1988. "The genesis of gendered subjectivity in the divorce tracts and in *Paradise Lost.*" In *Re-membering Milton: Essays on the texts and tradition*, edited by Mary Nyquist and Margaret Ferguson, pp. 99–127. New York: Methuen.

Parker, Patricia. 1979a. "Eve, evening and the labor of reading." *English Literary Renaissance* 9: 319–42.

———. 1979b. *Inescapable Romance: Studies in the poetics of a mode.* Princeton UP.

Parker, W. 1937. *Milton's Debt to Greek Tragedy in* Samson Agonistes. Baltimore: Johns Hopkins UP.

Patterson, F. A., and others, eds. 1931–36. *The Works of John Milton.* 18 vols. New York: Columbia UP.

Pecheux, Mother M. Christopher. 1978. "Milton and *kairos.*" *Milton Studies* 12: 197–211.

Prince, F. T. 1958. "On the last two books of *Paradise Lost.*" *Essays and Studies* 11: 38–52.

Quinones, Richard. 1972. *The Renaissance Discovery of Time.* Cambridge: Harvard UP.

Quint, David. 1999. "Expectation and prematurity in Milton's *Nativity Ode.*" *Modern Philology* 97: 195–219.

———. 1993. *Epic and Empire.* Princeton UP.

———. 1983. *Origin and Originality in Renaissance Literature: Versions of the source.* New Haven: Yale UP.

Radzinowicz, Mary Ann. 1977. "Medicinable tragedy: The structure of *Samson Agonistes* and seventeenth-century psychopathology." In *English Drama: Forms and development: Essays in honour of Muriel Clara Bradbrook,* edited by Marie Axton and Raymond Williams, pp. 94–122. Cambridge UP.

———. 1968. "Man as a probationer of immortality: *Paradise Lost* XI and XII." In *Approaches to* Paradise Lost, edited by C. A. Patrides, pp. 31–52. York UP.

Rajan, B. 1947. Paradise Lost *and the Seventeenth Century Reader.* London: Chatto.

Ricks, Christopher. 1963. *Milton's Grand Style.* Oxford UP.

Roberts, Deborah. 1982. "Parting words: Final lines in Sophocles and Euripides." *Classical Quarterly* 37: 51–64.

Robertson, David. 1995. "Soliloquy and self in Milton's major poems." In *Of Poetry and Politics: New essays on Milton and his world,* edited by P. G. Stanwood, pp. 59–77. Binghamton: SUNY P.

Rogers, John. 1996. *The Matter of Revolution: Science, poetry and politics in the age of Milton.* Ithaca: Cornell UP.

Rollin, Roger B. 1973. "*Paradise Lost:* 'Tragical-Comical-Historical-Pastoral.'" *Milton Studies* 5: 3–37.

Rumrich, John. 1995. "Milton's God and the matter of chaos." *Publications of the Modern Languages Association* 110: 1035–46.

Samuel, Irene. 1971. "*Samson Agonistes* as tragedy." In *Calm of Mind: Tercentenary essays on "Paradise Regained" and "Samson Agonistes,"* edited by Joseph Wittreich, pp. 235–57. Cleveland: Case Western Reserve UP.

Saurat, Denis. 1925. *Milton: Man and thinker.* New York: Dial.

Schwartz, Regina. 1988. *Remembering and Repeating: Biblical Creation in* Paradise Lost. Cambridge UP.

Sewall, Richard. 1959. *The Vision of Tragedy.* New Haven: Yale UP.

Shaw, William. 1985. "The Euripidean influence on Milton's tragedy of Adam." *Milton Quarterly* 19: 29–33.

———. 1975. "Milton's choice of the epic for *Paradise Lost.*" *English Language Notes* 12: 15–20.

Shawcross, John T. 1975. "Milton's choice of the epic for *Paradise Lost.*" *English Language Notes* 12: 15–20.

———. 1972. *Milton: The critical heritage, 1732–1801.* London: Routledge.

——. 1969. "The style and genre of *Paradise Lost*." In *New Essays on Paradise Lost*, edited by T. Kranidas, pp. 15–33. Berkeley: U of California P.

——. 1965. "The balanced structure of *Paradise Lost*." *Studies in Philology* 62: 696–718.

Spiller, Michael R. G. 1995. "Directing the audience in *Samson Agonistes*." In *Of Poetry and Politics: New essays on Milton and his world*, edited by P. G. Stanwood, pp. 121–29. Binghamton: SUNY P.

Steadman, John M. 1976. *Epic and Tragic Structure in* Paradise Lost. U of Chicago P.

Summers, Joseph. 1962. *The Muse's Method: An introduction to* Paradise Lost. Cambridge: Harvard UP.

Svendsen, Kester. 1949a. "Adam's soliloquy in Book X of *Paradise Lost*." *College English* 10: 366–70. Reprinted in *Milton: Modern essays in criticism*, edited by Arthur E. Barker, pp. 328–35. Oxford UP, 1965.

——. 1949b. "Milton's 'On his having arrived at the age of twenty-three.'" *Explicator* 7:53.

Thompson, Elbert N. S. 1957. "For *PL* XI and XII." *Philological Quarterly* 36: 376–86.

Tillyard, E.M.W. 1951. *Studies in Milton*. London: Chatto.

——. 1930. *Milton*. London: Chatto.

Waddington, Raymond B. 1971. "Melancholy against melancholy: *Samson Agonistes* as a Renaissance tragedy." In *Calm of Mind: Tercentenary essays on* Paradise Regained *and* Samson Agonistes *in honor of John S. Diekhoff*, edited by Joseph Wittreich, pp. 259–88. Cleveland: Case Western Reserve UP.

Williamson, George. 1935. "Milton and the mortalist heresy." *Studies in Philology* 32: 553–79.

Wittreich, Joseph. 1986. *Interpreting* Samson Agonistes. Princeton UP.

Woodhull, Marianna. 1907. *The Epic of* Paradise Lost: *Twelve essays*. New York: Putnam.

Wolfe, Don M., and others, eds. 1953–82. *The Complete Prose Works of John Milton*. 8 vols. New Haven: Yale UP.

Author Index

Subject Index